CHECKPOINTS WITH READINGS

Developing College English Skills

Second Canadian Edition

Jack Page
Merritt College

Leslie Taggart

Jane Merivale
Centennial College

Toronto

National Library of Canada Cataloguing in Publication

Page, Jack
   Checkpoints with readings : developing college English skills / Jack Page, Jane Merivale. — Second Canadian ed. rev.

Includes index.
ISBN 0-321-25349-3

1. English language—Rhetoric. 2. English language—Grammar. 3. College readers.
I. Merivale, Jane II. Title.

PE1408.P33 2004a   808'.0427   C2003-906992-3

Copyright © 2004, 2001 Pearson Education Canada Inc., Toronto, Ontario

Original edition published by Longman, an imprint of Addison Wesley Longman, Inc., a division of Pearson Education, New York, NY. Copyright © 2004 by Addison Wesley Longman, Inc.

This edition is authorized for sale in Canada only.

All Rights Reserved. This publication is protected by copyright, and permission should be obtained from the publisher prior to any prohibited reproduction, storage in a retrieval system, or transmission in any form or by any means, electronic, mechanical, photocopying, recording, or likewise. For information regarding permission, write to the Permissions Department.

ISBN 0-321-25349-3

Vice-President, Editorial Director: Michael J. Young
Sponsoring Editor: Andrew Winton
Marketing Manager: Toivo Pajo
Supervising Developmental Editor: Suzanne Schaan
Production Editor: Charlotte Morrison-Reed
Copy Editor: Susan Broadhurst
Production Coordinator: Peggy Brown
Page Layout: Jansom
Art Director: Mary Opper
Interior and Cover Design: Gillian Tsintziras
Cover Image: Veer

1 2 3 4 5   08 07 06 05 04

Printed and bound in Canada.

TABLE OF CONTENTS

Preface ix

Chapter 1 The Writing Process Begins with Reading — 1

Reading: The Infomedia Revolution — 2
    The Infomedia Revolution —Frank Koelsch — 3
Writing Process: An Overview of the Writing Process — 6
Prewriting: Brainstorming — 7
Sentence Mechanics: Spelling Troublemakers — 8
Wordcheck: Definitions — 14
Checkpost: Practise Using a Dictionary — 15

Chapter 2 The Paragraph — 16

Reading: Paragraphs with Topic Sentences — 16
    Why I'm Skipping the Olympics —Kaliya Young — 16
Writing Models: A Paragraph with a Topic Sentence — 18
Prewriting: Keeping a Journal — 22
Writing Assignment: A Paragraph with a Topic Sentence — 22
Sentence Structure: Identifying the Subject and Verb of the Sentence — 26
Wordcheck: Pronunciation — 34
Checkpost: Definite (the) and Indefinite (a/an) Articles — 34

Chapter 3 Paragraphs with Specific Details — 37

Reading: Specific Details Following a Topic Sentence — 37
    Grandmother of Us All —Brian Bethune — 37
Writing Models: A Paragraph with Specific Details — 39
Prewriting: Clustering — 41
Writing Assignment: A Portrait of a Person — 42
Writing Process: Revising the Paper — 43
Sentence Structure: Avoiding Fragments — 44
Wordcheck: Spelling — 49
Checkpost: Determiners — 50

Chapter 4 Paragraphs with Descriptive Details — 52

Reading: Description Adds Life — 52
    Land Is Holy . . . Sacred —Sharon Butala — 52
Writing Models: The Descriptive Paragraph — 54
Writing Assignment: a Descriptive Paragraph — 55
Writing Process: Writing a Summary — 57
Sentence Structure: Avoiding Clause Fragments — 58
Wordcheck: Spelling Compound Words — 67
Checkpost: More on Determiners — 67

Chapter 5 Paragraphs with Narrative Details — 69

Reading: Narrative Paragraphs Tell Stories — 69
    Traditions —Neil Bissoondath — 69
Writing Models: The Narrative Paragraph — 71
Prewriting: Nonstop Writing — 73
Writing Assignment: A Narrative Paragraph — 73
Sentence Structure: Avoiding Run-Together Sentences — 74
Wordcheck: Word Origins — 84
Checkpost: Adjectives–Using Comparatives — 84

Chapter 6 Developing Paragraphs Using Process — 86

Reading: Process Paragraphs Tell How Something Comes About — 86
    The Story of Roots —Michael Posner — 86
Writing Models: The Process Paragraph — 88
Prewriting: Asking How and Why — 90
Writing Assignment: A Process Paragraph — 92
Sentence Structure: Using Verbs Correctly — 94
Wordcheck: Verb Forms — 102
Checkpost: Using Comparatives and Superlatives — 103

Chapter 7 Developing Paragraphs Using Cause and Effect — 105

Reading: Analyzing Cause and Effect — 105
    Plague of Privatization Is Robbing Our Citizens —Dalton Camp — 105
Writing Models: The Cause and Effect Paragraph — 107
Prewriting: Audience — 108
Writing Assignment: A Cause and Effect Paragraph — 109
Sentence Structure: Making Subjects and Verbs Agree in a Sentence — 112
Wordcheck: Plurals — 118
Checkpost: Adjectives and Adverbs — 120

Chapter 8 Developing Paragraphs Using Examples — 122

Reading: Using Examples to Support a Point — 122
    Evacuees in Alberta —Joy Kogawa (extract from *Obasan*) — 122
Writing Models: The Example Paragraph — 125
Writing Assignment: An Example Paragraph — 126
Sentence Structure: Selecting the Right Pronoun — 128
Wordcheck: Synonyms — 136
Checkpost: Conditionals — 137

Chapter 9 Developing Paragraphs Using Comparison — 139

Reading: Paragraphs Comparing Similarities and Contrasting Differences — 139
    Pro-globalization Forces Get Taste of Own Medicine —Naomi Klein — 139
Writing Models: The Comparison Paragraph — 141
Writing Assignment: A Comparison Paragraph — 143

Sentence Structure: Pronoun Agreement and Clear Reference	144
Wordcheck: Usage Tips	152
Checkpost: Gerunds and Infinitives	152

Chapter 10 Developing Paragraphs Using Definition — 154

Reading: Definitions of Words	154
Beauty Myth Preserves Male Dominance —Michele Landsberg	154
Writing Models: The Definition Paragraph	156
Writing Assignment: A Definition Paragraph	158
Sentence Punctuation: Using Commas in Sentences	160
Wordcheck: Biographical Names	167
Checkpost: Participles–Present and Past	167

Chapter 11 Developing Paragraphs Using Opinion — 170

Reading: Expressing an Opinion	170
A Debt to a Neighbour —Jane Williams	170
Writing Models: The Opinion Paragraph	172
Writing Assignment: An Opinion Paragraph	173
Writing Process: Diction—Choosing the Right Word	175
Sentence Punctuation: Using Punctuation	176
Wordcheck: Word Choice	185
Checkpost: Modals	186

Chapter 12 Writing the Essay — 188

Reading: Developing an Idea	188
Fatherhood–It Has Its Moments —Winston F. Wong	188
Writing Models: The Essay	189
Writing Assignment: An Essay	192
Sentence Mechanics: Using Capitals, Figures, and Abbreviations	194
Sentence Structure: Being Consistent	199
Wordcheck: Places and Things	205

Chapter 13 The Classification Essay — 206

Reading: Using Categories to Convey Information	206
Saskatchewan's Indian People–Five Generations —Pat Deiter-McArthur	206
Writing Models: The Classification Essay	208
Writing Assignment: A Classification Essay	209
Sentence Structure: Achieving Sentence Variety	210
Sentence Structure: Building Effective Sentences	216
Wordcheck: Foreign Words	222

Chapter 14 An Essay Using Persuasion — 223

Reading: Persuading Others to Share One's Views	223
Mad Cows, Funny Plants, Uranium Dust and Such —Flora Lewis	223
Writing Models: Using Persuasion	225

Writing Assignment: A Persuasion Essay	227
Sentence Structure: Solving Sentence Problems	228
Wordcheck: Abbreviations	236

Chapter 15 Using Mixed Modes — 237

Reading: An Internet Success	237
Why Google Should Be Your First Choice —Simon Crerar	237
Hints for Successful Googling	239
Writing Models: The Mixed Mode Essay	241
Writing Assignment: An Essay on Life	243
Writing Process: Revising–Eliminating Wordiness	243
Writing Process: Adjectives and Adverbs	245
Writing Process: Coherence	247
Writing Process: Faulty Logic	249
Wordcheck: Miscellaneous Facts	254

Additional Readings

Education and Work	255
Studying Science, Playing Politics —Deborah Skilliter	255
Shedding Light on Confucius: A Window to East Asians in Canada —Douglas Todd	257
How to Find Your First Job —Lyric Wallwork Winik	259
Relationships and Partnerships	262
Babies Having Babies —Jocelyn Elders	262
Raising a Feminist —Sarah Vaughn Snyder	263
The "I Don't Care" Game —Susan Jacoby	265
Community and Society	268
Lessons Learned During Ramadan —Ameena El Jandali	268
Finding a Nationality That Fits —Isabel Vincent	269
Hang the Rich; Improve the Herd —H. S. Bhabra	271
Kick 'Em Again —Judy Rebick	273
Our Own Native Hong Kong —Meaghan Walker-Williams	275
Environment and Science	278
Exposing a Mysterious Development —Geoffrey Rowan	278
Individual Actions Can Have Huge Consequences —Ian Burton	280
The Good, the Bad and the Ugly of Skepticism —David Suzuki	281
Will *Survivor* Replace *Lord of the Flies*? —Christine McGovern	283
Health and Sports	285
So What's the Problem with *Wussy* Sports? —Mary Louise Adams	285
Alternative Medicine Gains Ground in Canada —Wallace Immen	289
Home Ice —Paul Quarrington	291
Dentistry Self-Drilled —Dave Barry	294
Writing Resource A: Writing a Summary	297
Reading: Finding the Main Points of an Essay	297
Lack of English, Not Good Will, Is the Culprit —Anna Nike Mineyko	297

Writing Models: The Summary	**299**
Writing Assignment: A Summary	**300**
Writing Resource B: Revising and Editing	**301**
Using a Computer	301
Revising and Editing a Paragraph	302
Editing	304
Writing Resource C: Using Outside Sources in Writing	**305**
Keep Your Ideas Separate from Your Sources' Ideas	305
Writing Resource D: For Students of ESL	**309**
Writing Resource E: Grammatical Terms – The Parts of Speech and Transition Words	**313**
Answer Key	**316**
Credits	**335**

PREFACE

Welcome to the second Canadian edition of *Checkpoints with Readings: Developing College English Skills.*

Those of you who are familiar with the first Canadian edition of this book will recognize the exciting features that help students acquire the language skills necessary to be successful today. It is filled with high-interest readings on current topics by Canadian and international writers, opportunities for writing paragraphs and essays in a process-oriented approach with ample space for editing and revising, and numerous exercises featuring all of the crucial grammatical features of clear, concise, and articulate writing.

Readings at the beginning of each chapter provide models of specific rhetorical modes that can then be practised in isolation before the student ultimately writes a more realistic mixed mode essay. Drawn from a range of subject areas and written by diverse authors, these readings will stimulate valuable discussion and foster ideas for writing. Some of the readings reflect an academic background while others are more journalistic; all of the articles, however, are appropriate for the first-year college-level student.

In each chapter, the reading is followed by Writing Models, Writing Practice, and a Writing Assignment. Students are also encouraged to keep a journal to help them with the writing process. The writing process, supported by grammar exercises, provides the student with ample opportunity to thoroughly understand how to produce clear and coherent writing. The student will advance from writing well-organized paragraphs in the initial chapters to composing informative essays in the final chapters.

There are more grammar exercises in this edition, coupled with those in the *Instructor's Manual*, that provide further practice for ESL students as well as students for whom English is a first language. The exercises are organized so that students can monitor their own progress, and teachers can use the final Checkpoints exercises as a review of each chapter's grammar points.

Also *new* to this edition, the Netcheck feature, weblinks relevant to each chapter's reading, provides opportunities for discussion and writing and is designed to help the student surf the Net efficiently and effectively.

There is also a substantial Writing Resource on Using Outside Sources in Writing that teaches MLA standards of how to quote from outside sources, and how to list Works Cited. Documentation is now more important than ever as students need to be aware of the consequences of plagiarism.

The Writing Resources also include tips on using a computer, discuss the process of revising and editing, and provide more material for the ESL student.

Finally, the additional readings provide fodder for lively discussion and informed written work. The essays have been chosen from writers who reflect our multicultural society. They will help develop students' evaluation and critical-thinking skills on a range of topics and ideas.

I wish to thank all of those who helped me in this production: my husband, who gave me a new dimension to work in; my son, who inspires me to help students on their writing journeys; Andrew Winton, for marvellously purposeful meetings (for meetings with no agenda!); Marta Tomins, for getting me wired and communicating e-ways with me in such a timely and helpful manner; and my dragon buddy Laura Brawn, for her encouragement.

Good luck to the students who will find that this book takes them on a reading and writing journey to become competent, critical, and concise writers.

THE WRITING PROCESS BEGINS WITH READING

Some people may consider reading and writing practically obsolete as a result of the changes in communication technology over the past decade. Certainly, new technology will continue to change our lives. However, as you no doubt already have discovered, good reading skills are essential for success in further education. It's hard to take part in class discussions, and impossible to do well on tests, if you don't understand the assigned readings.

In addition, reading can make you a better writer. Reading will show you how experienced writers make use of words, sentences, and paragraphs. Reading will improve your vocabulary and spelling skills, often without your even being aware of the change. And it will give you new ideas, information, and insights to add strength to your own writing.

Whether you are skipping through a biker magazine or struggling with a chemistry text, these suggestions can help you understand and remember what you read.

- *Preview* the material. The more you know ahead of time about what you are going to read, the easier and more efficient your reading will be.

  - Is there an *introductory note* with clues about the subject or the author's purpose? This note often appears at the beginning of the piece, before the title or before the first chapter, as in this text.

  - Look at the *title*. Sometimes it reveals or hints at the subject or purpose. Make a question from the title so that you can test your comprehension at the end.

  - What do you know about the *author*? On what is he or she an authority? What ideas or prejudices have come through in earlier writings that you have seen?

  - Are there *subheadings*—short titles within the work, usually set in contrasting type? These may signal points that the author wants to emphasize or show how the ideas are organized.

  - Read the *first and last paragraphs*. Writers often present their main idea at the beginning and restate it at the end. This will help you focus on the topic.

- Read the first sentence of each of the other paragraphs. This may be the *topic sentence*, which gives a summary of the entire paragraph. (This approach is less useful with the very short paragraphs often found in newspaper and magazine articles.)
- Read *actively*. Ideas and information are not going to leap off the page into your mind. You have to make an effort. Make sure you are studying in a place where you can concentrate.
  - Look for the *main idea*. Then, keep asking how other details relate to that idea.
  - Decide what the author's *purpose* is in writing. Is it to inform, to persuade, to describe, to entertain? Focus on those details that carry out the purpose.
- Mark up your book! *Underline key points*. When you review the material before a class discussion or a test, the most important details should be obvious. Underlining requires constant thought about what is and isn't important. Those who overdo it—who underline almost every sentence—are missing the point.
- *Read critically*. Just because something is in a book doesn't mean you have to accept it as true or worthwhile. Ask questions. Do the "facts" seem reliable? Are the opinions supported with sound evidence? Is the writer appealing mostly to your emotions or to your reason? Jot down your doubts and disagreements in the margin.
- Understand the *words*. If an unfamiliar word blocks your understanding of a passage, by all means look it up. But it isn't necessary to turn to the dictionary every time you come to a new word. Often you can guess what the word means from the way it is used, and you can skip over some unfamiliar words for the moment if they aren't essential to understanding. By the way, reading on a wide range of subjects is the best way to build up your vocabulary.
- When you've finished reading, *quiz yourself*. What was the thesis or main point of the material? What were the main supporting points? If necessary, read the material again to find the answers you missed. Rarely will reading the material just once provide the understanding expected in the classroom. The more you read, the faster a reader you will become. Practise by enjoying all the readings in this book.

READING: THE INFOMEDIA REVOLUTION

Precheck Frank Koelsch, an expert in information technology (IT) innovations, has been writing about changes to our lives as a result of technological innovation for some years. The following extract from his book *The Infomedia Revolution* describes the technological changes we have yet to experience. These changes may heavily influence our approaches to reading and writing.

Journal Topic

What are your own approaches to reading and writing now that you are in a post-secondary program? Have your reading habits changed? Will you be making the most of the communications technology available to you?

The Infomedia Revolution –*Frank Koelsch*

Computers and Communication

Sitting at a desk in downtown New York, an executive picks up the telephone to place a call to Tokyo. He is hoping to finalize the arrangements for a corporate merger. A family in Atlanta watches the Olympics in Lillehammer, Norway. They cheer wildly as David Jansen finally wins his first gold medal after his earlier heartbreaking attempts. They watch in awestruck wonder as Jean-Luc Brassard flies over the bumps to win the gold in moguls. An engineer sits at his desk in Los Angeles. He is connected to colleagues in Boston and London, England. They use their PC to exchange drawings, sketches, mail messages and product specifications. All of these scenarios have become so commonplace as to be unremarkable.

We simply expect to be able to pick up the phone and call anywhere in the world. We expect to turn on the TV and surf through 50 channels. We think nothing of connecting a PC to networks and computers around the globe. We simply expect this amazing technological infrastructure to be there and to function, quickly and efficiently, at any time of day or night. The sense of wonder that Bell and Watson experienced with the first telephone call is gone—today's technology makes theirs look like a child's toy.

Communications technology is pervasive and affects every aspect of our lives. Working, traveling, driving in our cars or relaxing at home, we are never out of reach of a phone, a radio or the TV. They have become the cornerstones of modern communication. As PCs become a ubiquitous part of our business and personal lives, data links are becoming commonplace. Communication in its many forms is shaping our economy and society, making our world a smaller place. It puts us in touch with people and events around the globe—in real time, any time.

This awesome power is available in every home and office at the flick of a dial or the touch of a keypad. It's easy to believe that we have reached the zenith of communications technology, that we have reached the limit of innovation and that any future changes will result only in minor variations or extensions to what already exists. Nothing could be further from the truth.

Communications technology, as advanced as it is today, is still in its infancy. We have yet to apply computing technology to the most basic communicating devices in any meaningful way. Most communicating devices—the TV, radio and telephone—are only just now being computerized. The transformation is just beginning. As computing technology converges with TVs, radios and telephones, these devices will take a huge technological leap forward. They will not be the same common household appliances to which we have grown accustomed. They are already beginning to change shape, to break out of their historic molds. As they are reborn, perhaps our sense of wonder will return.

---

product specifications design descriptions of a particular sales item

infrastructure all the components assembled to enable us to use technology

pervasive found everywhere

Network Convergence

The power of computing technology is simply this: it lets us reinvent things. It also lets us change the way we do things. Today's media appliances—the TV, radio and telephone—have non inherent intelligence or "smarts." Applying computer technology to these everyday products lets us rethink them entirely. We can start with a clean slate and ask questions like: "If I could invent the TV today, would I invent what I have in my living room?" The answer is, likely not.

If we had no preconceived notions about how TV should be, we would never design what we have today. The original TV was developed in the era of vacuum tubes; it predates the transistor by over 20 years. Today's TV owes its format to scheduled live shows and the technical limitations of a past age. The shows of the 1950s, when TV first became popular, were not taped; they were live broadcasts. Taping only came along later. The networks were assigned "channels" on which they could broadcast their scheduled shows. The original concepts and the original model for broadcast TV haven't changed significantly since their inception and formalization over four decades ago.

Today, we have more channels, pictures appear in color, screens are larger and electronic remote controls are common, but TV basics are still the same. We still watch a show when it's scheduled, on a specific channel. TV is still very much a one-way passive medium. As we sit mesmerized by the tube, the only active role we play is turning the set on and changing channels.

If we had a choice, clearly we would design TVs to be highly interactive—not passive. The TV is a window on the world around us, open to travel, science, history, action and mystery. Humans by nature want to interact with their world, not sit like vidiots passively watching it go by. Computers and modern communications technology let us do just that.

Think of it this way. We're not in control of the TV; the TV controls us. We don't watch what we want because it's never on when we're ready to watch. We endlessly graze on the channels looking for something to catch our interest, something that is really worth watching. We wander the pages of TV guides, searching for a show that looks worthwhile. When we find one, we wait like video zombies until start time. Our lives are scheduled around the evening news, *Bart Simpson, Bay Watch* and the Sunday night movie—each broadcast at the hour ordained by the network.

The TV networks decide how our evenings will be spent, not us. If we have night-school classes at 7:00 p.m., we won't be watching *Jeopardy* that evening. Our personal schedule of evening activities has little influence on NBC's program schedule. The network bosses decide when *Roseanne* will air, and that's that.

We have come to accept channelization and TV schedules as the norm. We wouldn't accept the same model for a minute on our PCs. If a computer were a TV, we would have to sit patiently waiting for the word-processing program to appear at its scheduled time. We would only work on our expenses or budgets when the spreadsheet program was scheduled to be active. We could only write letters between 4:00 p.m. and 5:00 p.m., the scheduled time for word processing. If the letter wasn't finished by 5:00 p.m., too bad; we would just have to wait until tomorrow to finish it.

Computer technology lets us change the nature of TV and all other communicating devices. It is being applied to the TV to make it interactive, responsive to *our* needs and schedules. Computers are being used today to make TVs

inherent "smarts" natural or inborn intelligence

"smart." Soon they will help us navigate vast media warehouses. These media repositories will contain thousands of TV shows, movies and documentaries, and even digital books, music and encyclopedias. We will be able to see what we want, when we want. If *Bart Simpson* conflicts with the dog's need to go for a walk—right now—no problem. Just call up the current episode, or last week's or any week's for that matter, when the chore is done.

14 The nature of TV will change in other ways as well. We will be able to move beyond *viewing* things to *doing* things on TV. When people want to check their bank balance, buy a new watch or shop for groceries, they will be able to do it all from the comfort of their living rooms. A range of new services will soon be available to the home. Almost anything we can do in a store today, we will be able to do at home.

15 As the TV becomes smart, it will become very PC-like. People will be able to use it to perform typical computing functions such as writing letters, managing the household budget and looking up grandma's favorite recipe for gingerbread cookies. It will be able to send electronic mail and faxes as well as connect to information networks like *CompuServ* and *America Online*. The line between PC and TV will eventually disappear.

16 Radio will change much like the television. Instead of tuning up and down the FM band or selecting a preset station, we will be able to program music selections to suit our taste and the mood of the moment. Music libraries will replace radio stations. Never again will we be forced to listen to the same stale news, every hour on the hour, when we really want to rock and roll.

Checking Meaning and Style

1. What device does the author use in the first paragraph to grab our attention?
2. What does "theirs" in paragraph 2, line **7** refer to?
3. What various things can we do now with this modern technology?
4. How is our use of television different from our personal computer (PC) use?

Checking Ideas

1. What idea is Frank Koelsch exploring in this excerpt?
2. Discuss with a partner the extent of your personal use of computer technology.
3. Now that other media are so pervasive, do you read and write less?
4. What are your predictions about the future uses of technology?

Netcheck

In each chapter, this feature will help you focus on aspects of the Internet. This may help you use the Internet effectively in your studies, as well as in your life in general.

Frank Koelsch is a well-known authority on information technology. When you read an article on the Internet, and you do not know anything about the author, how do you know whether you can believe the author's information? Check the following **WH Questions** when you are reading information on the Web:

When was the article posted on the Web?

Who is responsible for the information?

Where is the information consistent with other articles on the subject?

What is the source of the information?

How knowledgeable is the writer?

WRITING PROCESS: AN OVERVIEW OF THE WRITING PROCESS

This text is designed to help you acquire the writing skills necessary for success in college. Of course, language skills will help you in other ways—for example, in your social and family life and on the job. For now, it will be helpful to recognize that writing is not a single act. It is a process. It is a series of steps that result in a composition—whether a term paper in history or a job application letter—that is well thought out, carefully organized, and technically correct.

These steps should include the following:

1. Prewriting—getting ready to write
2. Writing—putting down a rough draft
3. Revising—improving the first version
4. Editing—correcting errors
5. Rewriting—copying the final draft

Learning about the stages of the writing process will help you with the assignments in each chapter of this book and also with the other writing you do in college. Each chapter of this text discusses one aspect of the writing process in detail. For now, here is a quick summary of each step in the process:

Prewriting

We have all probably found ourselves with a blank piece of paper in front of us that seems matched by the blank spot in our brains where all the words and ideas are supposed to come from. There must be an easier way to write a paper. One way to make writing easier is to do some prewriting first. Let's make a sentence for an example.

Silvia used the prewriting step of **brainstorming** when she thought about her personal computer and listed her ideas:

expensive   crashes   slow   out of date   three years old

Use the prewriting step to list some ideas you might include in a sentence about your use of a computer.

_____

_____

Writing

The most important point to remember in writing the first draft of any paper is that it is just a beginning. You will not be turning in this copy, and it does not have to be perfect.

After prewriting, Silvia was able to write this first sentence about her computer:

> My expensive, three years old computer is very slow and crashes alot.

Look at your prewriting ideas and write a sentence about your computer.

_____
_____

Revising

Even skilled writers do their "assignments" more than once. In other words, they need to revise their work to make it as good as possible. Revision literally means "seeing again." Be prepared to look at your paper again and to perform major surgery.

In the revision stage, Silvia was able to add details to her one-sentence description:

> My expensive, three years old, but out of date computer is very slow and crashes alot now.

Revise the sentence you wrote about your computer.

_____
_____

Editing

Editing your paper means finding and correcting errors in grammar, punctuation, capitalization, and spelling. Your editing skills will grow as you study these aspects of writing.

While editing her sentence, Silvia corrected some mistakes:

> My expensive, three-year-old, outdated computer is very slow now and crashes a lot.

Edit your own sentence.

_____
_____

Rewriting

When you are ready, write the final draft.

PREWRITING: BRAINSTORMING

Let's take a closer look at the first step in the writing process. As we have just seen, a common type of prewriting to use when you need ideas is **brainstorming**. As with any kind of prewriting, brainstorming can be used in an assignment for your composition class or for other types of writing and thinking you must do.

In brainstorming, jot down whatever ideas about your subject pop into your mind. Do not worry about grammar, spelling, or sentence structure. Do not even worry about whether the ideas are good. Just quickly make a list of all thoughts about a subject that occur to you, without stopping to reflect or censoring your ideas. When you are finished brainstorming, go back and circle all the ideas that could be useful.

Brainstorming is especially suitable for writing about a personal experience or a subject you know well. For a paper about a common experience, you might work with a group to brainstorm. Sharing ideas in a group can be helpful to all members.

A Student Demonstration

Joe had to write a paragraph describing the uses of the Internet. He decided to use brainstorming to put down his thoughts. Here are the results of Joe's brainstorming:

| shopping | research | music | videos | events | stock market |
| weather | currency conversion | news | languages | | |

Now You Try It

Let's say you are asked to write about your experiences of and feelings about reading and writing on the Internet. Without stopping to judge your ideas, write down as many points on the subject as you can think of. Your list may look something like this, but see if you can add to this list:

- types of reading material
- convenience
- problems with word processing
- learning new skills
- journals
- writing e-mails
- chat rooms
- talking books

Now narrow your ideas to three that relate to each other, such as the kinds of communications you use the Internet for. Write a few sentences using your three ideas.

_____
_____
_____
_____
_____
_____

SENTENCE MECHANICS: SPELLING TROUBLEMAKERS

Probably because the words sound alike, people often have trouble with little words such as *its* and *it's* and *their, there,* and *they're.* Since the words come up often in everyday writing, it's worth knowing how to get them right.

Its, It's

Let's take *its* and *it's* first. There's a simple rule to guide you here. Use *it's* only as a short form or contraction of *it is* or *it has*. The apostrophe (') means that one or more letters have been left out.

It's [It is] time to go home.

It's [it has] been a week since the lawyer called.

Use *its* without an apostrophe when you don't mean *it is* or *it has*.

The dog wagged its [not *it is*] tail when the burglar entered the house.

The car lost its [not *it is*] headlight in the collision.

Its is an example of a possessive pronoun. Some other pronouns that show possession and do not take an apostrophe are these:

his   hers   ours   theirs   yours

Spotcheck 1-1

Underline the correct word in parentheses. Remember to use it's *only if you mean* it is *or* it has.

1. A one-cent piece doesn't have the word "penny" on (its / it's) face.
2. Neither does the coin have "penny" on (its / it's) reverse side.
3. (Its / It's) common for the Queen's face to appear on Canadian stamps.
4. Wear a hat when (its / it's) cold. Your body loses 80 percent of (its / it's) heat through the head.
5. (Its / It's) been about 80 years since women were first allowed to vote in Canada.

They're, Their, and There

They're is a contraction of *they are*. Notice that the apostrophe goes where the letter *a* has been left out.

They're [They are] building a theatre on the corner of Maple and Elm streets.

Clint and Loretta said they're [they are] in the same biology lab.

Their is a possessive pronoun. It shows ownership.

The Mustang convertible is their car.

Their three sons are in the Canadian Armed Forces.

There shows location (not *here*) and is also a frequent sentence starter: *There is... There are...*

The deer was standing right over there.

There was no way to solve the puzzle.

Spotcheck 1-2

Fill in the blanks with they're, their, *or* there.

[1]The Changs are selling _____ house. [2]_____ planning to build a new one in Kenwood. [3]_____ son and his family live _____. [4]_____ may be a delay while _____ house is in escrow. [5]However, before long _____ sure _____ new home will be _____ in Kenwood.

Spotcheck 1-3

Write sentences using each of the words in parentheses.

1. (its) _____
2. (it's) _____
3. (there) _____
4. (their) _____
5. (they're) _____

Doublecheck 1-1

Underline the correct word in parentheses.

[1]Many Canadians observe holidays of the countries from which they or (they're / their / there) ancestors came. [2](They're / Their / There) are often celebrations of Bastille Day in Quebec. [3](Its / It's) observed on July 14, the day in 1789 when the French people rebelled against King Louis XVI. [4]Citizens entered the Bastille prison and freed (it's / its) prisoners. [5]Many Americans of Mexican descent observe May 5—*Cinco de Mayo*—as one of (they're / their / there) significant dates. [6](They're / Their / There) celebrating the victory of Mexican soldiers over a powerful French Napoleonic army. [7]Mexico celebrates (its / it's) Independence Day each September 16. [8]On that date in 1810, a priest named Miguel Hidalgo gave *el grito*, the call to freedom that led Mexicans to (they're / their / there) independence from Spain. [9]For Chinese communities in Canada, (they're / their / there) are festivities associated with the New Year. [10]The Vietnamese call (they're / their / there) New Year's celebration *Tet*.

More Troublemakers

Editing is the final step in the writing process. Here are some more often-used words that cause many people problems. Be sure you can use them correctly, and check for errors before you hand in your work.

a an   Use *an* before a word that begins with the sound of a vowel (*a, e, i, o, u*): an apple, an opportunity, an hour (silent *h*). Use *a* before a word that begins with the sound of any other letters (called *consonants*): a book, a Pontiac, a university (the *u* sounds like *y*).

a lot	Notice that it is two words—not *alot*.
are or our	*Are* is a verb: They *are* happy.
	Or separates two possibilities: Faizal or Aziz will drive the van.
	Our is a word showing ownership: That is *our* house on the corner.
have of	Don't use *of* for *have*: They should *have* (not *of*) phoned first.
hear here	*Hear* is what you do with your ear: We *hear* a bird singing.
	Here means "this place": Bring the book *here*.
than then	Use *than* in comparisons: Wanda is taller *than* Carol.
	Then refers to time: If I had known *then* what I know now, I wouldn't have bought the TV set.
there's theirs	*There's* is a shortened form of *there is*: *There's* a full moon tonight.
	Theirs shows ownership: That poodle is *theirs*.
to too two	*To* is a preposition: Rasheed is going *to* college.
	Too means *also:* Besides the ketchup, bring some mustard, *too*.
	Too can mean "excessively": Sam is *too* tired to study.
	Two is a number: The Chungs own *two* cars.
were we're where	*Were* is a verb: The cats *were* frisky.
	We're is a short form of *we are:* We will leave when *we're* ready.
	Where indicates place: That is *where* Antonio lives.
you're your	*You're* is a short form of *you are:* Let us know if *you're* uncomfortable.
	Your shows ownership: Is that *your* basketball?

Spotcheck 1-4

Underline the correct words in parentheses.

[1](Are / Our / Or) you going to the lake in (are / or / our) car (are / or / our) in Franklin's? [2]We should (have / of) planned ahead. [3]I (hear / here) that Judith forgot her swimsuit. [4]I have mine (here / hear) in my tote bag. [5]Monica is more excited (than / then) Karen about the trip. [6]However, Karen will be excited (to / too / two) when she arrives at the lake. [7](Were / Where) are Dwight and Mary? [8]They (were / where) supposed to roast the hot dogs. [9](You're / Your) supposed to bring ice for the soft drinks. [10]Let's use this picnic table over (hear / here). [11](Than / Then) everything will be just about perfect.

Doublecheck 1-2

Write sentences using the words in parentheses.

1. (than) _____
2. (we're) _____
3. (too) _____
4. (there's) _____
5. (your) _____
6. (hear) _____
7. (an) _____
8. (our) _____
9. (to) _____
10. (you're) _____

Doublecheck 1-3

In each sentence, underline the correct word in parentheses.

[1]The human brain is almost (to / too / two) amazing to be believed. [2](Its / It's) unlikely that a computer will ever do all that the brain can do. [3]The brain tells us what is happening in (are / or / our) world by processing messages from the eyes, ears, nose, and skin. [4]It controls bodily functions (to / too / two), such as the beating of the heart. [5]The brain stores information and memories, so (there's / theirs) a chance of learning and benefiting from experience. [6]Without a developed brain, the human species might (have / of) disappeared, as the dinosaurs did.

[7]By the time you were about 15, (your / you're) brain had reached (its / it's) full size. [8]By (than / then) it weighed about three pounds. [9]The brain of a genius is not necessarily bigger (than / then) that of a feeble-minded person. [10](Theirs / There's) no direct relationship between human intelligence and the size of the brain. [11]The brains of large animals, such as elephants, weigh more (than / then) those of humans, but (there's / theirs) are smaller in relation to body weight. [12]The animal with the largest brain in proportion to (its / it's) size is the ant.

SENTENCE MECHANICS: SPELLING TROUBLEMAKERS   13

¹³(You're / Your) brain is not a single organ like your liver. ¹⁴Each of (it's / its) many parts has special functions. ¹⁵(Your / You're) using different sections when speaking (are / or / our) driving a car, for example.

Editing Check 1

Edit the following paragraph to correct spelling troublemaker errors, if any. The first sentence has been done as an example.

¹Salt and pepper ~~our too~~ **are two** everyday items that we probably never even think about. ²However, a lot of people don't realize that when their putting salt and pepper on there food their using a valuable commodity. ³Salt was the first currency; Roman soldiers where paid in salt, or *salarium*—which explains *salary*. ⁴An eighth-century trader sold salt for gold, and pepper was very precious to. ⁵Peppercorns our still very expensive today as pepper heightens are desire too eat. ⁶Without salt and pepper, trade from Europe to Asia would never of begun and long-distance travel might never of happened.

Checkpoint 1-1

Write the correct word in parentheses in the blank at the left.

1. _____ (Are / Or / Our) chorus is getting better all the time.
2. _____ (Were / Where) you at the concert last night?
3. _____ (You're / Your) going to be sorry if you missed it.
4. _____ You can (hear / here) us again in two weeks.
5. _____ (Theirs / There's) going to be another performance.
6. _____ But you really should (have / of) heard us last night.
7. _____ We sang better last night (than / then) we ever had before.
8. _____ There was a large turnout (to / too / two).
9. _____ When (are / or / our) you going to sing with us?
10. _____ (Its / It's) good that you are a tenor.
11. _____ (Their / There / They're) always in demand.
12. _____ In fact, we could use (to / too / two) or three tenors right now.
13. _____ (Their / There / They're) voices are especially important in the folk songs.
14. _____ Soon we expect to be accompanied by (a / an) organ as well as a piano.
15. _____ (Than / Then) we will have a richer sound.

No answers are given for Checkpoint quizzes.

WORDCHECK: DEFINITIONS

A dictionary is one of the most valuable tools a writer can have, despite the advent of spell-check and e-dictionaries. We probably open a dictionary most often to find out what an unfamiliar word means, but then a problem may come up. The word may have more than one meaning. Suppose that you come across this sentence in your reading:

> The burglar rifled the bedroom dresser before taking my season tickets to the Canucks games.

You know that a rifle is a kind of firearm. Does the sentence mean the burglar shot at the dresser? No. The dictionary tells us that *rifle* is also a verb meaning "search and rob." When more than one meaning is given for a word, we need to decide which one fits the context, the other words surrounding the word in question.

Checkpoint 1-2

Use a dictionary to select the correct word and identify its part of speech.

1. The (councillor / counsellor) was asked his (advice / advise) on family planning.
2. People often argue (among / between) themselves about the best methods.
3. Everyone is (conscious / conscience) that it is a controversial issue.
4. No one could (quite / quiet) agree on the subject.
5. The reason is because / The reason is that) family planning is a personal decision.

Checkpoint 1-3

Use the context to guess the meanings of the underlined words. Then, look up the words in a dictionary.

1. Because of vacations, the office had only a skeleton staff.

   Definition: _____

2. In the photo, my grandfather wore a handsome handlebar.

   Definition: _____

3. Michel wouldn't dance the polka, but Simone was game.

   Definition: _____

4. The Williams sisters won the match three love.

   Definition: _____

5. Eloise pinch-hit in the accounting department when Françoise had her baby.

   Definition: _____

CHECKPOST: PRACTISE USING A DICTIONARY

First, use an English-as-a-second-language dictionary to check the spelling of these words. Then, look up their definitions in an electronic dictionary and discuss the differences between the two resources.

The (theatre / theater) was unable to (accomodate / accommodate) the large party that had (travelled / traveled) from the prairies (especially / specially) to see the play. The visitors were very (dissapointed / disappointed).

THE PARAGRAPH

READING: PARAGRAPHS WITH TOPIC SENTENCES

Precheck

Writers often organize a paragraph with an opening topic sentence followed by specific details that make their ideas clear and interesting to the reader. In the following selection about the Olympics, Kaliya Young discusses her reasons for not participating in the Games. Whenever the subject of the Olympic Games is raised, there is usually some controversy to comment upon—drug scandals, judging decisions, or other corrupt incidents. In her article, Young discusses her disillusionment with the Olympic movement.

In every paragraph, she uses details and examples to elaborate on the topic sentences. You will notice in several of the readings in this book that many experienced writers do not always write in complete sentences, or will use one-sentence paragraphs for effect. Pay special attention to the paragraphs that have model topic sentences followed by further, more specific details.

Journal Topic

How do you feel about the Olympic movement? Are the Games an international event of great significance to you?

Why I'm Skipping the Olympics *–Kaliya Young*

1   I was a three-time All-American at Cal in women's water polo and left college for a year to prepare for the Olympic Games with the Canadian National Team. In July, after the Pan-American Games, I had a change of heart about this decision. I walked away from the opportunity to go to the Olympics and returned to my studies at the University of California at Berkeley.

2   Everyone who knew me asked the same question: "Why?" After all, I had played for 13 years, and been part of the national team program for six years.

3   During my last year on the team, I looked deeper into the Olympic movement. I was deeply troubled by the corporate sellout of the event, by the hollowness of Olympic environmental claims and by the blatant lie that the competition served to "bring the world together."

4   Like all other hopefuls, I gave up a great deal to make the Olympic team. I moved away from friends and family, lived well below the poverty line for years and put my education on hold in order to hone my athletic skills. I made these sacrifices because I loved playing water polo and because I wanted to compete with the best.

perspective point of view, opinion

diminished made less significant

sustainable development a term used to describe a movement whereby a country or a group is given assistance to become self-sufficent and eventually independent of outside aid

initiatives innovative projects

My perspective on the Games gradually shifted. I began to see that my sacrifices were going to be used by the Olympic Games and their sponsors for ends that conflicted with my fundamental values. My competitive performance would not just be a part of a world community gathering to compete in the spirit of fair play, good will and global unity, but rather it would be sold to the highest corporate bidder for their own commercial gain. The profits of this sale would go not to the performing athletes, but rather to the International Olympic Committee, national Olympic committees and sponsors.

The spirit of the Games has been diminished by becoming a platform for multinational companies to promote their unhealthy products to the world, with the Olympians as their unwitting promoters. Coke is not what athletes drink, and McDonald's hamburgers are not what they eat. They are not part of an athlete's healthy diet. I began to question whether I could commit myself to promoting these kinds of products by performing under their logos since, by doing so, I was suggesting that they were "healthy" and commendable.

The environment became the third pillar of the Olympic movement in 1994, along with culture and athletics. The IOC also signed an "Earth Pact" with the U.N. Environmental Program and changed its charter to include sustainable development as a goal. The goal was to have the Olympic movement play an active role in helping sustainable development occur throughout the world. I question the ability of "the movement" to do this when it does not question the consumption patterns that they are ultimately promoting via their corporate sponsors.

This pact, called Agenda 21, is rhetorical in nature and reflects more generally the rhetorical shift of the corporate world, which pays for the staging of the Games to "Green-wash" their images. A deeper look at the Games and the corporate system that supports them is needed. The Olympic movement is a "light" green movement that has raised some public awareness of environmental issues and environmentally friendly alternatives. The Olympic villages use solar water-heating, do water remediation and recycling. While these initiatives address the technical problems of being environmentally friendly, they do not address the truly fundamental value system changes that are needed to prevent global environmental disaster.

The 2000 Games were awarded to Sydney, in part, because of its environmental platform. Part of the platform was that an independent monitoring body, Green Games Watch Inc., ensure that they fulfilled the promises that earned them the Olympic bid. Report cards were issued during the lead-up to the Games, and it became clear that their own ecological criteria might not be met. In the fall of 1999, the government funding of Green Games Watch Inc. was cut off. The detailed environmental platforms of Sydney's Olympic Games and the criteria set out for all games in the IOC's Agenda 21 are completely meaningless without independent monitoring.

The Games themselves create villages that are supposed to reflect the real world. However, only those with credentials (elite athletes, coaches, managers, officials and volunteers who serve the aforementioned) are allowed in, and then only after a security search. Enormous resources are required to feed and care for the athletes, officials and media. The underlying culture is elitist. The Games ironically reinforce nationalist, ethnocentric feelings, imperialistic attitudes and promulgate a culture of consumption.

What this world needs is a festival of true cooperation that brings a diverse mix of rich and poor together—not to compete against each other—but to find common ground and to work together to imagine a brighter, fuller future. If this celebration of all that is best in humanity emerges, I will then seek to be a participant.

Checking Meaning and Style

1. What sacrifices did Kaliya Young have to make to become a member of the Olympic team?
2. Why did she not wish to be an "unwitting promoter" of multinationals' products?
3. Look at each paragraph and decide what the topic sentences are. In what way does Young support her paragraph topics?
4. What is the third pillar of the Olympic movement, and what initiatives are taken as a result?
5. How does Young conclude her article?

Checking Ideas

1. What is supposed to be the purpose of the Olympic Games?
2. For what did Young think her performance would be used?
3. Why does she describe the Olympic village as "elitist"?
4. What is her opinion of the environmental initiatives, and who is using them as "Green-wash"?
5. Do you agree with Young? Would you prefer to see a different kind of international celebration?

Netcheck

A lot has been written about *sustainable development* in recent times. See what you can find out about the subject by going to www.google.ca. Are there any references to the Earth Summit on sustainable development that took place in Johannesburg in September 2002?

WRITING MODELS: A PARAGRAPH WITH A TOPIC SENTENCE

For good reasons, most writing is broken into paragraphs. One reason is that paragraphs help the reader follow the flow of the writer's ideas. Since a traditional paragraph discusses only one idea, a new paragraph alerts the reader that a new idea is coming up. Another reason for paragraphs is that they help writers organize their thoughts. In this section, you will examine three model paragraphs in which the writers' thoughts are well organized.

We can recognize the beginning of a paragraph because it is usually indented. That is, it starts several spaces in from the left side of the page, as in the model paragraphs below. However, typewritten or word-processed material is sometimes written in block form; a new paragraph is indicated by an extra space between paragraphs, and there is no indenting.

Kaliya Young's essay has a thesis sentence in the first paragraph that establishes the focus of the whole selection:

WRITING MODELS: A PARAGRAPH WITH A TOPIC SENTENCE   19

> In July…I had a change of heart about this decision.

The paragraphs that follow begin with a topic sentence and elaborate on Young's decision. Here are some examples of paragraphs with topic sentences that have further details that support or develop the main idea:

> Paragraph 4—Like all other hopefuls, I gave up a great deal to make the Olympic team.
>
> Paragraph 6—The spirit of the games has been diminished by becoming a platform for multinational companies to promote their unhealthy products to the world, with the Olympians as their unwitting promoters.
>
> Paragraph 7—The environment became the third pillar of the Olympic movement in 1994, along with culture and athletics.

Kaliya Young's entire essay can be reduced, with very little alteration, to a paragraph of the main points by focusing on the topic sentences.

> In July, after the Pan-American Games, I had a change of heart about this decision. Everyone who knew me asked me the same question: "Why?" During my last year on the team, I looked deeper into the Olympic movement. Like all other hopefuls, I gave up a great deal to make the Olympic team. My perspective on the Games gradually shifted. The spirit of the Games has been diminished by becoming a platform for international companies to promote their unhealthy products to the world, with the Olympians as their unwitting promoters. The environment became the third pillar of the Olympic movement in 1994, along with culture and athletics. The "Earth Pact," called Agenda 21, is rhetorical in nature and reflects more generally the rhetorical shift of the corporate world, which pays for the staging of the games to "Green-wash" their images. The 2000 Games was awarded to Sydney, in part, because of its environmental platform. The Games themselves create villages that are supposed to reflect the real world. *However, it is elitist in nature.* What the world needs is a festival of true cooperation that brings a diverse mix of rich and poor together.

Notice that this skeleton becomes less interesting without all the details for each topic. Study the model paragraphs that follow. Observe how the opening topic sentence establishes the *focus* of the paragraph. The other sentences add interesting details that clarify each topic sentence.

Model Paragraph #1

The topic sentence has been underlined

Notice how the details support the writer's topic sentence.

>   Recent milk advertisements suggest that natural, nutritional products have to be given a "product identity" to sell. In one advertisement, a hockey celebrity is wearing the black-and-white design of a cow! He is jogging with extra energy. The ad suggests that he gets his vitality from milk; if we drink milk, we can be like him. Milk now has a designer image.

What details have been added to enhance the topic sentence?

Model Paragraph #2

The underlined topic sentence states what the paragraph will discuss

<u>Walking is a healthful form of exercise that avoids some of the problems of running or jogging.</u> Running places stress on the ankles and knees and can cause injury; walking is much gentler to the body. Runners often risk their lives in auto traffic, while walkers tend to stick to the safer sidewalks. The flashing legs of a runner are of much greater interest to neighbourhood dogs than is the slower stride of a walker. Runners need a shower after their workout, but walkers can take a brisk noontime stroll and return to the office without fear of offending. Doctors say that walking rapidly for a half-hour or more several times a week can be beneficial in keeping a person's heart and lungs operating efficiently.

State three specific advantages of walking over running.

Unified

A paragraph should be *unified*; that is, it should deal with only one subject. **The topic sentence says what the main point of the paragraph is.** Putting the topic sentence first is most helpful in writing a unified paragraph.

Spotcheck 2-1

Support each topic sentence with sentences giving examples of your own. Be careful of your spelling and punctuation.

1. The Olympic Games have become highly controversial. _____
   _____
   _____
   _____
   _____

2. There are three pillars of the Olympic movement. _____
   _____
   _____
   _____
   _____

3. The athletes' village is considered elitist. _____
   _____
   _____
   _____
   _____

WRITING MODELS: A PARAGRAPH WITH A TOPIC SENTENCE   21

Spotcheck 2-2

Provide a topic sentence for each of the following paragraphs.

1. _____

   The kids use the computer mostly for playing games, such as Zoop and SimCity, but ten-year-old Billy has a program to help him with his spelling. The teenager, Sally, enjoys a program that casts horoscopes for her and her friends. My wife works out the family budget with an accounting program. I, meanwhile, try to catch up on some of my office correspondence in the evenings with the word-processing program—if no one else is using the computer.

2. _____

   We arrived at the lake early, about 9:30 a.m., when the air was still cool and the lake so still that the surrounding mountains were reflected as in a mirror. Alex suggested that we go to an old miner's cabin on the opposite shore. We walked through a cool pine forest along the edge of the lake, scaring up a few ducks as we went. After a picnic lunch near the cabin, I took a nap while Alex scouted around for good photo subjects. When we got back to the car, the sun was hot, and we were glad to take a dip in the lake.

3. _____

   I have liked animals since I was a little girl. While I was growing up, my pets included rabbits, snakes, guinea pigs, and a series of kittens. Another reason is that veterinarians provide a useful service in helping animals stay healthy, and they make a good living while doing it. Furthermore, the nearby university has a respected program in veterinary medicine.

Spotcheck 2-3

Two of the sentences in this paragraph do not stick to the topic sentence (underlined). In the blanks that follow the paragraph, write the numbers of the sentences that violate the unity of the paragraph.

   [1]The ancient Egyptians were pioneers in the use of eye makeup. [2]By 4000 B.C., they were emphasizing the eyes as the facial feature that most clearly revealed inner thoughts and feelings. [3]The Egyptian queen Cleopatra was famed for her beauty. [4]Green eye shadow was a favourite cosmetic. [5]Made from a copper ore, it was used on both upper and lower eyelids. [6]A paste made from a variety of substances outlined the eyes and darkened the eyebrows and lashes. [7]"Eyebrow pencils" were made of sticks of wood, metal, or ivory. [8]Both men and women used an eye glitter made from crushed beetle shells. [9]The ancient Egyptians are also famous for their huge pyramids, which were used as tombs for royalty.

   _____
   _____

PREWRITING: KEEPING A JOURNAL

If you were learning to play the guitar, the more you practised the better you would get. In the same way, the more you practise writing the more you will improve. One way to get in some extra practice is to keep a journal. Journal writing can also be a way to explore a topic before writing a paragraph or an essay. Many writers attribute their success to the journals they have kept.

A journal is a notebook in which you jot down thoughts about whatever has interested you that day or in the past few days. A loose-leaf or spiral notebook would do nicely. In addition, you might want to carry a smaller pad or a piece of paper during the day to make reminders of ideas and experiences. Entries should be made at least several times a week, ideally at the same time each day, such as at bedtime.

Your journal might include such things as how you felt when you got back your latest math quiz, your feelings about the math instructor or the person who sits next to you in class. Did you have a disagreement with a friend or family member, or enjoy a movie or TV show? What are your goals in life—job, money, family? Include something that was especially significant or interesting that your sociology instructor said about the causes of poverty, or the joke she told that you might want to use some day. How did you feel about the man playing the trombone in the subway? And so on.

Spotcheck 2-4

Write a short journal entry on one of the topics that will appear in the next writing assignment: computers, television, or radio.

_____
_____
_____
_____
_____
_____

WRITING ASSIGNMENT: A PARAGRAPH WITH A TOPIC SENTENCE

The topic of a paragraph is what it is about. You could write a paragraph about computers, television, or radio. Each one could be a topic of a paragraph. However, you would not have a **topic sentence** until you said something about your topic that led you into the paragraph. Notice how the three topics just mentioned could become parts of topic sentences:

1. <u>Computer</u> technology has changed completely over the past ten years.

Now you can give specific details and examples.

2. <u>Television</u> will have become a different entity by 2010.

Now add details about the ways in which TV might be different then.

3. <u>Radio</u> is still a major form of communication.

Discuss ways in which radio is used around the world.

Be sure that your topic sentences lead easily into a discussion of the topic. If you state only facts, there will be nothing to discuss. Stating an opinion leads to a more interesting paragraph. Avoid "so what?" sentences that lead nowhere, such as these:

Computers are often grey in colour. *(So what?)*

Radios are displayed in Future Shop. *(Who cares?)*

Spotcheck 2-5

*In the blanks at the left, write **good** for effective topic sentences that would lead to fully developed paragraphs. Write **weak** for those that seem to lead nowhere.*

1. _____ My writing skills have improved since I started reading more books and magazines.

2. _____ Mayor Lee wants to improve the city's park system.

3. _____ Canada's highest mountain is 5959 metres.

4. _____ Banff's mile-high altitude affects visiting athletes.

5. _____ There are three boys and three girls in my family.

Narrowing the Focus of the Topic Sentence

Topic sentences should not be too broad; that is, they should not try to cover too much ground. After all, you are writing a paragraph, not a book. Narrow your subject so that it can be discussed in a worthwhile way in the few sentences of a paragraph.

(too broad) The weather in British Columbia is sometimes uncomfortable.

(better) <u>The weather in Lytton</u> is sometimes uncomfortable.

(too broad) <u>Dogs</u> are devoted pets.

(better) <u>My grandfather's poodle Fifi</u> is a devoted pet.

Further Practice in Topic Sentences

From the following subjects, narrow the topics into suitable topic sentences.

1. Using public transportation

2. Violence policies in schools

3. The fishing industry

4. Public broadcasting

5. Winter sports

6. Learning a second language

Spotcheck 2-6

Rewrite the subjects at the left twice, each time making them less broad and more suitable for discussion in a single paragraph.

EXAMPLE:

| outdoor activity | gardening | growing roses |

1. work
2. buildings
3. music
4. students
5. books

Being Specific

Having narrowed your topic, be sure that what you say about it is specific, not general or vague.

(vague) The CBC <u>has good programs</u>.

(specific) The CBC <u>features the kind of news programs that I like</u>.

(vague) Montreal <u>is an interesting city</u>.

(specific) Montreal <u>has many outstanding restaurants</u>.

(more specific) Montreal <u>is a good place to find French cuisine</u>.

Spotcheck 2-7

*In the blanks at the left, write **weak** for topic sentences that are broad or vague. Write **good** for the others.*

1. _____ Mr. and Ms. Hameed are good people.
2. _____ Baseball is one of Canada's favourite sports.
3. _____ The woman at the checkout counter is nice.
4. _____ My new pickup truck costs a great deal in loan payments, insurance, and maintenance.
5. _____ Most of the "romance" novels sold at supermarkets are poor.
6. _____ Running eight kilometres several times a week can improve a person's health.

Spotcheck 2-8

Turn the listed topics into topic sentences by saying something specific about each one. Ask yourself if each sentence would lead easily to a full paragraph.

EXAMPLE: Professional football—Watching professional football on TV takes up too much of my time in the fall.

1. My favourite sport _____

2. My neighbourhood _____

WRITING ASSIGNMENT: A PARAGRAPH WITH A TOPIC SENTENCE   25

3. Christmas shopping _____
   _____

4. My English class _____
   _____

5. My cousin _____
   _____

Write a Paragraph

As final preparation for your own paragraph, first write a topic sentence for each of the broad topics listed below. Then narrow the topic to one particular example—one television show, for example—and make a specific point about it. You may find ideas in your journal exercise.

The Olympic Games _____
_____

The Internet _____
_____

The radio _____
_____

Television _____
_____

Music _____
_____

Now write a paragraph of five to ten sentences that begins with one of the topic sentences you just wrote.

Writing Assignment Checklist

✓ Use the brainstorming technique discussed in Chapter 1 or the journal writing discussed in this chapter to find details to develop your paragraph.

✓ Start with a topic sentence that makes clear the main point of the paragraph.

✓ Be sure that your paragraph is unified, with all sentences sticking to the topic sentence.

✓ If you have a chance, discuss the assignment and your paragraph with a classmate.

✓ In this and all other writing assignments in this text, observe the guidelines that follow. Of course, your instructor may have additional or different requirements.

Manuscript Preparation

Procedure for Papers Written with Word Processors

1. Use standard white paper, 8½ by 11 inches.
2. Double-space the lines.
3. Be sure that your toner or ribbon is fresh enough to print clearly.
4. Leave margins on both sides—1½ inches on the left and 1 inch on the right.
5. Number each sheet in the upper right-hand corner, starting with the second sheet.
6. Fold the paper lengthwise (do not staple it) and write your name and the date on the *front* cover.

Procedure for Handwritten Papers

1. Use a pen (never a pencil) with blue-black or black ink. Write as neatly and clearly as you can.
2. Use standard lined notebook paper. Avoid the spiral-bound kind that leaves a ragged edge when you tear out a sheet.
3. Write on every other line.
4. Write on only one side of the paper.
5. Follow items 4 to 6 in the instructions for word processors above.
6. Other instructions

_____
_____
_____
_____

SENTENCE STRUCTURE: IDENTIFYING THE SUBJECT AND VERB OF THE SENTENCE

To write acceptably, we have to write in **sentences**. Most of us do that most of the time without thinking about it. But sometimes we may write something that looks like a sentence—that starts with a capital letter and ends with a period—but isn't a sentence. Here is an example:

Driving into the parking lot while following a green Mercedes.

Since a complete sentence needs a subject and a verb, we need to be able to recognize these sentence parts. Recognizing subjects and verbs is not worth much in itself. But if you can do it, you will be able to deal later with some very real problems in writing: **sentence fragments, run-together sentences, lack of subject–verb agreement, inconsistencies in person and tense,** and **errors in punctuation**.

Finding the Subject of the Sentence

The subject tells *who* or *what* the sentence is about. The underlined words in the following sentences answer the question "Who?" or "What?"

Lee arrived early.

Winnipeg is the capital of Manitoba.

Glass breaks.

We always sing before supper.

Parts of Speech

The subject is usually a noun or a pronoun. A *noun* is the name of a person, place, or thing (*Lee, Winnipeg, glass*). A *pronoun* is a word that takes the place of a noun. *We* is an example of a pronoun. *He, she,* and *it* are other examples of pronouns.

The words underlined in the examples just given are the *simple subjects* of their sentences. A *complete subject* is the simple subject plus any words that describe it. In the following example, the complete subject is underlined once and the simple subject (*car*) twice:

The blue car with the damaged fender struck a tree yesterday.

In this text, the phrase *the subject* refers to the simple subject.

Spotcheck 2-9

*Underline the subject in each sentence. To find the subject, ask **who** or **what** the sentence is about.*

1. The electricity went out at 11 p.m.
2. Swimming is good exercise.
3. Ms. Jackson bought a new dress.
4. Our new calendar has a picture of Stanley Park.
5. The hard-working plumber finished the job.
6. The average person can see 93 million miles—when looking at the sun.
7. Air conditioning was invented to control humidity, not temperature.
8. George Ferris invented the Ferris wheel in 1893.
9. Jupiter, the largest planet, is three times bigger than Earth.
10. Less snow falls at the South Pole than in parts of the United States.

Finding the Verb of the Sentence

There are two kinds of verbs.

1. **Action verbs** tell what the subject *does* (or did, or will do).

   Geese fly south in the winter.

   Maria's brother attended Concordia University.

2. **Linking verbs** connect the subject to words that say something about the subject.

> Marcia <u>was</u> overjoyed at getting the job.
>
> Roberto <u>seems</u> tired tonight.

The verb *was* links the subject *Marcia* to information about the subject: that she was overjoyed. The verb *seems* links the subject *Robert* to the description *tired*.

One group of linking verbs consists of forms of the verb *to be*:

> am is are was were been

Another group of linking verbs contains words such as these:

> seem appear look become feel taste smell

Some of these words can be either linking or action verbs.

> Rudy <u>looked</u> happy. [linking verb]
>
> Rudy <u>looked</u> at the magazine. [action verb]

Spotcheck 2-10

Underline the verbs. In the blanks, indicate whether they are action verbs (A) or linking verbs (L).

1. _____ The firefighters fought the blaze for two hours.
2. _____ They were happy to be home.
3. _____ The water in Lake Huron looked dirty last fall.
4. _____ The third baseman hit two home runs.
5. _____ The spectators cheered for the home team.

Spotcheck 2-11

Underline the verbs. In the blanks, indicate whether they are action verbs (A) or linking verbs (L).

1. _____ Many birds eat twice their weight each day.
2. _____ Today's blue whales are bigger than the biggest dinosaurs.
3. _____ Lobsters look red only after boiling.
4. _____ Dolphins and monkeys have better memories than elephants.
5. _____ Ants live on every continent except Antarctica.

Doublecheck 2-1

Draw one line under the subject and two lines under the verb in each sentence.

1. French soldiers fought an odd battle in the First World War.
2. German soldiers threatened to cross the Marne River.
3. The river was only 50 kilometres from the French capital, Paris.

4. The French cause seemed lost.
5. The army needed reinforcements at the front immediately.
6. The reinforcements arrived in time—and in style—as passengers in the taxicabs of Paris.

Crossing Out Prepositional Phrases to Find the Subject

Often it is easier to find the subject if you first cross out all prepositional phrases in a sentence. Look at this example:

~~Behind the house,~~ Mr. Olson was napping ~~in a hammock~~.

After you cross out the two prepositional phrases, *Behind the house* and *in a hammock*, it is clear that the subject is *Mr. Olson*.

IMPORTANT: A word in a prepositional phrase is never the subject of a sentence.

Prepositional phrases are groups of words that begin with a preposition and end with a noun or pronoun. Here are some common prepositions:

about	beside	of
above	between	on
according to	by	over
across	during	through
after	for	to
among	from	toward
around	in	under
at	into	upon
before	near	with

Spotcheck 2-12

Use eight different prepositions to form prepositional phrases with these words.

EXAMPLE: <u>near</u> the window

1. _____ the two trees
2. _____ the binoculars
3. _____ the leaves
4. _____ our car
5. _____ the roof
6. _____ town
7. _____ friends
8. _____ ten o'clock

Spotcheck 2-13

Cross out the prepositional phrases and underline the subject.

EXAMPLE: ~~In the office,~~ the <u>president</u> stood ~~near his desk~~.

1. Of the three singers, Charles is best.
2. Between the tall buildings, a tree turned to the sunlight.
3. One of the ducks on the pond is tame.
4. For some reason, the instructor gave an "A" to everyone in the class.
5. Between you and me, the award should go to Sylvia.

Doublecheck 2-2

Draw one line under the subject and two lines under the verb in each sentence.

1. The new neighbours have three children.
2. The prom queen removed her crown after the dance.
3. Eric's 1975 Chevy is ready for the scrap heap.
4. Your stew tastes like my mother's.
5. Lawrence was a good source of gossip at the office.

More Tips on Finding the Subject of the Sentence

The subject usually appears at the beginning of the sentence, but it may appear elsewhere.

>Flitting from flower to flower was a <u>hummingbird</u>. (The usual word order: A hummingbird was flitting from flower to flower.)

Although it often starts a sentence, *there* is never the subject.

>There were three books lying on the table. (*Books* is the subject of the verb *were lying*.)

A sentence can have more than one subject.

>The <u>oil</u> and the <u>filter</u> need to be changed.

In sentences that express a command, the unwritten but understood subject is *you*.

>[You] Bring home a loaf of bread after work.

Sometimes it is easier to find the subject if you pick out the verb first, then ask *who* or *what* questions.

>   **subject**   **verb**
>In the spring, the <u>poppies</u> on the hillsides <u>appear</u> first.

Spotcheck 2-14

Draw a line under each subject.

1. College athletes have little chance of joining a professional team.
2. In football, for example, only 1 player in 100 has a chance of turning professional.
3. There is only 1 chance in 500 of succeeding in the National Basketball Association.
4. Even then, the average sports career is short—4.2 years in football and 3.2 years in basketball.
5. Remember these statistics when dreaming about sports instead of doing homework.
6. Less likely than other students to complete a degree are athletes at university or college.

Quickcheck on Subjects of a Sentence

✓ Every complete sentence must have a subject.
✓ The subject tells who or what the sentence is about.
✓ The subject usually appears at the beginning of the sentence, but it may appear elsewhere.
✓ A prepositional phrase is never the subject.
✓ In commands, the unwritten but understood subject is *you*.

More Tips on Finding the Verb of the Sentence

If the subject performs more than one action, there will be more than one **verb**.

The car swerved to the left and hit a tree.

The verb may consist of more than one word. The main verb may have one or more *helping verbs*.

The hikers had walked 15 kilometres before noon.

Here are some examples of helping verbs with forms of the verb *work*:

can work	does work
is working	has been working
might have been working	should have worked
had worked	will work
will have worked	will be working

NOTE: A word ending in *-ing* cannot be the verb without one or more helping verbs. A verb preceded by *to* (*to work*) is an *infinitive* and cannot be the verb.

Sometimes the verb is broken by words that are not part of the verb. Words that often separate parts of a verb are *not* (and its contraction *-n't*), *never, always, just,* and *only*.

Mr. Ochoa had never seen a redwood tree before.

The fire hadn't been started in the fireplace when we arrived.

Sometimes the verb has an *object*—the person or thing acted upon by the verb. The object of a verb is **never** the subject of a sentence.

      verb   **object**
The landlord raised the rent twice this year.

Spotcheck 2-15

Underline the verb or verbs in each sentence.

1. The Barbie doll first appeared in 1958 and achieved instant popularity.
2. It was invented by Ruth Handler for the Mattel toy company.
3. Before Barbie, North American dolls had usually resembled infants.

4. Noticing her daughter's fondness for full-figured paper cutout dolls, Mrs. Handler developed a shapely adult doll.

5. As a full-sized person, Barbie would have a 39–23–33 figure.

6. A large wardrobe and other accessories for Barbie were soon offered.

7. Taking his place with Barbie on toy store shelves in 1961 was Ken.

8. Barbie and Ken were named after the Handlers' daughter and son.

Quickcheck on Verbs in a Sentence

✓ Every complete sentence must have a verb.

✓ Action verbs tell what the subject *does*; linking verbs tell what the subject *is*.

✓ A sentence may have more than one verb.

✓ A verb can be more than one word—a main verb plus helping verbs.

✓ To be a complete verb, a verb form ending in *-ing* always needs a helping verb.

Doublecheck 2-3

In the following paragraph, draw one line under each subject and two lines under each verb. Finding the subjects may be easier if you cross out prepositional phrases first.

¹Education in Japan is different in many ways from education in the United States. ²For one thing, only 7 percent of Japanese students drop out. ³In the United States, the dropout rate is about three times higher. ⁴The quality of the Japanese education system is often credited for Japan's success in technological fields. ⁵For many Japanese, education has been the only path to social and economic status. ⁶Starting in grade one, Japanese schools stress hard work, endurance, and concentration. ⁷These same values are reinforced in the students' homes. ⁸The status of a Japanese woman depends in large part on the success of her children in school. ⁹Nearly half of the high-school students attend tutoring centres after school. ¹⁰They worry about passing the difficult college entrance exams. ¹¹Four hours of sleep at night is common for serious students. ¹²Surprisingly, Japanese colleges often receive low marks from some American observers. ¹³Americans sometimes have been critical of the emphasis in Japanese schools on memorizing facts. ¹⁴Too much emphasis on learning facts may hamper creativity.

Checkpoint 2-1

Enter the subjects and verbs of each sentence in the blanks.

1. _____   The history of advertising goes back thousands of years.
   _____

2. _____   Street peddlers long ago called out the praises of their goods.
   _____

SENTENCE STRUCTURE: IDENTIFYING THE SUBJECT AND VERB OF THE SENTENCE **33**

3. _____   The ancient Greeks advertised the sale of cattle and slaves.
   _____

4. _____   In Rome, signs on walls informed the public of upcoming gladiator contests.
   _____

5. _____   In the Middle Ages, handbills often contained pictures to help the illiterate.
   _____

6. _____   The first newspaper in England was the *Weekly Newes*.
   _____

7. _____   It appeared in 1622 and contained an ad for the return of a stolen horse.
   _____

8. _____   During the plague of 1665, many ads for pills for "preventing sickness" appeared.
   _____

9. _____   King Charles II cracked down on the numerous shop signs "shutting out the air and the light of the heavens."
   _____

10. _____ In 1752, the *Halifax Gazette* carried the first formal ad in Canada.
    _____

Checkpoint 2-2

Write the subject(s) of each sentence in the first blank(s) at the left and the verbs— with any helping verb(s)—in the remaining blanks.

1. _____   Our next-door neighbours may return Tuesday.
   _____

2. _____   The chemistry teacher and the students left the lab after the explosion.
   _____

3. _____   Never accept a ride from a stranger.
   _____

4. _____   There is a music collection in the library.
   _____

5. _____   After studying all night, Susan slept during the exam.
   _____

No answers are given for Checkpoint quizzes.

WORDCHECK: PRONUNCIATION

Let's suppose that you aren't quite sure how to pronounce the word *psychology*. Looking it up in a dictionary, you will find something like this right after the entry for the word:

[saiˈkɒlədʒi]

The accent mark (ˈ) means that the following syllable is emphasized in speaking. Other pronunciation marks are explained in a key usually found at the front or back, or at the bottom of one of the two pages you see when you open the dictionary. The upside down *e* (ə) in the third syllable is pronounced *uh*, like the *a* in *ago* or *around*.

Using a dictionary, copy the pronunciations of the following words. Use the pronunciation key in the dictionary to practise pronouncing the words. If more than one pronunciation is given, the first one is used more often.

photographer   Mozart   ask   pronunciation   nuclear

CHECKPOST: DEFINITE (THE) AND INDEFINITE (A/AN) ARTICLES

Definite and indefinite articles are used before nouns and convey information about the nouns. A number of rules for the use of definite and indefinite articles concern count and noncount nouns.

Count nouns are nouns of person, place, or thing that can be counted:

toy(s), pear(s), girl(s), sheet(s) of paper, piece(s) of wood

Noncount nouns refer to items and abstractions that cannot be counted:

water, paper, knowledge

Sometimes, a noncount noun will be used in a countable way:

"What are these papers doing here?"

Rules

- *A/An* is used to introduce a count noun for the first time. After the first mention of the noun, *the* is used.

    A man came into view. The man limped, clutching his thigh.

- *The* is used for all kinds of nouns—count and noncount, singular and plural.

- In general, no article is used with plural count nouns and noncount nouns.

- *The* can be used for generic statements that include concepts, ideas, or categories.

CHECKPOST: DEFINITE (THE) AND INDEFINITE (A/AN) ARTICLES   35

  The buffalo was brought back from near extinction.

  The sun seems hotter than it used to be.

- *The* is used with plural proper nouns.

  the United States, the Solomon Islands

- *The* is **not** used for plural or noncount nouns that express "all."

  Wheat is a staple in Eastern Europe.

  Ponds are expensive to install.

- *The* is **not** used with most singular proper nouns or abstract nouns.

  Nathan Phillips Square, Stanley Park, love, beauty

  Envy is a sin. *But:* The envy he feels is making him sick.

Remember

- The sound of *the* rhymes with *sea* when it is spoken before a noun with a vowel sound.

  the air / the bear

- Use *an* for vowels, *y* and the soft *h*, but not for words that start with "a hard" *u* (*union, university*).

Checkpost 2-1

Use a/an or the, or nothing, in the following blanks.

1. _____ Rockies are exquisite to view in the early morning.

2. _____ Hudson's Bay Company was established in 1670.

3. _____ vegetarian is often _____ very healthy person.

4. _____ van crashed into our car on _____ Trans-Canada, but it was _____ van, not our car, that was damaged.

5. Although Ji Yong loves _____ lemonade, she offered me _____ bottle of ginger beer.

6. The newspaper was delivered by a boy on _____ bicycle.

7. _____ price of _____ gold is very low at present.

8. She is not _____ most intelligent girl in the world, but she certainly tries hard.

9. _____ sun is so hot, you must wear sunblock.

10. Henry loves studying _____ biology.

11. _____ bicycles are _____ environmentally friendly way of travelling.

12. _____ teachers should be sensitive to their students' needs.

13. _____ stitch in time saves nine.

14. It is hard to find _____ honest used car salesperson.

15. She is employed at _____ hourly rate.

Checkpost 2-2

Use articles appropriately with these count/noncount nouns.

1. _____ Lake Superior is very deep; _____ volume is 12 000 cubic kilometres, whereas _____ volume in _____ Lake Ontario is 1640 cubic kilometres. _____ water in both lakes is polluted.

2. Since _____ computers became popular, writing with _____ ink has gone out of fashion. Many children don't know how to write with _____ fountain pen; they can only use _____ ballpoint pen, _____ pencil, or _____ computer.

3. _____ universities are becoming very expensive. _____ students can't afford to pay _____ fees. Now _____ work is hard to find for _____ students; it is often impossible for them to get _____ money.

4. _____ tea is grown in Sri Lanka. It is _____ popular drink in Europe where it is drunk with _____ sugar and _____ piece of lemon, not with _____ milk.

3

PARAGRAPHS WITH SPECIFIC DETAILS

READING: SPECIFIC DETAILS FOLLOWING A TOPIC SENTENCE

Precheck Are you a fan of science fiction? Do you watch sci-fi films? In the following article, Brian Bethune celebrates the latest publication by Phyllis Gotlieb, who, at 76, is still writing science fiction. Until Gotlieb's success in this genre, Canadian writers had not gained recognition or a foothold in the sci-fi market internationally. Bethune furnishes the reader with details about Gotlieb's long career as a poet and sci-fi writer and describes the influences on her development as an author.

Journal Topic In your journal, write about a famous person whose life you admire.

Grandmother of Us All *–Brian Bethune*

Phyllis Gotlieb is the first to agree she fits the classic profile of the science fiction writer. "Like quite a few of us—Robert Silverberg, Frederik Pohl, my friend Judy Merril," she rhymes off, "I was an only child." And if that wasn't enough to predetermine an imaginative girl's future, there's also how she used to spend her Saturday afternoons. The daughter of a man who ran a series of movie houses in Depression-era Toronto, Gotlieb would "go to whatever theatre my father was running, and spend the day there with my movie mags and my pulps *Doc Savage* and *The Shadow* especially. I had such a pop culture background, Mickey Mouse was my hero." So it's easy to visualize a straight line from such a childhood to this month's publication, on the eve of her 76th birthday, of *Mindworlds*, the final volume of Gotlieb's acclaimed *Flesh and Gold* trilogy.

Except very little in Phyllis Gotlieb's writing career has followed a straight line. By the time she was 11, she was determined to become a writer, but it was poetry more than stories that delighted her. Only when Gotlieb was enduring a writer's block in the early 1950s ("I have a lot of those," she says of a career more notable for longevity than output) did her husband, Calvin, a physicist turned pioneering University of Toronto computer scientist, strike a chord by suggesting

trilogy a set of three books, all related to each other

strike a chord to sound like a good idea

37

she try science fiction. The first result was completely unexpected. "My poetry had dried up, but as soon as I started SF, it came back."

By the next decade the two mutually reinforcing strands of Gotlieb's writing were both in full flower. Her poetry, which would bring her a 1970 Governor General's Award nomination for *Ordinary Moving*, coincided with a surge of national interest in the genre. The Canada Council frequently dispatched poets, including Gotlieb, across the country to give readings in schools and libraries. In 1964, during a week she has never forgotten, Gotlieb was one of a quartet sent to Montreal, Ottawa and London, Ont. The other three were Leonard Cohen, Irving Layton and Earle Birney, stars then and now of the CanLit galaxy. "Let's just say I was pretty much *suppressed* by my companions," Gotlieb sighs. But on a tour that had no shortage of towering egos, Gotlieb was no one's main target. "Last I saw of Earle, he was in the back of a taxi, with his thumbs at his ears, waggling his fingers at Leonard and Irving." Not at you? "Oh no; if I'd thought that, I'd have given him the finger."

suppressed held down, out of the spotlight

During the same period, while her poetry was finding an audience and she still had three children at home, Gotlieb finally emerged from a painful sci-fi apprenticeship. After years of rejections, Gotlieb broke through in 1964 with *Sunburst*, Canadian science fiction's seminal novel. "That's when she became the grandmother of us all," says Robert Sawyer, the most prominent author in a now-flourishing national scene. "She was the one—till the '80s, the only one who proved you could sit in Toronto and write major science fiction and sell it to major American publishers." *Sunburst*, which has given its name to an award for the best Canadian sci-fi book of the year, marked a final change of course for Gotlieb, who eventually no longer had "poem-shaped ideas." (Since then, she says, "my aliens write poetry.")

Sunburst also brought to the fore what would be Gotlieb's perennial theme over the next four decades—telepathy. Gotlieb is second to none in creating detailed universes, full of exotic aliens in the mode of *Star Wars* (itself a direct descendant of the movies she watched as a kid). And she's miles beyond most in evoking her creatures with beautifully crafted images. But the telepathic powers that drive her stories are more than plot devices. "I hope it's clear that telepathy in my writing is shorthand for understanding and communication," she says. It's clear to John Robert Colombo, prolific compiler of Canadian cultural lore and long-time friend of Gotlieb. "She's a quintessential Canadian writer, preoccupied with what constitutes identity, and with communication between peoples."

telepathy communication through thoughts, not with words

quintessential most representative

That doesn't lead to the tidy, upbeat endings so beloved of classic sci-fi. Gotlieb recalls an early rejection from John W. Campbell, the legendary editor of *Astounding* magazine, who said her story "denies the whole premise of science fiction." By that Campbell "seemed to mean it didn't have a happy ending," she says in some wonderment, adding: "In my books most of my characters—not all, but most—are still standing at the end. That's my idea of a happy ending. Standing is good." She smiles. "I'm still standing."

Checking Meaning and Style

1. What occasion prompted this article?
2. What details does the author give of Phyllis Gotlieb's career highlights?
3. What is the topic sentence that introduces the subject?
4. What prompted Gotlieb to start writing sci-fi?

Checking Ideas

5. What details do we learn of her private life?
6. What does Bethune mean by the expression "The Canada Council frequently dispatched poets"? What details do we learn of Gotlieb's tour?
1. What two influences shaped Phyllis Gotlieb as a sci-fi writer?
2. Why is she so important to other sci-fi writers?
3. Why does Colombo call her "a quintessential Canadian writer"? Do you know of any other Canadian writers who have the same themes?
4. Why was one of Gotlieb's early stories rejected?
5. Is sci-fi a favourite genre of yours, or do you prefer another type of fiction?

Netcheck

If you wanted to know more about Phyllis Gotlieb's books, what site would you go to on the Net?

WRITING MODELS: A PARAGRAPH WITH SPECIFIC DETAILS

The late-night TV host Johnny Carson used to open his show with a line such as "Boy, was it hot today!" His studio audience always shouted back, "How hot was it, Johnny?"

There's a lesson for writers in that exchange. People aren't satisfied with generalities. They want specific details. They want to know not just that it was hot but that the thermometer hit 35 degrees Celsius, that downtown office workers waded in the courthouse fountain at lunchtime, and that highway traffic was snarled by overheated cars.

Using specific details is one of the best ways to develop the general idea of a topic sentence. Specific details help make a paragraph interesting, convincing, and clear.

Being Specific

As we have seen, writing that doesn't get down to specifics—writing that is general or vague—is uninteresting and often unclear.

(vague) Susan <u>can't be trusted</u>.

(specific) Susan <u>borrowed my reggae album two weeks ago and hasn't returned it</u>.

(vague) Jason has a new <u>dog</u>.

(specific) Jason has a new <u>attack-trained Chihuahua</u>.

(vague) Kevin lives in a <u>big house</u>.

(specific) Kevin lives in a <u>14-room mansion that has 6 bathrooms, 4 garages, and an indoor swimming pool</u>.

Spotcheck 3-1

Fill in the blanks so that vague words are on the left and the most specific are on the right.

EXAMPLE:

Animal	farm animal	cow

1. breakfast cereal — hot cereal — _____
2. recreation — _____ — _____
3. _____ — African languages — Swahili
4. books — college texts — _____
5. fruit — citrus fruit — _____

Spotcheck 3-2

Rewrite these sentences to make the vague words (underlined) more specific. Your sentences will probably be longer than the originals.

EXAMPLE:

My parents are <u>nice</u>.

My parents <u>give me money whenever I want it</u>.

1. Larry was <u>angry</u>. (Say what Larry *did* that showed anger.)
   _____

2. Yolanda has a new <u>car</u>.
   _____

3. Naomi brought a <u>snack</u>.
   _____

4. Carlos is <u>handsome</u>.
   _____

5. Jonathan ate <u>a big dinner</u>.
   _____

To prepare for the next writing assignment, study the following portrait of an officer in the armed forces.

Writing Paragraphs with Specific Details

Model Paragraph with Specific Details #1

<u>Major Cartier was one of the most intimidating men I had ever met.</u> His smile had the same effect as an axe-killer's smile; it screamed, "I'm dangerous!" Standing six-feet-five, he had a Mr. Universe build. His growling, snarling voice earned him the nickname "The Bear," and his eagle eyes never missed a recruit's slightest misstep. To top it all, his mind was quicker than a computer.

Notice that the topic sentence states what the focus of the portrait will be—that the major was "intimidating." Note, too, how specific details show that the major was indeed intimidating.

PREWRITING: CLUSTERING

Clustering is another type of brainstorming that many writers find useful. Clustering helps you organize your thoughts and produce the details that make your writing interesting. This is how clustering works: First, choose a word or phrase as the starting point. Put it in the middle of a blank page and circle it. Let your mind make connections with the topic word. Write your new ideas down, forming a web around the centre word. Put ideas that seem related near each other. When done, use the cluster as an outline of your paragraph (or essay). Here is an example that will help you with your next writing assignment, a portrait of a person.

Teaching
3rd grade
Jackson Elem.
Teacher of the Year
retired 1992

Grandchildren
four
babysitting
evenings
weekends
doctor trips
birthdays

GRANDMA RUTH

Strength
5' 10"
190 lbs.
arm wrestling

Gardening
liked flowers
marigolds, azaleas
county fair honours

The second model paragraph could be written from the "Grandma Ruth" cluster.

Model Paragraph with Specific Details #2

<u>Grandma Ruth played an important part in the lives of many children</u>. She taught grade three at Jackson Elementary School for 35 years, retiring in 1992. The city had honoured her as Teacher of the Year in 1985. After retiring, she devoted much of her time to her four grandchildren. She spent many evenings and weekends babysitting them when their parents wanted to go to a movie or attend an out-of-town event. Sunday dinner was always held at Grandma's, even though her small house was overflowing when everyone attended. If both of a child's parents were at work, Grandma could be counted on to drive the child to a doctor's or dentist's appointment. She never forgot a birthday. It's no wonder that so many people appreciated Grandma's role in their lives.

The topic sentence is underlined. The cluster items about Grandma Ruth's appearance and gardening activities have been left out because they don't develop the topic sentence idea—that she was important to many children.

Another use of clustering would be to choose one of the topics in the cluster and put that in the centre of a new cluster. That way you could have a more detailed paragraph on, for example, Grandma Ruth's teaching years.

WRITING ASSIGNMENT: A PORTRAIT OF A PERSON

With the model paragraphs in mind, write a one-paragraph portrait of a person you know well.

Begin with a topic sentence that focuses on *one quality* of the person. For example, if your topic sentence says

> Mrs. Schaffer always dresses in the latest fashions.

you would discuss only Mrs. Schaffer's clothing, not her favourite TV shows or how many children she has.

Notice how each of these sample topic sentences could lead to a limited, unified paragraph.

> I can never count on my husband to do anything on time.

> My neighbour loves to listen to rock and roll music, unfortunately.

> When I was in the hospital, my nurse, Ms. Beresford, was very helpful.

Be sure to check that none of your details are vague or uninteresting.

GRAMMAR CHECK: As well as checking for punctuation, spelling, and sentence structure, you must also look for fragments.

Writing Assignment Checklist

- ✓ Use a topic sentence to provide a focus for the paragraph.
- ✓ Use the prewriting technique of clustering to develop and organize your paragraph.
- ✓ Use specific details to make your writing interesting and clear.
- ✓ If possible, collaborate with a classmate when revising the paragraph.
- ✓ Proofread the final draft, looking especially for spelling troublemakers.

In this and all writing assignments, remember to revise your work, as demonstrated in the example that follows.

WRITING PROCESS: REVISING THE PAPER

Even skilled writers usually have to do their "assignments" more than once. In other words, they need to *revise* their work to make it as effective as possible. The famous novelist Ernest Hemingway said he wrote the last page of *A Farewell to Arms* thirty-nine times before he was satisfied. Even if you don't keep up with Hemingway, you should expect to go over your writing more than once. Consider your first effort as a *rough draft*, not the final product.

If time permits, let your first draft sit for a while. When you come back to it, your opportunities for making improvements will stand out more clearly. (*Revision* literally means "seeing again.") It may not be necessary, but be prepared to perform major surgery: to cut, add, and change.

Revision Checklist

Here are some questions you might ask about a paragraph written for this class:

- ✓ Does it have a *topic sentence* that says clearly what the paragraph is about?
- ✓ Is it *unified*? Do all the other sentences stick to the topic?
- ✓ Is it adequately *developed* with specific details to make it interesting and convincing?
- ✓ Does it contain errors in spelling, punctuation, grammar, or sentence construction? (Many of these problems will be discussed in later chapters.)

Compare the following draft of a paragraph describing a person called Nonnie with the revised version that follows. Weaknesses in the original are underlined, with marginal comments. Problems indicated in the margin will be covered in later chapters.

vague topic sentence
comma splice
sentence fragment
punctuation error
spelling error
nonparallel structure
lack of unity

Nonnie <u>was my mother</u>. She listened to the same radio programs each morning as she had breakfast<u>,</u> then she put on her blue uniform and caught a ride to her job at the tobacco factory. <u>Cutting the hard ends off tobacco leaves</u>. She always took her lunch to work. After supper she read the *Durham Sun*<u>,</u> and made sure the <u>childern</u> completed their chores. Saturdays were her days for washing the clothes, ironing, and <u>she worked</u> in the garden. Sunday afternoons she would visit her friends. She was content with this routine. <u>Her neighbour, Claudia, worked in a general store</u>.

Here is a revised version:

Nonnie, my mother, lived a structured life. She listened to the same radio programs each morning at breakfast. Then she put on her blue uniform and caught a ride to her job at the tobacco factory, where she cut off the hard ends of tobacco leaves. She always took her lunch to work. After supper, she read the

Durham Sun and made sure the children completed their chores. Saturday was her day for washing the clothes, ironing, and working in the garden. Sundays she visited her friends. She was content with this routine.

SENTENCE STRUCTURE: AVOIDING FRAGMENTS

In the last chapter you learned how to recognize subjects and verbs. Now you can put that knowledge to good use as we move on to writing sound sentences, a skill that lies at the heart of effective writing. A complete sentence has three characteristics:

1. A sentence has a *subject* (that tells who or what the sentence is about).
2. A sentence has a *verb* (that tells what the subject does or that links it to words that describe the subject).
3. A sentence *expresses a complete thought* (makes sense by itself).

Fragments are pieces of sentences that look like sentences because they start with a capital letter and end with a period, but they are not sentences unless they meet the three tests just listed. An example:

The man on the white horse.

The man on the white horse is a fragment. It has a subject, *man*. (You know *horse* is not the subject because it is the object of the preposition *on*. The object of a preposition is never the subject of a sentence.) But *The man on the white horse* is not a sentence because it lacks a verb (what did the man *do?*) and because it is incomplete (it does not make sense by itself).

The man on the white horse waved.

When we add the verb *waved*, the words express a complete thought and become an acceptable sentence.

Remember that an *-ing* word is not a complete verb.

(fragment) The politician <u>speaking</u> for two hours.

Such verbs need helping verbs such as *is*, *was*, and *has been*.

(complete sentence) The politician <u>has been speaking</u> for two hours.

Spotcheck 3-3

The following paragraphs contain fragment errors. At the end of each paragraph, indicate which "sentences" are really fragments by writing the appropriate letters in the blanks. Then circle S, V, or Both to indicate whether the fragments lack a subject, a verb, or both.

NOTE: Fragments are more obvious if you read backwards—from the last sentence to the first.

1. [A]In the 1980s, Canadians still travelled more to the United States than to anywhere else. [B]According to Statistics Canada. [C]In 1989, 204 visits were made to South America, compared to 56 in 1980.

   Fragment _____ lacks: S V Both

SENTENCE STRUCTURE: AVOIDING FRAGMENTS   45

2. ᴬTokyo is a very expensive city to visit. ᴮEven for an overnight stay. ᶜIn 1988, a hotel room cost an average of $742. ᴰMaking it the most expensive city in the world.

   Fragment _____ lacks: S V Both

   Fragment _____ lacks: S V Both

3. ᴬIn all of human history, there have been about 250 different alphabets. ᴮAbout 50 still in use today, including our own ABCs. ᶜOf the 50 alphabets, half are in one country. ᴰIndia.

   Fragment _____ lacks: S V Both

   Fragment _____ lacks: S V Both

4. ᴬJoe was "cool" in high school. ᴮHe usually cut classes to hang out. ᶜHe hardly ever did assignments. ᴰHe said he could attend a community college even if he didn't pass his high-school courses. ᴱHe was "cool" in college, too. ᶠCutting classes and ignoring assignments. ᴳHe flunked out after one term.

   Fragment _____ lacks: S V Both

5. ᴬA bicycle is a good choice if one wants cheap transportation. ᴮA good bike costs far less than a car. ᶜUses muscle power instead of expensive and polluting gasoline. ᴰIt also promotes good health.

   Fragment _____ lacks: S V Both

Spotcheck 3-4

The following paragraphs contain fragment errors. At the end of each paragraph, indicate which "sentences" are really fragments by writing the appropriate letters in the blanks. Then circle S, V, or Both to indicate whether the fragments lack a subject, a verb, or both.

1. ᴬBill Gillen set the mile record in five-object joggling. ᴮA sport involving running while juggling. ᶜGillen ran the mile in 8 minutes, 28 seconds. ᴰAnother joggler, Albert Lucas, completed the Los Angeles marathon of 26.2 miles in just over 4 hours while juggling 3 balls all the way.

   Fragment _____ lacks: S V Both

2. ᴬThe amazing Brazilian soccer player known as Pelé scored 1281 goals during his career. ᴮHe played from 1956 until his retirement in 1977. ᶜFinished his career playing for the New York Cosmos of the North American Soccer League. ᴰA French magazine named him "Athlete of the Century."

   Fragment _____ lacks: S V Both

3. ᴬThe first table tennis games were played by English university students in 1879. ᴮThey hit a champagne cork over books stacked in the middle of a table. ᶜLater, balls made of rubber and then celluloid replaced the cork. ᴰWith a net taking the place of the books.

   Fragment _____ lacks: S V Both

4. ᴬThe Chinese language is made up almost entirely of one-syllable words. ᴮThere are only 405 syllables in Chinese. ᶜThe same word, therefore, may have several meanings. ᴰThe meaning depending on how the syllable is pronounced. ᴱThe word *wan* can mean "to bend," "to finish," "late," or "10 000."

Fragment _____ lacks: S V Both

5. ᴬLearning to write in the Chinese language is very difficult. ᴮWith some 3000 characters to be memorized for a basic vocabulary. ᶜElementary pupils in China spend half their time learning the language. ᴰTyping in Chinese seems nearly impossible. ᴱTypewriters having 2200 keys.

Fragment _____ lacks: S V Both

Fragment _____ lacks: S V Both

Completing Sentence Fragments

Each of the following groups of words breaks at least one of the three rules for complete sentences. These fragments can be changed into sentences by adding the necessary subjects or verbs.

Left the party at midnight.

The subject is missing. *Who* left the party?

(correction) Cinderella left the party at midnight.

The man in the blue cape.

The verb is missing. *What* does the man (subject) *do*?

(correction) The man in the blue cape can leap tall buildings at a single bound.

On a tropical island.

Both the subject and the verb are missing. *Who* does *what* on a tropical island?

(correction) Robinson Crusoe [subject] lived [verb] on a tropical island.

Snow White living with seven dwarfs.

A complete verb is missing. Remember, an *-ing* word such as *living* cannot be the main verb of a sentence. Such verbs need helping verbs, such as *is, was,* and *has been.*

(correction) Snow White was living [or lived] with seven dwarfs.

Spotcheck 3-5

Add subjects or verbs or both to turn the following fragments into complete sentences.

EXAMPLE: Reading a book. The third-grader was reading a book.

1. A small airplane. _____
2. While eating lunch. _____
3. After the movie. _____
4. The dog barking at passing cars. _____
5. A clerk in the shoe department. _____

SENTENCE STRUCTURE: AVOIDING FRAGMENTS

Spotcheck 3-6

Add subjects or verbs or both to turn these fragments into complete sentences.

EXAMPLE: Eating his lunch. Tom was eating his lunch.

1. A red convertible. _____
2. While driving home. _____
3. Before the exam. _____
4. The plumber fixing the sink. _____
5. A cashier at the theatre. _____

Joining Sentence Parts

Often a sentence fragment should really be part of the complete sentence before or after it. Study these examples:

We set out for the fairgrounds. <u>Hoping to watch the fireworks</u>.

The underlined fragment can be corrected by making it part of the first sentence.

(joined) We set out for the fairgrounds, hoping to watch the fireworks.

Mr. Williams planned to do some fishing. <u>And enjoy the beauties of nature</u>.

(joined) Mr. Williams planned to do some fishing and enjoy the beauties of nature.

<u>Lurking in the bushes</u>. The cat eyed the bird bath.

(joined) Lurking in the bushes, the cat eyed the bird bath.

(Put a comma after fragments that lead up to the words that could be a sentence by themselves—for example, "The cat eyed the birdbath." There will be more about commas in Chapter 10.)

Spotcheck 3-7

Get rid of any sentence fragments in the following items by joining the fragments to neighbouring sentences. Change punctuation and capital letters as needed.

1. In Egypt stands the Great Pyramid of the pharaoh Cheops. The largest stone structure in the world.
2. Covering 5 hectares of desert. It is as tall as a 40-storey building.
3. It is made up of about 2.5 million stone blocks. Some weighing 70 000 kg each.
4. Hundreds of thousands of workers toiled for 20 years. To build a monument considered one of the wonders of the world.
5. The workers hauled the blocks upward with ropes made of reeds. And their own muscle power.
6. Fifty centuries after being built. The pyramid still inspires awe in the viewer.

Editing Check 3

The following paragraph contains seven sentence-fragment errors. Underline them. Then, in the space below, revise the paragraph. Correct all fragments by supplying needed subjects or verbs or by joining each fragment to a neighbouring sentence.

¹Helen Keller provides an inspiring example. ²Of a person who overcame great physical handicaps. ³She was made deaf and blind by illness. ⁴Before the age of two. ⁵With the help of a teacher, Anne Sullivan. ⁶Helen learned to communicate by spelling out words on a person's hand. ⁷She learned to speak by the time she was 16. ⁸As a result of her own hard work and Miss Sullivan's patience. ⁹Graduating from Radcliffe College in 1904 with honours. ¹⁰She began working to improve conditions for the blind. ¹¹By writing books, lecturing, and appearing before legislative bodies. ¹²Two movies tell of her life. ¹³*The Helen Keller Story* and *The Miracle Worker*.

_____
_____
_____
_____
_____
_____
_____
_____
_____
_____
_____

Each sentence can be corrected in more than one way.

Quickcheck on Sentence Fragments

✓ A sentence must have a subject and a complete verb, and it must express a complete thought.

✓ You can often correct a fragment by joining it to a neighbouring sentence.

✓ Any fragments in your writing may stand out more clearly if you edit your paper by starting at the last sentence and reading toward the first.

WORDCHECK: SPELLING

Checkpoint 3-1

In the blank spaces below, write C if the word group is a complete sentence. Write F if it is a fragment.

1. _____ Toronto's CN Tower, the world's tallest free-standing structure.
2. _____ Measuring 553 metres tall.
3. _____ It was completed on April 2, 1975.
4. _____ By taking a high-speed elevator.
5. _____ You can go to the top.
6. _____ Where there is a revolving restaurant.
7. _____ Offering magnificent views of the city.
8. _____ The giant structure attracts many visitors.
9. _____ Particularly as it is right next to the SkyDome.
10. _____ At the base, there is a simulated space ride.

Checkpoint 3-2

Some of the "sentences" in this paragraph are really fragments. In the blanks below, indicate which sentences are complete (C) and which are fragments (F).

[1]For centuries, Native Americans in Mexico had chewed gum from the chicle tree to keep their mouths moist on long hikes. [2]Chewing gum wasn't offered as a commercial product until 1872. [3]Developed by Robert Adams, a photographer from Staten Island, New York. [4]Adams had experimented with gum for two years. [5]Trying to find a substitute for rubber. [6]One day he put a piece in his mouth. [7]And enjoyed chewing it. [8]Unable to interest a manufacturer in the product, he decided to make it himself. [9]Became a national fad. [10]By 1890, Adams had a 6-storey chewing gum plant and 250 employees.

1 _____   2 _____   3 _____   4 _____   5 _____
6 _____   7 _____   8 _____   9 _____   10 _____

No answers are given for Checkpoint quizzes.

WORDCHECK: SPELLING

You can improve your spelling by checking any words you are unsure of and by listing (and studying) words misspelled in your college papers. If there are homonyms of the word, however, or you are using an American English checker, spell-check may not help, and you will need to use a dictionary.

Put the underlined words through the spell-check on your computer and see what happens.

1. The captain couldn't <u>sea</u> through the fog.

2. The pair tasted deliciously refreshing.
3. It was a great honor to have been invited to the Oscars.
4. The gun blast was herd in the next town.
5. The weight was too long, she decided not to see the doctor that day.

CHECKPOST: DETERMINERS

Using *some / any / many / much* can be confusing for people. Here are a few rules and guidelines to follow—then apply them in the exercise.

- Verb forms: Interrogative (the question form), imperative (the command form), and both positive and negative forms are important to consider when choosing the right word for a count or noncount noun.
- *Some* and *any* are used with either countable or uncountable nouns.
    - *Any* is used for negative statements and in questions.
    - *Some* is used for affirmative statements and in questions.
- *Much* is used for uncountable nouns, and *many* is used for plural countable nouns. *Much* is only commonly used in negative statements and questions.

Checkpost 3-1

Fill in the blanks with the determiners some / any / much / many.

1. How _____ oil is there in the car?
2. Have you _____ milk?
3. There are _____ sugar lumps in the dish.
4. Do you have _____ work to do on weekends?
5. Is there _____ cream for the coffee?
6. There aren't _____ tourists in Winnipeg.
7. _____ newcomers to Canada settle in Montreal.
8. How _____ staff do you have in your company?
9. There is _____ cough mixture in the cupboard.
10. Are there _____ animals in the room?

Remember

- There is a difference between *too* and *very*.

    This cup of coffee is very full. = There is a lot of liquid in the cup.

    This cup of coffee is too full. = The liquid is spilling over the cup.

- It is important to distinguish between *too* and *not + enough*.

    This cup of coffee is <u>too</u> hot to drink = hot/I can't drink it.

    This cup of coffee is<u>n't</u> hot <u>enough</u> to drink. = cold/I can't drink it.

  Remember the difference:

    Raymond is <u>too</u> old to drive. Pierre is <u>not</u> old <u>enough</u> to drive.

    Jean does <u>not</u> earn <u>enough</u> to have a car. He earns <u>too</u> little to have a car.

    An elephant is <u>too</u> large to fit in a regular car. An elephant is <u>not</u> small <u>enough</u> to fit in a regular car

Checkpost 3-2

Make ten sentences using much / many / some / any / too / very / not enough.

1. _____
2. _____
3. _____
4. _____
5. _____
6. _____
7. _____
8. _____
9. _____
10. _____

4

PARAGRAPHS WITH DESCRIPTIVE DETAILS

READING: DESCRIPTION ADDS LIFE

Precheck   Descriptive writing gives us a clear picture of a person, place, or event. In the following reading, we experience the sensations of a place called Old Man On His Back; it is a place in the prairies that is very special to the writer, Sharon Butala. Places are often special to us for what they look like and what they mean to us. An effective description will enable the reader to see what you see. Sharon Butala describes the landscape and the effect that living in the wilderness in Saskatchewan has had upon her.

Journal Topic   Describe a special person or a place.

Land Is Holy...Sacred –Sharon Butala

In 1996 Saskatchewan rancher Peter Butala and his wife, best-selling author Sharon, donated their family ranch to the Nature Conservancy of Canada, establishing the core of Old Man On His Back Prairie and Heritage Conservation Area. Sharon Butala has written before in The Perfection of the Morning *(1994) and* Wild Stone Heart *(2000), about OMB's 13 000 acres of almost untouched grassland and the deep spiritual meaning it has for her. Award-winning photographer Courtney Milne is a similarly passionate advocate for wilderness preservation. Now they have joined together to produce* Old Man On His Back: Portrait of a Prairie Landscape, *a tribute to a unique place preserved for all time.*

For most of the year the hills are a pale gold, varying to tones of buff, cream, beige, and copper, and at sunrise and sunset, tinted shades of rose and gold, or mauve and a luminescent blue. In dull winter light they're coated with silver, and on sunny days they gleam a polished white that, as night descends, turns to indigo and purple. In spring, those same fields and hills are the palest blues and greens, and shimmer gently in the rising heat, the sky-line a gently wavering band of

luminescent a radiating-light quality

blue-green light that invites the traveller to walk to it, and on into some other world of perfect peace and beauty. Such is the OMB: a place where the human soul may find both its roots and renewal.

I came into this place in 1976—I like to say that I came into the landscape to live—when I was already in my mid-30s. I came as a new bride into a world about which I knew virtually nothing, and into a landscape I had not even known existed in Saskatchewan, despite my having lived nearly all my life here. I think now, although I'd never have admitted it then, nor for years afterward, that I married this stunning landscape as much as I married Peter. To live in such beauty seemed to me nothing short of a gift from God.

I hadn't bargained for the difficulties of an urban, single-parent academic marrying into rural agricultural life. I often felt that people were speaking another language—although they all spoke English—and for years I could not even get a grip on how to be a person, a woman, in this strange environment. I lost my footing then; I fell into confusion; as the years passed I sometimes hovered on the brink of despair. I had thought that I would live in beauty. I had not conceived of what that beauty consisted beyond endless vistas of grassy hills, a sky so vast that early settlers—women—sometimes went mad and ran from it until their lungs burst and they died.

I, who couldn't remember dreaming at all, began to have vivid, beautiful dreams. I believe that happened because every night as I went to the outdoor toilet I walked under a sky brilliant with stars, the very history of the universe riding on my shoulders, because the presence of the moon and her monthly passage had become part of my life. The lives of birds and animals began to fit in for me with the seasons, and I began to get a sense of the way the chain of life operated. Most miraculously of all, I could understand my womanhood in the light of the rhythms of nature, as part of nature.

I began to see that behind daily or seasonal vicissitudes nature was entirely serene. I began to see it as omnipresent, as all-powerful, and we humans, with our sense of control, as puny, arrogant, mild in the face of it, and despite our delusions of might, essentially helpless.

I have been taught enough to understand that there are reasons that far outweigh the gathering of wealth that require humans to preserve in an undisturbed state places like OMB. Wilderness, it turns out, is an absolute value in itself. It is our last connection with creation and, as such, contains all possibilities for life. We human beings know in our bones and our blood that we need it, that it contributes to our happiness, to our sense of belonging on this earth. Perhaps most important of all, its existence reminds us of our spiritual nature, of what it is to be human, of where we have come from and where we are going when we die. In such a sense, land is holy; it is sacred. And it belongs to all of us.

virtually almost, nearly

vicissitudes changes in life from one condition to another

delusions mistaken beliefs or ideas

Checking Meaning and Style

1. How does the opening sentence attract the reader's attention?
2. Where is the topic sentence in the first paragraph? Discuss its impact on the reader.
3. Why did Sharon Butala have difficulties in adjusting to life in the wilderness?
4. What images does she evoke to describe the night sky?
5. To what sense does Butala appeal most?

Checking Ideas

1. What does Sharon Butala mean by the idea that she married both her husband and the landscape?
2. What happened to early women settlers? Do you think the landscape would affect you in a similar way?
3. According to Butala, what overall importance does wilderness have for humans?

Netcheck

Can you find any readings about pioneer women who settled in rural Canada in the 1800s or 1900s? Try looking up Susanna Moodie and her literary classic *Roughing It in the Bush*.

WRITING MODELS: THE DESCRIPTIVE PARAGRAPH

The following paragraphs are examples of *descriptive* writing that brings the word to life by appealing to our senses—sight, sound, touch, smell, and taste.

In this paragraph, Margaret Laurence describes two people in a photograph. From the description of the photo, can you conjure up the couple, their relationship, and their lives?

Model Descriptive Paragraph #1

The man and woman are standing stiffly on the other side of the gate. It is a farm gate, very wide, dark metal, and old—as is shown by its sagging. The man is not touching the woman, but they stand close. She is young, clad in a cotton print dress (the pattern cannot be discerned) which appears too large for her thin frame. Looking more closely, one can observe that her slight and almost scrawny body thickens at the belly. Her hair is short and fluffy, possibly blonde. The man's head is bent a little, and he is grinning with obvious embarrassment at the image-recorder who stands unseen and unrecorded on the near side of the gate. The man appears to be in his early thirties. He is tall and probably strong, narrowly but muscularly built. His hair is dark and somewhat unruly, as though he had combed it back with his fingers an instant before. In the far background, at the end of the road, can be seen the dim outlines of a house, two-storey, a square box of a house, its gracelessness atoned for, to some extent, by a veranda and steps at the front. Spruce trees, high and black, stand beside the house. In the further background there is a shadow-structure which could be the barn. Colon Gunn and his wife, Louisa, stand here always, in the middle 1920s, smiling their tight smiles, holding their now-faded sepia selves straight, hopeful, their sepia house and sepia farm firmly behind them, looking forward to what will happen, not knowing the future weather of sky or spirit.

Morag Gunn is in this picture, concealed behind the ugliness of Louisa's cheap housedress, concealed in her mother's flesh, invisible. Morag is still buried alive, the first burial, still a little fish, connected unthinkingly with life, held to existence by a single thread.

Study the use of descriptive details in the two model paragraphs that follow.

Model Descriptive Paragraph #2

Last week I arrived at work with a small head cold; by the time I left, I felt like I had the Hong Kong flu. Usually I don't mind helping the workers on the construction site with their hammering and sawing. Because of my cold, however, the <u>buzzing</u> of the electric saw <u>vibrated in my head as if a fly were in my ear</u>. The strong <u>smell of damp wood cleared my sinuses</u> at first, but later it only <u>stuffed them up</u>. The sawdust in my nostrils <u>felt like an itch that I just couldn't scratch the right way</u>. The <u>hammering</u> was no better. Since the rooms had no furniture, the <u>pounding was amplified</u> at least ten times. It was as though someone was <u>using my head as a drum</u>. By the time I got home, I was in no condition for school or work the next morning.

Notice how the sensory details (underlined) enable us to suffer along with a student describing the start of a bad cold. The description lets us hear the buzzing of the saw and the hammering; see and hear the unfurnished, echoing room; feel the itch in the nose and the stuffed-up sinuses, the head vibrating as if a fly were in the ear, the head being pounded like a drum; and smell the damp wood.

In addition to helping us see a place and feel an experience, descriptive paragraphs can also make it possible for us to meet people.

Model Descriptive Paragraph #3

Oliver was an extremely cheerful-looking young man. The upturned corners of his mouth always seemed to be dancing in a smile. His clear blue eyes twinkled when he spoke. His voice, too, had a ring of laughter that always made one happy to be near him.

1. What does this description tell you about Oliver?
2. Which senses are appealed to in this paragraph?
3. Which words and phrases bring Oliver to life?

WRITING ASSIGNMENT: A DESCRIPTIVE PARAGRAPH

The model descriptive reading was about a place (OMB in Saskatchewan) and the model descriptive paragraphs described people and a thing (the common cold). When describing people, places, and things, the sentences are often more effective if they appeal to the senses of sight, sound, touch, smell, and taste. Sharon Butala used a variety of colours to effectively convey the landscape's beauty.

Write a Description Paragraph

Write a paragraph using specific descriptive details on one of the following topics:

1. A room in your house or apartment
2. An unpleasant experience (Model #2)
3. A favourite object
4. A favourite recreation spot
5. A person whose looks you like or dislike

Your topic sentence should make clear what impression you want to create, as in the following examples:

1. Anyone who looks at my room knows at once that I enjoy sports. (This topic sentence would lead to a description that appeals to the sense of sight.)
2. Running my first marathon was a combination of agony and ecstasy. (Observe how this topic sentence would lead you to write about how it feels to run a first marathon.)
3. My grandfather's gold watch is a thing of beauty. (This topic sentence opens the paragraph for a description of how the gold watch looks, feels, and sounds.)

After you write your topic sentence, you will need to follow it with sentences containing specific descriptive details. Make notes for your first draft on the form below. (Your description may not involve all the senses.)

(Your own topic sentence) _____

_____

(Sight notes) _____

_____

(Sound notes) _____

_____

(Touch notes) _____

_____

(Smell notes) _____

_____

(Taste notes) _____

_____

Revise your first draft. Eliminate any sentence fragments by making sure that each sentence has a subject and a verb and expresses a complete thought. Don't forget to edit for spelling and punctuation errors.

Writing Assignment Checklist

✓ Use the clustering prewriting technique—perhaps using separate clusters for sight, sound, and smell, for example—to come up with descriptive details that appeal to the senses.

✓ Use a topic sentence that makes clear what impression you want to create, as in these examples:

> OMB is a place where the human soul may find its roots and renewal.
>
> The park across from my house is a good place to relax.
>
> I still remember the wonderful smells in my grandmother's kitchen at Thanksgiving.

✓ When revising the first draft, be sure the descriptive details are strong and interesting.

✓ Check especially for sentence fragments and the kinds of problems marked in recent papers.

✓ Proofread the paper before turning it in.

WRITING PROCESS: WRITING A SUMMARY

A good way to test your understanding of a reading is to write a brief summary of the material, putting the main ideas in a few sentences. This practice sharpens both your reading and your writing skills. Follow these steps:

1. Identify and make a note of the main ideas of the reading.

2. Jot down the most important details that explain or support those ideas.

3. Write the summary, using the main idea and supporting details. It should be no longer than half the length of the original material and will probably be less.

4. In the first sentence, give the title and author of the work you are summarizing.

5. Omit your opinion of the material summarized.

More help on summaries can be found in Writing Resources A.

Now You Try It *Summarize the reading from The Infomedia Revolution in Chapter 1.*

_____
_____
_____
_____
_____
_____
_____

SENTENCE STRUCTURE: AVOIDING CLAUSE FRAGMENTS

The sentence fragments we looked at in the last chapter were made up of **phrases**. Phrases are groups of related words that do not contain both a subject and a verb. These are phrase fragments:

> Covering 5 hectares of wilderness. (no subject, no complete verb)
>
> Before she arrived in the wilderness. (no subject, no verb)

Now we are going to look at another kind of word group—the **clause**. A clause *does* contain a subject and verb. Here are some examples of clauses:

> The <u>wilderness</u> [subject] <u>covered</u> [verb] 5 hectares of prairie.
>
> <u>She</u> [subject] <u>became</u> [verb] depressed about the landscape.

If you think those clauses look a lot like sentences, you are right. They meet the three tests of the sentence: (1) each has a subject, (2) each has a verb, and (3) each expresses a complete thought—it makes sense by itself. So is a clause the same thing as a sentence? Not always. Look at these clauses:

> Because the <u>wilderness</u> [subject] <u>was</u> [verb] vast.
>
> While <u>the Butalas</u> [subject] <u>lived</u> [verb] in rural Saskatchewan.

Each one is a clause because it has a subject and a verb. But neither one is a sentence because neither one expresses a complete thought. Each needs more words to finish the idea.

> Because the wilderness was vast, <u>Sharon felt lost</u>.
>
> While the Butalas lived in rural Saskatchewan, <u>Sharon developed a deep love for the land</u>.

Without the added words, each is an example of our enemy, the fragment.

So we now have two kinds of clauses. *Independent clauses* are complete in themselves and can stand alone as sentences. *Dependent clauses* depend on other words to complete their meaning.

IMPORTANT: Every sentence must contain at least one independent clause.

Test yourself on the following examples by marking the independent clauses **Ind** *and the dependent clauses* **Dep**.

1. _____ Alicia arrived early at work yesterday.
2. _____ Because Alicia arrived early at work yesterday.
3. _____ Mrs. Ng admired the roses.
4. _____ Although Mrs. Ng admired the roses.
5. _____ The Alexopouloses moved to Prince Edward Island.
6. _____ Until the Alexopouloses moved to Prince Edward Island.

All six are clauses because they have subjects and verbs. Examples 1, 3, and 5 are independent clauses. They are complete sentences and make sense by themselves. Examples 2, 4, and 6 are dependent clauses. They depend on other words to complete their meaning. They are sentence fragments.

What is it that turns the complete sentences into sentence fragments? It is just one word in each case: *because* in example 2, *although* in example 4, and *until* in example 6. Since they turn independent clauses into dependent clauses, we will call such words **dependent words**.

Here is a longer list of dependent words. Study it carefully. When you edit your work, checking for fragments wherever you use these words will help you write well.

after	in order that	whenever
although	since	where
as	so that	wherever
as if	than	whether
because	that	which
before	though	whichever
even if	unless	while
even though	until	who
ever since	what	whom
how	whatever	whose
if	when	why

Spotcheck 4-1

Fill in the blanks with the dependent word that best completes the meaning of the sentence.

1. _____ the 1967 centennial celebrations were held all over Canada, the community colleges were founded in Ontario.

2. _____ many of us are on diets, the average North American eats about 16 pounds of candy a year.

3. Ice cream actually makes us feel warmer _____ it contains so many calories.

4. Early experiments with electric vehicles took place in Europe _____ an electric cart was built in 1887.

5. _____ his team loses, the coach locks himself in his office for several hours.

Spotcheck 4-2

In the blank spaces that follow the paragraph, write the numbers of the "sentences" that are actually fragments and the dependent word that makes each a fragment.

¹Two Latin-American poets who won worldwide praise were Octavio Paz and Pablo Neruda. ²Who both won the Nobel Prize in literature. ³Paz (1914–98) was born in Mexico City. ⁴Where he founded a literary journal at age 17 and published his first book of poetry at 19. ⁵He wrote many of his best-known works. ⁶While he served in Mexico's diplomatic corps in such places as France, Switzerland, and India. ⁷These works include a book of essays, *El Laberinto de la Soledad* (*The Labyrinth of Solitude*). ⁸Which is considered his masterpiece. ⁹Pablo Neruda (1904–73), a Chilean, also served in the diplomatic corps, representing Chile as ambassador to France. ¹⁰Like Paz, Neruda began to write poetry at an early age. ¹¹When he was still in his teens. ¹²Although both writers were enormously influential in Latin America. ¹³Their admirers are found throughout the world.

NO.	DEPENDENT WORD
____	_____
____	_____
____	_____
____	_____
____	_____
____	_____

Spotcheck 4-3

*In the blank spaces, write **C** for a complete sentence and **F** for a fragment. Underline the dependent words in the fragments.*

1. _____ Because Dave had sold more TV sets than anyone else at Smith's Department Store in January.

2. _____ Dave and his wife, Liz, won an all-expenses paid vacation to Palm Springs.

3. _____ The temperature was balmy when they arrived.

4. _____ Even though it was snowing back home.

5. _____ Before they went out to dinner.

6. _____ They took a swim in the pool at their resort.

7. _____ Since many movie stars have homes in Palm Springs.

8. _____ Liz thought it would be fun to drive around and look at some of the houses.

9. _____ Later she suggested that they take a ride on the aerial tramway that climbs to an elevation of more than 2550 metres above Palm Springs.

10. _____ Although she knew that Dave didn't like heights.

Joining Fragments to Sentences

You can usually correct a *dependent-word fragment* by joining it to the sentence before it or after it.

> When his computer stopped working [fragment]. Gordon was glad the warranty hadn't expired.

> **(corrected)** When his computer stopped working, Gordon was glad the warranty hadn't expired.

The fragment has been added to the sentence following it.

> Jim will gain weight. Unless he stops drinking so much beer [fragment].

> **(corrected)** Jim will gain weight unless he stops drinking so much beer.

The fragment has been added to the sentence before it.

Notice that a comma separates the two clauses in the first example but not in the second. Here is the rule: Use a comma if the dependent-word clause comes first; do not use a comma if the independent clause comes first.

Another way to correct this kind of fragment is simply to get rid of the dependent word.

> **(fragment)** Because Sean bought a Porsche.

> **(corrected)** Sean bought a Porsche.

Spotcheck 4-4

Make complete sentences by adding an independent clause before or after these dependent clauses. Underline the dependent words. Remember to use a comma when the dependent clause comes first.

1. Although the wind was blowing _____.

2. _____ because it was Ahmed's birthday.

3. Whenever Kimberly entered the classroom _____
   _____.

4. _____
   _____ as Curtis picked up the phone.

5. Since it was raining _____.

Are you sure the words you added make independent clauses? Could they stand by themselves as complete sentences?

Using Who, Which, and That in Sentences

Sometimes a dependent word is the subject of the dependent clause. Words often used that way are *who*, *which*, and *that*.

                  subject   **verb**
Mr. Mohamed is a friend <u>who</u> <u>can be trusted</u>.

The subject of the dependent clause is the dependent word *who*. The verb is *can be trusted*. (The independent clause is *Mr. Mohamed is a friend*. Remember that every sentence must have at least one independent clause.)

Sometimes the dependent clause is in the middle of the sentence.

A friend <u>who can be trusted</u> is valuable.

The dependent clause, *who can be trusted*, interrupts the independent clause, *A friend is valuable*.

Sometimes the dependent word *that* is left out.

(correct) The officials assumed <u>that the queen would be present</u>.

(also correct) The officials assumed <u>the queen would be present</u>.

Spotcheck 4-5

These sentences use who, which, *and* that *to introduce dependent-word clauses. Underline the entire dependent clause.*

EXAMPLE: Winnie, <u>who works harder than anyone else</u>, should be paid more.

1. April 30, which is the day taxes are due, should be a national holiday.
2. A specialist is a person who knows more and more about less and less.
3. "O Canada" has a French version that we sing.
4. Celine Dion stocked her show, which was scheduled to appear in many cities, with 130 speakers and 124 computerized lights.
5. A province that has many mountains is British Columbia.

Choosing among Who, Which, and That in a Sentence

Use *which*, not *who* or *whom*, to start a clause about animals or things.

> Sandra was feeding her horse, which [not *who*] had a sore leg.

Use *who*, not *which*, to start a clause about people.

> On the bus were the teachers who [not *which*] were attending the conference.

Whose may be used with people, animals, or things.

> All photos *whose* colours are fading should be protected from light.

Use *which* and commas for dependent clauses that are not essential to the meaning of the sentence.

> *Crash, which I have seen three times,* will be on TV again tonight.

Use *that* with dependent clauses that are essential to the meaning of the sentence.

> A movie that I have seen three times will be on TV tonight. (no commas)

That may also be used to refer to unnamed people.

> Where is the taxi driver that was supposed to be here 15 minutes ago?

Spotcheck 4-6

Underline the correct word in parentheses.

1. Mr. Simpson, (who / which / that) lives next door, has the flu.
2. People (which / that) pay off their credit cards each month will save money.
3. It was the zoo's giraffe (who / which / that) had a sore throat.
4. Under the front porch, (who / which / that) needed repair, were two raccoons.
5. The section of the Amazon River (which / that) we travelled lies in Peru.

Quickcheck on Clauses and Phrases

✓ A clause contains a subject and a verb.

✓ If a clause expresses a complete thought, it is an *independent* clause.

✓ If a clause depends on other words to complete its meaning, it is a *dependent* clause.

✓ Dependent clauses begin with *dependent words*, such as *although*, *because*, and *since*.

✓ The dependent words *who*, *which*, and *that* often are the subjects of dependent clauses. Use *who* to refer to people; use *which* to refer to animals or things.

✓ A dependent clause written as a sentence causes the error called a sentence fragment.

64 CHAPTER 4 PARAGRAPHS WITH DESCRIPTIVE DETAILS

Doublecheck 4-1

Write sentences using the dependent words in parentheses.

1. (unless) _____
2. (after) _____
3. (while) _____
4. (who) _____
5. (because) _____

Doublecheck 4-2

Several of the sentences in this paragraph contain dependent clauses. Underline the dependent word in each case.

[1]Canadians, who love doughnuts, spend millions of dollars a year on these treats. [2]They usually buy them in the coffee shops that occupy every second or third shop in every city and small town, which has to be the greatest proportion of any retail type. [3]While the chains of coffee shops like Coffee Time are increasing, the local, homegrown variety is still popular. [4]Tim Horton's, which is a Canadian chain, has to compete with local and international ventures like Dunkin' Donuts and Mr. Sub. [5]The gourmet shops like Timothy's and Second Cup have to compete with upscale shops like Starbucks, which have grown in popularity recently. [6]Starbucks is especially popular on the west coast where people adopt new trends easily. [7]While these more sophisticated coffee shops serve a gourmet, varied kind of coffee, they don't sell doughnuts, which probably means the old-fashioned coffee shops that serve regular brew will hold their own for years to come.

Doublecheck 4-3

Underline any dependent clauses in these sentences, and write the dependent words in the blanks at the left. Write X if the sentence contains no dependent clause.

1. _____ Canada, which is the largest country in the Western Hemisphere, has a total of 9 970 610 square kilometres.

2. _____ It stretches from Cape Spear, Newfoundland, to the Yukon–Alaska border, which is a distance of 5514 kilometres.

3. _____ There are four major physiographic regions.

4. _____ The Canadian Shield, which is also known as the Precambrian Shield, is located in the central part of the continent.

5. _____ In fact, the Shield, which is composed of ancient rock, covers over half of Canada.

6. _____ Although the Shield's rock is ancient, the mountains of the Appalachian Region to the east are younger.

7. _____ To the west of the Shield, everyone knows of the Prairies' distinctive flatness.

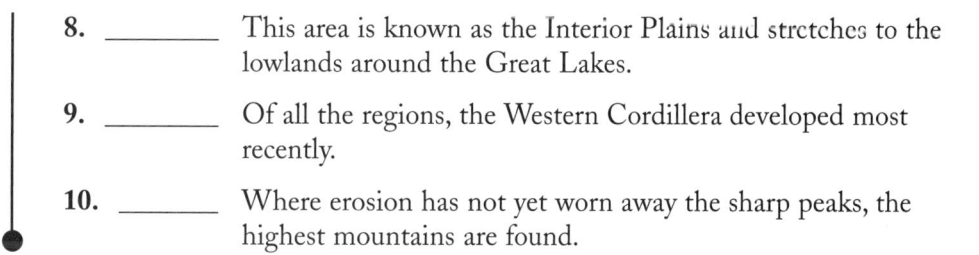

8. _____ This area is known as the Interior Plains and stretches to the lowlands around the Great Lakes.

9. _____ Of all the regions, the Western Cordillera developed most recently.

10. _____ Where erosion has not yet worn away the sharp peaks, the highest mountains are found.

Editing Check 4

Edit these paragraphs on the martial arts to correct the fragments in them. (The first fragment has been corrected as an example.) The fragments may be either phrases or clauses. Correct them by adding subjects and verbs or by joining the fragments to neighbouring sentences.

¹The term *martial arts* covers a variety of fighting methods based on ancient Asian combat skills. ²The martial arts are practised today for a number of reasons. , iIncluding self-defence, physical fitness, and sports competition. ³Styles, techniques, and teaching methods vary. ⁴Even within a given branch of martial arts, such as karate. ⁵Although adherence to ancient traditions is usually emphasized.

⁶Although the exact origins are uncertain. ⁷The Asian styles of the martial arts seem to have come to China from India and Tibet. ⁸Where they were used by monks for exercise and protection against bandits. ⁹The arts flourished in Japan. ¹⁰Although Japan was among the last of the Asian nations to learn them. ¹¹For a time, practice of martial arts was restricted to the Japanese warrior class, but the peasants practised in secret.

¹²Martial arts can be divided into two categories. ¹³Those that use weapons and those that don't. ¹⁴In the weaponless methods, such as karate and kung fu, the contestant depends on kicks and hand and arm blows. ¹⁵As well as various holds, chokes, and twists, to subdue an opponent. ¹⁶In one of the branches using weapons, kendo, based on ancient Japanese sword fighting. ¹⁷Contestants today use bamboo swords cased in leather.

[18]T'ai chi is the most gentle of the martial arts. [19]Slow, graceful movements that bear little resemblance to the original blows and blocks on which the movements are based. [20]Used today for conditioning and flexibility. [21]Some use it as a form of meditation.

Checkpoint 4-1

At the end of the following paragraph, write the numbers of any sentence fragments you find. Then write the dependent words contained in the fragments. The fragments may be more obvious if you give the paragraph a second reading, starting with the last sentence.

[1]Icebergs are huge chunks of ice floating in the ocean. [2]They are made of frozen fresh water. [3]That breaks off from glaciers. [4]The icebergs in the North Atlantic come from Greenland. [5]Which is an island almost entirely covered by a sheet of ice hundreds of feet thick. [6]Because icebergs are made of fresh water, sailing ships used to replenish their drinking water supply from pools formed on the ice. [7]Of course, icebergs are a danger to ships. [8]One of the greatest sea disasters occurred in 1912. [9]When the ocean liner *Titanic* sank after hitting an iceberg. [10]While it was on its first transatlantic trip. [11]An estimated 1517 people lost their lives. [12]The danger to ships is less today. [13]Because the Coast Guard keeps a lookout for icebergs.

NO. DEPENDENT WORD   **NO. DEPENDENT WORD**   **NO. DEPENDENT WORD**

___ _____   ___ _____   ___ _____

___ _____   ___ _____   ___ _____

Checkpoint 4-2

The paragraph below contains fragments caused by dependent clauses written as sentences. In the blanks below the paragraph, write the number of each of the five sentence fragments and the dependent words causing the fragments.

[1]The salt water in the ocean contains all the minerals found on land. [2]Seawater contains, for example, many tonnes of gold that are not recovered. [3]Since the cost of removing it would be greater than the value of the gold. [4]Another product of the sea is pearls. [5]Which are gathered from the ocean bottom by divers. [6]Seaweeds are used for food. [7]Although that is not all they are used for. [8]They are used in making medicines, ice cream, candy, and cosmetics. [9]Because it is expensive to remove the salt. [10]Seawater is not used to supply nations that are short on fresh water. [11]One of the main problems for the ocean is people. [12]Who dump all kinds of things into the water, polluting it.

NO. DEPENDENT WORD   **NO. DEPENDENT WORD**   **NO. DEPENDENT WORD**

___ _____   ___ _____   ___ _____

___ _____   ___ _____   ___ _____

No answers are given for Checkpoint quizzes.

WORDCHECK: SPELLING COMPOUND WORDS

Is this the correct spelling of *good bye*? Is it two words, one word, or one hyphenated word? Your dictionary will tell you. (It's one word: *goodbye*; *good-bye* is also acceptable.)

Should the following be written as one word, two words, or hyphenated? Write in the correct forms where appropriate.

1. self conscious
2. sea bird
3. week end
4. brother in law
5. south paw
6. fire arm
7. early bird
8. two thirds

CHECKPOST: MORE ON DETERMINERS

Rules
- *A lot of* and *lots of* can be used instead of *much* and *many* in informal or colloquial English. They go before both countable and uncountable nouns in affirmatives, negatives, and questions.
- *Little* can only modify uncountable nouns; *few* modifies countable nouns.
- *A little / a few* indicates a small amount.

    There is a little milk left, not enough for everyone's coffee.

    There are a few chocolates left, but not many.

    Both determiners often take *only*.

    There are only a few Canadian TV stars in Hollywood.

    There is only a little money in the Canadian film industry.

- *Quite a few* indicates a reasonable amount and is used with countable nouns.

    Quite a few children don't read before the end of grade one.

    A few means not many in number.

    A few children can't read in grade two.

    Few is less than *a few* in quantity; it means a minority or a very small amount.

    Few children can read in junior kindergarten.

- *No* can be used for countable and uncountable nouns.

    I have no time to learn Mandarin.

    There are no assistants in department stores.

Checkpost 4-1

Use the appropriate determiner in the blanks.

1. There are _____ trained singers in the church choir.
2. Is there _____ one to help me?
3. There is _____ money in my account; I am just about broke.
4. I like _____ of my teachers.
5. There's only _____ salt on my potatoes; please give me some more.

Checkpost 4-2

Fill in the blanks with singular or plural verbs.

1. There _____ a few apples on the tree.
2. _____ there quite a few doctors at the camp?
3. There _____ a little honesty left in the world.
4. _____ there a few Canadian athletes at the games?
5. There _____ few women in engineering classes.

Subjects and Verbs

- Make sure you have a subject in your sentence. If the subject is not at the beginning of a sentence, use *there* or *it* at the beginning of the sentence.

    <u>Wayne Gretzky</u> (subject) has hundreds of trophies; <u>there</u> (expletive at the beginning, in place of subject) are many advantages to playing great hockey. It is hard to skate as well as Gretzky.

- Make sure the subject is only written once in its own clause.

    Mary (she) had a little lamb.

    The lamb that went to school (he) was sent home.

5 PARAGRAPHS WITH NARRATIVE DETAILS

READING: NARRATIVE PARAGRAPHS TELL STORIES

Precheck

Writing that tells a story, that relates "what happened," is called *narration*. Often the story makes a point. In the following narration, novelist Neil Bissoondath recalls his family's traditional Christmas in Trinidad.

Journal Topic

Write about a tradition that is important in your family.

Traditions *–Neil Bissoondath*

arrowing marking the stalks for cutting

Hindu person who practises Hinduism, the major religion of East India

1. December in Trinidad, the land of my birth, meant gray skies, rain and temperatures that were chilling after the great summer heat. January would herald dry heat and the arrowing of the sugarcane stalks that preceded the cutting, but before that there was Christmas—as elsewhere, a time of family gatherings, parties, and gifts around the tree.

2. My father, the grandson of immigrants from India, was born into a Hindu household in a society that was, at the time, largely Christian. He was not a man of many stories but this one tale of Christmas in the late 1940s has shaped itself into a fullness in my mind. His childhood memory informs mine and has become, through the vibrancy of imagination, as fully part of me as it was of him. This is how it goes:

3. His brother breathed deeply in undisturbed sleep beside him, but the boy had been awake for some time, listening to the silence of the predawn darkness, searching in vain through the darkened windowpanes for any hint of morning light. There was nothing to be seen, not the shadows of the orange tree he knew to be out there, not the outline of the neighbouring house that sat just beyond the tree. He pulled the blanket to his neck, burrowed more comfortably into the soft mattress.

4. His brother stirred. "Stop movin'," he mumbled sleepily.
5. "You think he come yet?"
6. "Pa get up for prayers?"
7. "No."
8. "Well, he ain't come yet. Go back to sleep."

fastidious fussy, particular

dhoti Indian garment for the lower body
hibiscus bright, tropical flower

fathom understand
Hindi language of East India

But the question would not let him sleep: had Santa Claus come yet? 9

Somewhere in the distance a cock crowed. Not many minutes later, the floorboards creaked. His father was up. A fastidious man, he would, even on cool mornings, take a cold-water shower out back, slapping the cold away, shivering aloud. Then, he would dry himself off and, wearing his cotton shirt and dhoti, wander about the garden in search of fresh hibiscus for his prayers. 10

These prayers remained a mystery to the boy. His father had not yet explained the rituals or their meanings, so he did not know why Krishna and Hanuman and the other gods needed to be offered fresh flowers every morning, saw only simple beauty in the flame in the holy lamp, could not fathom the Hindi words his father chanted so effortlessly. 11

He thought of the young American soldiers—"Hey, Joe, got some gum?"— at the base not far away, wondered what they did with their time now that the war, so recently savaging Europe, was over. Were they too awake in their beds, wondering whether Santa Claus had visited yet? 12

The darkness outside began to break up. Shadows—the branches of the orange tree, the roof of the house next door—took shape against a field of gray. 13

From deeper in the house came the sound of worship: the tinkling of the brass bell, the musical murmur of his father's voice. 14

His brother, eyes blinking open, whispered, "So, he come yet?" "Don't know." 15

They eased out of bed and quietly opened the door to the living room. It was large and dark, the louvered windows glowing dull with the light outside. And there, on the lace doilies that covered the gramophone, sat proof that he had indeed come. For there, side by side, were the gifts he had left for them: an orange, an apple, and a can of soda biscuits each. 16

The boy, my father, could not suspect it in the excitement of the moment, but the years to come would bring changes bewildering in scope. All religious observance would fall by the wayside: he was never to understand the rituals, never to learn the words. He would have family of his own, and we, his children, would write letters to Santa Claus demanding impossible things, letters he would promise to mail. We would sing Christmas carols before a twinkling Christmas tree, eyes bright with longing at the stacks of colorfully wrapped boxes crowded round it. 17

But no gift—none of the toys, none of the games—would retain so central a place in our memories as would the orange, the apple, and the soda biscuits in his. For none of the gifts he would give us could speak quite so eloquently of the distance traveled between generations, of the visions that inevitably came to change expectations forever. 18

eloquently with particular grace and force

Checking Meaning and Style

1. The story told in paragraphs 3 to 16 of "Traditions" has been handed down to Neil Bissoondath. How important is it to him?

2. How did Bissoondath's father feel about Christmas time in Trinidad? How do we know?

3. What influences may have prevented Bissoondath's father from ever being able to "fathom the Hindi words his father chanted so effortlessly"?

4. In what way were Bissoondath's childhood Christmas seasons different from those of his father? Which have more significance?

Checking Ideas

1. Do you participate in the celebration of Christmas or do you have a different special day? Is it different in the way it is celebrated now than when your parents were young?
2. What point does the story make beyond the narration of a Christmas experience?
3. Are there traditions, rituals, or languages that your parents know, but that you don't understand?

Netcheck

Look up information about a religion that is unfamiliar to you. How can you check that the source is reliable?

WRITING MODELS: THE NARRATIVE PARAGRAPH

Narration tells a story. A story is just a series of events with a beginning and an end. The story usually makes a point of some kind. The point Neil Bissoondath's story makes is that vast lifestyle changes have occurred between one generation and another. The events in the story lead up to the revelation of these cross-generational differences.

Starting in childhood, we get much of our information and entertainment through stories. The child says, "Read me a story," and the parent gets out *Franklin Goes to School* for the umpteenth time. Stories continue to entertain us as we go through life—in books and magazines, on television, and at the movies.

We request stories of a different kind when we want to know "what happened." What happened in the crisis on the stock exchange? What happened at the tenants' meeting? What happened on Tom's date with Sylvia on Saturday night? In such cases, we want a story that gives us information, although it may be entertaining too.

Don't be shy about using anecdotes from your own life in your writing. Let's say you are writing an essay on crime in your community. The essay will be more interesting and believable if you include a short account of your personal experience. Or, if you want to make the point that holidays have become too commercialized, you could relate an experience you had shopping at the mall when the season was in full swing.

A close look at Bissoondath's narrative reveals this sequence:

1. Background about Christmas in Trinidad
2. His father's Christmas in the late 1940s
3. The boys' wait for Santa Claus
4. Christmas morning sounds
5. The gifts Santa brought

Bissoondath could have written one sentence about each event. He could have put the sentences together into a narrative paragraph that might have looked something like this:

Model Narrative Paragraph #1

Notice how a topic sentence comes before the other sentences.

<u>My father's story of a Christmas in Trinidad reveals just how different life is for us today.</u> While his brother was sleeping, on Christmas Eve, he lay awake, waiting for Santa. When morning came, he heard his own father performing many Hindu rituals. He would never understand these mysteries. When the morning noises finally woke his brother, the two boys got up to see whether Santa had come yet. They found their gifts: an orange, an apple, and a can of soda biscuits. No gifts that I have ever received have been as important to me as those gifts my father got from Santa, which shows clearly how much has changed in our lives.

In the two narrative models that follow, notice how the student writers develop their topic sentences with specific details about the events in their stories.

Model Narrative Paragraph #2

Notice how the writer describes the events in order, saving the surprise ending for the last sentence.

¹<u>Children need to understand that frustration and failure are not only inevitable but often helpful.</u> ²Over the weekend my husband and I tried to teach my daughter to ride her new bike. ³Each time one of us wasn't holding her up, Sue fell over. ⁴After falling again and again, she became frustrated and started to cry. ⁵I couldn't get her to try again. ⁶Then my neighbour talked to her, and Sue decided to give it one more attempt. ⁷My daughter ran over bushes and sprinklers. ⁸She tried to ride up walls. ⁹But by the end of the day she had a smile on her face that couldn't be wiped off. ¹⁰Sue had learned to ride her bike.

1. What is the point of this narrative paragraph?
2. What event happens in sentence 2?
3. What event happens in sentence 10?
4. What made the daughter successful?

Model Narrative Paragraph #3

¹<u>When I was six years old, I decided, against my mother's advice, that I could pet bees.</u> ²The sun was warm on my back, and the bees were buzzing around the sweet-smelling flowers of the lemon tree. ³Some of the bees were sitting so still that I just had to touch one. ⁴The bee felt soft and furry, and I could feel its "buzziness." ⁵Then I let out the loudest yell I could make. ⁶I thought my finger was going to explode. ⁷My mother yelled out the back door, "I told you so!" ⁸She pulled out the stinger and put ice on my finger. ⁹The cold ice dulled the pain, and I knew that I was going to live.

What is the point of this narrative paragraph?

PREWRITING: NONSTOP WRITING

Before going on to the next writing assignment, let's look at one more way of brainstorming for ideas. This method is called freewriting or nonstop writing. In this method you put your pen to a blank paper, or your fingers to a keyboard, and then write without stopping for three minutes or so. If you can't think of anything new about a topic, you just repeat the last word until something new comes to mind. The important rule is to keep writing without stopping. Don't worry about such things as spelling or punctuation.

Nonstop writing puts you in touch with your thoughts and gives you some ideas to use in your first draft. Let's say that Bill wants to write about a memorable experience or person. He starts his nonstop writing.

> memorable memorable memories memories are hard to remember remember I always have a hard time remembering things I hate memorizing we always had to memorize poetry in school and recite it i used to race through my poem when it was my turn my turn didn't want to forget it so I raced through so fast the teacher probably couldn't understand a word of it once a teacher required the class to memorize part of "The Shooting of Dan McGrew" by Robert Service and I remember I was able to say it in 30 seconds at home but in class she made me say it slowly no, I could only say it fast

Bill's nonstop writing put him in touch with a long-forgotten memory. After he finished, he read over the material and underlined the part he felt could be used—the lines about the "Dan McGrew" experience. Now he had the information to write his first draft.

Practise nonstop writing on one of these subjects: holidays, accidents, or relatives. Write for three minutes without stopping.

WRITING ASSIGNMENT: A NARRATIVE PARAGRAPH

With the earlier model paragraphs as examples, write a narrative paragraph—one that tells "what happened"—on one of the numbered topics that follow.

1. The first day I attended college classes
2. A funny or embarrassing incident
3. The day I learned how to drive (swim, dance, etc.)
4. The time I learned an important lesson

Use this structure for your paragraph

(Topic sentence) _____

(First detail) _____

(Second detail) _____

(Third detail) _____

(Fourth detail) _____

(Fifth detail) _____

Now, using this outline as a starting point, write a first draft of a narrative paragraph with no more than 12 sentences. Make sure you have a strong topic sentence and specific details. Check the first draft to be sure that each sentence has a subject and a verb before writing the final draft. Try to join sentences with conjunctions other than and, then, or but!

Writing Assignment Checklist

✓ Use prewriting techniques such as nonstop writing, brainstorming, and clustering to get ideas for your topic.

✓ State the point of your story in the topic sentence, as in these examples:

> Uncle Ed made a fool of himself at the family reunion last week.
>
> I'll never forget my excitement on Christmas Eve.

Develop the topic sentence with interesting details—for example, by explaining how or why Uncle Ed made a fool of himself or why you got embarrassed.

✓ Start at the beginning of the story and continue step by step to the end. Include only those details that support your main point.

✓ Revise the paper as often as needed. Watch especially for sentence fragments and spelling troublemakers.

✓ Proofread the final copy for such things as overlooked misspellings and punctuation errors.

SENTENCE STRUCTURE: AVOIDING RUN-TOGETHER SENTENCES

This writing is hard to read:

> Raymond was supposed to meet Jennifer in the library at 3 o'clock he got there 15 minutes early he sat down to read a copy of *Maclean's* magazine, it was so interesting that he didn't look up again until someone tapped him on the shoulder it was Jennifer, Raymond looked at his watch it was 4:30 "hi," she said.

Of course it's hard to read. That's because the reader expects to see a **capital letter** at the beginning of each sentence and a **period** at the end. Without these guides, the reader quickly gets lost.

SENTENCE STRUCTURE: AVOIDING RUN-TOGETHER SENTENCES

The paragraph is full of **run-together sentences**, which result when two or more sentences are written as if they were one.

Sometimes there is no punctuation used to separate the sentences, resulting in a **fused sentence** or **run-on**.

It was snowing the road to the cabin was blocked.

Sometimes a comma is used, causing a **comma splice**.

It was snowing, the road to the cabin was blocked.

A sentence, you will remember, has a subject and a verb and expresses a complete thought. Both *It was snowing* and *The road to the cabin was blocked* qualify separately as sentences. A comma cannot separate them.

Use a Period and a Capital Letter

Run-together sentences can be corrected in five different ways. The first is to use a period and a capital letter to make two sentences.

It was snowing. The road to the cabin was blocked.

Spotcheck 5-1

Correct these run-together sentences by adding a period and a capital letter between the two independent clauses.

EXAMPLE: England is smaller than Manitoba. Its people founded one of the world's largest empires.

1. Most of England's colonies became independent after the Second World War its empire has all but vanished.

2. Traditions are important to the English they hold the royal family in affection.

3. Elizabeth II became queen in 1952 she has been a popular monarch.

Use a Comma and a Connecting Word

Use a comma and one of the following **connecting words** (coordinating conjunctions):

and but or for nor yet so

(It's a good idea to memorize this short list.)

It was snowing, and the road to the cabin was blocked.

Note that there is an independent clause (a sentence) on each side of the connector, *and*.

Spotcheck 5-2

Correct these run-together sentences by adding a comma and a connecting word between the two independent clauses.

EXAMPLE: England is smaller than Manitoba, ^yet its people founded one of the world's largest empires.

1. Most of England's colonies became independent after the Second World War its empire has all but vanished.
2. Traditions are important to the English they hold the royal family in affection.
3. Elizabeth II became Queen in 1952 she has been a popular monarch.
4. Canada has had close ties with England many of the earliest settlers came from that country.
5. Canadian visitors to England will probably spend much of their time in London they may enjoy touring the beautiful countryside instead. It depends on their interests.

Spotcheck 5-3

Correct these run-together sentences by adding one of the connecting words between the two independent clauses. The first sentence has been done as an example.

¹It may be hard to believe, <u>but</u> today's hair dryer was based on a combination of the vacuum cleaner and the milkshake blender. ²Manufacturers noticed that hot air came out of the vacuum's exhaust, ____ they soon advertised their machine as a two-in-one product. ³With the hose attachment provided, buyers could vacuum rugs, ____ they could blow-dry their hair. ⁴This was a popular but awkward setup, ____ the manufacturers looked for a better way. ⁵They found it in the newly developed milkshake mixer, ____ its small, efficient motor permitted a dryer that could be held in the hand. ⁶The hand dryer was at first used almost exclusively by women, ____ it found new users in the 1960s when men started wearing their hair long.

Spotcheck 5-4

Use the connecting words shown to write sentences containing two independent clauses. Use a comma after the first clause.

EXAMPLE: (yet) Timothy has a good job, <u>yet</u> he is always borrowing money.

1. (and) _____

2. (but) _____

3. (or) _____

SENTENCE STRUCTURE: AVOIDING RUN-TOGETHER SENTENCES   77

4. (so) _____

_____

Make One Clause Dependent

Make one of the clauses dependent by using a *dependent word* such as *because, since, while,* or *unless.* (You may want to review the list of dependent words on page 59.)

<u>Because</u> it was snowing, the road to the cabin was blocked.

Spotcheck 5-5

Correct the following run-together sentences by changing one of the independent clauses into a dependent clause by using a dependent word. Be sure that the punctuation and capitalization are correct.

Although
EXAMPLE: ^ Carlos had a full-time job, he got good grades.

because
EXAMPLE: Carlos got good grades ^ he studied hard.

1. Mother gets home early we will have a good dinner.
2. The bulldozer knocked down the trees the neighbours watched in dismay.
3. She was already ten minutes late Yolanda decided not to go to class.
4. We always have a good time we go camping.
5. The electricity went out Terry lit some candles.

Spotcheck 5-6

Use the dependent words shown to write sentences containing one independent clause and one dependent clause. (Put a comma after the dependent clause if it begins the sentence.)

EXAMPLE: (while) The sun went down <u>while</u> we were fishing.

1. (before)_____

_____

2. (unless)_____

_____

3. (although) _____

_____

Use a Semicolon

Use a **semicolon**. This mark suggests a closer relation between the two clauses than a period would.

It was snowing; the road to the cabin was blocked.

(Be sure that you always have independent clauses on *both sides* of the semicolon.)

Spotcheck 5-7

Correct these run-together sentences with a semicolon.

EXAMPLE: Pierre got into his car; it wouldn't start.

1. Canadians have great faith in education they believe it is the solution to most problems.
2. Education can help people "get ahead" it produces citizens who can make intelligent decisions when they vote.
3. Many parents read to their small children those children are likely to enjoy reading as adults.

Use a Semicolon and a Transitional Word

Use a semicolon and a **transitional word** (conjunctive adverb) or **phrase** that reflects the change (transition) from the first part of the sentence to the second.

It was snowing; therefore, the road to the cabin was blocked.

(A period may be used instead of a semicolon. In that case, be sure to capitalize the next word. A comma is usually placed after the transitional word when the word comes at the beginning of the clause.)

Following are some more examples of transitional words. You will notice that they have about the same meaning as the more common connecting words (*and, but,* etc.). The transitional words make your writing seem somewhat more formal, which may or may not be desirable.

Transitional words similar in meaning to *and:*

furthermore   moreover   also   besides   in addition

Transitional words similar in meaning to *but:*

however   instead   nevertheless   on the other hand

Transitional words similar in meaning to *so:*

therefore   consequently   thus   as a result

Other transitional words:

still	for example	next
meanwhile	in fact	then
even so	first	finally
otherwise	second	

Spotcheck 5-8

Use a semicolon and a transitional word to correct these run-together sentences. Put a comma after the transitional word.

however,
EXAMPLE: Wilson got into his car; ^ it wouldn't start.

1. Canadians have great faith in education they believe it is the solution to most problems.

SENTENCE STRUCTURE: AVOIDING RUN-TOGETHER SENTENCES   **79**

2. Education can help people "get ahead" it produces citizens who can make intelligent decisions when they vote.

3. Many parents read to their small children those children are likely to enjoy reading as adults.

4. People tend to think of education as something that takes place in schools we learn in many ways outside of school.

5. Most experiences are "educational" television teaches us more than we realize.

Spotcheck 5-9

Use a semicolon and the transitional words shown to write sentences containing two independent clauses. (Put a comma after the transitional word.)

EXAMPLE: (nevertheless) Today is Mohamed's birthday; <u>nevertheless</u>, he plans to work until eight o'clock.

1. (furthermore) _____

_____

2. (otherwise) _____

_____

3. (however) _____

_____

4. (for example) _____

_____

Doublecheck 5-1

*Each of the following sentences contains two clauses. Draw one line under the subject and two lines under the verb in each clause. In the blanks at the left, write **RTS** for a run-together sentence or **C** for a correctly punctuated sentence.*

_____C_____   **EXAMPLE:** <u>We</u> <u>take</u> cars for granted, but <u>they</u> <u>haven</u>'t always <u>been</u> around.

_____ 1. The automobile was introduced in North America at the end of the nineteenth century; it brought many changes.

_____ 2. Farmers could easily drive to the city, and city dwellers could go to the country for recreation.

_____ 3. Highways and motorways made long-distance travel easy, motels were built along the roads.

_____ 4. When families owned cars, they could move to the new suburbs to live.

_____ 5. Cars made shopping centres practical; moreover, drive-in movies, drive-in restaurants, and even drive-in banks became common.

Doublecheck 5-2

*Each of the following sentences contains two clauses. Draw one line under the subject and two lines under the verb in each clause. In the blanks at the left, write **RTS** for a run-together sentence or **C** for one that is correct.*

_____ 1. If you are a typical North American, you eat about 50 litres of popcorn a year.

_____ 2. The Indians brought popcorn to the first Thanksgiving in 1621, the Pilgrims apparently liked it.

_____ 3. Popcorn is a good snack since 1 litre of dry-popped popcorn contains only 100 calories.

_____ 4. Even if you add cooking oil and salt, popcorn compares favourably with potato chips or corn chips.

_____ 5. Oil-popped popcorn has one-third the calories of potato chips, it has one-fourth the fat of potato chips.

Doublecheck 5-3

Add connecting words, dependent words, and transitional words to complete these paragraphs.

Bathing suits did not make an appearance until the middle of the 1800s _____ recreational bathing was not popular before then; _____, at that time doctors began to prescribe the "waters" for a variety of ailments. Europeans flocked to the streams, the lakes, and the ocean _____ they sought relief from "nerves" or other disorders. Standards of modesty were different in those days, _____ bathing suits covered more of the body than they do today. Women wore knee-length skirts in the water; _____, they wore bloomers and black stockings under the skirts. _____ a wet bathing suit could weigh as much as the bather, the accent was on *bathing*, not swimming.

_____ she wanted greater privacy, a woman could use a "bathing machine" at the ocean. Attendants would wheel her and the portable dressing room into shallow waters. _____ she had changed into a loose head-to-toe gown, she would step down a ramp into the surf _____ attendants shooed away any interested males.

A Danish immigrant to the United States named Carl Jantzen revolutionized swimwear in 1915 _____ he invented a knitting machine that yield-

SENTENCE STRUCTURE: AVOIDING RUN-TOGETHER SENTENCES   81

ed a stretchy fabric. The fabric resulted in a body-clinging fit; _____, swimsuits still had sleeves and reached to the knees. Swimsuits became more revealing in the 1930s _____ narrow straps and backless models paved the way for the two-piece suit.

It wasn't until 1946 that the bikini made its appearance. The Second World War had recently ended, _____ the United States was testing an atom bomb in the Pacific. A French designer was about to introduce a skimpy swimsuit model, _____ he didn't have a catchy name. _____, the atomic blast at Bikini Atoll on July 1, 1946, gave him the name for the "explosive" suit he displayed to the world four days later.

Doublecheck 5-4

Correct each run-together sentence in three ways: (a) with a connecting word, (b) with a dependent word, and (c) with a semicolon and a transitional word or phrase. Use the correct punctuation.

EXAMPLE: Most people waste a large part of their lives, they spend five years standing in line.

a. . . . their lives, for they spend...

b. . . . their lives because they spend...

c. . . . their lives; for example, they spend...

1. Mrs. Frisbee has been with the company five years, she will get a raise.

   a. _____
   b. _____
   c. _____

2. Ruth is a hard worker, she will not get a raise.

   a. _____
   b. _____
   c. _____

Editing Check 5

Edit this paragraph to correct run-together sentences. Use one of the five methods listed in the editing Quickcheck that follows the paragraph. The first error has been corrected as an example.

                                                    for

[1]The Great Wall of China is remarkable, ^ it is the only human structure large enough to be seen from outer space. [2]The wall is about 17 metres high and 5 metres wide at the top, it stretches for 2400 kilometres. [3]It was built between 300 B.C. and A.D. 1646 as a fortification against enemies, it once had 40 000 watchtowers. [4]The wall required 300 million cubic metres of material, that is enough to build a 2-metre-high wall around the Earth at the equator. [5]The wall's construction required an enormous number of labourers, when construction was at its peak, one-third of all Chinese males were required to work on the project. [6]Hundreds of thousands of workers died, their efforts did not succeed in keeping out invaders.

Quickcheck on Run-Together Sentences

✓ You can correct a run-together sentence in five ways.

1. Use a period and a capital letter.
2. Use a comma and a connecting word (*and, but,* etc.).
3. Use a dependent word (*although, because,* etc.).
4. Use a semicolon by itself.
5. Use a semicolon and a transitional word (*however, therefore,* etc.) with a comma after it.

✓ A comma cannot be used alone to separate two independent clauses. A semicolon or period is required.

✓ A semicolon must have an independent clause (sentence) on each side of it. You can test your use of a semicolon by asking if you could use a period instead. If not, the semicolon is wrong.

✓ Be sure you understand the differences between the connecting words (*and, but,* etc.), the transitional words (*however, therefore,* etc.), and the dependent words (*since, although, because,* etc.). Study the punctuation that goes with each type.

SENTENCE STRUCTURE: AVOIDING RUN-TOGETHER SENTENCES   **83**

Checkpoint 5-1

In the blank to the left of each paragraph, write the letter of the run-together sentence in that paragraph.

_____ 1. ᴬAutomobiles were introduced in the 1890s. ᴮAt first, they seemed very strange, in fact, they were displayed in circuses. ᶜBefore cars, most long-distance travel was done in horse-drawn carriages, which explains why the first autos were called "horseless carriages."

_____ 2. ᴬThe first vehicles that could move themselves were built as early as the eighteenth century; however, they were powered by steam, not gasoline. ᴮA steam carriage in England in the 1830s reached a speed of 25 kilometres an hour, and some of the vehicles carried as many as 22 passengers. ᶜThe success of steam-powered road vehicles worried the railway people, they got laws passed limiting the use of steam carriages.

_____ 3. ᴬCars powered by electric batteries were the most popular. ᴮThey were cleaner and quieter than those powered by steam or gasoline, but they had major drawbacks, they couldn't go fast, and their batteries had to be recharged every 80 kilometres. ᶜGasoline-powered cars gradually replaced steam and electric cars.

_____ 4. ᴬAlthough the gasoline-powered car originated in Europe with such men as Gottlieb Daimler and Karl Benz, the first successful North American car of that type is usually credited to two brothers, Charles and Frank Duryea. ᴮThat car was built in 1894, in 1895 the Duryeas started the first company to manufacture gasoline-powered cars. ᶜMen such as Henry Ford and Ransom Eli Olds soon were also making cars.

_____ 5. ᴬIn the United States, the young car industry was helped in 1901 by the discovery of huge oil fields in Texas, in addition, mass production methods were introduced to make cars cheaper. ᴮOne no longer had to be rich to afford a car. ᶜNot surprisingly, cars became a popular means of transportation.

_____ 6. ᴬThe Olds Motor Works in Detroit had the first auto assembly line. ᴮParts for the cars were made at a variety of machine shops; they were then brought to a central factory to be assembled into cars. ᶜThis made the work go faster, production jumped from 425 cars in 1901 to 5000 cars in 1903.

_____ 7. ᴬHenry Ford wanted to make a car that almost everyone could afford, to do that he introduced the moving assembly line. ᴮA conveyor belt moved the frame of the car through the plant while workers on each side of the belt added parts brought to them on other conveyor belts. ᶜThis method cut the time needed to assemble a car from 12.5 hours to 1.5 hours.

_____ 8. ᴬBy cutting assembly time, Ford was able to cut costs. ᴮThe famous Model T Ford dropped in price from $850 to less than $400, making it cheaper than any other car. ᶜMore than 15 million Model Ts were sold between 1908 and 1927, half the cars sold in America in that period were Fords.

CHAPTER 5 PARAGRAPHS WITH NARRATIVE DETAILS

Checkpoint 5-2

In the blanks below the following paragraph, indicate whether each sentence is correct (C) or run together (RTS).

[1]The dolphin is believed to be among the most intelligent animals and is the star performer in many aquarium shows. [2]The bottle-nosed dolphin can be trained to leap high in the air to grab fish from a trainer's hand, it can also be taught to jump through a hoop or retrieve a ball or stick. [3]Using clicks, whistles, and barks, dolphins are able to communicate with each other. [4]They use the underwater echoes of their sounds to locate enemies or other objects, a system similar to the sonar used by submarines. [5]Some scientists rank the dolphin's intelligence between that of the dog and the chimpanzee, others say the dolphin is smarter than the chimpanzee. [6]Bottle-nosed dolphins live in coastal waters, grow up to 3 metres in length, and can weigh as much as 362 kilograms. [7]The smaller common dolphin lives in warm ocean waters and was considered a sign of good luck by sailors. [8]Therefore, the sailors refused to eat the dolphins. [9]Dolphins were considered sacred in ancient Greek mythology. [10]Dolphins are sometimes confused with porpoises, but porpoises lack the dolphins' "beak."

1. ____   2. ____   3. ____   4. ____   5. ____
6. ____   7. ____   8. ____   9. ____   10. ____

No answers are given for Checkpoint quizzes.

WORDCHECK: WORD ORIGINS

Many words have histories that are interesting in themselves and that sometimes help us remember a word's meaning. The dictionary lists a word's origin or derivation in brackets.

Look up the origins of these words:

1. sandwich
2. smog
3. bonbon
4. dandelion
5. sinister

CHECKPOST: ADJECTIVES—USING COMPARATIVES

Forming comparatives from basic adjectives is straightforward if you follow these rules:

Rules
- Words of one syllable add *-er* to the end:

    fast – faster

- For adjectives with -e on the end, don't repeat the e.

    nice – nicer

- For words that end with a single consonant, double the letter:

    hot – hotter

Remember

- The word *fun* does not change in the comparative or superlative form.

- For words of two syllables that end in -y after a consonant, change the y to i and then add -er:

    witty – wittier; friendly – friendlier

- For words of two syllables that end in -er already, add -er:

    bitter – bitterer; clever – cleverer

- For other words of two or more syllables, use more:

    helpful – more helpful

    honest – more honest

    handsome – more handsome

Checkpost 5-1

Make comparative sentences using the following.

1. Canada/USA: large

2. Niagara Falls/Lethbridge: tourists

3. St. Lawrence Seaway/Mississippi River: polluted

4. Margaret Atwood/Farley Mowat: interesting

5. Keanu Reeves/Sean Connery: famous

DEVELOPING PARAGRAPHS USING PROCESS

READING: PROCESS PARAGRAPHS TELL HOW SOMETHING COMES ABOUT

Precheck

Most people have heard the name Roots, even if they do not personally own any Roots clothing. The success of Roots is a story that spans three decades and emphasizes successful marketing strategies. The following article discusses the process, or stages, by which this success came about.

Journal Topic

Do you know of any business success stories?

The Story of Roots –Michael Posner

1   One could argue that the dawn of Roots was in the summer of '55, when two Americans, Don Green and Michael Budman, spent the summer at Camp Tamakwa, on Tea Lake, Algonquin Park. After that summer's experience with nature, the boys never looked back: Budman has spent the best part of thirty years in the park; Green twenty. Without the formative and enduring influence of Algonquin and its magnetic tug, it's fair to say that the friendship between Budman and Green would never have been sealed, and that they would never have settled in Toronto or gone into business together.

2   Without the camp experience, there would have been no Roots, the little counterculture shoe store that the entrepreneurial young Americans opened in August 1973, immediately and cleverly appropriating that most Canadian of logos—the beaver. Two decades later, as it closes in on $100 million in annual sales, Roots is a major success story—an international, 500-employee, vertically integrated, privately owned empire in progress. Today, with sales increasing annually, it has fifty-one stores in Canada, five in the U.S., two in Japan and more on the way; its wide product range has been tailored to the tastes of the rich and famous, who have been assiduously cultivated and used to promote Roots products.

formative influential

appropriating taking to use for one's own purposes

assiduously with great concentration, effort

It all began in the late '60s when, after a summer as a Tamakwa camp director, Budman bought a cottage on Smoke Lake and moved up to Toronto from Detroit. Green joined him there eventually, after first travelling with Budman from Quebec to Jamaica's Negril.

On their settling in Toronto, with a view to changing their "economic reality," the boys investigated many products before being directed to a Michigan lifestyle store that was selling Earth Shoes, the improbably designed negative heel which laid claim to orthopaedic correctness by daring to suggest that this was precisely how God had intended humankind to walk, with our toes an inch above our heels.

Having decided to make their own version of this shoe, they pooled their savings and then approached a manufacturer under B in the yellow pages, tiny Boa Shoes, owned by Jan Kowalewski, scion of seven generations of Polish shoemakers. He modified the Earth design and produced several styles: moccasin, desert boot, city, and sport. Looking for a name organic enough to rival the competition, Green discovered the word "roots" in a textbook on trees. "Your feet are connected to the ground, like a tree is," he says. "Really, your feet are your roots."

On opening day in their rented store at Yonge and Davenport, August 15, 1973, they sold seven pairs of shoes. The second Saturday, they sold thirty pairs, and after three weeks it had become an Event—with lineups down the block.

By year's end, Budman and Green had bought Kowalewski's business and moved the operation into larger premises with new equipment. They went from making thirty pairs of shoes a day to 2000 within a year. Within eighteen months, there were Roots shoe stores across the continent.

In their marketing, they stressed Kowalewski's made-in-Canada craftmanship, and ran sepia-toned advertisements featuring Jan and sons in work aprons, implying each Roots shoe had been lovingly handmade. With that native American genius for marketing, the Roots boys have turned what might have been just another retail chain into a legitimate cultural icon. It says something about the crisis of identity in contemporary society, the desperate longing to belong to something, that Budman and Green have been able to persuade millions of North Americans that wearing the Roots logo confers instant membership in a not-so-private club—their club, Team Roots.

Even more remarkably, they have somehow managed to transplant the ideology of conservation onto its very antithesis—the act of consumption—making the purchase of a Roots sweatshirt synonymous with selfless, ecological virtue and oneness with Nature. They've packaged the wilderness and sold Canadians back their own myths. A marketing ploy? You bet—but one rooted in their authentic and unmistakable love for Algonquin Park.

By 1976, even though the negative heel was going the way of the bell bottom pant, Budman and Green were churning out rubber-soled versions of other shoe styles, as well as a new line of leather jackets and handbags. After the birth of Green's first child, Roots launched the baby and kids' line, with immediate success.

But the real accumulation of gold was literally spun from cotton—the sweatshirt. Between '85 and '87, the country seemed overcome by fleece frenzy. "It started very small," an associate recalls. "A few sweatshirts in a basket in a corner, more for staff than anything else. And it evolved. The numbers became unbelievable. We couldn't give enough floor space, time, effort to it. I remember a Boxing Day at the Eaton Centre store, bringing product out from the back and being almost killed by customers."

By 1990, Roots was not alone in experiencing sweat fatigue; the entire retail sector was spinning into a black hole. Ironically the recession may be one of the best things to have happened to Roots, a much needed wake up call. "Their work habits had become pretty slack," says one former Roots employee. That changed, literally overnight.

Rima Greenberg, an employee of the company, credits the company's survival to the durability of the Roots name, the flexibility of factory ownership and the push to expand the wholesale division, which sells leather jackets, sweatshirts, etc., to sports clubs, movie crews and corporations and now accounts for a third of all revenues.

"We've learned it over and over," says Green. "Your results in business are directly proportionate to the time you give it. It's not a complicated formula." Indeed, for the Roots boys it has been a most successful one.

Checking Meaning and Style

1. Why does Michael Posner see the beginning of Roots in Budman and Green's stay in Algonquin Park?
2. How was the Earth Shoe intricately linked to the beginning of Roots?
3. What events prompted Roots to diversify and expand?
4. How have the Roots stores managed to survive the recessions Canada has been through?

Checking Ideas

1. What does Posner see as remarkable about the use of the beaver as the Roots logo?
2. What are the features of a "vertically integrated" management style?
3. What does this article illustrate about entrepreneurial success in North America?
4. Do you choose your clothes with brand names in mind? Are there any brand names that have particular meaning for you?

Netcheck

Can you find a reading that traces the development of a successful business enterprise or entrepreneur on the Web? Compare the information you find with what is in *The Canadian Almanac*.

WRITING MODELS: THE PROCESS PARAGRAPH

To describe a process is to tell, step by step, how something is developed: how to teach a dog to roll over, how to make a good chili, how Canada became a confederation. Most of "The Story of Roots" is an example of process writing. The article discusses the steps by which Budman and Green developed an extremely successful retail chain. These were the major stages:

1. In 1973, Budman and Green began selling their version of Earth Shoes at Yonge and Davenport in Toronto.

WRITING MODELS: THE PROCESS PARAGRAPH   **89**

2. By the middle of 1975, they had a chain of stores across Canada.

3. By 1976, they had branched into new lines of shoes; they had also begun selling handbags and jackets.

4. In 1985, their Roots sweatshirt stormed the market.

5. In the 1990s, restructuring saved Roots from the recession.

The amount of detail the author adds depends on whether the writing is a paragraph, an essay, or a book. Consider also what transition words will be needed.

The following is a process paragraph based on these significant steps in the reading selection. Notice the transition words used to link the sentences in these process paragraphs.

Model Process Paragraph #1

The underlined topic sentence states what process is being examined.

The development of the Roots retail success began in 1973. By 1975, Budman and Green were selling a type of Earth Shoe in Roots stores across Canada. In 1976 they began to manufacture other leather goods, such as handbags and jackets, as well as offer other shoe styles. Their fame and financial success were cemented in 1985, when they began to sell the famous Roots sweatshirts. In the early 1990s, they restructured for the recession years. Nowadays, the Roots beaver logo is seen everywhere.

Read the following process paragraph, and then answer the questions below it.

Model Process Paragraph #2

Notice how the first sentence establishes the topic of the paragraph.

Levi Strauss arrived at the riveted blue jeans so popular today through a series of major developments. First, he made a pair of pants from canvas for a California Gold Rush miner who wanted sturdy trousers. Other miners put in requests. When an order for more canvas was not filled, he made pants from "denim," a tough brown cloth made in Nîmes, France. Almost from the beginning, he had his cloth dyed the distinctive indigo that gives blue jeans their name. Later, he adopted riveted pockets after a miner complained that the pockets weren't strong enough to hold ore samples.

1. What did Strauss do first?

2. What did Strauss do when he could not get more canvas?

3. What colour did Strauss dye the denim?

4. Why did he rivet the pockets to the pants?

The answers to these four questions identify the steps Levi Strauss went through in the process of developing his famous blue jeans.

Study the organization of the following step-by-step description of how to judge a car in a used-car lot.

Model Process Paragraph #3

Observe the underlined transition words that help keep track of steps.

If you're thinking about buying a used car from a dealer, *Consumer Reports* magazine says you can learn a good deal about a car by examining it carefully in the lot. <u>First</u>, look for leaks. Oil spots under the car or greenish-white stains on the radiator could mean trouble. <u>Next</u>, examine the body. Fresh welds, fresh paint on a car under three years old, panels that don't match the rest of the car—all could mean the car has been in an accident. Look for rust on the door edges and trunk floor; lift the floor covering to check the metal underneath. <u>Now</u>, inspect the tires. Uneven wear suggests an accident or an alignment problem. To check the suspension, grab the top of each front wheel and push and pull; it shouldn't move or clunk. <u>Finally</u>, go over the interior. Look for stains from water leaks; sniff for the musty odour of mildew. Check the seat belts, seat adjustments, and other interior hardware. Test the wipers, radio, air conditioner, and other accessories. If you're still interested, take the car for a test drive.

PREWRITING: ASKING HOW AND WHY

"The Story of Roots" explains how and why the stores came about. Those questions can often be useful in obtaining details to develop a topic.

Let's say that you're looking at this topic sentence:

Education and on-the-job training are increasingly necessary for job success.

Like most topic sentences, it is rather general. You need specific details to make the paragraph interesting and convincing. Ask yourself why education and training are necessary. Then jot down ideas that answer that question. Remember, you are brainstorming, so don't worry if all the ideas are good. You can get rid of the bad ones later.

- technological changes—new skills needed
- jobs less secure these days
- layoffs and downsizing, even for veteran workers
- blue-collar jobs more complicated
- college grads make more money

Then ask how the skill training might be obtained.

- finish high school
- go to college or trade school
- look for on-the-job training opportunities
- take night classes

These ideas should provide enough details for a paragraph. After crossing out any details that don't fit and rearranging others, you might write a paragraph like the next model.

Model How-and-Why Paragraph

More than ever, education and training throughout a worker's life are important to job success. Changes in technology can make old skills obsolete, and downsizing and layoffs may mean the need to enter another line of work. Continued education usually produces bigger paycheques; the average college graduate earns considerably more than the average high-school graduate. Blue-collar workers need solid math and communication skills as jobs grow more complex and workers take part in the teams that are used more and more in factories. Clearly, a person should get as much schooling as he or she can. Beyond that, job applicants might do well to join a company that offers on-the-job training when new skills are needed. Formal education should continue, too. For example, night classes at the local community college can keep a worker up to date or provide skills in a new field.

Sometimes, only one of the how–why questions will work. If, for example, the boss asks for a memo on why you should get a raise, you will leave it to the boss to worry about how to pay for it. In a process paragraph, emphasis will be on how the process takes place.

Now You Try It

Ask "how?" or "why?" to get specific details to develop each general statement.

EXAMPLE: Spring is my favourite season.

    a. The flowers and fruit trees are in blossom.

    b. Baseball season opens.

    c. I can wear lightweight clothes.

1. The Internet is useful for the elderly.

   a. _____

   b. _____

   c. _____

2. Yesterday was one of the worst days of my life.

   a. _____

   b. _____

   c. _____

3. The Olympic Games are surrounded by controversy.

   a. _____

   b. _____

   c. _____

WRITING ASSIGNMENT: A PROCESS PARAGRAPH

The topic sentence of a process paragraph usually says something about the process, such as that it is easy, fun, or worthwhile. Here are three examples:

> Changing the wallpaper in your kitchen is not an easy task, but the job can be simplified if you follow these steps.
>
> A bill follows a complex path in Parliament before it becomes a law.
>
> Developing an idea into a sound business is not easy unless you follow certain steps.

Transition words or phrases, such as those underlined in Model Process Paragraph #3, can be helpful in making the steps of a process clear. However, do not overdo them; use transition words only when they help. Here are some more examples:

to start with	the first step	second
the next step	after that	the last step

Write a Process Paragraph

Write about a process that can be described in one paragraph. Write on one of these subjects:

1. How to plan a wedding
2. How to spend a pleasant Sunday with a child
3. How to do something around the house (not a recipe)
4. How to do something in sports or as a hobby
5. How to become a citizen of Canada
6. How to make something (Model #2)
7. How to buy something (Model #3)

To get started on your process paragraph, do the exercises below. If your mind is blank, use the prewriting techniques discussed earlier (nonstop writing and brainstorming).

1. Write a topic sentence for your process paragraph.

   _____

   _____

2. What is the *first step*?

   _____

   With what transition word or phrase will you start?

   _____

3. What is the *second step*?

   _____

What will be your next transition word or phrase?

_____

4. What is the *third step*?

_____

What will be your next transition word or phrase?

_____

5. What is the *fourth step*?

_____

What will be your final transition word or phrase?

_____

Before you write your process paragraph, be sure that all steps in the process are included and that each step is clear. You may need more than four steps.

Writing Assignment Checklist

✓ Use whatever prewriting techniques seem useful: listing, clustering, asking how and why, etc.

✓ Start with a topic sentence that leads easily into the steps of the process.

✓ Be sure that each step is described clearly and that all necessary steps are included.

✓ Check your use of transition words. Make sure you have variety.

✓ Revise the paragraph as needed. Does the topic sentence say something about the process? Does the paragraph include clear and interesting details? Do transition words make the process clear?

✓ Watch especially for spelling troublemakers, sentence fragments, and run-together sentences.

✓ Proofread the final copy.

SENTENCE STRUCTURE: USING VERBS CORRECTLY

Verbs change their form to show changes in time. Most verbs are regular; that is, they show past time in a consistent way, by adding *-ed* or *-d* to the present-time form.

Present Time	Past Time
jump	jumped
dance	danced
hope	hoped

But that isn't true of all verbs. Look at the verbs in these past-time sentences:

Angela <u>knowed</u> the words to all the Top 40 songs.

Alexandra <u>losed</u> her wedding ring in the potato salad.

Obviously, adding *-ed* or *-d* to *know* or *lose* just results in embarrassing errors. They are irregular verbs. Their past-time forms are made in irregular or inconsistent ways. Those sentences should have been written this way:

Angela <u>knew</u> the words to all the Top 40 songs.

Alexandra <u>lost</u> her wedding ring in the potato salad.

To avoid mistakes with irregular verbs, we have to memorize the past-time form and the past participle for each one. The past participle is the form used with the helping verbs *has*, *have*, and *had*.

Present time	Today Violet <u>sings</u>.
Past time	Yesterday Violet <u>sang</u>.
Past participle	Violet <u>has sung</u> all week long.

Unfortunately, the list of irregular verbs is rather long (the following list is not complete).

Present	Past	Past Participle (used with the helping verbs *has, have, had*)
arise(s)*	arose	arisen
become(s)	became	become
begin(s)	began	begun
bite(s)	bit	bitten
blow(s)	blew	blown
break(s)	broke	broken
bring(s)	brought	brought
buy(s)	bought	bought
catch(es)	caught	caught
choose(s)	chose	chosen
come(s)	came	come
do (does)	did	done
draw(s)	drew	drawn
drink(s)	drank	drunk

---

*Present-time verbs add an *-s* or *-es* if the subject is *he*, *she*, or *it*.

drive(s)	drove	driven
eat(s)	ate	eaten
fall(s)	fell	fallen
feed(s)	fed	fed
feel(s)	felt	felt
fight(s)	fought	fought
find(s)	found	found
fly (flies)	flew	flown
forget(s)	forgot	forgotten
get(s)	got	got *or* gotten
give(s)	gave	given
go (goes)	went	gone
grow(s)	grew	grown
hurt(s)	hurt	hurt
keep(s)	kept	kept
know(s)	knew	known
lay(s) (to place)	laid	laid
lead(s)	led	led
leave(s)	left	left
let(s)	let	let
lie(s) (to recline)	lay	lain
lose(s)	lost	lost
make(s)	made	made
meet(s)	met	met
pay(s)	paid	paid
ride(s)	rode	ridden
ring(s)	rang	rung
run(s)	ran	run
say(s)	said	said
see(s)	saw	seen
send(s)	sent	sent
shoot(s)	shot	shot
shut(s)	shut	shut
sing(s)	sang	sung
sit(s)	sat	sat
slide(s)	slid	slid
speak(s)	spoke	spoken
spend(s)	spent	spent
steal(s)	stole	stolen
swim(s)	swam	swum
take(s)	took	taken
teach(es)	taught	taught
tell(s)	told	told
think(s)	thought	thought
throw(s)	threw	thrown
wear(s)	wore	worn
win(s)	won	won
write(s)	wrote	written

To see if any of the irregular verbs are a problem for you, cover the past and past participle columns and test yourself. Make up sample sentences for the present, past, and past participle forms. The sentences don't have to make a lot of sense to serve your purpose. For example:

Today I <u>write</u> a letter. Yesterday I <u>wrote</u> a letter. I <u>have written</u> two letters.

Today Mrs. Hassan <u>wears</u> a suit. Yesterday she <u>wore</u> a dress. She <u>has worn</u> different outfits every day this week.

Put a check beside any verbs you had trouble with; then practise them again and again until the correct forms seem natural. Errors in verbs show up in both your speaking and your writing, so time spent on these problems will be time well invested.

Note: Present-time verbs are used not only to express an action that is going on right now but also to express an action that continues from the past into the present and future. Examples:

Loretta <u>sings</u> in the choir at First Baptist Church.

A dissatisfied car buyer <u>tells</u> his troubles to an average of 22 people.

Spotcheck 6-1

Use all three forms of the verbs in italics—present, past, and past participle (in that order). Remember that the present-time verb ends in -s if the subject is he, she, *or* it. *The past participle is always used with one of the following helping verbs:* has, have, *or* had.

EXAMPLE: Six-year-old Billy likes to *draw*. He <u>draws</u> whenever he gets a chance. He <u>drew</u> a Corvette for his dad's birthday. He has <u>drawn</u> since he was two years old.

1. Baby birds quickly learn to *fly*. They _____ within days of being hatched. A baby robin _____ for the first time this morning in my yard. By October it will have _____ to a warmer location.

2. Some people *eat* more than is good for them. For example, Tom usually _____ between meals. He _____ two doughnuts this morning during coffee break at work. By bedtime, he has usually _____ a chocolate bar or two.

3. It is really discouraging to *forget* what one has learned in class. I _____ the forms of irregular verbs if I don't review them frequently. In a test yesterday, I _____ the past participles of *forget* and *swim*. I'm afraid I have also _____ the difference between *affect* and *effect*.

4. Jacqueline likes to *go* dancing. She _____ almost every Saturday night. Last week she _____ to a club called the Top Hat. She didn't like the band; she says she has _____ there for the last time.

5. It is easy to *hurt* oneself skiing. Curtis and Jake usually _____ themselves at least once each season. Curtis _____ his ankle at Horseshoe Valley last weekend. Jake has _____ his arm three times in two winters.

Spotcheck 6-2

Underline the correct verb form in parentheses.

1. Sandra (buy/bought) a new motorcycle yesterday.
2. She had (gave/given) the purchase a good deal of thought.
3. Finally, she (threw/throwed) aside all her doubts.
4. The salesman at the cycle shop (tell/told) her she should buy a helmet, too.
5. He mentioned statistics that the Canadian Automobile Association had (brung/brought) out on motorcycle safety.
6. After hearing these statistics, Sandra (begins/began) to think she should learn more about driving safely.

Spotcheck 6-3

Write the correct form of the verb given in parentheses.

1. (teach) Mr. Tam has _____ at Acadia University for 15 years.
2. (sing) Louis and Besonda have _____ together on a local television program.
3. (fly) Charles Lindbergh _____ alone across the Atlantic Ocean in 1927.
4. (eat) Cathy had _____ two bags of potato chips while watching a horror movie on TV.
5. (drink) Meanwhile, Farida had _____ a six-pack of root beer.
6. (speak) Monica and Mark have not _____ to each other since the college dance.
7. (see) Marilyn _____ the movie six times.
8. (write) Have you _____ your sociology term paper yet?
9. (spend) Corporations have _____ large sums to get their products displayed in movies.
10. (pay) A cigarette manufacturer is said to have _____ actor Sylvester Stallone $500 000 to use its brands in five films.

Spotcheck 6-4

Write sentences using the verb forms in parentheses. Use helping verbs where needed.

1. (seen) _____
   _____
2. (became) _____
   _____
3. (rang) _____
   _____

4. (known) _____

_____

5. (driven) _____

_____

Past Participles as Adjectives

Sometimes the past participle is used not as a verb but as an adjective, a word that describes a noun or a pronoun. In those cases it will come after a linking verb or before a noun.

The runner was <u>exhausted</u>. (after the linking verb *was*)

The <u>stolen</u> car was soon recovered. (before the noun *car*)

Spotcheck 6-5

Underline past participles used as adjectives.

1. The mayor looked excited when the news came.
2. A frightened rabbit hurried across the road.
3. Two grown men were swinging in the playground.
4. The speaker seemed annoyed at the interruption.
5. The shopper thought the clerk was prejudiced.

Three Verbs to Watch Out For

Three irregular verbs that sometimes cause trouble are *be*, *have*, and *do*. Be sure you are familiar with the forms of each.

Present Time (*be*)		Past Time (*be*)	
Singular	**Plural**	**Singular**	**Plural**
I am	we are	I was	we were
you are	you are	you were	you were
he (she, it) is	they are	he (she, it) was	they were

Present Time (*have*)		Past Time (*have*)	
Singular	**Plural**	**Singular**	**Plural**
I have	we have	I had	we had
you have	you have	you had	you had
he (she, it) has	they have	they had	they had

Present Time (*do*)		Past Time (*do*)	
Singular	**Plural**	**Singular**	**Plural**
I do	we do	I did	we did
you do	you do	you did	you did
he (she, it) does	they do	he (she, it) did	they did

Spotcheck 6-6

Underline the standard verb form in parentheses.

1. Libya (be / is / are) the only country with a flag of a single colour—green.
2. Nepal is the only country that (have / has) a nonrectangular flag.
3. Country music (have / has) gained many new fans in recent years.
4. Barney usually (does / do) 100 metres in around 10 seconds.
5. However, yesterday he (do / did / done) it in over 11 seconds.
6. The MacGees (have / has) a boat.
7. Yesterday you (be / was / were) late for your music class.
8. The albatross is a bird that (have / has) a reputation for bringing bad luck.
9. From the fifth century to the ninth, the average human life span (be / was / were) 36 years.
10. Despite its name, the College of William and Mary (do / does / did) not admit women students for 255 years, until 1918.

Verb Endings

The *-s* and *-ed* endings of regular verbs sometimes get dropped (or added) when they shouldn't be.

No: John <u>hope</u> to get a job at the foundry.
Yes: John <u>hoped</u> (or <u>hopes</u>) to get a job at the foundry.

No: Cindy always <u>play</u> the piano at our parties.
Yes: Cindy always <u>plays</u> the piano at our parties.

No: The restaurant serves <u>home-cook</u> meals.
Yes: The restaurant serves <u>home-cooked</u> meals.

Following are the standard forms for a typical regular verb. If any of them don't "sound right," they are worth practising until they do.

Present Time		**Past Time**	
Singular	**Plural**	**Singular**	**Plural**
I work	we work	I worked	we worked
you work	you work	you worked	you worked
he (she, it) works	they work	he (she, it) worked	they worked

Notice that the past-time forms are all the same and that the only change in the present-time forms is the *-s* added in the singular ("he *works*").

Spotcheck 6-7

Underline the correct form in parentheses.

1. Marlene's three-year-old daughter (know / knows) the alphabet by heart.
2. Wasn't Raymond (suppose / supposed) to paint the garage over the weekend?
3. The instructor (ask / asked) the class to write 500 words on 1 of the 4 topics.
4. Lucy (say / says) she won't be home for dinner.
5. Sandra and Rashid (run / runs) five kilometres every day.

Doublecheck 6-1

Orville and Wilbur Wright invented the first practical airplane. As an exercise, change the underlined words in the following paragraph to give all the credit to Wilbur. Change the subjects and verbs from the plural to the singular, as in the first sentence. Put all the verbs in the present tense.

¹~~Orville and Wilbur Wright introduce~~ **Wilbur Wright introduces** the age of air travel when, in 1803, ~~they make~~ **he makes** the first successful powered flight. ²Without even finishing high school, <u>the two bicycle makers discover</u> complicated principles of aerodynamics that make flight possible. ³On that historic day, on a beach in Kitty Hawk, North Carolina, <u>they fly</u> a homemade, 12-horsepower craft for 12 seconds. ⁴<u>They travel</u> 40 metres. ⁵After that first flight, <u>they complete</u> three more on the same day, December 17, 1903, the longest trip covering 284 metres. ⁶Then <u>the brothers watch</u> in dismay as a gust of wind blows the flimsy craft along the beach, wrecking it. ⁷Undiscouraged, <u>they build</u> another model. ⁸At first, <u>they receive</u> little attention for the historic accomplishment. ⁹Today, however, <u>they are</u> honoured by a national memorial near Kitty Hawk.

Doublecheck 6-2

In the blanks to the left of each sentence, write the correct form of the verbs in parentheses. Use past-time verbs in the first five sentences. Then switch to present-time verbs in the last five sentences.

_____ 1. Emily Carr (be) the name of a British Columbian painter and author who is now recognized as a great Canadian painter.

_____ 2. She (live) in a strict, disciplined atmosphere in Victoria in the 1890s.

_____ 3. In 1891, after her parents' death, she (go) to study at the California School of Design in San Francisco.

SENTENCE STRUCTURE: USING VERBS CORRECTLY   101

_____ 4. When she (return) two years later, she set up art classes for children in Victoria.

_____ 5. The trip to England that she (take) in 1902 resulted in an illness that lasted until 1904.

Use present-time verbs for the next five sentences.

_____ 6. She then (go) to France where her art develops under the influence of post-Impressionism.

_____ 7. She (begin) to paint the Indian sites she had begun to record in 1908.

_____ 8. After several years, she (produce) a tremendous record of vanishing native villages, houses, and totem poles.

_____ 9. She (meet) the Group of Seven on a trip to eastern Canada that revitalizes her art.

_____ 10. After this time, her art work (receive) the recognition it still enjoys today.

Editing Check 6

Edit the paragraph that follows to change all the underlined subjects and verbs from the plural to the singular, as in the first sentence.

Sam walks   **he needs**

[1]~~Sam and Joe walk~~ over to the library because ~~they need~~ some information to write a psychology class paper on hypnotism. [2]They ask a librarian for help. [3]They are told that the *Readers' Guide to Periodical Literature* lists articles from about 200 magazines. [4]They look under "hypnotism" and see the titles of many articles on the subject. [5]They decide to request the April 1982 issue of *Essence* because they are attracted to an article called "Hypnosis: Put Your Mind Power to Work."

Checkpoint 6-1

In the blank to the left of each sentence, write the correct form of the verb in parentheses.

_____ 1. The manufacturer says this breakfast cereal has been (shoot) from cannons.

_____ 2. You could see that Muriel had (lie) in the sun too long while at the beach.

_____ 3. Luis said the movie had already (begin) when he and Martina arrived.

_____ 4. The car (run) onto the shoulder of the road before tipping over.

_____ 5. Have all the students (bring) their books to class?

_____ 6. I wonder where all the cookies (go) that I bought yesterday.

_____ 7. Timmie said he had no idea where they had (go).

_____ 8. If Lynn had (know) that Paris was a town in Ontario, she would have had a perfect score on the test.

_____ 9. She knew it last week, but by test time she had (forget).

_____ 10. The estimated value of the average housewife's labour has (rise) to $40 000 a year.

Checkpoint 6-2

In the blanks to the left of each sentence, write the correct form of the verb in parentheses.

_____ 1. Sandra usually (buy) new shoes every month.

_____ 2. Has Marie (choose) her wedding gown yet?

_____ 3. It (begin) to rain as we left the theatre.

_____ 4. Mohamed was (name) to the all-star team.

_____ 5. Today, George (like) Sylvia best.

_____ 6. The Olsons (grow) vegetables in their backyard last year.

_____ 7. We waited until the phone (ring) four times.

_____ 8. Oscar has (lose) his chance for promotion.

No answers are given for Checkpoint quizzes.

WORDCHECK: VERB FORMS

There is ice on the pond. You want to write that the pond behind the barn has... *froze? frozen?* Your dictionary lists the past-time and past participle forms of irregular verbs. It will tell you that *frozen* (the past participle of *freeze*) is the form of *freeze* to use with the helping word *has*. The forms are usually printed in boldface (dark) type in the dictionary.

Look up the past time and past participle of these verbs:

1. shake _____ _____
2. put _____ _____
3. swear _____ _____
4. forgive _____ _____
5. sink _____ _____

CHECKPOST: USING COMPARATIVES AND SUPERLATIVES

Rules

Comparatives

- Look out for these irregular adjectives:

    good – better
    bad – worse
    far – farther
    little – less than/littler than
    much – more than
    many – more than

- Always use the subject pronoun, not the object pronoun, in a comparison, or the meaning will change drastically:

    He likes her more than I (do). [The helping verb is not essential] = I don't like her very much; he likes her.

    He likes her more than me. = He prefers her to me.

Remember

- Use *fewer* with countable nouns, and *less* with uncountables.

    She works fewer hours now so she spends less time in her office.

Superlatives

- Follow the rules for one and two syllable comparatives by adding *-est* and using *the*.

    The MacKenzie Range is the highest in the country.
    Gloria Steinem is the most famous feminist.
    Houdini was the cleverest escape artist.

- Irregular cases:

    good – the best
    bad – the worst
    far – the farthest
    little – the least
    much – the most
    many – the most

Remember

- Distinguish between *the most/most of the* and *most*.

    Most of the guests are from out of town.
    or Most guests are from out of town.

    I like Lawren Harris the most of all the Group of Seven.
    Victoria is the most beautiful place to visit.

Checkpost 6-1

Use the following adjectives in superlative sentences.

1. pleasant

2. bad

3. many

4. important

5. quiet

6. fun

7. smart

8. intelligent

9. terrific

10. fast

7

DEVELOPING PARAGRAPHS USING CAUSE AND EFFECT

READING: ANALYZING CAUSE AND EFFECT

Precheck Many services that used to be regarded as government owned and in the *public* sector—some postal and car licensing services, for example—are now in the hands of the *private* sector. This "privatization" is supposedly meant to improve services. In the following article, well-known columnist Dalton Camp argues otherwise. Notice how he cites the effects of privatization on ordinary citizens to argue his case against it.

Journal Topic As a consumer, have you made use of a service lately? How well were you treated?

Plague of Privatization Is Robbing Our Citizens –Dalton Camp

1 A friend, standing in line at a railway station washroom in Britain, observed the following sign, erected by the management: "Due to service improvement, there are reduced toilet facilities on this floor."

2 This, in the lexicon of the academic community, is known as "plastic speech," in which vacuity is employed with the intention of assuring the ignorant and the helpless that someone is in control and all is well, all evidence to the contrary. My favourite has always been that of Secretary of Defence Robert MacNamara during the rigorous brutality of the *ancien régime* in Vietnam against the enemy: "Autocratic methods within a democratic framework were required to restore order."

vacuity emptiness (of statements)

3 These methods, under the rubric of "autocratic methods" permitted torture, the routine abasement of human dignity and worth, but are justified by bureaucratic vapidity.

abasement degradation, demoralizing

4 British Rail, once a wholly public owned railway, has been sacrificed to the gods of privatization. Instead of one publicly owned railway, privatization gave Britons 25 new railways. These, Britons were assured, would provide improved service, healthy competition, lower fares and further delights.

The result has been chaos. Apart from much plastic speech, there was an awesome decline in the quality of passenger service, frequent delays and cancellations, not to mention the increased danger to life and limb now provided by a public service driven by the lust for private profit.

And profits there are; privatized railroading has proved a gravy train for the investor. As for the public, its rewards have been few and, of course, the government is still shelling out millions of pounds in subsidy for maintenance and other infrastructure costs. The British experience speaks eloquently to the high public cost of free market capitalism.

eloquently very clearly

Consider the illusionary bonanza of deregulation of the airline industry both in Canada and the United States. While the public was promised the benefits of open skies, which would include more competition, lower fares, and improved service, Canada now has a high cost, non-competitive industry in which flying has become a luxury. In the United States, where its citizens are raised to believe that patriotism and capitalism are synonyms, air travel has become a health hazard and will soon become a near monopoly business. Given the lack of regulation, America's open skies have become filled with bankrupt airlines and high altitude mergers.

We could, I suppose, travel by bus. But could we live without power? The citizens of California are in the process of finding out. Four years ago, the California state legislature voted unanimously to deregulate its power industry given the assurance, in the language of *The New York Times*, "that market forces would bring power costs down." This was, *The Times* adds, "a dramatic miscalculation as it turned out."

As of this hour, California's two largest private utilities are "sliding into bankruptcy." Responding to the growing crisis, the government of the state, proclaiming deregulation a failure, has promised, in *The Times'* description, "to reassert the state's control over its power market." This would include steps to control power plants, grids, and prices. Privatizers and free market theorists will complain of these developments, but Californians will likely think it better than sitting in the dark.

The plague of privatization has robbed the citizens of their joint properties—railroads, airlines, air terminals, "the King's highways" and public space. And as its dark twin, deregulation, brings only misery to the general population, someone might think to ask if there is any mechanism or method of accountability somewhere. John Locke put it very simply: Members of the society authorize others to act for them "to make laws… as the public good of the society shall require." But then, we have this spell whereby the legislators make laws only as the private good may require.

dubious suspect

All this may have been more tolerable were it not for the fact that so much was done in the name of a dubious philosophy, part of which argued that government could not serve the public interest nearly as well as could private interests.

If we have learned anything, out of all this misadventure, inconvenience and risky business, it is that it just ain't so.

Checking Meaning and Style

1. How does Dalton Camp begin his essay?
2. What is "plastic speech," and what example does Camp give of it?
3. What is meant by "gravy train for the investor"?
4. What example of privatization in Canada does Camp use?
5. What effect does the use of "ain't" have in the last paragraph?

Checking Ideas

1. How would you explain "bureaucratic vapidity"?
2. What was the effect of the privatization of British Rail on the public and the investors?
3. What was the supposed result of Canada's airline deregulation? Were these results apparent?
4. What has happened to the power industry in California?
5. What is your opinion of Locke's statement?

Netcheck

Look up John Locke and see what you can find out about the man and his philosophies.

WRITING MODELS: THE CAUSE AND EFFECT PARAGRAPH

What is the result of privatization on ordinary citizens? Dalton Camp argues that the effects caused by privatization and deregulation are not in the best interests of the public. Here is a breakdown of some of his analysis:

AIRLINES IN CANADA

Cause: Deregulation   Effects: Poor services
                                 Increased health risks
                                 Higher costs

POWER IN CALIFORNIA

Cause: Deregulation   Effects: Rising costs
                                 Increased job losses
                                 More power cuts

Study the following three model paragraphs to see how cause and effect arguments are used.

Model Cause and Effect Paragraph #1

The topic sentence states that this paragraph will explain causes.

Experts say reckless and hostile freeway driving—even to the point of shooting at other motorists—has several causes. Cars give us a sense of power. At the same time, they protect our identity and give us a chance to escape after we have been rude or hostile. Moreover, as we creep along in congested traffic, our blood pressure rises, and we are quick to get angry when someone cuts in front of us. Finally, the television programs and advertising we see often suggest that violent behaviour is acceptable.

Model Cause and Effect Paragraph #2

In this example, the effect is mentioned first; then, two causes are described.

Two reasons why many students drop out of college are that they hang around with the wrong crowd, or they have to go to work to support their family. If they associate with students who go to school just to socialize, they are likely to neglect their studies and possibly fail their courses. Their friends may encourage them to cut classes to "hang out." If they fall behind in their classes, they may drop out altogether. Other students drop out because they are the only ones to support the family. They may have done well in school, but now they need to work full time.

1. What effect is discussed in this paragraph?
2. What two causes are mentioned for this effect?

This paragraph might have been improved if the writer had given all his attention to just one of the two reasons. Then he could have given more details about that one reason, making the paragraph more interesting and worthwhile, as in Model Paragraph #3. Do not try to cover too much ground in a single paragraph.

Model Cause and Effect Paragraph #3

Here the topic sentence—the first sentence—leads into a discussion of causes

My friend Ali had to drop out of college to support his family. Ali's father has been unemployed since the local steel mill shut down. His mother quit her job as a nurse years ago because of back trouble. His two brothers are still in elementary school, and his sister is in high school. Even though Ali had been working from 4 p.m. to midnight at a gas station and his father receives employment insurance, the family was having trouble making house payments. So Ali added a 2 to 6 a.m. job stocking shelves at a supermarket. He tried to continue his classes, too. However, when he found that he was coming to classes unprepared and often dozing off, he decided to postpone his college education until the family finances were in better shape.

1. What is the main effect discussed in this paragraph?
2. What caused other members of Ali's family not to contribute more to its support?
3. What seems to be the final factor that caused Ali to take a second job?
4. What two factors finally caused Ali to drop out of school?

PREWRITING: AUDIENCE

We have discussed prewriting methods for getting in touch with your ideas through brainstorming, keeping a journal, clustering, nonstop writing, and questioning. The ideas in your paper are very important, of course, but another point to consider is the **audience** you are writing for. Look back at the articles you have read so far; at what kind of audience was each of them originally aimed?

Now You Try It

We all have different ways of speaking, depending on whom we are speaking to. We talk differently to a child than to an older person and to a close friend than to a boss.

Imagine that you were unable to go to work today and you called in to report this. Demonstrate how your audience would influence your approach.

You (talking to a co-worker over the phone): _____
_____
_____

You (talking to your boss over the phone): _____
_____
_____

WRITING ASSIGNMENT: A CAUSE AND EFFECT PARAGRAPH

Your college instructors may call on you to analyze a subject in terms of cause and effect: What caused the First World War? What are the causes of the high divorce rate in Canada? What were the effects of the invention of electric lights? How does television viewing affect students' grades?

When writing a cause and effect paragraph, you analyze either the causes or the effects of something. You do not analyze both the causes and the effects at the same time.

Start with a topic sentence that may look similar to one of these:

Acid rain is caused by burning fossil fuels.

A major cause of teen drug use is peer pressure.

My life has been miserable since I met Lucy. (effect)

Obtaining my high-school diploma had a positive effect on my life.

This is a good time to look at the difference between the words *affect* and *effect*. *Affect* is an action verb meaning "influence."

The medicine <u>affected</u> Brad's driving ability.

Effect is a noun meaning "result."

Did the medicine have an <u>effect</u> on Brad's driving?

Write a Cause and Effect Paragraph

Write a cause and effect paragraph. Choose your subject from the two lists that follow. The six suggested subjects are dependent-clause fragments. Be sure that your topic sentence is a true sentence, not a fragment.

Subjects Emphasizing Cause

1. Why I chose to attend this college
2. Why I bought the kind of car (bicycle, motorcycle) I did
3. Why I am a liberal (vegetarian, jogger, etc.)

Take Topic 1 as an Example

Observe how all four reasons are part of the same *cause*.

I. Topic sentence about the effect

I chose to attend this college in order to save money.

Explanation about the cause

A. Night classes, so could work days

B. Community college tuition is less

C. Could live at home and save on expenses

D. Nearby, so save on transportation costs

Subjects emphasizing *cause* could use this outline:

For Your Own Notes

II. Topic sentence about the effect

_____

_____

Explanation of the cause

A. _____
B. _____
C. _____
D. _____

Subjects Emphasizing Effect

1. How my life has changed since I quit smoking (started drinking, joined a church, etc.)
2. How driving affects my emotions and behaviour
3. How friends improve (spoil) my life

Take Topic 1 as an Example

I. Topic sentence about the cause

My life has changed since I quit smoking.

Observe how all four reasons are part of the same *effect*.

Explanation about the effect

A. Have more money to spend on food
B. Food tastes better now
C. Put food in mouth instead of cigarette
D. Have put on a few pounds

Subjects emphasizing *effect* could use this outline:

For Your Own Notes

II. Topic sentence about the cause

_____

_____

Explanation about the effect

A. _____
B. _____
C. _____
D. _____

Develop your topic sentence by writing at least half a dozen sentences of explanation or examples. When revising, watch out for fragments and run-together sentences.

Writing Assignment Checklist

✓ You might try writing nonstop or asking how and why—or both—to develop your topic. Asking *why* you chose this college (what *caused* your decision), you might come up with a list like this one:

close to home   low tuition   friends attending
chance to play football   good music department

✓ Start with a true sentence, not a fragment. The six subject suggestions begin with a dependent word—*why* or *how*—and are dependent clause fragments.

✓ Be sure that your paragraph sticks to the causes or effects of your subject.

✓ When revising your first drafts, make sure that your paragraph includes clear explanations or examples. Look especially for sentence fragments, run-together sentences, and verb errors.

✓ Ask a classmate or a friend to read the paragraph and to tell you if it seems well organized, interesting, and convincing.

✓ Remember to proofread the final copy for overlooked mistakes.

SENTENCE STRUCTURE: MAKING SUBJECTS AND VERBS AGREE IN A SENTENCE

Subjects and verbs must agree. That means that singular (one-item) subjects need singular verbs and plural (more-than-one-item) subjects need plural verbs.

Usually we don't have problems with subject–verb agreement:

> Mary attends college. (subject and verb both singular)
>
> The Olson boys attend college. (subject and verb plural)

A complication to keep in mind: A plural subject usually ends in *-s* (*boys*), while a singular verb often ends in *-s* (*attends*).

Here are some other situations to consider.

Subjects Joined by And

Subjects joined by *and* are usually plural.

> Latanya and Baroum have [not *has*] announced their engagement.
>
> Swimming and walking are [not *is*] good exercise.

Spotcheck 7-1

Underline the correct verb in parentheses.

1. Anagrams and Scrabble (is/are) word games.
2. Mr. and Mrs. Choy always (plays/play) bridge when they get a chance.
3. Four cats and one dog (runs/run) down the street.

Subjects Joined by Either...or or Neither...nor

When subjects are joined by *either... or* or *neither... nor*, the verb agrees with the nearer subject:

> Either Jim or his parents are meeting the plane. (The plural verb *are meeting* agrees with the nearer subject, *parents.*)
>
> Neither the Kims nor their daughter has reservations. (The singular verb *has* agrees with the nearer subject, *daughter.*)

Or rewrite the sentence:

> The Kims don't have reservations. Neither does their daughter.

Spotcheck 7-2

Underline the correct verb in parentheses.

1. Either Terrie or Jonathan (plans/plan) to bring the games to tonight's party.
2. Of course, neither Naomi nor Richard (expects/expect) to attend the party because of final exams coming up.
3. Neither Joey nor his parents (enjoys/enjoy) word games.

SENTENCE STRUCTURE: MAKING SUBJECTS AND VERBS AGREE IN A SENTENCE   113

Beware of Words That Separate Subject and Verb

Words that come between the subject and verb may cause confusion. Phrases that begin with *in addition to*, *along with*, or *as well as* do not affect the number of the verb.

   Phil, along with several friends, is attending Caribana.

   The apple pie, in addition to two dozen cookies, was eaten by the squirrels.

Remember

A word in a prepositional phrase is never the subject of the verb. To help pinpoint the subject, you might cross out the prepositional phrases, as in these examples:

   The stamps ~~in the desk drawer~~ belong ~~to Harold~~.

   Only one ~~of the books~~ is overdue.

Some of the common prepositions are *of, in, into, for, on, at, by, to, from, with, above, below, through, during, among, before,* and *after*. The noun or pronoun that comes after the preposition completes the prepositional phrase.

Spotcheck 7-3

Draw one line under the subject and two lines under the correct verb in parentheses. Cross out any prepositional phrases if that will help you locate the subject.

1. One of Canada's best-known writers (is/are) Margaret Atwood.
2. The cause of the computer's problems (is/are) static electricity.
3. A banana, along with whole grains, (adds/add) important nutritional value at breakfast.
4. Several workers in the front office (is/are) getting raises.
5. The woman wearing the hat and carrying the roses (thinks/think) she is a princess.

Sometimes the subject comes after the verb instead of before it. Remember that the word *there* is never the subject.

              verb   **subject**
~~Inside the boxes~~ was a collection ~~of old magazines~~.

      verb   **subject**
There are not many clues ~~in the case at this time~~.

Spotcheck 7-4

Draw one line under the subject and two lines under the correct verb in parentheses.

1. At the edge of the trees (is/are) an old abandoned house.
2. There (is/are) also the remains of two rusty cars.
3. Across the street (is/are) the tombstones of the local cemetery.
4. There (is/are) a scary quality about the whole area.
5. Inside my stomach (is/are) some nervous feelings.

Indefinite Pronouns Are Always Singular

Words called **indefinite pronouns** are almost always singular, even though some of them seem to be plural. Here are some examples:

    each   either   neither   everyone   everybody   someone

    somebody   anybody   nobody   something   everything

When one of those words is the subject, the verb must of course be singular.

    Everybody has [not *have*] to bring a hot dish or a salad to the party.

    Everything the committee planned is [not *are*] taking place on schedule.

However, *both, few,* and *several* always take a plural verb.

    Both of the vases are to be auctioned.

    (compare) Neither of the vases is to be auctioned.

Spotcheck 7-5

Draw one line under the subject and two lines under the correct verb in parentheses. You may want to cross out prepositional phrases to make the subject more obvious.

1. One of our neighbours (owns/own) a complete set of the novels of Charles Dickens.
2. Both of the family bicycles (has/have) flat tires.
3. Everyone in the cast of the school play (was/were) invited to a party.
4. Each of the pies (tastes/taste) delicious.
5. Nobody among Scott's friends (is/are) going to lend him money.

Beware of *Who, Which, That*

When *who, which,* or *that* is used as the subject of a dependent clause, its verb may be singular or plural. It is singular if the word the pronoun stands for is singular; it is plural if the word it stands for is plural.

    Whistler is a resort area that is very popular. (The verb is singular because *that* stands for a word that is singular, *area*.)

    Whistler is one of those resort areas that are very popular. (The verb is plural because *that* stands for a word that is plural, *areas*.)

Spotcheck 7-6

Underline the correct verb in parentheses.

1. The vice-president of the company is a woman who (has/have) a master's degree in business administration.
2. Winnipeg has residents who (doesn't/don't) mind the winter cold.
3. Motorists who (drives/drive) Highway 401 know the meaning of boredom.
4. The leader of the expedition into the Himalayas is one of those people who (loves/love) adventure.
5. David's Camaro, which (costs/cost) him $90 a month just for insurance, will have to be sold.

Group Nouns Are Usually Singular

Group nouns look plural but are usually singular. Here are some examples of group nouns:

    family   team   class   committee   audience   band

    flock   herd   group   department store   gas company

They usually require singular verbs:

    The Dupree family <u>has</u> a cabin on Lake Simcoe. (The family is one unit or group.)

    This year's class <u>was</u> the largest in ten years. (The class is a single unit.)

However, sometimes when we use group nouns we are thinking of individual members of the group acting separately. We are thinking "they" rather than "it." Then we need a plural verb.

    The Dupree family <u>have</u> interesting jobs. (Individual members have separate jobs.)

    This year's class <u>are</u> getting good job offers. (*Class* refers to individual members.)

Spotcheck 7-7

Draw one line under the correct verb in parentheses.

1. The audience always (gives/give) a standing ovation after the orchestra plays.
2. The law class (plans/plan) a field trip to the courthouse tomorrow.
3. The army (is/are) holding manoeuvres near the river.

Beware of Singular Nouns Ending in *-s*

Some nouns end in *-s* and look plural but take a singular verb: *politics, news, measles, mathematics, physics, economics,* etc.

    The <u>news</u> from home <u>was</u> encouraging.

    Dave said <u>physics</u> <u>is</u> his most difficult course.

Spotcheck 7-8

Draw one line under the correct verb in parentheses.

1. Politics (seems/seem) like an attractive field to Harry.
2. The news about her mother (has/have) brightened Sylvia's day.
3. Mathematics (is/are) difficult for some people.

Doublecheck 7-1

Draw one line under the correct verb in parentheses.

1. Everyone in the boats (knows/know) how to swim.
2. There (was/were) a beautiful rainbow after the storm.
3. Luis is one of those guys who (is/are) reliable when the going gets rough.
4. Among the crowd at the theatre (was/were) Mr. and Ms. Greenberg.

5. The average Canadian household (watches/watch) TV for about seven hours a day.//
6. Neither the Mighty Ducks nor the Calgary Flames (is/are) going to win the Stanley Cup this year.
7. Centennial College, which (was/were) founded in 1967, was the first community college in Ontario.
8. The dishes in the sink (needs/need) to be washed before dinnertime.
9. Where (is/are) the ribbons for wrapping these presents?
10. Everybody in the back row (has/have) to move to the front row.

Quickcheck on Subject–Verb Agreement

✓ Singular subjects take singular verbs; plural subjects take plural verbs.
✓ Subjects joined by *and* are plural.
✓ When two subjects are joined by *either... or* or *neither... nor*, the verb agrees with the nearer subject.
✓ Don't mistake the object of a preposition for the subject of the verb.
✓ The subject usually comes before the verb, but sometimes it comes after.
✓ *There* is never the subject of the sentence.
✓ Indefinite pronouns such as *each*, *either*, and *everybody* are always singular.
✓ When used as subjects, *who*, *which*, and *that* agree with the words they stand for.
✓ Group nouns such as *committee*, *audience*, and *team* are usually singular.

Editing Check 7

Some of the underlined verbs do not agree with their subjects. If the verb is wrong, write the correct form above the line. Underline the subject also. The first sentence is an example.

    are
¹There <u>is</u> many <u>people</u> these days who are taking aerobic exercise classes or building muscles with weight training. ²Which one of the two kinds of exercise do you think <u>has</u> more health benefits? ³The answer to that question <u>lie</u> in understanding the terms **aerobic** and **anaerobic**. ⁴The first of the terms <u>mean</u> "with oxygen," while **anaerobic** means "without oxygen." ⁵One of the sports that <u>stimulates</u> beneficial activity of the heart and lungs is aerobic. ⁶Activities such as brisk walking, running, cycling, and swimming <u>are</u> healthfully aerobic. ⁷They make the body work hard and <u>increases</u> the demand for oxygen. ⁸Lifting

weights, on the other hand, <u>is</u> anaerobic—building muscles but not strengthening the heart and lungs. ⁹Either walking or swimming <u>produce</u> good aerobic results without the risk of injury that is a drawback in running. ¹⁰Aerobic exercise, <u>says</u> medical experts, can increase endurance, lower blood pressure, and reduce stress.

Checkpoint 7-1

In the blanks at the left, write the subject (s) and the correct verb (v) form for each sentence.

(s) _____
(v) _____
1. Provincial parks in summer (is/are) crowded with campers.

(s) _____
(v) _____
2. Of all her courses, biology and chemistry (is/are) Rosanne's favourites.

(s) _____
(v) _____
3. There (is/are) no trees in Iceland.

(s) _____
(v) _____
4. The election committee (is/are) going to meet Tuesday evening.

(s) _____
(v) _____
5. The neighbours have one of those dogs that (barks/bark) night and day.

(s) _____
(v) _____
6. Flitting about among the many blossoms in the garden (was/were) two hummingbirds.

(s) _____
(v) _____
7. Either Mr. Jong or Mrs. Daniels (is/are) driving the scouts to the museum.

(s) _____
(v) _____
8. Neither of the parents (was/were) eager to make the trip.

(s) _____
(v) _____
9. The waterfalls in Banff (is/are) usually at their best in the spring.

(s) _____
(v) _____
10. Neither the players nor the coach (is/are) ready for the tournament.

(s) _____
(v) _____
11. There (is/are) many advantages in knowing how to speak standard English.

(s) _____
(v) _____
12. The audience (was/were) less rowdy than the theatre manager had expected.

Checkpoint 7-2

In the blanks at the left, write the correct form of the verb for each sentence.

_____ 1. Neither Ian nor his brothers (drinks/drink) tea.

_____ 2. The teacher, as well as the students, (has/have) the measles.

_____ 3. Everyone on both teams (expects/expect) to win.

_____ 4. A dog is one of those animals that (is/are) usually friendly.

_____ 5. A committee of three doctors (was/were) appointed.

_____ 6. Directly behind the bears (was/were) a coyote.

_____ 7. There (is/are) no chocolate chips in my cookie.

_____ 8. Inside the box (was/were) a dozen letters.

_____ 9. Mr. and Mrs. Holt (sings/sing) in the choir.

_____ 10. The road that connects the two towns (is/are) bumpy.

No answers are given for Checkpoint quizzes.

WORDCHECK: PLURALS

Using a dictionary when necessary, write the plural form of each word in the following list. The dictionary gives the plural form only for irregular plurals—those formed in some way other than by adding -s to the word. (The recommended plural spelling is usually given just after the pronunciation guide.)

| woman | potato | company | sheep |
| wolf | scissors | business | mother-in-law |

Review Checkup

This review quiz covers important terms used so far. Put the letter of the correct answer in the blank to the left of each definition.

_____ 1. A part of a sentence written as a complete sentence
   A. independent clause
   B. fragment
   C. run-together sentence

_____ 2. The connectors that go with commas and independent clauses
   A. words such as *although* and *since*
   B. words such as *of, with, on, to, by*
   C. the words *and, but, or, for, nor, yet, so*

_____ 3. The term for a word such as *he, she, it, they*
   A. pronoun
   B. preposition
   C. clause

SENTENCE STRUCTURE: MAKING SUBJECTS AND VERBS AGREE IN A SENTENCE   **119**

_____ 4. A word that says what the subject does or is
   A. pronoun
   B. dependent word
   C. verb

_____ 5. A group of words containing a subject and a verb
   A. clause
   B. transitional words
   C. phrase

_____ 6. A group of words that could be a sentence
   A. fragment
   B. dependent clause
   C. independent clause

_____ 7. The name of a person, place, or thing
   A. noun
   B. verb
   C. preposition

_____ 8. The term for two sentences written as if they were one
   A. dependent clause
   B. run-together sentence
   C. fragment

_____ 9. A word such as *although, since, because*
   A. dependent word
   B. fragment
   C. connecting word

_____ 10. The term that names who or what a sentence is about
   A. subject
   B. object
   C. verb

_____ 11. A word such as *of, to, on, from,* or *with*
   A. dependent word
   B. verb
   C. preposition

_____ 12. Transitional words that can be used after semicolons
   A. *while, unless, although*
   B. *however, nonetheless, in fact*
   C. *through, among, between*

CHECKPOST: ADJECTIVES AND ADVERBS

Rules

Order

- Remember the order of adjectives if more than one modifies a noun: assessment – appearance (size, shape, condition) – age – colour – origin/material

    That <u>comfy, deep, leather, ancient, green</u> armchair had to be thrown out.

Comparison Using Adjectives

- To compare two items equally, use *as _____ as*.

    The semesters are <u>as long as</u> the terms.

    You are <u>as pretty as</u> your mother.

    That river is <u>as deep as</u> the lake.

- To show similarity between two nouns, use *the same as* or *as _____ as*.

    This dress is <u>the same as</u> that one.

    Showcase costs <u>the same as</u> Bravo TV.

    She is <u>as stubborn as</u> a mule.

- To contrast, use *different from*.

    Your house is very <u>different from</u> ours.

    Her sister's nature is very <u>different from</u> her brother's.

Comparison Using Adverbs

- Follow the same rules to form comparatives with adverbs as you do for comparison using adjectives.

    She sings <u>as beautifully as</u> he does.

- Adverbs can take *more than* and *the most*.

    She sings <u>more beautifully than</u> he does.

    She sings <u>the most beautifully</u>.

- Adverbs of time (*early, late, soon*) and three adverbs of manner (*slowly, quickly, loudly*) take *-er* or *-est*.

    He arrived soon<u>er</u> than she did.

    The plane was late<u>r</u> than had been expected.

- There are some irregular adverbs:

    hard – harder – hardest

    fast – faster – fastest

    well – better than – the best

    badly – worse than – the worst

    far – farther than – the farthest

    much – more than – the most

    little – less than – the least

Checkpost 7-1

Complete the following sentences using comparisons.

1. Sheila's cooking is very different _____.

2. Aminah has a better _____.

3. Roger, of all the mechanics I've known, is the _____.

4. Most of _____.

5. Compared to her brother's results, Patricia's _____.

6. Salim is much _____.

7. Minnie Mouse is more _____.

8. Ben Johnson runs _____.

9. Mark is not as clever _____.

10. Joseph is the most _____.

8

DEVELOPING PARAGRAPHS USING EXAMPLES

READING: USING EXAMPLES TO SUPPORT A POINT

Precheck

The history of Japanese Canadians during the Second World War may not be well known. Here is an example of one particular family's ordeal. Joy Kogawa's family was moved from their home and into a camp during the Second World War, when the government classified Japanese Canadians as "enemy aliens." In her novel *Obasan,* Kogawa describes the family's ordeal; the following selection is about their forced work in Alberta's sugar beet fields. While searching through her Aunt Emily's belongings, the novel's protagonist comes across a file with the label "Facts about Evacuees in Alberta." In this, she finds a newspaper clipping about how industrious and productive the Japanese workers had been. Below the picture is the caption "Grinning and happy." In the following extract, Kogawa cites many examples of just how unhappy the evacuees really were.

Journal Topic

Have you, or someone close to you, experienced hardship? What were the circumstances? How was the difficulty managed?

Evacuees in Alberta —*Joy Kogawa (extract from* Obasan)

evacuees persons moved from their homes, in this case by law

pervasive spreading everywhere

1 Facts about evacuees in Alberta? The fact is I never got used to it and I cannot, I cannot bear the memory. There are some nightmares from which there is no waking, only deeper and deeper sleep.

2 There is a word for it. Hardship. The hardship is so pervasive, so inescapable, so thorough it's a noose around my chest and I cannot move any more. All the oil in my joints has drained out and I have been invaded by dust and grit from the fields and mud is in my bone marrow. I can't move any more. My fingernails are black from scratching the scorching day and there is no escape.

3 Aunt Emily, are you a surgeon cutting at my scalp with your folders and your filing cards and your insistence on knowing all? The memory drains down the

sides of my face, but it isn't enough, is it? It's your hands in my abdomen, pulling the growth from the lining of my walls, but bring back the anaesthetist turn on the ether clamp down the gas mask bring on the chloroform when will this operation be over Aunt Em?

    Is it so bad?   **4**

    Yes.   **5**

    Do I really mind?   **6**

7 Yes, I mind. I mind everything. Even the flies. The flies and flies and flies from the cows in the barn and the manure pile—all the black flies that curtain the windows, and **Obasan** with a wad of toilet paper, spish, then with her bare hands as well, grabbing them and their shocking white eggs and the mosquitoes mixed there with the other insect corpses around the base of the gas lamp.

8 It's the chicken coop "house" we live in that I mind. The uninsulated unbelievable thin-as-a-cotton-dress **hovel** never before inhabited in winter by human beings. In summer it's a heat trap, an incubator, a dry sauna from which there is no relief. In winter the icicles drip down the inside of the windows and the ice is thicker than bricks at the ledge. The only place that is warm is by the coal stove where we rotate like chickens on a spit and the feet are so cold they stop registering. We eat cloves of roasted garlic on winter nights to warm up.

9 It's the bedbugs and my having to sleep on the table to escape the nightly attack, and the welts over our bodies. And all the swamp bugs and the dust. It's Obasan uselessly packing all the cracks with rags. And the muddy water from the irrigation ditch which we strain and settle and boil, and the tiny carcasses of water creatures at the bottom of the cup. It's walking in winter to the reservoir and keeping the hole open with the axe and dragging up the water in pails and lugging it back and sometimes the water spills down your boots and your feet are red and itchy for days. And it's everybody taking a bath in the round **galvanized** tub, then Obasan washing clothes in the water after and standing outside hanging the clothes in the freezing weather where everything instantly stiffens on the line.

10 Or it's standing in the beet field under the maddening sun, standing with my black head a sun-trap even though it's covered, and lying down in the ditch, faint, and the nausea in waves and the cold sweat, and getting up and tackling the next row. The whole field is an oven and there's not a tree within walking distance. We are tiny as insects crawling along the grill and there is no protection anywhere. The eyes are lidded against the dust and the air cracks the skin, the lips crack, Stephen's flutes crack and there is no energy to sing any more anyway.

11 It's standing in the field and staring out at the heat waves that waver and shimmer like see-through curtains over the brown clods and over the tiny distant bodies of Stephen and Uncle and Obasan miles away across the field day after day and not even wondering how this has come about.

12 There she is, Obasan, wearing Uncle's shirt over a pair of dark baggy trousers, her head covered by a straw hat that is held on by a white cloth tied under her chin. She is moving like a tiny earth cloud over the hard clay clods. Her hoe moves rhythmically up down up down, tiny as a toothpick. And over there, Uncle pauses to straighten his back, his hands on his hips. And Stephen farther behind, so tiny I can barely see him.

13 It's hard, Aunt Emily, with my hoe, the blade getting dull and mud-caked as I slash out the Canada thistle, dandelions, crab grass, and other nameless non-beet plants, then on my knees, pulling out the extra beets from the **cluster**, leav-

---

Obasan Aunt (Japanese)

hovel shack

galvanized made of iron sheeting

cluster group

ing just one to mature, then three hand spans to the next plant, whack whack, and down on my knees again, pull, flick flick, and on to the end of the long long row and the next and the next and it will never be done thinning and weeding and weeding and weeding. It's so hard and so hot that my tear glands burn out.

And then it's cold. The lumps of clay mud stick on my gumboots and weight my legs and the skin under the boots beneath the knees at the level of the calves grows red and hard and itchy from the flap flap of the boots and the fine hairs on my legs grow coarse there and ugly. **14**

I mind growing ugly. **15**

I mind the harvest time and the hands and the wrists bound in rags to keep the wrists from breaking open. I lift the heavy mud-clotted beets out of the ground with the hook like an eagle's beak, thick and heavy as a nail attached to the top of the sugar-beet knife. Thwack. Into the beet and yank from the shoulder till it's out of the ground dragging the surrounding mud with it. Then crack two beets together till most of the mud drops off and splat, the knife slices into the beet scalp and the green top is tossed into one pile, the beet heaved onto another, one more one more one more down the icy line. I cannot tell about this time, Aunt Emily. The body will not tell. **16**

We are surrounded by a horizon of denim-blue sky with clouds clear as spilled milk that turn pink at sunset. Pink I hear is the colour of llama's milk. I wouldn't know. The clouds are the shape of our new prison walls—untouchable, impersonal, random. **17**

There are no other people in the entire world. We work together all day. At night we eat and sleep. We hardly talk anymore. The boxes we brought from Slocan are not unpacked. The King George/Queen Elizabeth mugs stay muffled in the *Vancouver Daily Province*. The camera phone does not sing. Obasan wraps layers of cloth around her feet and her torn sweater hangs unmended over her sagging dress. **18**

Down the miles we are obedient as machines in this odd ballet without accompaniment of flute or song. **19**

"Grinning and happy" and all smiles standing around a pile of beets? That is one telling. It's not how it was. **20**

muffled silenced

Checking Meaning and Style

1. Where is the main point of this essay?
2. Where do the examples of what Joy Kogawa's protagonist couldn't bear about the evacuees' life in Alberta start?
3. What is the effect of starting many paragraphs with "It's"?
4. Why is paragraph 15 only one sentence?
5. What other devices does Kogawa use to make the extract affect the reader? For example, why are there few commas in paragraph 3?

Checking Ideas

1. During the Second World War, did this kind of discrimination happen to any other group of people living in Canada?
2. Do you think that treating a group of people this way can ever be justified?
3. Have you, your family, or your friends ever experienced discrimination because of race or religion?

WRITING MODELS: THE EXAMPLE PARAGRAPH

Netcheck — Find an article about the history of Japanese Canadians during the Second World War. What did former Prime Minister Brian Mulroney's government agree to do for the Japanese community?

Joy Kogawa's essay is full of examples of the terrible hardships endured by the evacuees. The essay could be reorganized into the five-paragraph format using Kogawa's own words. In each paragraph, the topic sentence has been underlined.

Model Example Paragraphs #1

Evacuees in Alberta

1. Introduction with topic sentence underlined

Facts about evacuees in Alberta? <u>The fact is I never got used to it and I cannot, I cannot bear the memory.</u> There are some nightmares from which there is no waking, only deeper and deeper sleep. There is a word for it. Hardship. The hardship is so pervasive, so inescapable, so thorough it's a noose around my chest and I cannot move any more. Do I really mind?

2. Body with 1st support; topic sentence underlined

<u>Yes, I mind.</u> I mind everything. Even the flies. The flies and flies and flies from the cows in the barn and the manure pile—all the black flies that curtain the windows, and Obasan with a wad of toilet paper, spish, then with her bare hands as well, grabbing them and their shocking white eggs and the mosquitoes mixed there with the other insect corpses around the base of the gas lamp.

3. Body with 2nd support; topic sentence underlined

<u>It's the chicken coop "house" we live in that I mind.</u> The uninsulated unbelievable thin-as-a-cotton-dress hovel never before inhabited in winter by human beings. In summer it's a heat trap, an incubator, a dry sauna from which there is no relief. It's the bedbugs and my having to sleep on the table to escape the nightly attack, and the welts over our bodies.

4. Body with 3rd support; topic sentence underlined

<u>Or it's the work we had to do.</u> It's standing in the beet field under the maddening sun, standing with my black head a sun-trap even though it's covered, and lying down in the ditch, faint, and the nausea in waves and the cold sweat, and getting up and tackling the next row. It's standing in the field and staring out at the heat waves that waver and shimmer like see-through curtains over the brown clods and over the distant bodies of Stephen and Uncle and Obasan miles away across the field day after day and not even wondering how this has come about.

5. Conclusion with final message underlined

"Grinning and happy" and all smiles standing around a pile of beets? That is one telling. <u>It's not how it was.</u>

The three body paragraphs in the rewrite of Kogawa's essay give examples to support her thesis statement. In the following paragraph, a woman discusses parents in general by using her own parents as real-life examples:

Model Example Paragraph #2

Observe the opening topic sentence

Even though it may sometimes be difficult, parents should give their teenage children considerable privacy. When my parents realized that it was embarrassing for me to talk to boyfriends on the phone in the kitchen, they had a phone installed in my bedroom. If I was in my room with the door closed, they always knocked and asked if it was all right to come in. Of course, I can't know for sure, but I'm confident they never searched my room for drugs or whatever else it is parents are often suspicious about. They respected my privacy, so I always tried to behave in a way that justified their trust.

1. How many examples about her parents does the writer give?
2. In each example, what did her parents do?

The next paragraph, which takes a different view of privacy, uses hypothetical parents or "parents in general" as examples.

Model Example Paragraph #3

Observe the opening topic sentence

With more teenagers getting into serious drug trouble these days, parents need to keep a close watch on their children, even if that means "invading" their privacy now and then. Parents should listen in on their children's phone conversations and be sufficiently acquainted with slang to know that Johnny's remark about "snow" might not be about a ski trip. When Mom puts clean clothes in the kids' dresser drawers, she should keep an eye out for suspicious bags or surprising wads of money. Dad might call the attendance office at school now and then just to be sure that's where Susie is spending her days. Parents may not like playing the role of narcotics agents, but that may save their children from the real narcs later on.

1. What names does the writer give to the four members of this hypothetical family?
2. Why do you suppose the writer chose to use these names?
3. How many examples about these parents does the writer give?
4. In each example, what are the parents doing?

WRITING ASSIGNMENT: AN EXAMPLE PARAGRAPH

When you write an example paragraph, you have a couple of decisions to make. You have just seen a demonstration of the difference between using a true example from your own life and a hypothetical example that you made up. Another choice you have to make is whether you will give one extended example or several short examples.

John had decided to write an example paragraph about the way some teachers can bring out the worst in students. He was going to base his example on his own grade six teacher, Mr. Clark. John had several true examples in mind:

1. Mr. Clark would assign homework but never collect or grade it, so no one did it.
2. Mr. Clark never started class until everyone was ready, so students never got ready.
3. Mr. Clark would laugh at students' mistakes, so they never volunteered to answer questions.

John liked all of these true examples about his former teacher, but he decided that his paragraph would have more power if he just used one of these examples and fully developed it. Here is what John finally wrote:

> Some teachers bring out the worst in their students. I remember my grade six teacher, Mr. Clark. Every day at the end of math class he would assign us a page of practice problems. The first night just about everyone did them, but the next day he did not collect the homework or grade it. The second time he assigned homework, fewer people bothered doing it. By the end of the week, no one was doing the math homework. Then came our first midterm test in math. Everyone had a horrible time on the test because we had never practised the problems he had demonstrated on the board each day. I still blame my poor background in math on Mr. Clark's careless attitude.

Write an Example Paragraph

Write a unified paragraph on one of the following numbered subjects. Use either real-life or hypothetical examples to support the topic sentence.

1. Women (Men) can be hard to understand.
2. Some teachers bring out the best (worst) in a student. (see example above)
3. Mothers who work outside the home usually have busy lives.
4. Small children can be a real joy (headache) to their parents.
5. People who use drugs are inviting trouble.
6. Parents should (should not) respect their children's privacy. (Models #2 and #3)

Will you use several examples to write about one subject, or will you use only one example but develop it fully? Use the planning form below to make some notes about what you might include in your example paragraph.

(Topic sentence) _____

_____

_____

(First example) _____

_____

_____

(Second example) _____

_____

_____

(Third example) _____

_____

_____

Does one of these examples seem considerably more interesting than the others? Would your paragraph be better with all three examples or with just the most interesting one fully developed? Decide on the best way to organize your example paragraph.

In revising your first draft, be sure to correct any sentence fragments, run-together sentences, or faulty verb forms.

Remember the language to use in exemplary writing. Although Joy Kogawa lists her examples in a literary fashion, in general, the following phrases will be used:

such as   for instance   for example   to illustrate   to demonstrate

Writing Assignment Checklist

✓ Start with a topic sentence that makes clear your central point. (One of the previous numbered topics may be used as a topic sentence.)

✓ Develop the topic with a prewriting technique. Brainstorming, nonstop writing, or asking how and why would seem most useful.

✓ While revising your first draft, be sure that the topic sentence leads to a unified, convincing paragraph. Correct any sentence fragments, run-together sentences, or faulty verb forms.

✓ Proofread the final copy, looking for small, overlooked mistakes.

SENTENCE STRUCTURE: SELECTING THE RIGHT PRONOUN

Pronouns are words used to take the place of nouns. If we did not have pronouns, our writing might read something like this:

> The man asked the woman if the woman knew what time it was. The woman told the man the time was ten o'clock. The man thanked the woman.

With pronouns, we can avoid the annoying repetition of nouns:

> The man asked the woman if <u>she</u> knew what time it was. <u>She</u> told <u>him</u> that it was ten o'clock. <u>He</u> thanked <u>her</u>.

Subject and Object Forms of Pronouns

The pronouns *she, her, he, him,* and *it* take the place of the nouns *woman, man,* and *time* to make the writing smoother.

Most pronouns change their form, or *case,* depending on whether they are used as the subject or the object of a sentence. In the example just given, we noticed that *she* and *her* both refer to *woman.*

Here are the subject and object forms of the personal pronouns, both singular and plural:

Singular		Plural	
Subject	**Object**	**Subject**	**Object**
I	me	we	us
you	you	you	you
he	him	they	them
she	her	they	them
it	it	they	them

Spotcheck 8-1

Enter the appropriate pronoun forms in the blanks.

	Subject	Object		Subject	Object
1.	he	_____	5.	I	_____
2.	_____	them	6.	_____	us
3.	it	_____	7.	you	_____
4.	_____	her	8.	_____	him

Subject, Direct Object, Indirect Object, and Object of a Preposition Forms of Pronouns

Use the **subject form** when the pronoun is the subject of the sentence.

<u>I</u> will deliver the message.

<u>They</u> travelled in Europe.

Notice that subject form pronouns usually come *before* the verb.
Use the **object form** in these situations:

1. When the pronoun is acted upon by the verb (is the **direct object**).

    verb object
The boss praised *her.*

    verb object
The biology test confused *me.*

2. When the pronoun is the **indirect object** of the verb. (To find an indirect object, ask *for whom* or *to whom* something is done.)

The doctor gave *us* blood tests.

130   CHAPTER 8   DEVELOPING PARAGRAPHS USING EXAMPLES

To whom were the tests given? To *us*. *Us* is the indirect object of the verb *gave*. (*Tests* is the direct object.)

Martin has done *me* many favours.

For whom were the favours done? For *me*. *Me* is the indirect object of the verb *has done*. (*Favours* is the direct object.) Notice that direct object pronouns and indirect object pronouns usually come after the verb.

3. When the pronoun follows (is the object of) a preposition

The letter was addressed <u>to</u> *her.*

The ball rolled <u>between</u> *us.*

Spotcheck 8-2

Indicate whether the underlined pronoun is the subject (S), direct object (DO), indirect object (IO), or object of a preposition (OP).

_____ 1. The store sent <u>her</u> a refund for the returned blouse.

_____ 2. <u>They</u> ate their lunch in the park.

_____ 3. When will you mail <u>them</u> the cheque?

_____ 4. The farmer walked with <u>us</u> to the gate.

_____ 5. Whoever hears <u>him</u> in a concert is lucky.

_____ 6. On our way to work, <u>we</u> stopped at Harvey's.

_____ 7. The clerk gave <u>us</u> a big smile.

_____ 8. The spotlight struck <u>her</u> in the eyes.

Spotcheck 8-3

Substitute a pronoun for the underlined words. Say whether the pronoun is the subject, direct object, indirect object, or object of a preposition. Write your answers in the blanks.

EXAMPLE: The government sent <u>Mr. Nelson</u> a big income tax refund.

   him   indirect object

1. <u>The Nelsons</u> built a swimming pool in their backyard.

   _____   _____

2. Workers finished <u>the pool</u> in four weeks.

   _____   _____

3. The crew boss gave <u>Mr. Nelson</u> a pair of fins.

   _____   _____

4. Mr. Nelson gave the fins to <u>his son</u>.

   _____   _____

5. The son uses <u>the fins</u> almost every day.

   _____   _____

Knowing about Pronouns in Compound Subjects and Objects

Usually we don't have much trouble using the correct pronoun form. For example, we're not likely to say or write, "*Me* saw *she* at the movies."

But there are a few times when pronoun errors are likely to appear. One of them is when there is more than one subject or object. Which pronoun is correct in the following sentences?

1. Between you and (I/me), Jason should have got the job.

   The object form *me* is needed as the object of the preposition *between*.

2. The family sent Mark and (he/him) thank-you letters.

   Him is the indirect object of the verb *sent*.

3. The Zhangs and (we/us) deserve credit for the job.

   We is part of the subject, along with *The Zhangs*.

4. The audience applauded the violinist and (she/her).

   Her is the object of the verb *applauded,* along with *violinist*.

Tip for Pronoun in Compound Subject

If you had trouble with any of those, here is a tip that should clear up your problem: When the pronoun is accompanied by another word in a compound subject or object, *cross out the other word.* Your ear will then probably tell you the correct form.

The audience applauded ~~the violinist and~~ (she/her).

Of course, the audience applauded *her.* In the same way, your ear would tell you that the family sent *him* a letter (sentence 2 above).

NOTE: It is considered a courtesy to refer to the other person first in such uses as "Mildred and I went..." or "... sent to my husband and me."

Spotcheck 8-4

Underline the correct pronoun after crossing out any accompanying words that might cause confusion.

EXAMPLE: The package was addressed to ~~Anthony and~~ (I/<u>me</u>).

1. Sam and (I/me) don't have dates for tomorrow night's dance.
2. The teacher gave Justin and (he/him) a scolding for arriving late.
3. (We/Us) NDPers have to stick together.
4. The stampeding elephants frightened (we/us) tourists.
5. The dishwashing duties are shared by my wife and (I/me).

6. The police officer gave the other hikers and (we/us) tickets for jaywalking.
7. The LaFlairs and (she/her) will vacation together.
8. The convention featured a debate between the senator and (he/him).

(Note that the crossout method doesn't work with the preposition *between*.)

Pronouns in Comparisons

Problems in choosing the right pronoun can also appear in comparisons. Which pronoun is right in the following comparison?

Alfredo studies harder than (I/me).

At least in somewhat formal writing, *I* would be preferred. Why? Because *I* is the subject of the implied verb *study*. Look at the following comparisons in which the verb is implied but not stated:

We go to the movies more often than they [do *or* go].

Calvin is not as interested in jazz as I [am].

Comparison sentences usually contain the word *than* or *as*.

Spotcheck 8-5

Underline the formally correct pronouns.

1. Margaret earns more money than (I/me).
2. Richard doesn't waste as much time as (I/me).
3. They go shopping more than (we/us).
4. Michele is not as interested in football as (he/him).

Who and Whom

Many people feel a little uncomfortable when they have to choose between the pronouns *who* and *whom*. Keep in mind that *who* is the subject form and *whom* is the object form.

Mr. Lee saw the thief who had robbed his market the night before. (*Who* is the subject of the verb *had robbed*.)

It was Irene whom the class elected. (*Whom* is the object of the verb *elected*.)

To whom was the package addressed? (*Whom* is the object of the preposition *to*.)

Whom is not much used in conversation or in informal writing. It seems too fancy or pretentious. For instance, many people would prefer to say "Who was the package addressed to?"—avoiding the formally correct *whom*. You will have to decide when the formal approach is better, but remember that *whom* can never be the subject of a verb. If in doubt, use *who*.

Spotcheck 8-6

Underline the formally correct pronouns.

1. (Who/Whom) did you see at the mall?
2. Chantelle is the friend (who/whom) is always ready to help out.

3. John saw the child (who/whom) was missing.
4. To (who/whom) should I address this letter?

-self Pronouns

Careful writers do not use *-self* pronouns such as *myself* and *themselves* in place of regular pronouns (*me, them,* etc.).

> The premier awarded medals to Sergeant Foster and *me* [not *myself*].
>
> Nancy and *you* [not *yourself*] will arrange the centrepiece.

The *-self* words have two uses: to provide emphasis and to reflect an action back to its performer.

> The premier *himself* presented the medals to us. (emphasis)
>
> Nancy stuck *herself* with a pin while arranging the flowers. (reflects action back to performer)

NOTE: Avoid using *hisself* for the standard *himself*. Also avoid using *ourself* for *ourselves*. Use *themselves* rather than *themself* or *theirselves*.

Spotcheck 8-7

Underline the formally correct pronouns.

1. Frank addressed the letter to (himself/hisself).
2. The first prize was shared by Sharon and (me/myself).
3. They can do the job (themselves/theirselves).
4. Paul and (you/yourself) are invited.

Doublecheck 8-1

Underline the correct pronouns.

1. (We/Us) club members will provide transportation.
2. Just between you and (I/me), the boss is incompetent.
3. Antoine weighs less than (I/me) since going on a diet.
4. It was William Lyon Mackenzie King (who/whom) said, "Not necessarily conscription, but conscription if necessary."
5. Ahmed wrote the poem for (hisself/himself), not for Judith.
6. The Halls are the couple (who/whom) we met on vacation.
7. The second-year students will have to decorate the gym (theirselves/themselves).
8. My wife and (I/myself) attended the awards dinner.
9. An argument broke out between Mr. Eng and (she/her) over the mayor's policies.
10. Sell the car to the person (who/whom) offers the most cash.

11. I hope that you and (they/them) can resolve your problems.

12. The choir director sent the altos and (we/us) our parts for Tuesday's rehearsal.

13. Either the Swedes or (we/us) Canadians will host the next Olympics.

14. Ms. Galvez is the person (who/whom) I believe will run for MPP.

15. (I and the auditor/The auditor and I) will inspect the firm's books.

16. (We/Us) young drivers have to pay high car insurance premiums.

17. Although those of (we/us) drivers between 16 and 24 make up only 20 percent of licensed drivers, we are involved in 42 percent of alcohol-related traffic deaths.

18. Experts say that traffic accidents are the biggest killer for people (who/whom) are between the ages of 15 and 19.

Doublecheck 8-2

Write sentences using the words in parentheses.

1. (herself) _____

2. (whom) _____

3. (me) _____

4. (themselves) _____

5. (who) _____

6. (Patrick and she) _____

7. (Kimberly and me) _____

8. (yourself) _____

SENTENCE STRUCTURE: SELECTING THE RIGHT PRONOUN 135

Editing Check 8

Edit the following paragraph to correct any pronoun errors, as in the first sentence.

                    me

¹"This is just between you and I," Helen said to her friend Gloria. ²"I don't trust Bill for a minute. ³He said he would pick up Francine and myself at nine o'clock outside the library. ⁴Francine and me stood there until ten without any sign of Bill. ⁵Luckily, the last bus was still there for Francine and me. ⁶This morning Bill told us that we women are always taking advantage of he and the other guys. ⁷He said that he hisself has been stood up by women plenty of times. ⁸I don't doubt it, him being the way he is. ⁹Guys like Bill should straighten theirselves out before it's too late." ¹⁰"No one knows that better than me," Gloria responded.

Checkpoint 8-1

Write the formally correct pronouns in the spaces at the left.

_____ 1. Except for you and (I/me/myself), no one seems to know what is going on.

_____ 2. Alex is the kind of person (who/whom) is friendly with everyone.

_____ 3. To (who/whom) should the telegram be delivered?

_____ 4. Henri is more industrious than (he/him).

_____ 5. The coach should have stopped the fight (himself/hisself).

_____ 6. He is the man (who/whom) we saw on the train.

_____ 7. Many people enjoyed the skit put on by Pat and (I/me/myself).

_____ 8. The roses were meant for Mrs. Holloway and (you/yourself).

_____ 9. I will never be able to play the piano as well as (he/him).

_____ 10. There was great friendship between Suresh and (we/us).

_____ 11. Bruce was excited when the company president sent (he/him) an answer to his letter.

_____ 12. Is Shania Twain the singer (who/whom) we heard last season?

_____ 13. On Tom's team, it's every man for (himself/hisself/theirselves).

_____ 14. Ruth can run a kilometre a lot faster than (I/me).

_____ 15. The psychic said that Harry and (I/me) will be millionaires before we're 30.

Checkpoint 8-2

In the spaces at the left, write the form of the pronouns in parentheses that would be preferred in formal situations.

_____ 1. Anthony and (you/yourself) are expected to win.

_____ 2. Between you and (I/me), this party is boring.

_____ 3. The provinces require (we/us) hunters to buy licences.

_____ 4. Eric always drives faster than (I/me).

_____ 5. The arrow fell between the target and (I/me).

_____ 6. (We/Us) chess players will meet Friday night.

_____ 7. Everybody should do the work (himself/hisself).

_____ 8. Was it Felix (who/whom) gave the speech?

_____ 9. The class report was assigned to Bonnie and (I/me).

_____ 10. The judge gave Winston and (she/her) suspended sentences.

No answers are given for Checkpoint quizzes.

WORDCHECK: SYNONYMS

Synonyms are words with the same or similar meanings—*car* and *automobile*, for instance. A dictionary lists synonyms after the definitions of some words. Notice that two synonyms do not usually mean exactly the same thing.

List at least two synonyms for each of these words:

1. mysterious
2. magic
3. poor
4. anger
5. deceive

CHECKPOST: CONDITIONALS

Rules   Conditionals are used to convey three basic types of meaning.

- The condition is probable or likely (predictable events).

    Present tense + present tense

    > When a penny drops, it falls to the ground.

    If/when + present tense + *will* + verb's root form
    If/when + present tense + present tense

    Use of *if* indicates a real probability.

    > If it rains, I will take an umbrella.

    Use of *when* indicates an increased certainty.

    > When I get married, I'll live in my own apartment.

- The condition is improbable or unlikely (but not impossible). This is the conditional form that is used for *hypothetical speech*—for expression of imaginary ideas and events—as well as in polite conversation.

    If + past tense + *would* + verb's root form

    > If I were rich, I'd live in a mansion.

    > If the Flames were to return to Calgary, they would win the Cup.

    > If dentists didn't earn so much, dental care would be cheaper.

    > If I ate fewer candies, my teeth wouldn't be so rotten.

- The condition is impossible, in a past time, or about an event that did not occur.

    If + past perfect + *would* + present perfect (or reverse order)

    > If Simon had bought a good alarm clock, he wouldn't have been fired for being late.

    > Had Abdul heard the news, he would have joined the celebration.

    > I would have been born in Bermuda if my mother hadn't moved to England.

    > Marta would have spoken French better if she had employed a good teacher.

Checkpost 8-1

Complete the following sentences, and mark which are hypothetical (H) and which are real possibilities (P).

1. If only I were rich, _____.

2. When I find a partner, _____.

3. If my grades in high school were higher, _____.

4. When a whistle kettle boils, _____.

5. If I were president of the college, _____.

6. When it snows, _____.

7. If I had a swimming pool, _____.

8. I wouldn't have finished my homework _____.

9. When I watch TV, _____.

10. If I could act, _____.

11. I would have passed the exam _____.

12. When you go to Regina, _____.

13. If the prime minister was a woman, _____.

14. If I ever get to Corner Brook, _____.

15. If the banks would support small businesses, _____.

9

DEVELOPING PARAGRAPHS USING COMPARISON

READING: PARAGRAPHS COMPARING SIMILARITIES AND CONTRASTING DIFFERENCES

Precheck

"Globalization" is a term that one cannot miss on any newscast covering our society, our economy, and our environment. Whenever there is a summit, a meeting among the most powerful nations, there is usually an "alternative" summit, formed to protest the discussions in the other camp. Naomi Klein, the author of *No Logo*, is a well-known critic of current trends in the process of globalization. In the following article Naomi Klein compares the summit and alternative summit that took place in 2001.

Journal Topic

Do you follow the news? Do you watch your local news station or a broader newscast such as CNN? What sort of news coverage are you most interested in?

globalization the process whereby every nation state becomes dependent on other nations for its economic and social well being

Pro-globalization Forces Get Taste of Own Medicine –*Naomi Klein*

No fair! That's what they are screaming from the mountaintop in Davos this week. [1]

Every year since 1971, executives of the richest multinational corporations have met with the most powerful heads of state in an alpine village in Switzerland. Davos is where Bill Clinton and Bill Gates put their differences aside, where flaky Internet gurus and name-brand Harvard economists get together to agree that the world would be an infinitely better place with freer markets. [2]

infinitely completely, totally

But what they really do at Davos, which begins tomorrow, is pray. They pray not to a god, but to an idea: competitiveness. The bible of Davos is the "Global Competitiveness Report," measuring the success of nations based on a "Growth [3]

Competitiveness index." At an altitude of 1,560 meters, there seems to be no problem that more competition cannot fix.

So what has these high priests of competition crying foul? A tax hike? A wave of government regulation? Hardly. Their enemy is a not a foe but a friend: competition. This year, for the first time, the World Economic Forum in Davos has some serious competition.

It's called the World Social Forum—colloquially, "the Anti-Davos." It will take place on precisely the same days as the Davos summit (January 25 through January 30), in Porto Alegre, Brazil. And the force that broke up Davos' intellectual monopoly was yet another traitorous pal: supply and demand.

At protests around the world, loud questions are being asking about the effects of increased competition, sometimes called "turbo capitalism": what has it done to workers? To the environment? To democracy? More to the point: if the widening economic **disparity** of the past two decades has been the result of "unprecedented prosperity," what can we look forward to in a downturn?

To borrow the language of Davos, there is a demand for something else. Bringing together over 1,000 organizations, the World Social Forum is a critical stage in moving from protests against the free market's assaults on the public sphere to an **articulation** of concrete alternatives. The forum slogan—as optimistic as anything heard at Davos during the dot-com craze—is, "Another World is Possible."

The significance of this competitive threat hasn't been lost on the organizers of the World Economic Forum. Last year, the WEF summoned a handful of its critics to the mountain, holding special sessions on the "backlash against globalization." And the conference was "carbon neutral": the planetary debt incurred by ferrying oil executives by helicopter was wiped clean, apparently, by planting some trees in Mexico. Or so the organizers declared, to much fanfare.

This year, economic euphoria isn't even on the agenda at Davos. The somber theme is "Sustainable Growth and Bridging the Divides." The captains of industry are, they say, ready to listen.

Only wait a minute: where is everybody?

Gone South. Davos Director Claude Smadja complained to reporters that the opposition has been poaching his "civil society" delegates. And Klaus Schwab, founder of the WEF, insists that "the best place for dialogue is inside the Congress Centre." Not in the messy, unwieldy, outside world.

And that is the heart of the dispute between these battling global gatherings. The World Economic Summit, by its own admission, assembles the world's "leadership team"—superheroes of the global stage who "are fully engaged in the process of defining and advancing the global agenda." Unconcealed elitism is the governing structure of Davos: attendance is by invitation only and even journalists are hand-selected. This exclusivity is protected at all costs—even when the cost is inviting a few pesky critics to be part of the "leadership team."

The World Social Forum, on the other hand, won't be gathering a competing league of experts to draft an equally dogmatic set of global prescriptions. Yes, Nobel laureates such as East Timor's Jose Ramos Horta will be in attendance, as will civil society leaders such as Canada's Maude Barlow and activists such as Jose Bove, France's McDonald's-battling cheese farmer.

But the real goal of Porto Alegre is to transform globalization from a site of experts-only **oligarchy** into an arena of genuine democracy. The forum's founding premise is that decision-making that affects us all should be open to everyone who wants to participate.

That's why the gathering is organized on the principle of participatory democracy: whoever wants to get involved can do so. Originally, estimates were that 2,500 people would attend. Now that number is up to 10,000, with some predicting twice that. At last count there were over 400 self-organized workshops scheduled and a giant campground has been set up to catch the hotel overflow.

Compared to Davos, the World Social Forum promises to be sprawling, chaotic, even frustrating. I'm going anyway because, well, I'm invited. So is everyone else.

And when it comes to global democracy, that gives Porto Alegre a distinct competitive advantage.

Checking Meaning and Style

1. Why is the first paragraph so short?
2. Who is the "they" that Klein refers to in the first and third paragraphs?
3. Paragraph four has many rhetorical questions for effect. How could you paraphrase it?
4. What is meant in paragraph five by "traitorous pal'?
5. What differences in the two conferences does Klein highlight?

Checking Ideas

1. What is the main purpose of the Davos meeting?
2. Why are the leaders at Davos upset?
3. How have people been affected by "turbo capitalism"?
4. What is the difference between the memberships of the World Economic Forum and the World Social Forum?
5. What is the principle of participatory democracy that the World Social Forum is based on?

Netcheck

What newscast can you find on the Internet? Try going to www.CBC.ca and listening to the news on the Internet. How does the broadcast differ from the way you normally listen to the news?

WRITING MODELS: THE COMPARISON PARAGRAPH

There are two basic ways of organizing a comparison of two items. One is the **block method**. In this approach, all of the details about one of the items are presented, followed by all of the details about the second item. The **point-by-point method** goes back and forth between the two items, discussing one point of similarity at a time.

This will be clearer if we take Naomi Klein's topic and outline how we might write about the meetings using first the point-by-point method and then the block method.

Point-by-Point Method

Point 1: Difference in location and size of meetings
- WEF: Davos, Switzerland; select participants
- WSF: Porto Alegre, Mexico; thousands of participants

Point 2: Difference in focus of meetings
- WEF: Global competitiveness
- WSF: Democratic alternatives to competition

Point 3: Difference in organization
- WEF: guests by invitation only
- WSF: everyone welcome

Block Method

Block A: World Economic Forum
1. Davos, Switzerland; select members
2. Discussion of global competitiveness
3. Entry by invitation only

Block B: World Social Forum
1. Porto Alegre, Mexico; thousands of participants
2. Focus on alternatives to competition
3. Everyone welcome

Which method should you use—point-by-point or block? Use the method that helps you present your ideas and information in the clearest, most interesting way. It is up to you.

Here is how "Pro-globalization Forces Get a Taste of Own Medicine" might have been written in a single paragraph, using first the point-by-point method and then the block method.

Look carefully at the underlined transition words used to express contrast.

Model Comparison Paragraph #1

<u>Although</u> they are happening at the same time, there are fundamental differences between the WEF and the WSF. The WEF is meeting in wealthy Switzerland, <u>while</u> the WSF is being held in Mexico. The WEF will focus on global competitiveness; in contrast, the WSF will seek alternatives to this. Finally, <u>whereas</u> the WEF is by invitation only and only a select few will attend, the WSF has an open invitation, so there will be thousands of participants.

Model Comparison Paragraph #2

<u>Although</u> they are happening at the same time, there are fundamental differences between the WEF and the WSF. The WEF is taking place in wealthy

Switzerland, the discussion will focus on competitiveness, and the participants will attend by invitation only. <u>On the other hand</u>, the WSF is being held in Porto Alegre, Mexico, the discussion will focus on alternatives to competitiveness, and there will be thousands of guests since there is an open invitation.

Study the following paragraph on similarities and determine whether it is organized by the point-by-point method or the block method.

Model Comparison Paragraph #3

Notice the transition words underlined.

As we have so much <u>in common</u>, one would never guess by looking at us that Carla and I aren't sisters. Carla is tall and slender: five-seven and 120 pounds; <u>similarly</u>, I am five-six and 115 pounds. We <u>both</u> have blonde hair, which we cut and perm in the latest style. Carla has blue eyes and fair skin; <u>likewise</u>, my eyes are a deep blue and my skin is very fair. To complete the similarities, we both adore dancing and go out as often as we can. To complete the picture, our boyfriends *are* brothers!

1. Is this paragraph organized using the point-by-point method or the block method?
2. Name the areas in which the writer compares Carla and herself.
3. Using the block method, outline the information given about Carla and the writer.

WRITING ASSIGNMENT: A COMPARISON PARAGRAPH

In everyday life, you continually make comparisons: between your car and your friend's car, between high school and college, between Rosa's new hairdo and her old one, between Brand X toothpaste and Brand Y, between becoming a beach bum and becoming a nuclear physicist.

In college, exams and term papers often ask that you "compare and contrast" two poems, two characters in a play, or two economic policies. (*Comparison* emphasizes the ways in which things are similar; *contrast* emphasizes differences. However, *comparison* can cover both similarities and differences.)

Write a Comparison Paragraph

Write one paragraph of comparison using the point-by-point method or the block method. Write on one of these topics.

1. Two movie stars or two musicians
2. College classes and high-school classes
3. You and a family member
4. Two houses or neighbourhoods in which you have lived
5. Two styles of dress

Writing Assignment Checklist

✓ Develop your ideas through journal writing, nonstop writing, clustering, or one or more of the other prewriting methods discussed earlier.

✓ Start with a topic sentence that makes clear the point of your comparison. Examples:

> College courses are more challenging than high-school courses in several ways.
>
> Life is more comfortable since my family moved from an apartment to a house.

Your topic sentence:

_____
_____
_____

✓ Answer the questions that follow to outline your paragraph.

1. What two people, places, or things are you comparing?

_____

2. List three different ways you will compare the two.

_____
_____
_____

3. Will you organize the paragraph with the point-by-point method or the block method?

✓ Check that your examples support the point of your comparison.

✓ Look out for pronoun and verb errors and the kinds of problems marked on earlier papers. Remember to use appropriate transition words.

✓ As always, proofread the final copy before turning it in.

SENTENCE STRUCTURE: PRONOUN AGREEMENT AND CLEAR REFERENCE

The word that a pronoun refers to is called its **antecedent**. In this sentence, *Marta* is the antecedent of the pronoun *she:*

Marta was given a scholarship because she is a talented violinist.

A pronoun must *agree* in number with its antecedent; that is, both must be singular or both must be plural.

The robin has left its nest. The robins have left their nest.

It's easy to see that the singular pronoun *its* agrees with the singular antecedent *robin*, and the plural pronoun *their* agrees with the plural antecedent *robins*. But you probably won't be surprised to learn that things are not always that simple.

Each of the men brought (his/their) own tools.

You may have been tempted to choose *their*, but *his* is right. The singular pronoun *his* agrees with the singular subject *each*. (*Men* is the object of the preposition *of* and not the sentence's subject.)

These *indefinite pronouns* are always singular:

one	someone	each
anyone	everybody	either
everyone	nobody	neither

The indefinite pronouns *both*, *several*, and *few* are always plural.

Spotcheck 9-1

Underline the correct pronouns. It may help to cross out prepositional phrases first.

1. Each of the television sets was missing (its/their) antenna.
2. Both of the orchestras have (its/their) good points.
3. Neither Christopher nor Ross could find (his/their) textbook.
4. Someone left (her/their) purse on the counter.
5. Everybody who goes into carpentry will find (his/their) situation challenging.
6. A woman who studies engineering will find (her/their) work rewarding.

Avoid Sex Bias

You may not have liked the answer given for sentence 5 in Spotcheck 9-1. You might have asked yourself why *everybody* should take the masculine pronoun *his* when the word could refer just as easily to women as to men. In the past, indefinite antecedents (neither masculine nor feminine) have worked that way. However, many people today believe that that method gives a sexist bias to the language. Unfortunately, there is no easy way around the problem.

The most common "solution" is to use the plural pronoun *their*, which is neither masculine nor feminine. Thus we would have "*Everybody* should pay *their* taxes." But this combination of plural pronoun and singular antecedent is ungrammatical and, at least in writing, should be avoided.

A somewhat better possibility is to say *his or her* in such situations, but this solution can be awkward if the words must be repeated very often.

> **(awkward)** Each applicant should bring his or her resumé to the office and be prepared to discuss his or her work experience with his or her interviewer.

A better approach is to make the antecedent plural when possible. This permits use of the gender-free pronoun *they*.

> **(revised)** All *applicants* should bring *their* resumés to the office and be prepared to discuss *their* work experience with *their* interviewers.

Other ways of wording a sentence sometimes can be used.

(awkward) Did everyone remember to bring his or her sweater?

(better) Did everyone remember to bring a sweater?

(biased) Everyone should pay his taxes by April 30.

(better) Taxes should be paid by April 30.

Spotcheck 9-2

Rewrite the following sentences to avoid sex bias and pronoun disagreement.

1. Everybody at the picnic brought his own lunch.
   _____

2. Each of the drivers had to show their licence.
   _____

3. If a person takes a shower instead of a bath, he uses only about half as much hot water.
   _____

4. A fan who brings his ticket stub from the rained-out game will get in free.
   _____

Use Singular Pronouns with Group Nouns

Group nouns—such as *team, committee,* and *flock*—refer to more than one person or thing but are usually regarded as referring to a single unit. They therefore take singular pronouns.

The committee will hold its [not *their*] next meeting Tuesday. The gas company promised to lower its rates before winter.

Spotcheck 9-3

Underline the correct pronoun in parentheses.

1. The Sparks family will take (its/their) vacation in Prince Edward Island this summer.
2. A neighbourhood street gang lost (its/their) leader in a shootout with police.
3. After deliberating for three days, the jury finally delivered (its/their) verdict.
4. The skiing team announced that (it/they) will enter the Winter Olympics.
5. When I saw them, the Barenaked Ladies rock band was on (its/their) third tour of England.

Doublecheck 9-1

Put a check mark in front of the better sentence in each of the following pairs.

_____ **1a.** One of the companies gave its employees turkeys at Christmas.

_____ **1b.** One of the companies gave their employees turkeys at Christmas.

_____ **2a.** Anyone who sings well should put his name on the list.

_____ **2b.** Those who sing well should put their names on the list.

SENTENCE STRUCTURE: PRONOUN AGREEMENT AND CLEAR REFERENCE   147

_____ **3a.** Neither France nor Germany would change their policy.

_____ **3b.** Neither France nor Germany would change its policy.

_____ **4a.** Not everyone will admit it when he has made a mistake.

_____ **4b.** Some people won't admit it when they have made a mistake.

_____ **5a.** The Girl Guides of Saskatchewan will hold their annual convention in Saskatoon.

_____ **5b.** The Girl Guides of Saskatchewan will hold its annual convention in Saskatoon.

_____ **6a.** A fool and his money are soon parted.

_____ **6b.** Fools and their money are soon parted.

_____ **7a.** Everybody brought a "We're No. 1" banner to the football game.

_____ **7b.** Everybody brought his "We're No. 1" banner to the football game.

_____ **8a.** The Bay will hold their "White Sale" on Monday.

_____ **8b.** The Bay will hold its "White Sale" on Monday.

_____ **9a.** People who buy Speedo cars should have their heads examined.

_____ **9b.** A person who buys a Speedo car should have his head examined.

_____ **10a.** One of those lipsticks cost more than they're worth.

_____ **10b.** One of those lipsticks costs more than it's worth.

Make Pronoun References Clear

Pronouns such as *he* and *they* have no meaning in themselves. They get their identity from the words they refer to, their antecedents. This connection must always be clear. Consider this sentence:

> Chris told his father <u>he</u> needed a haircut.

Who needs a haircut, Chris or his father? The pronoun *he* does not have a clear antecedent. Assuming it is the father who needs a haircut, the problem could be solved this way:

> Chris told his father, "You need a haircut."

In the next example, is it Matthew or Eric who is in college?

> **(unclear)** Matthew phoned Eric once a week when he was in college.
>
> **(clear)** When Eric was in college, Matthew phoned him once a week.

Here's a real-life example from the broadcast of an outfield play in a baseball game (find the lost pronoun):

> Winfield goes back to the wall. He hits his head on the wall, and it rolls off. It's rolling all the way back to second base!

Spotcheck 9-4

Rewrite the following sentences to make the pronoun references clear.

1. As the umpire and the coach argued, <u>his</u> voice got louder and louder.
   _____
   _____

2. Frank told the instructor that <u>he</u> had a poor understanding of the subject.
   _____
   _____

3. When Ms. Stemley saw Ms. Wright, <u>she</u> gave <u>her</u> a big smile.
   _____
   _____

4. The truck hit the police car, but <u>it</u> wasn't damaged.
   _____
   _____

5. The hail was followed by a high wind; <u>it</u> caused extensive damage.
   _____
   _____

Avoid Vague Pronoun References

A pronoun should refer clearly to a specific word or group of words. The pronouns *it*, *this*, *that*, and *which* sometimes appear without clear antecedents.

(weak) Mr. Armajani gave his wife a dozen roses. <u>This</u> pleased her. (*This* has no specific antecedent.)

(revised) Mr. Armajani gave his wife a dozen roses. The gift pleased her.

(weak) Sharon had always wanted to go into law, so she was excited when she finally achieved <u>it</u>. (*It* has no antecedent.)

(revised) Sharon had always wanted to go into law, so she was excited when she finally got her law degree.

Avoid the vague use of the pronouns *you*, *they*, and *it*. Be specific about the subject of the sentence.

(weak) When you take an English course, <u>you</u> should revise your papers carefully.

(revised) Students who take English courses should revise their papers carefully.

(weak) <u>They</u> say a storm is on the way.

(revised) The weather bureau says a storm is on the way.

(weak) In the newspaper, <u>it</u> says the Don Valley Parkway will be closed for repairs.

(revised) The newspaper says the Don Valley Parkway will be closed for repairs.

Spotcheck 9-5

Revise the following sentences to avoid weak pronoun references.

1. Johanna did weight training for a year before <u>it</u> became noticeable.

2. Jeffrey wants to be a rodeo rider, but he has never attended <u>one</u>.

3. When <u>you</u> drive on a highway, <u>you</u> have to stay alert.

4. <u>They</u> always listen to the one who complains the loudest.

5. I did not respond to her invitation, <u>which</u> was impolite.

6. Mr. Chan goes to the gym every day because <u>it</u> is good exercise.

Doublecheck 9-2

Rewrite these sentences to correct weaknesses in pronoun agreement or reference.

1. When visiting Paris, you should see the Louvre museum.

2. If a car needs premium gasoline, don't buy it.

3. According to this magazine, it says the polar ice cap is melting.

4. When suffering dizzy spells, you should see a doctor.

5. On the radio, they said rainy weather is expected.

6. The Jayanathans did not meet their neighbours until they invited them to a PTA meeting.

7. The committee finally made their recommendation at 1 a.m.

8. Neither of the golfers lost their ball in the rough on the final round.

9. Emile told Winston he was certain to win the race.

10. Not everyone knows his way around the Trans-Canada Highway.

Editing Check 9

Edit this paragraph to correct weaknesses in pronoun agreement and reference, as in the first example.

Moviegoers
¹~~Everyone~~ would have a hard time recognizing the cowboy depicted in films if they had actually lived in the "Wild West" themselves. ²For one thing, they say cowboys were greatly outnumbered—about a thousand to one—by his neighbours, the unglamorous farmers. ³Although a person wouldn't guess it from watching old-time westerns, at least a quarter of them were black or Mexican. ⁴Furthermore, even a resident of Dodge City, which had a reputation as one of the toughest towns in the West, would scratch their heads in puzzlement at the sight of all those gunfights on the screen. ⁵The town had only 34 bodies in their famous Boothill Cemetery, and almost all died of natural causes. ⁶The shootout at the O.K. Corral and the killing of Wild Bill Hickok became talked about just because this was so uncommon. ⁷In studies of the period, they say that the romanticized version of the Old West was largely due to two Easterners, Owen Wister and Zane Grey. ⁸Wister wrote a novel about cowboys called *The Virginian*. ⁹Zane Grey, a New York dentist who had never been out west, produced dozens of novels with a western setting. ¹⁰It included such "classics" as *Riders of the Purple Sage* and *West of the Pecos*. ¹¹His books are still read today; it's often found at bookstores and in the paperback section at drugstores.

Checkpoint 9-1

*In the blanks, write **weak** for sentences with faulty pronoun agreement or reference, including sex bias. Write **okay** for sentences without such problems.*

_____ 1. Ruth called her mother before she left for work.

_____ 2. You see a lot of violence on television.

_____ 3. The phone company gave its employees a holiday bonus.

SENTENCE STRUCTURE: PRONOUN AGREEMENT AND CLEAR REFERENCE   151

_____ 4. Rowena buys cotton blouses because it is cooler than synthetic fabrics.

_____ 5. Anyone planning to travel abroad should order his passport well in advance.

_____ 6. Philip wanted to be a chemist, but he changed his mind after getting a C− in it.

_____ 7. Neither of the brothers mows his own lawn.

_____ 8. Sarah refused the gift, which surprised Richard.

_____ 9. They say that the world's population is growing too quickly.

_____ 10. Each of the actresses owed her success to hard work and talent.

_____ 11. Everyone who forgets their book will have to go home and get it.

_____ 12. The counsellors who are on duty will give their advice to students who ask for it.

_____ 13. A dog usually barks when they see a cat.

_____ 14. Anyone who missed the exam should see their instructor about making it up.

_____ 15. You need a lot of money to spend your vacation in New York City.

Checkpoint 9-2

Put an X in front of the sentences that have an error or weakness in pronoun use. Write "C" in front of the sentences that are correct.

_____ 1. The jury will announce its verdict at noon.

_____ 2. Everyone in the office gave their suggestions.

_____ 3. Celyne told Erica she needs a new boyfriend.

_____ 4. Most people believe that you shouldn't tell lies.

_____ 5. A baseball player gets upset when they strike out.

_____ 6. Neither Pat nor Mike have finished their term paper.

_____ 7. Wanda and Donna came to class without their texts.

_____ 8. Shoppers Drug Mart celebrated its thirtieth anniversary.

_____ 9. A police officer sometimes risks his life.

_____ 10. They say rain is expected this weekend.

No answers are given for Checkpoint quizzes.

WORDCHECK: USAGE TIPS

A dictionary will give special usage suggestions for some words. Look up the underlined words to see which construction is recommended.

<u>farther</u>—<u>further</u>

1a. The gas station was farther than we thought.

1b. The gas station was further than we thought.

<u>enthused</u>—<u>enthusiastic</u>

2a. Marilyn was enthused about her new job.

2b. Marilyn was enthusiastic about her new job.

<u>infer</u>—<u>imply</u>

3a. Are you inferring that I took your pen?

3b. Are you implying that I took your pen?

<u>former</u>—<u>latter</u>

4a. We saw Tom, Dick, and Harry, the former being home from college.

4b. We saw Tom and Dick, the former being home from college.

<u>fewer</u>—<u>less</u>

5a. There were less students in class today.

5b. There were fewer students in class today.

CHECKPOST: GERUNDS AND INFINITIVES

Remember

Gerund = Verb + -*ing*
Infinitive = *to* + root verb form

Rules
- Some verbs take gerunds, some take infinitives, and others take either. It is important to know which is which because the meaning can change completely.

    She stopped <u>to smoke</u>. (= She had a cigarette.)

    She stopped <u>smoking</u>. (= She gave up the habit.)

    He tried <u>to save</u> her. (= He attempted to help.)

    He tried <u>saving</u> her. (= as one way of helping her)

Similarly, be careful of these two verbs:

forget   remember

- These verbs take either gerund or infinitive:

  begin   hate   like   love   start   continue

- Some verbs take an unmarked infinitive (with no *to*), which is followed by a noun or pronoun.

  She let him <u>pay</u> for lunch.

  The nurse makes the patient <u>take</u> the medicine.

- Gerunds can be objects of prepositions.

  Susan believes in <u>dieting</u>.

  She is afraid of <u>growing</u> in size.

- Gerunds can also be used in time phrases.

  Always wear gloves when <u>shovelling</u> snow.

  Since <u>visiting</u> St. John's, she hasn't eaten fish.

- These are some verbs that must take gerunds:

admit	avoid	appreciate	consider	deny	discuss
enjoy	escape	finish	give up	go	imagine
mind	miss	postpone	practise	put off	quit
recall	recommend	resist	risk	suggest	tolerate

Checkpost 9-1

Complete the following exercises by making sentences using gerunds or infinitives.

1. Would you mind _____?
2. He recommended _____.
3. Mary enjoyed _____.
4. Let's put off _____.
5. The committee discussed _____.
6. Begin _____.
7. Stop _____.
8. The doctor suggested _____.
9. The gangster admitted _____.
10. The little boy is afraid _____.

10 DEVELOPING PARAGRAPHS USING DEFINITION

READING: DEFINITIONS OF WORDS

Precheck — Many essays are written to clarify and explain definitions of words or phrases in current use—"Generation X" or "the information highway," for example.

In the following essay, well-known columnist Michele Landsberg defines "the beauty myth" that writer Naomi Wolf claims preserves male dominance in our society.

Journal Topic — How would you define beauty? What do you think informs the way in which you view the concept of beauty? Do you agree with the popular ideas of beauty?

Beauty Myth Preserves Male Dominance
–Michele Landsberg

Ever wonder why you can't convince your teenage daughter that she's perfectly lovely as she is? That her thighs aren't too fat, her bottom too big, her breasts too small, her hair too flat, her nose too pointed?

"Aaw Mum, you just say that because you're my mum."

According to Naomi Wolf's strongly argued book, *The Beauty Myth*, just published by Random House, that teenager is in the grip of a North American obsession. The beauty myth, spread through our culture by millions of images of ideal feminine beauty, is a belief system designed "to keep male dominance intact."

dominance control of power

"Our families can't inoculate us," Wolf told me in an interview. "There's a disease in the air."

self-loathing strong dislike of oneself

The disease is women's physical self-loathing. "We are in the midst of a violent backlash to feminism that uses images of female beauty as a political weapon against women's advancement," she writes.

obsession persistent idea that won't go away

gender roles function of males, females in society

adamant firm, insistent

mutilation injury, wound

6   It's no wonder that young women are not carrying on the feminist fight; they're "weakened and paralyzed by their obsession with appearance and half of them are living on the same semi-starvation caloric intakes as prisoners in World War II Japanese prison camps."

7   "The beauty myth isn't a conscious conspiracy," said Wolf. "It doesn't have to be. Societies invent necessary fictions, and both men and women in our society are stunned and panicky about the rapidity of change in gender roles. An obsession with beauty keeps women divided and distracted."

8   When Wolf read from her book at the Women's Book Store in Toronto last week, an overflow crowd stayed to talk excitedly for four hours. "It was like a consciousness-raising session," she laughed.

9   She may have hit a nerve. Her argument is all the more persuasive since she herself is 27 years old, brilliant, slender, blue-eyed and beautiful. A Yale graduate and a Rhodes scholar, the San Francisco–born Wolf is adamant that "it's a lie that there are winners in the beauty game. Beautiful women may be heaped with rewards they didn't earn, but they are divided from other women, who are trained to hate and envy them, and can never be sure they are valued or loved for themselves."

10   The beauty myth is big business. The diet industry rakes in $32 billion a year; cosmetics, $20 billion; cosmetic surgery, the fastest growing medical specialty, is already worth $300 million annually, according to her book.

11   Wolf's book has caused a firestorm of controversy in Britain (it won't be published in the United States till next spring) where it has leaped on to the bestseller lists. Reviewers have compared her work to Germaine Greer's or Kate Millett's.

12   What's certain is that she draws together the current evidence in a powerful way. Even skeptical readers will find it hard to wave aside her blood-curdling chapter on the violence of the beauty business. Stomach-stapling, jaw-wiring, intestinal bypasses, liposuction, chemical skin peeling, facelifts, breast alterations—how different are these painful tortures, really, from Chinese foot-binding and the genital mutilation practised on millions of African women?

13   All are painful, dangerous and done in the near-religious belief that they will enhance the woman's sexual value. "Breast surgery very often leads to loss of all sensation in the nipples, yet the ecstatic women report that they are more sexually fulfilled. Amazing, isn't it? We are trained to identify with the male erotic response to the female body."

14   The most menacing of Wolf's findings are those relating to work. All through the '70s, as women surged back into the labour force, U.S. and British courts were piling up judicial decisions that a woman's beauty was a "bona fide qualification" for many kinds of work, from television anchor to senior manager. The Catch 22: sex harassment cases are frequently thrown out because the woman's beauty "caused" the harassment.

15   Wolf's book left me newly appalled by the deadening anxieties imposed on today's young women. They ought to be the most free, vibrant and hopeful young women ever. Instead, 60 per cent of U.S. female students suffer from eating disorders.

16   I won't soon forget Wolf's vision of those privileged young women, dulled and apathetic, moving like death camp zombies across the grassy quadrangle—followers of the cult of hunger in the midst of intellectual and material plenty.

trajectory path of a moving item

Besides, Wolf points out, the rigid scale on which women's worth is judged reverses the usual trajectory of success: once her youthful beauty fades, the woman's worth declines as the man's stature, income, and security rise.

Wolf argues that there's nothing natural about our artificial norms of female beauty—or about our reversal of the natural order, in which male animals compete with their beauty to attract the fertile female. In any case, "beauty" is a standard that changes with the times.

anorexic eating disorder: patient unable to eat for fear of becoming fat

"My age group is the first to grow up as the anorexic–pornographic generation. The images of soft porn are everywhere in advertising; they inescapably define the ideal woman for us."

Checking Meaning and Style

1. What occasion was this article written for?
2. For whom do you think Michele Landsberg is writing?
3. How is "the beauty myth" defined in this article? Where does it come from?
4. Why is the word "myth" used?
5. What is the result of this "beauty myth," according to Naomi Wolf?

Checking Ideas

1. Do you agree that there is a "beauty myth"?
2. What does Wolf mean by "The beauty myth isn't a conscious conspiracy"?
3. Look at the list of practices in the beauty business. Many people might add piercing and tattooing. What do you think of the efforts people make to change their looks?
4. Do you agree with Wolf that there is a difference in attitudes about men and women as they get older?
5. Is this "beauty myth" purely a female problem, or do you think men have something similar to contend with?

Netcheck

Words often change in meaning over the years; sometimes they retain their original meaning, but often the original definition is no longer in usage. "Spam" was a processed meat that the British ate in the lean times of the 1940s and 1950s. Now *spam* refers to the junk mail you no doubt receive on your computer. Fraud is a growing concern on the Internet. If you receive an e-mail from an address containing !!!s or xxxs in its name, it is undoubtedly a con. Outlook Express has rules in its Tools feature to get rid of such mail. Also, the National Consumer Association Web site is www.fraud.org. There is even a Web site to check the authorship of a paper: www.turnitin.com. Check these sites for future reference.

WRITING MODELS: THE DEFINITION PARAGRAPH

Not everybody would understand what was meant by "the beauty myth" if it weren't defined clearly. In "Beauty Myth Preserves Male Dominance," Michele Landsberg helps make Naomi Wolf's definition clear to everyone. Here is a definition paragraph based on Landsberg's essay.

WRITING MODELS: THE DEFINITION PARAGRAPH   157

Model Definition Paragraph #1

The opening sentence states what is being defined.

The phrase "beauty myth" defines an obsession that is gripping teenagers in North America. It is spread through our culture by millions of images of ideal feminine beauty and is designed "to keep male dominance intact." It isn't a conscious conspiracy, says Naomi Wolf; it is a fiction invented by society that keeps women divided and distracted. The beauty myth reverses the natural order of the animal species where the males usually compete with their beauty in order to attract the females. In our society, the beauty myth makes females go to all sorts of lengths—from dieting to surgery—in order to attract males. Instead of letting women be free and vibrant, the beauty myth keeps women dull and apathetic.

In the following paragraph, the writer defines the term *bad habit* by giving specific details about how a bad habit changed his life.

Model Definition Paragraph #2

Observe how the paragraph begins with a topic sentence.

Smoking was a bad habit that threatened my health, irritated others, cost too much, and weakened my marriage. Every pack carried a warning that smoking was damaging to my health. At work and in restaurants, people complained if I lit up, making me feel like a criminal. My wife, who doesn't smoke, pointed out that we could go out to dinner once in a while with the money saved if I didn't smoke. She also complained that my foul-smelling clothes and breath didn't exactly excite her. Quitting wasn't easy after ten years at two packs a day, but I'm glad I finally did it.

1. What term is the author defining?
2. What activity is the writer focusing on to define *bad habit*?
3. Name four specific details that made the habit bad.

The next paragraph demonstrates how a person can be used as an example to demonstrate specific details about a word the writer wants to define.

Model Definition Paragraph #3

Observe how the paragraph begins with a topic sentence.

My friend Anthony practically defines the word "ambition." He wants to be a lawyer. He takes a full course load at a community college, attending classes from 8 a.m. to noon five days a week. He works 40 hours a week for a janitorial service, cleaning office buildings at night. On weekends, he catches up on his sleep and his school homework—when he isn't doing yard work for others. Tony says he can become a lawyer in six or seven years and cash in with a high-paying job with a big law firm—if he lives that long.

1. What word is being defined?
2. What example does the writer use to define *ambition*?
3. What three specific details show how ambitious Anthony is?

WRITING ASSIGNMENT: A DEFINITION PARAGRAPH

The dictionary definition of a word is called its **denotation**. The emotional meanings that attach themselves to a word are its **connotations**. The following words all denote *policeman*. Do they have favourable or unfavourable connotations? Are some neutral—neither favourable nor unfavourable?

    officer   peace officer   cop   pig

Good (or bad) examples of the use of connotations often appear in political language. For example, troops trying to overthrow a foreign government are called "freedom fighters" if we want them to win; otherwise, they are "rebels" or "terrorists." Advertising also provides many examples of language used to sway our emotions. Consider the cigarette brand Marlboro. This English name was originally meant to suggest elegance and sophistication. Because of advertising, what are its connotations today? What are the connotations of these perfumes: Obsession, Passion, Scoundrel?

We need to be alert to the connotative value of words for two reasons. One is to make our own writing clear, precise, and, yes, persuasive. Another is to detect efforts by others to influence our opinions through emotional language or "loaded" words.

Spotcheck 10-1

In the following comparisons, describe yourself by using words with favourable connotations and describe the other person with words that have similar denotations but negative connotations.

    EXAMPLE: I am hard-working. You are ___a workaholic___.

1. I am slender. You are _____.
2. I am lively. You are _____.
3. I am punctual. You are _____.
4. I am _____. You are old.
5. I am _____. You are childish.
6. I am _____. You are lucky.
7. My clothes are colourful. Yours are _____.
8. I am firm in my beliefs. You are _____.

Spotcheck 10-2

After each sentence below are several words with similar denotations but different connotations. Fill in each blank with the word that is most appropriate.

1. Claudette says she will never forget the love of her _____.
   (female parent   old lady   mother   mommy)

2. The Patels have built a charming _____ at the lake.
   (cottage   shanty   shack)

3. Mr. Turco criticizes his son-in-law as a mere _____.
   (lawyer   attorney   ambulance chaser)

4. Grandmother boasted that little Sammy got good grades because he was so _____.
   (bookish   studious   nerdy)

5. The driver said in court that he had been only a little tipsy, but the police officer testified that he had been _____.
   (pickled   boiled   stewed   intoxicated)

Write a Definition Paragraph

Write a paragraph in which you define one of the following terms. Do not try to imitate a dictionary definition. Instead, you may want to use examples to make the meaning clear. Or you might tell a story (narrative) that illustrates the word's meaning. For that, you could start with a topic sentence along the lines of "I learned the meaning of fear the night our house caught fire" or "My aunt Brenda is a good example of a person with common sense."

common sense	friendship
forgiveness	a good neighbour
ambition (Model #3)	a bad habit (Model #2)
macho	"cool"

Start with a topic sentence that includes the term you plan to define and identifies the specific person or event that will be used to define the term:

_____

_____

_____

After you write your first draft of the definition paragraph, revise the paragraph; give special attention to fragments, run-together sentences, verb forms, and subject–verb agreement. Make your writing as lively as possible through your choice of words.

160 CHAPTER 10 DEVELOPING PARAGRAPHS USING DEFINITION

Writing Assignment Checklist

✓ Develop the topic through prewriting techniques such as journal writing and nonstop writing. Be sure to make your definition interesting with examples, specific details, an anecdote, or other methods discussed so far.

✓ Start with a topic sentence that includes the term you plan to define. Then build on that idea with supporting details, or, if an anecdote is used, the steps in that story.

Topic sentence: _____

First supporting detail: _____

Second supporting detail: _____

Third supporting detail: _____

Fourth supporting detail: _____

Fifth supporting detail: _____

✓ In revising the paper, look especially for errors in pronoun use, as well as the kinds of problems indicated on recent papers.

✓ Proofread the paper before turning it in.

SENTENCE PUNCTUATION: USING COMMAS IN SENTENCES

We might be forgiven for turning to our TV sets if we came across much writing like this:

> Having forgotten to let out her dog the faithful Poochie Isabel had to turn around at Medicine Hat Alberta and drive back home a trip of two hours.

That sentence makes a good deal more sense with the addition of a few commas:

> Having forgotten to let out her dog, the faithful Poochie, Isabel had to turn around at Medicine Hat, Alberta, and drive back home, a trip of two hours.

Unfortunately, commas are the punctuation marks most likely to cause despair among inexperienced writers. Following are five occasions for using them.

Use Commas before Connecting Words

Use commas before the connecting words *and, but, or, for, nor, yet,* and *so* when they join two complete thoughts or independent clauses. You may want to return to the section on clauses (Chapter 4) for a quick review.

> The job is boring, but the pay is good.

> Mike liked the movie, so he told Fran to see it.

Be sure you are joining two independent clauses. In the following sentence, no comma is needed:

> Mike liked the movie and told Fran to see it. (single clause with one subject and two verbs)

Spotcheck 10-3

Use a comma and one of the connectors and, but, or, for, nor, yet, *or* so *between independent clauses.*

EXAMPLE: The book is valuable, but you may borrow it.

1. Dinner isn't ready _____ you can take a nap first.
2. Rick is always late _____ he never has an excuse.
3. You should get a raise _____ you deserve one.
4. That boy will apologize _____ I will tell his parents.
5. Cats are nice pets _____ they claw the furniture.

Spotcheck 10-4

Write three sentences, each using one of the connectors and, but, *or* so *between independent clauses.*

1. _____
   _____

2. _____
   _____

3. _____
   _____

Use Commas after Introductory Expressions

Use commas after introductory expressions—words that lead up to the main part of the sentence (the independent clause).

> After a long and snowy winter, we were eager for spring to come. (introductory prepositional phrase)
>
> Because the dog was limping, Arnold took it to the vet. (introductory dependent clause)

The comma is often omitted if the introductory expression is short.

> On Friday [no comma] the entire office staff played a game of softball in Stanley Park.

However, commas are used after such opening words as *well, yes,* and *no.*

> Yes, I returned the book to the library on time.

Spotcheck 10-5

Put a comma after the introductory words in each sentence.

1. Grown in California and Oregon nectarines resemble peaches without fuzz.
2. To drink the juice of a coconut puncture a hole in the shell.
3. Known in the Mediterranean area as "the poor man's fruit" figs are eaten fresh or dried.
4. No breadfruit is not used to make bread, but in the South Seas the wood of the plant is used to make canoes.

Use Commas to Separate Items in a Series

Use commas to separate items in a series. A series is a list of three or more items.

> The hairdresser took out his comb, brush, and scissors. (Some writers omit the comma before *and*.)
>
> The truck driver jumped into the cab, turned on the ignition, and pressed her boot against the accelerator.
>
> The instructor opened the book and started to read. (No comma—two items do not make a series.)

Spotcheck 10-6

Put commas between the items in series.

1. The Chinese eat kumquats fresh preserve them or make them into jams.
2. Most papayas in Canada come from Florida Texas Hawaii Mexico or Puerto Rico.
3. Figs contain calcium phosphorus and iron.

Spotcheck 10-7

Write two sentences using commas to separate items in a series.

1. _____
_____

2. _____
_____

Write two sentences using commas to set off introductory expressions.

3. _____
_____

4. _____
_____

Use Commas to Set Off Interrupting Words

Use commas to set off words that interrupt the sentence if those words are not essential to the main idea. This rule will be clearer after you study these examples:

Marie, who completed all the work, will pass the course.

Any student who completed the work will pass the course.

In the first example, the main idea, *Marie will pass the course,* makes sense without the interrupting words *who completed all the work.* Since the extra words add nonessential information, they are set off by commas.

In the second example, the main clause, *Any student will pass the course,* is clearly nonsense. The interrupting words are essential to complete its meaning. Therefore, the interrupter is not set off by commas.

Here are some more examples of essential and nonessential interrupters.

(nonessential) William Leong, who has been elected four times, will run for mayor again this year.

The interrupter *who has been elected four times* adds interesting but nonessential information. It is set off by commas.

(essential) A man who has been elected four times will run for mayor again this year.

The main (underlined) clause does not make sense without the help of the interrupter. The interrupter is *not* set off by commas.

(nonessential) We read a poem, "I Died for Beauty," in English class.

(essential) We read the poem "I Died for Beauty" in English class.

Use commas to set off expressions such as *on the other hand* and *it seems to me* that interrupt the sentence.

Kelvin, of course, has no intention of asking Jill to marry him.

Columbus, according to some historians, was not the first European to find America.

Spotcheck 10-8

Add commas to set off nonessential elements and interrupting expressions.

1. Bill's Diner which looks like it survived a tornado is a favourite student hangout.
2. My history teacher Mr. Jefferson has written a book on the Charlottetown Referendum.
3. The mating call of the Mediterranean fruit fly according to experts has the same frequency as the musical note F-sharp.
4. A goat that seems to be eating a tin can is probably just enjoying the glue on the can's label.
5. Pound cake which is one of my favourite desserts got its name from the pound of butter used in making it.

CHAPTER 10 DEVELOPING PARAGRAPHS USING DEFINITION

6. That fact of course won't keep me from enjoying pound cake—and putting on pounds.

7. Money is a bad master it has been said but a good servant.

8. Billy Bishop who failed RMC became Canada's ace pilot in 1917.

Use Commas in Place Names, Addresses, and Dates

Use commas to separate geographical names and items in addresses and dates.

Ming lived in Taipei, Taiwan, before coming to Canada.

Susan was born on Tuesday, September 15, 1966, in Calgary.

The letter was addressed to 91 Wilfrid Laurier Avenue, Québec, Quebec.

NOTE: Use postal code abbreviations (ON, AB, QC, and so on) only in addresses at the tops of letters.

Write a sentence in which you give the month, date, and year of an event significant to you and the city and province (or country) where it happened. Be careful with the commas.

_____

_____

Spotcheck 10-9

Add commas where needed.

1. The highest temperature ever recorded in Canada was 45°C recorded July 5 1937 at Midale and Yellowgrass Saskatchewan.

2. The lowest temperature ever recorded in Canada was −63°C at Snag Yukon Territory on February 3 1947.

3. The package was mailed to Mr. Robert Wong 213 West Pender Street Vancouver British Columbia.

4. Her son was born in Lethbridge Alberta on January 4 1962.

Doublecheck 10-1

Add commas where needed.

[1]Herbert Marshall McLuhan usually known as Marshall McLuhan was a world-renowned communication theorist. [2]He was born in Edmonton on July 21 1911 and died in Toronto on December 31 1980. [3]Because of his studies on the effects of the media he became famous in the 1960s. [4]He received a Ph.D. from Cambridge in 1943 and he was a professor at the University of Toronto where he became famous for his thoughts on the media. [5]A deeply literate man he formulated theories about modern culture. [6]His ideas were highly significant but he was misunderstood by a lot of people because of his revolutionary theories. [7]He made a distinction between "hot" and "cool" media where television for example conveys less information but requires more intensive listening. [8]When McLuhan published *Understanding Media* in 1964 he became famous worldwide. [9]In 1967 *The Medium Is the Message* was published and it soon became popular internationally. [10]He founded the Centre for Culture and Technology at the University of Toronto and the McLuhan Teleglobe Canada Award was cre-

ated in 1983 in his memory. [11]This award is very popular today because it carries a cash value of $50 000. [12]McLuhan asked us to change not only the way we considered information but also how we perceived knowledge.

Do Not Overuse Commas

The final rule is this: Don't use a comma unless you know why you're using it. If in doubt, leave it out.

Take care not to use commas where they are not needed. Here are some of the spots where unnecessary commas are most likely to appear:

- Before a connector (*and, but, or, for, nor, yet, so*) that does *not* join two independent clauses:

    (no comma) Marianne could read French, but couldn't speak it. (one independent clause with two verbs)

    (correct) Marianne could read French but couldn't speak it.

    (correct) Marianne could read French, but she couldn't speak it. (two independent clauses joined by *but*)

- Between a subject and its verb, especially if the complete subject (italicized in the following examples) is long:

    (no comma) *Fools and their money*, are soon parted.

    (no comma) *A knife, some string, and some matches*, are useful on a camping trip.

- Between a verb and its object:

    (wrong) The supervisor said, that she would be back at three.

    (compare) The supervisor said, "I will be back at three."

    (wrong) The snowplow has finished, clearing our driveway.

- Before the first or after the last item in a series:

    (no comma) We could get along without, pollution, poverty, and war.

    (no comma) She found a brush, comb, and mirror, on the dresser.

    (no comma) The sunset was a beautiful, breathtaking, inspiring, sight.

Spotcheck 10-10

Circle the unnecessary commas.

1. Throughout Canada, almost anyone, can buy a pack of cigarettes these days.
2. Confronted with the evidence, Susan admitted, that she had broken the vase.
3. Ford's new car is, economical, dependable, and quite handsome.
4. Making the dean's honour list, was Terry's goal for the semester, but he knew he would have trouble with math.
5. Yuko, who hated baseball, decided to attend the Expos game with her family.
6. Under the cushion, Debra found, two quarters, a dime, and three pennies.

7. The camp counsellor, Alice Koyama, rowed out to the island in a canoe, and built a fire on the beach.

8. Next semester I will have to take algebra, history, and, English.

Editing Check 10

Add commas where appropriate in this paragraph.

[1]According to archeologists men shaved their faces as far back as 20 000 years ago. [2]Drawings on caves show both bearded and beardless men and graves have contained the flints and shells that were the first razors. [3]As soon as humans learned to work with iron and bronze razors were hammered out of these materials. [4]Ancient Egyptians who sought status shaved their faces. [5]Greek soldiers shaved regularly because a beard was a handicap in hand-to-hand fighting. [6]In the New World Indian men used tweezers made from clams to pull out their beards one hair at a time.

Checkpoint 10-1

Some of the sentences below contain comma errors. Find the kind of error in the following list and write the number of the rule being illustrated in the blank to the left of each sentence.

1. Use commas with *and, but, or, for, nor, yet,* and *so* to join two independent clauses (complete thoughts).
2. Use commas after introductory elements that lead up to the main clause of a sentence.
3. Use commas to separate items in a series.
4. Use commas to set off nonessential words that interrupt a sentence.
5. Use commas to separate geographical names and items in addresses and dates.
6. If a sentence contains no error, write *6* in the blank.

_____ 1. Giovanni's restaurant which serves great spaghetti is on Main Street.

_____ 2. It will be closed next Monday and Tuesday.

_____ 3. The office lunch gang will be unhappy but they will just have to find another restaurant.

_____ 4. It wouldn't hurt them of course to fix a lunch and bring it to work.

_____ 5. A person who won't eat a bag lunch is going to spend a lot of money on food.

_____ 6. When I worked at Weston and Co. nearly everyone brought a bag lunch.

_____ 7. We ate our sandwiches in the company cafeteria or we took them to the little park across from the office.

_____ 8. I have been working for Darwin and Associates which is a big law firm for six months.

_____ 9. I joined the company on Monday April 16.

_____ 10. What I like about the company are the flexible work hours the medical benefits and the lunches at Giovanni's.

Checkpoint 10-2

*In the blanks to the left of each sentence, write **X** for sentences that contain comma errors and **C** for those that are correct.*

_____ 1. Scott was born on Tuesday, January 4, 1970.

_____ 2. Ed Morris, who farms north of town, won the lottery.

_____ 3. The television screen flickered, and then went blank.

_____ 4. Norway as you know is part of what is called Scandinavia.

_____ 5. Since Katlyn has a bicycle, she left her car at home.

_____ 6. Don't forget to buy, eggs, milk, and butter.

_____ 7. Any driver, who drives too fast, may get a ticket.

_____ 8. The newlyweds were shown the photographs, which were quite flattering.

_____ 9. The man on the bus was reading the novel *Alias Grace*.

_____ 10. Our new neighbours, came from Vancouver, British Columbia.

No answers are given for Checkpoint quizzes.

WORDCHECK: BIOGRAPHICAL NAMES

A dictionary may list the names of famous people in the main section or in a special biographical section at its end. Use a dictionary to identify and learn the birth dates and significance of these people:

Louis Riel	John A. Macdonald	Christopher Plummer
Giovanni Caboto	Maurice Richard	Elijah Harper

CHECKPOST: PARTICIPLES—PRESENT AND PAST

Rules

- Participles are used as adjectives and can be in the present (*-ing*) or past (*-ed*).
- When participles that end in *-ing*, the present participle form, modify nouns, they are placed before the noun. They describe someone or something causing an experience.

  The <u>boring</u> film was panned by the critics.

  The <u>interesting</u> play had good notices.

  The <u>fascinating</u> lecturer will be speaking again next year.

- Present participles may also follow linking verbs; they are in the active voice.

    Celine Dion is <u>exciting</u>.

    This exercise is very <u>tiring</u>.

    Are these examples <u>interesting</u>?

- When participles that end in *-ed*, and other past forms, modify nouns, they are placed before the noun. They describe a person or thing affected by an action.

    The <u>depressed</u> child refused to go to the funeral.

    The <u>hidden</u> treasure lay buried for years.

    The <u>focused</u> student gets good results.

- Participles that end in *-ed*, or other forms of past participle, may also follow linking verbs; they are in the passive voice. They describe someone or something having an experience.

    The crowd was <u>fascinated</u> by the lecture. = The lecture was fascinating.

    The students were <u>confused</u> (by the instructor). = The instructor was confusing.

    The teacher was <u>satisfied</u> with the results.

    He was <u>depressed</u> by the tragic news of Diana's death.

Remember

- Do not confuse the *-ing* forms, which can be gerunds used as nouns, with the adjective form.

    <u>Flying</u> can be fun. (n.)

    The <u>crying</u> child found her mother. (adj.)

Verb Forms

- Phrasal verbs—verbs followed by prepositions that entirely change the meaning of the verb—are very common. The most used verb in the English language is *set*, and with every preposition, its meaning changes.

    He <u>set</u> the table.

    He <u>set out</u> for Nova Scotia.

    She <u>set down</u> the heavy mailbag.

    The sun <u>set over</u> the ocean.

- Some phrasal verbs can take a noun or pronoun between the verb and the preposition; if you are not sure, check the dictionary.

    (both correct) The pet shop <u>gave</u> the hamster <u>away</u>. / The shop <u>gave away</u> the hamster.

    (incorrect) The shop <u>gave away</u> it.

    (incorrect) He <u>hung</u> the branch <u>onto</u> for safety.

    (correct) He <u>hung onto</u> the branch for safety.

CHECKPOST: PARTICIPLES—PRESENT AND PAST   169

Checkpost 10-1

Complete each sentence in this exercise using participles.

1. My classmates are interested in writing stories. Writing stories is _____.

2. Her audition results were disappointing. She was very _____ in her results.

3. The detective was puzzled by the mysterious crime. It was a _____ crime.

4. When they went out together, the son was embarrassed by his mother. His mother was very _____.

5. He was annoyed by her loud voice. Her habit of talking too loudly was _____.

Checkpost 10-2

Make sentences with the following phrasal verbs.

1. put up _____

2. put off _____

3. set up _____

4. come across _____

5. fill out _____

6. take up _____

7. touch down _____

8. touch up _____

9. hand in _____

10. hand out _____

DEVELOPING PARAGRAPHS USING OPINION

READING: EXPRESSING AN OPINION

Precheck

As U.S. Memorial Day approached, in the wake of the events of September 11, 2001, and the subsequent war on terrorism, Jane Williams argued that it is important to remember the suffering of people outside the United States as well. Americans should be aware, she wrote, that the war in Afghanistan claimed the lives of four Canadian soldiers through an accident of "friendly fire." Williams wrote the following article for her local newspaper in Waco, Texas.

Journal Topic

Every major event has an impact on each of us. Looking back now at the tumultuous events of recent years, how have you and your family been affected? What do you remember of the events Jane Williams writes about, and has anything changed for you since then?

A Debt to a Neighbour –Jane Williams

At church in Waco, Tex., in 1955, a local girl met a U.S. Air Force navigator training at the local base, married him the following year, and gained a Canadian connection. Bruce Williams' father had emigrated to Detroit from Minnedosa, Man., in the 1920s, and there met Bruce's mother, another Manitoban from Clanwilliam, only 20 km away. In 1967, Williams, by then a major, was killed in action in Vietnam. Last week, his widow, Jane Williams, a senior business lecturer at Baylor University in Waco, submitted this appreciation of Canada's recently fallen soldiers to her local newspaper, the Waco Tribune-Herald.

As we approach Memorial Day and prepare to honour those who have died in the cause of freedom, let us also remember that this year, we are not alone. In this current war against the forces of international terror, our neighbours in the international community are making sacrifices, too.

irony when one event serves to contradict another and the unexpected occurs

mobilized organized, acted (to help)

inadvertently not intentionally

empathize identify with someone else's feelings

On April 18, four Canadian Forces soldiers were killed in Afghanistan, and eight more were seriously injured as a result of a "friendly fire" accident. And it is the bitterest irony that this "friendly fire" was from an American air force pilot.

When America was attacked on Sept. 11, Canada lost no time in extending assistance in addition to her condolences. By early that afternoon, U.S.-bound flights had been safely diverted to airports across Canada. When these cities and towns needed food, bedding and shelter to put up our fellow Americans, it was the Canadian civilians that mobilized. Many of the Canadian hosts wept with their unexpected guests as if the loss were their own. And the Canadian government committed its military to assist ours in the war against terror.

Now it is the Canadians who are hurting and—however inadvertently—we have been the cause. For the first time since the Korean War, Canadians have had to endure the terrible sight of flag-draped caskets carrying home the remains of their own soldiers killed in combat, their "fallen heroes." To his credit, President Bush moved quickly (although less rapidly than some would have wished) to do everything a president could to make it up to our northern friend and neighbour. Unfortunately, our media seems to have assumed that Americans are less than interested in Canadian current events. Certainly there has not been the coverage that there ought to have been in the days since their four boys were killed serving beside ours in Afghanistan. In fact, an employee of the CBC told a member of my family, "We are all very aware that this is being ignored by CNN." To the extent that this is true, we have added insult to injury.

It was only because one of my sons, who now lives in Winnipeg, videotaped the live telecast of Sgt. Marc Léger's funeral that I was able to watch while the event was still timely. Let me assure you that a Canadian "full military honours" service is indescribably moving. And in a press statement she insisted on delivering herself soon after learning of the death of her husband, Marley Léger said, "I just want everyone to know what kind of man my husband was. I loved him very much and I'm extremely proud of him and what he's done for his country."

Sadly, there are many of us who can empathize. This month will mark 35 years since my husband was buried here in Waco with full military honours. I, too, wanted people to know this good man, the only child of Canadian immigrants, whose love I shared. I remember Bruce's devotion to his Canadian family members, including his "Grandma McPherson," who lived in Windsor, Ont., just across the border from his hometown of Detroit. And I still keep in touch with his Aunt Myrtle Beddome, a retired farm wife in Minnedosa, who sent him cards, letters and homemade fruitcake when he was posted overseas. A patriotic American officer, my husband was nevertheless proud of his Canadian roots and he loved his Canadian family dearly.

Because Bruce served in several missions under UN mandates, he was also privileged to work with members of the Canadian military. He had the greatest respect for the Canadian Forces, and he often told me so. My husband would have been very affected by this recent tragedy in Afghanistan. His grief over this loss would have been the same as if these men had been buddies from his own unit, and his heart would have gone out to the family members these four soldiers have left behind.

At the church service for Cpl. Ainsworth Dyer, the man who would have become his father-in-law urged the large crowd to "think of the pilot" (our pilot, who released the bomb that killed his son) and to pray for him, to forgive him,

compassion a sense of deep understanding for someone's actions or situation

to consider the burden on his conscience and to have compassion. How many of us could do the same thing?

The American people needed to know about these events; most of us would have wanted to know. I am certain that my husband and his buddies would have wanted us to know—and to remember. Let us not forget that they are also our heroes, and that in America we, too, owe them a debt of compassion and gratitude. 9

Checking Meaning and Style

1. What is the purpose of Memorial Day and what is the Canadian equivalent?
2. What is the topic sentence in the opening paragraph?
3. How did Jane Williams hear of the deaths in Afghanistan? What was the bitterest irony about the tragedy?
4. What was Jane Williams' husband's Canadian connection? In what war did he serve his country?
5. Explain "the man who would have become his father-in-law" in the penultimate paragraph.

Checking Ideas

1. Why do Americans not receive a great deal of news coverage about their neighbour to the north?
2. What was Jane Williams' opinion of a Canadian military funeral?
3. How was it that Williams could empathize with Marley Léger?
4. What informs Williams' opinion of these news items, and why does she think they should be publicized in the U.S.?

Netcheck

Do some research on Canadian heroes. Whom do you admire in Canada's history? Who are some of the Canadians who made sacrifices to achieve their goals?

WRITING MODELS: THE OPINION PARAGRAPH

Here is how Williams' article might look if it were condensed in a single paragraph:

Model Opinion Paragraph #1

Notice that the opinion is clearly stated in the final sentence.

As Memorial Day approaches, Jane Williams argues that it is important to remember not only American heroes but also the suffering of others who have experienced pain and sacrifices in the same causes. In the war against terrorism, recently in Afghanistan, four Canadians lost their lives and eight more were seriously wounded. American media have not publicized this event; many Americans do not even know the tragedy occurred. As a war widow herself, Jane Williams can understand the suffering of the families in Canada. She feels that her husband, who respected the Canadian military and had family connections in Canada, would have been very affected by the deaths. He would have wanted people to know about them. In Williams' opinion, Americans need to know; they owe these four Canadians a debt of gratitude.

In the next two paragraphs about the difficulties, or otherwise, of dating, look at the two contradictory opinions.

Model Opinion Paragraph #2

Observe how the opening sentence clearly states the opinion.

The anniversary of the Pill prompts a reflection on how easy it *used to be* to find a partner: to meet someone, fall in love, and get married. These days, however, dating has become a difficult task. Before getting married, don't you have to fall in love? And before falling in love, don't you have to meet someone, somehow? This process has become less than simple, given the current obsession with date rape and sexual harassment. The workplace used to be the best place to find a mate, but it has become a minefield. Similarly, the university campus used to be a logical place to meet a mate, but it isn't now. Of course, people do still manage somehow to fall in love and get married, sometimes with computer help. But still, I would hate to be 20 and waiting for a date.

Here is how a paragraph stating the opposite opinion might look:

Model Opinion Paragraph #3

Romantic-style marriages are back, which is great because meeting someone and falling in love are easier than ever. This process has become much simpler as a result of the new date rape and sexual harassment laws. People in the workplace and on campuses are much more careful in the way that they treat each other. This makes it easier to feel safe with people, to get to know them, and to become friends. It is wonderful to be 20 and looking forward to finding a date.

WRITING ASSIGNMENT: AN OPINION PARAGRAPH

We usually like to give our opinions on a variety of topics—the new model Mini Cooper car, the Canadiens' chances of winning the Stanley Cup or the drinking age. Other people are more likely to listen to our opinions if we state them clearly and in a reasonable way.

Opinion and Facts

One way to state an opinion effectively is to back it up with some supporting facts. Opinions can be argued endlessly, but facts are statements that can be checked to see if they are true. Consider the following examples:

(opinion) Duke Ellington was the greatest American composer of the twentieth century.

(fact) Ellington's compositions include "Warm Valley," "Mood Indigo," and many concert suites.

(opinion) Canadian women have easier lives than men.

(fact) Canadian women outlive men by several years.

Practise distinguishing between opinions and facts in the following exercise.

Spotcheck 11-1

In the blanks, write fact *or* opinion *to identify each sentence.*

_____ 1. Roger Bannister of England was the first person to run a mile race in under four minutes.

_____ 2. Singer Dean Martin was born Dino Paul Crocetti.

_____ 3. *The Diviners* is a greater novel than *The Stone Angel*.

_____ 4. Eating yogurt every day is good for people.

_____ 5. Newfoundland's salmon is not as tasty as British Columbia's.

_____ 6. Samuel Maclure (1860–1929) was a west coast architect.

_____ 7. German car designers are the best in the business.

_____ 8. The earth is about 150 million kilometres from the sun.

Write an Opinion Paragraph

Write an opinion paragraph on one of these topics:

1. Ordinary citizens should (not) be allowed to carry guns.
2. (Name of team) is the most exciting team in (football, basketball, baseball).
3. The most shocking music group today is (name of group).
4. Smoking is a public (personal) decision.
5. The Internet should be (not be) regulated by government.

Writing Assignment Checklist

✓ Develop your ideas through journal writing, nonstop writing, or one of the other prewriting methods discussed earlier.

✓ Start your paragraph with a topic sentence that makes clear the opinion you want to put across and support your opinion with persuasive facts and examples.

Topic Sentence: _____

First Support: _____

Second Support: _____

Third Support: _____

Fourth Support: _____

✓ Use a style (see "Diction: Choosing the Right Word" below) appropriate to a college assignment.

✓ In revising the first draft, be sure that you have included facts and examples to support your opinion. Check carefully for comma errors and the kinds of mistakes marked on recent assignments.

✓ Proofread the final copy.

WRITING PROCESS: DICTION—CHOOSING THE RIGHT WORD

An author can use an informal, conversational style to great effect—refer back to Naomi Klein's essay in Chapter 9 and look at her diction. She uses colloquialisms such as "no fair!," as well as exclamation marks, question marks, and short sentences, which all make her essay very informal.

You might write informally in this way to a friend, but there are many occasions when this style would not be appropriate. You would not write a job application letter in this informal style, nor a report to your boss, nor a college term paper on the Group of Seven. You would handle those subjects in a more formal style.

A good writing style, then, is *appropriate*—for its readers and its subject. Here are some specific points to keep in mind:

- *Slang* words and expressions are acceptable in only the most informal writing. Words such as *groovy* quickly go out of fashion and mark their users as the opposite of "cool." Slang is also usually vague and unclear.

- *Clichés* or trite expressions were originally colourful and full of life but now are worn out from overuse. Avoid expressions that pop into your mind fully formed: *neat as a pin, sadder but wiser, last but not least.*

- *Jargon* is the specialized language of a particular group or occupation, such as football players, computer programmers, or doctors. The following memo contains jargon (in italics) that a group of business consultants found objectionable: "Your new *agenda*: Be *proactive* and *interface* with customers. Start *networking*. *Finalize* sales. Rack up the *done deals* that will *impact* the *bottom line*. We've got *world-class, state-of-the-art, user-friendly* products. That's our *competitive edge*."

- *Big words* are often hard to resist. We like to sound impressive. But the person who lives in a *residence* instead of a house, or prefers to *commence* something instead of to start it, is on the wrong track. "Write to express, not to impress." Your first goal is to be clear.

- *Wrong words* must be corrected, of course, by checking a dictionary. "The teacher ~~inferred~~ implied that I had copied the paper."

Spotcheck 11-2

Correct the underlined examples of slang, clichés, jargon, big words, and wrong words.

EXAMPLE: Rudy is really ~~uptight~~ about tomorrow's game.
                            nervous

1. Sally is the most <u>pulchritudinous</u> woman I know.
2. George wants to <u>interface</u> with me at lunch.
3. The city council wasn't <u>crazy</u> about the mayor's idea.
4. Most critics said the movie was <u>gross</u>.
5. Please <u>inquire of</u> your boss if you can leave early.

6. Despite her long trip, Amy <u>was the picture of health</u>.
7. Someone stole Peter's new <u>wheels</u> last night.
8. The Petersons have bought a new <u>domicile</u>.
9. <u>Irregardless</u> of Tim's feelings, the family will vacation again at Lac Edouard.
10. Samantha was <u>green with envy at</u> Julia's success.

SENTENCE PUNCTUATION: USING PUNCTUATION

For clear writing, knowing how to punctuate correctly is essential. This section covers the following ten punctuation marks:

period	.
exclamation mark	!
question mark	?
quotation marks	" "
underlining	___
apostrophe	'
semicolon	;
colon	:
dash	—
parentheses	( )

Periods, Exclamation Marks, and Question Marks

Show that a sentence is completed by using a period, an exclamation mark, or a question mark.

A period marks the end of a statement.

Good grief! I thought you knew that an exclamation mark shows strong emotion.

Do you always remember to put a question mark at the end of a question?

Be sure to note the difference between a direct question and an indirect question. An indirect question is actually a statement and ends with a period, not a question mark.

(direct) Lee asked me, "Are you going home?"

(indirect) Lee asked me if I was going home. (This statement tells what Lee asked.)

A sentence may contain both a question mark and a period.

"Are you going home?" Lee asked me.

SENTENCE PUNCTUATION: USING PUNCTUATION **177**

Spotcheck 11-3

Supply the correct end punctuation for each of the sentences.

1. Did Frank remember to fill the gas tank
2. Look out That gun is loaded
3. Jerome asked Julie if she had a spare dime
4. "What time is it" William asked
5. William wondered what time it was

Quotation Marks with Written and Spoken Language

Use quotation marks around direct quotations—the *exact* words of a speaker or writer. Do not use quotation marks around indirect quotations—the idea of the speaker or writer put into your own words.

(direct) "Reading is to the mind what exercise is to the body," said Sir Richard Steele. (his exact words)

(indirect) Sir Richard Steele said that reading develops the mind in the way that exercise develops the body. (his idea, your words)

(You will often find the word *that* before an indirect quotation.)

Study the use of quotation marks in the following examples. Note especially the relation of the marks to other punctuation and to capital letters.

1. "The plane will be 20 minutes late," the flight attendant said.
   - The words identifying the speaker (*the flight attendant said*) are separated from the quotation by a comma.
   - All commas (and periods) go *inside* the ending quotation marks.
2. The captain said, "Prepare to abandon ship."
   - The quotation begins with a capital letter if it is a complete sentence.
3. "The time to relax," wrote Sydney J. Harris, "is when you don't have time for it."
   - If the quotation is interrupted, the next part doesn't begin with a capital letter unless it is a complete sentence.
   - Be sure to put quotation marks around the quoted words only, not around the words naming the speaker.
4. Angela protested, "That's not fair. You should have told me that I was expected to attend class. I don't want to flunk."
   - When the quotation goes on for more than one sentence without interruption, use quotation marks only at the beginning of the first sentence and at the end of the last.

Spotcheck 11-4

Supply quotation marks and any other needed punctuation.

1. According to Northrop Frye literature is conscious mythology.
2. Marriage is a great institution said Mae West. But I'm not ready for an institution.
3. I did it for Canada said Marilyn Bell after her marathon swim.
4. No Mr. Speaker said Elijah Harper.
5. In the seventeenth century John Comenius said We are all citizens of one world; we are all of one blood. To hate a man because he was born in another country, or because he speaks a different language, or because he takes a different view on this subject or that, is a great folly.

Quotation Marks, Italics, and Underlining in Titles

Use quotation marks around the titles of short works such as essays, short stories, songs, book chapters, and magazine or newspaper articles.

Underline (or type in *italics*) the titles of longer works, such as books, magazines, plays, movies, and television or radio shows.

> Wanda read an article titled "Buying Your First Home" in the September issue of <u>Canadian Living</u>.

> For Monday, the class is supposed to read the short story "The Painted Door" in the book <u>Best Canadian Stories</u>.

Use single quotation marks for a quotation or title within a quotation.

> "We read the poem 'Cat Dying in Autumn' in class," Mario said.

Spotcheck 11-5

Supply quotation marks, underlining (italics), and commas. Remember that quotation marks go outside commas and periods.

1. What are you doing tonight? Mary asked.
2. Oh, I don't know Cathy answered. I'll probably just stay home and watch a rerun of Star Trek on TV.
3. Mary said that she thought television was a waste of time.
4. So what are you going to do, Miss Intellectual? Cathy wanted to know.
5. Mary said I'll probably do some reading. There's an article called Lipstick and You in the new Teen World that looks good.

Apostrophes in Contractions

An apostrophe is used to show where one or more letters have been left out in a contraction of two words into one. Some examples:

isn't = is not	can't = cannot	they've = they have
I'm = I am	here's = here is	won't = will not

Do not confuse the following contractions with other sound-alike words.

it's = it is	we're = we are	they're = they are
you're = you are		

SENTENCE PUNCTUATION: USING PUNCTUATION

Spotcheck 11-6

In the blanks, write the contractions of the words shown in parentheses. Be sure to put the apostrophe where one or more letters have been left out.

1. (I have) My boss was surprised at how much _____ learned in English class.
2. (cannot) I _____ believe that final exams are here already.
3. (has not) Lyman is worried because he _____ had a letter from his fiancée in three weeks.
4. (they are) When the baseball teams finish spring training, _____ ready for action.
5. (you are) If _____ ready, we'll leave now.
6. (there is) _____ a new drugstore on the corner.
7. (could not) Tim _____ remember where he had left the car keys.
8. (you have) Congratulations! _____ won first prize.
9. (will not) The dog _____ surrender the bone.
10. (we will) Unless it rains, _____ return Tuesday.

Apostrophes to Show Possession

Apostrophes are also used to show possession or ownership.

Alec's book	children's games
two mothers' opinions	the car's brakes

A common problem is not knowing whether the apostrophe comes before or after the *-s*. Why is it *Alec's book* (apostrophe before the *-s*) but *mothers' opinions* (apostrophe after the *-s*)?

You can solve the problem by asking yourself this question: Whom (or what) does it belong to? If the answer does not end in *-s*, add *-'s* to the word. If the answer does end in *-s*, add only an apostrophe.

> Whom does the book belong to? (Alec)

Since *Alec* does not end in *-s*, add *-'s:* It is Alec's book.

> Whom do the games belong to? (the children)

Since *children* does not end in *-s*, add *-'s:* They are the children's games.

> Whom do the opinions belong to? (the two mothers)

Since *mothers* ends in *-s*, add only an apostrophe: They are the mothers' opinions.

> What do the brakes belong to? (the car)

Since *car* does not end in *-s*, add *-'s:* They are the car's brakes.

Be sure to place the apostrophe clearly in front of or behind the *-s*. Don't cheat by putting it on top of the *-s!*

The following possessive pronouns, although they end in -s, never take apostrophes:

his   hers   yours   ours   theirs   its

Almost all nouns form the plural by adding an -s. Be sure that a word shows ownership before giving it an apostrophe.

Two cats sat on the fence. (no ownership, no apostrophe)

Spotcheck 11-7

Put apostrophes in the correct position in the possessive words below.

1. the mens wages
2. three horses stalls
3. a weeks work
4. the countries borders
5. the radios volume
6. both flowers petals
7. the two cars headlights
8. a lifetimes effort

Spotcheck 11-8

Add apostrophes where needed.

1. The history books cover was worn from hard use.
2. Duncans attitude has improved since he got a raise.
3. These notebooks belong to Monica.
4. Both boys wagons were on the sidewalk.
5. The caddies brought the womens golf carts to the clubhouse.

Spotcheck 11-9

Write sentences using the words in parentheses.

1. (men's) _____

2. (farmers') _____

3. (Jennifer's) _____

4. (players) _____

Doublecheck 11-1

Add quotation marks, apostrophes, and underlining (italics) as needed.

1. Why are you calling me at three in the morning? he yelled into the phone.
2. The college drama class is putting on Shakespeares The Taming of the Shrew.

SENTENCE PUNCTUATION: USING PUNCTUATION 181

3. Im sure I saw you last night at Joes party.

4. We had to memorize John McCraes poem In Flanders Fields in grade three.

5. Surely, Joyce said, you don't expect me to drink day-old coffee.

6. Is that bicycle yours, or is it ours?

7. That used to be Charles car, but now it belongs to Karen.

8. The two cowboys horses were tied to the hitching post.

9. Look before you leap is an old saying.

10. Jacques says that he will never forget the goal he scored in his high schools hockey game.

The Semicolon

A semicolon may be used between two closely related independent clauses that are not joined by *and, but, or, for, nor, yet,* or *so*. (You may want to review the discussion of independent clauses in Chapter 4.)

The rain stopped; we decided to continue our walk.

A semicolon may also be used when the second clause contains a transition word such as *however* or *consequently*.

The rain stopped; therefore, we decided to continue our walk.

Periods could have been used instead of the semicolons. In fact, a good test of the semicolon is to ask if a period might have been used instead. A semicolon indicates a closer link between the two sentences.

Another use of the semicolon (in which the preceding test does not apply) is to separate series items that already contain commas.

The new club officers are Hilda Jones, president; Franklin Hill, vice-president; and Rick Okamura, secretary-treasurer.

Spotcheck 11-10

Put semicolons in the correct spots in the following sentences.

1. The sun came up the dew quickly dried.

2. Michael Jordan wanted to play major-league baseball however, he never made the grade.

3. The highest-paid entertainers in 1990 and 1991 were pop musicians New Kids on the Block, $115 million TV comic Bill Cosby, $113 million talk-show host Oprah Winfrey, $80 million and singer Madonna, $63 million.

The Colon

Use a colon *after a complete statement* to introduce one of the following: a list, an explanation, or a long quotation.

(list) Everyone should bring these items to class: the text, a notebook, and a pen.

(explanation) There are two things I like about Gerry: his sense of humour and his loyalty to his friends.

(quotation) The commencement speaker quoted Mark Twain: "When I was a boy of 14, my father was so ignorant I could hardly stand to have the old man around. But when I got to be 21, I was astonished at how much he had learned in seven years."

Spotcheck 11-11

Supply colons as needed.

1. Here's what you should bring to the picnic paper plates, paper cups, and plastic forks.

2. Monica has a quality I really admire enthusiasm.

3. Before you leave home, be sure to turn off the lights, turn down the furnace, and put out the cat.

Dashes and Parentheses

Use a *dash* to show an abrupt change in thought or to provide emphasis.

(abrupt change) We were married in 1982—no, in 1981.

(emphasis) Our neighbour—the scoundrel—still hasn't returned our lawn mower.

Use *parentheses* to set off extra information that is not emphasized.

Jason said weight training (which he took up in January) helped him with the batting title.

The battle is discussed in Chapter 6 (pages 123 to 134).

Spotcheck 11-12

Add dashes and parentheses as needed.

1. I'd like a girlfriend just like Marsha a knockout!

2. The construction of the St. Lawrence Seaway completed in 1959 was an exceptional engineering feat.

3. My wife Mildred I mean Agnes went to visit her mother.

4. My friend Brad who owes me money by the way was just named a vice-president at the bank.

5. Tina's brother in fact her whole family is a little odd.

Doublecheck 11-2

Add semicolons, colons, dashes, and parentheses as needed.

1. Among the largest cities of the world are Bombay, India Cairo, Egypt Jakarta, Indonesia London, England and Tokyo, Japan.

2. Uncle Alfred he's my mother's late brother once went over Niagara Falls in a barrel.

3. The curtain rose the performance began.

4. Be sure to bring these on the camping trip a knife, a first-aid kit, and a can of bear repellent.

5. Ludwig van Beethoven 1770–1827 was probably the greatest composer ever known.

6. Allison lost would you believe it? ten pounds in two weeks.

7. Jan lost ten pounds in two months however she gained them back in one.

8. Everything the Garcias owned furniture, clothing, family keepsakes was destroyed in the fire.

9. The Blue Jays won the World Series in 1992 moreover they won it again in 1993.

10. Katharine Hepburn do you remember her? won the Academy Award for best actress in 1981.

Editing Check 11

Edit this paragraph about the McDonald's restaurant chain to supply needed apostrophes, semicolons, colons, dashes, parentheses, quotation marks, and question marks. Notice that the name McDonald's has an apostrophe when it refers to the restaurants.

[1]Ill bet you didnt know that back in 1950 North Americans ate more pork than beef however 20 years later they were eating twice as much beef as pork. [2]Half of that was in the form of you guessed it hamburger. [3]The hamburgers success really took off in the 1950s. [4]Can you guess what name is most closely associated with that success [5]Yes, of course, its McDonalds. [6]The McDonalds were two brothers. [7]Almost everything were likely to think of when we think of fast food can be traced to the McDonalds the drive-through service, the simple menu, the single dressing for the meat, and the specialized labour one task per person. [8]The McDonald brothers even had the golden arches and a sign out front announcing Over 1 Million Sold. [9]Though pioneers in the fast-food business, the McDonalds arent the ones were likely to think of today when we think of the Golden Arches. [10]Better known is Ray Kroc, a salesman who bought the McDonalds name in 1954 and by the end of the century had Golden Arches all over the world. [11]If youre one whos been to McDonalds lately, you have lots of company about 10 percent of Canadians visit on any day.

Checkpoint 11-1

One sentence in each of the following pairs contains a punctuation error. Place a check mark in front of the correct sentence in each pair.

_____ **1a.** Who is that at the front door?

_____ **1b.** Its probably just the newspaper boy.

_____ **2a.** I asked him if he would put the paper inside the screen door.

_____ **2b.** He said that "he would."

_____ **3a.** I enjoy reading The Edmonton Sun every day, don't you?

_____ **3b.** Well, I'd rather watch <u>The National</u> on TV.

_____ **4a.** I like the special reports, especially the international features, they're really interesting.

_____ **4b.** However, I do wish they would cover more local news.

_____ **5a.** My mother likes listening to Dick Gordon on This Morning on CBC Radio.

_____ **5b.** She says "She's a very good interviewer."

_____ **6a.** "I don't like the radio; it's boring."

_____ **6b.** "Thats a ridiculous thing to say," James told me.

_____ **7a.** One part of <u>The Toronto Star</u> that I do like is the column Careers.

_____ **7b.** One of the columnists, Janis Foord Kirk, is pretty clever.

_____ **8a.** Did you read her item about what to write in a resumé?

_____ **8b.** It is not appropriate to mention, your marital status, or how old you are.

_____ **9a.** On the other hand she said you must mention your experience.

_____ **9b.** "Your experience," she said, "must be mentioned."

_____ **10a.** She said "we must think of the employers when we write."

_____ **10b.** She told us that we must think of the employers when we write.

Checkpoint 11-2

Put an X in front of any sentence that contains an error in punctuation. Put a C in front of any sentence that is correct.

_____ 1. You will need to buy: a swimsuit, a towel, and sandals.

_____ 2. Sir John A. Macdonald 1815–1891 was the first prime minister of Canada.

_____ 3. The two cowboy's horses were tied to the rail.

_____ 4. Ms. Greene should'nt overwater her violets.

_____ 5. Are those tickets ours or theirs?

_____ 6. "Hitting the Road" is a chapter in the book "Bike Touring."

_____ 7. The children's toys were scattered around the room.

_____ 8. "The mail is here, Veronica said. Did I get a letter from Christopher?"

_____ 9. The waiter said, "Your table is ready".

_____ 10. The sun slowly disappeared; the lake grew calm.

No answers are given for Checkpoint quizzes.

WORDCHECK: WORD CHOICE

Just because a dictionary lists a word doesn't mean that the word is suitable for all occasions. These are some of the terms dictionaries use to guide us:

obsolete or *archaic*—words no longer in use

dialectal or *regional*—used only in certain areas of the country

nonstandard or *illiterate*—not used by educated people

colloquial or *informal*—more suited to conversation than to formal writing

slang—popular words that usually soon go out of fashion; suitable for only the most informal writing

Use a dictionary to see what labels are given to the italicized words in these sentences.

1. Marcia's boyfriend is a good-looking *dude*.
2. Who *hath* seen the wind?
3. Alonzo fixed the car *hisself*.
4. Some words *ain't* in my dictionary.
5. Billie Joe carried the groceries home in a *poke*.

CHECKPOST: MODALS

Rules   Modals add a particular meaning to the verbs that they combine with.

- Verb forms that are used as modals have to be learned. Here is a list of the modals:

  can – could
  may – might
  shall – should
  will – would
  must – must
  need – needed

- A root verb always follows the modal in either the active or passive voice.

  You <u>must</u> do something! Something <u>must</u> <u>be</u> done!

- *Can* has three meanings:

  a. possibility

      Keeping horses <u>can</u> be expensive.

  b. ability

      I <u>can</u> ride a horse.

  c. permission

      <u>Can</u> I have a horse?

- *May* signifies

  a. permission and requests

      <u>May</u> I help you?

  b. conjecture about the future

      We <u>may</u> live under the sea in the year 3000.

  c. conjecture about the past

      We <u>may</u> have ruined our environment.

      We <u>might</u> have had an accident in that ice storm.

- *Must* means

  a. necessity

      We <u>must</u> fight poverty in our society.

  b. prohibition

      We <u>must</u> not smuggle cigarettes.

  c. deduction

      Conrad Black <u>must</u> be very rich.

- *Must* is stronger in meaning than *have to*. *Must* is often concerned with authority and laws, while *have to* is used when the concerns are more trivial.

    I <u>must</u> check the exhaust emissions from my car. (by law)

    I <u>have to</u> get my car washed—it's filthy.

- *Must not* and *not have to* are completely different in meaning.

    I <u>must not</u> steal; it is against the law.

    You do<u>n't have to</u> vote if you don't want to; it is voluntary.

Checkpost 11-1

Fill in the blanks with the most suitable modal: must, should, can, could, might, may, need, would.

¹Mitra's little boy didn't eat his dinner, so she thought he _____ be sick. ²She called her doctor although she knew she _____ not because it was so late. He didn't answer the phone. ³"He _____ be still at the hospital," she thought. ⁴"He _____ not have gone home already; he never leaves before nine. ⁵He _____ be in his car; I'll try his cellphone." ⁶There was no answer—his phone _____ be switched off, she decided. After half an hour of trying, Mitra took her son to the hospital. ⁷"The doctor _____ not have got my messages, or he _____ have called," she told the nurse. After the examination, she learned that her son had a mild cold. ⁸"You _____ not keep him away from school, but you _____ dress him warmly. ⁹He _____ play with his friends, but he _____ not stay outside. ¹⁰You _____ not bring him back to see us unless he develops a temperature. ¹¹If he has a fever, you _____ bring him back at once," advised the nurse.

12 WRITING THE ESSAY

READING: DEVELOPING AN IDEA

Precheck Being the parent of small children isn't always a joy, says physician Winston F. Wong in the following Father's Day essay. Still, he says, the pleasures outweigh the pains. Notice that the main idea of the essay is stated in the first paragraph and that each of the next three paragraphs begins with a topic sentence. Observe also the use of specific details to develop the paragraphs.

Journal Topic What do you think are the pleasures and pains of parenthood?

Fatherhood—It Has Its Moments –Winston F. Wong

1   Sometimes the last thing I want to eat is a McDonald's french fry, and I've stopped counting how many times I've seen "Sesame Street" videos. I've stuck my hand in my coat pocket only to find a lint-covered Gummi Bear. I've gone to work unaware that my baby spat up on my clean shirt. Being a father of three small children hasn't been a constant string of pleasures, but I can't think of a more fulfilling and rewarding adventure, and it's allowed me to relive the joys of being a child.

contemporary modern
repertoire set of skills

doodle scribble aimless designs

2   Like a lot of contemporary dads, I've taken on chores and responsibilities my own late father never had in his repertoire. Part of my routine includes giving the kids a bath, changing diapers, and bringing them shopping. But like my dad, I have fun with the kids. I really get a kick when I doodle with my 6-year-old daughter, play "dinosaurs" with my 3-year-old son, and build a tent for my 18-month-old daughter.

3   I especially like to laugh with my kids. I guess I picked up a certain corniness from my father, who always seemed to crack a joke and poke a gentle tease even though he had other responsibilities. In my work as a family physician, I've worked in Chinatown with young immigrant families that remind me of my own childhood and father. As my parents did, these families struggle to learn a new language and culture—and make ends meet. The fathers that seem to cope well seem to really enjoy their kids, despite these pressures. Humour has kept them going.

4   I'm both pleased and a bit embarrassed today when my children and I laugh together at the same slapstick humour I enjoyed as a kid watching the Three

Stooges. I know it's not educational TV, but the laughter we share is precious. Hopefully, my kids will learn to laugh like I did as a kid growing up in San Francisco. That's why when Alisa, Connor, and Maya try to tickle me, ask me to make that "funny face" or scream, "Daddy, you're so silly!" I can't think of anything more complimentary.

So, while being a dad is a lot of responsibility, it's equally a ball. After all, being a dad is supposed to be FUN! 5

Checking Meaning and Style

1. What is the thesis or central idea of the essay? (Paragraph 1)
2. What are some of the "chores and responsibilities" that fathers have? (Paragraph 2)
3. What are some of the pleasures? (Paragraphs 2, 3, and 4)
4. What helps immigrant families "keep going"? (Paragraph 3)
5. What is the function of the final paragraph?

Checking Ideas

1. If fatherhood is so rewarding, as Winston F. Wong says, why are so many families without fathers?
2. Do immigrant families have a greater need for a sense of humour than other families, as Dr. Wong suggests? If so, why?
3. How has the role of fathers changed in recent years for many men?
4. What are some examples of conflicts that might arise between the generations as far as parenting is concerned?

Netcheck

What current ideas of parenting do you come across on the Internet? Who is the latest guru of the best parenting practices? If you were a new parent, what sources of information would you look for to help you?

WRITING MODELS: THE ESSAY

Wong's essay on parenthood and the student composition that follows are models for the essay, the kind of writing you will do for the rest of the term. Notice how Dr. Wong's essay starts with an introductory paragraph that states the main idea or thesis of the essay—that being a father can be rewarding. Paragraphs 2, 3, and 4 start with topic sentences that give the main idea of those paragraphs. The concluding paragraph sums up the writer's ideas. The student essay that follows is an example that is worth analyzing in detail.

Model Five-Paragraph Essay

A Double Standard

The Women's Movement has helped improve the lives of women in North America in many ways. We can work at jobs formerly closed to us. We are more likely to get pay comparable to that of men. We are less likely to hear men call

190   CHAPTER 12   WRITING THE ESSAY

Introduction: The final sentence is the thesis statement for the whole essay.	us "baby" and more likely to have them treat us as adults. But the Women's Movement hasn't had much impact on my family, especially on the way my brother and I are treated. <u>Just because he is male, he has many privileges and advantages that are denied me just because I am female.</u>
Body I: The first sentence is the topic sentence for the paragraph.	<u>Even though he is two years younger than I, he is much more free to stay out late and to come and go as he pleases.</u> If I come home after midnight, my dad throws a fit. He wants to know where I've been, who I was with, and who drove me home. Even if I tell him I went to a church meeting and had a pizza afterwards with several girlfriends, he tells me that if it happens again I won't be allowed out of the house after dark for a month. Meanwhile, my brother's coming home at one or two in the morning, and all my dad says the next day is, "Well, did you have a good time last night?"
Body II: The first sentence is the topic sentence for the paragraph.	<u>It irritates me that my brother doesn't have to do nearly as much work around the house as I do.</u> I'm expected to set the table for all meals, help Mom with the cooking, and wash the dishes by myself. On Saturdays, it's my job to mop and wax the kitchen floor and vacuum all the rugs. And what does Little Brother do? Once in a while he carries out the garbage. He's supposed to keep the lawn mowed, but somehow he always seems to have baseball practice or some other crucial activity just when the grass gets a bit long. So Dad does it, saying he needs the exercise anyway.
Body III: The first sentence is the topic sentence for the paragraph.	<u>Then there's the matter of the car.</u> You can guess who gets to use it, and who doesn't. He drives to classes. I take the bus to my morning job and the bus to my afternoon classes. I told my friend Shauna that I thought I could get the car to take us to the new Spielberg movie on Saturday night. But Brother gets the car to drive his buddies to a rock concert at the auditorium. Mother said it was too dangerous for him to take the bus to that part of town.
Conclusion: The first sentence summarizes the three body paragraphs.	<u>It isn't fair that my brother has more freedom than I, that he gets out of household chores, and that he monopolizes use of the car.</u> Whoever said it's a man's world must have been peeking into our house.

Until now we have concentrated on writing paragraphs. It is time to tackle the larger challenge of writing an essay. If you have been having success with paragraphs, you should not have much trouble with the essay. A paragraph is a brief development of one idea. An essay is a longer development of one idea or subject.

You have been urged to use a topic sentence to express the main idea of each paragraph. You are now urged to use a **thesis sentence** to express the main idea of the entire essay.

We will focus on writing the kind of essay that is standard in many college composition courses: the five-paragraph essay. The five paragraphs look like this:

Paragraph 1	The *introduction*, including a *thesis sentence* that states the main point of the essay.
Paragraph 2	*First support paragraph* to back up the thesis sentence. Starts with a *topic sentence*.
Paragraph 3	*Second support* paragraph, with a topic sentence.
Paragraph 4	*Third support paragraph*, with a topic sentence. (Paragraphs 2, 3, and 4 make up the *body* of the essay.)
Paragraph 5	The *concluding paragraph*, which brings the essay to a satisfying end, perhaps with a summary or restating of the main points.

Here is the essay in diagram form:

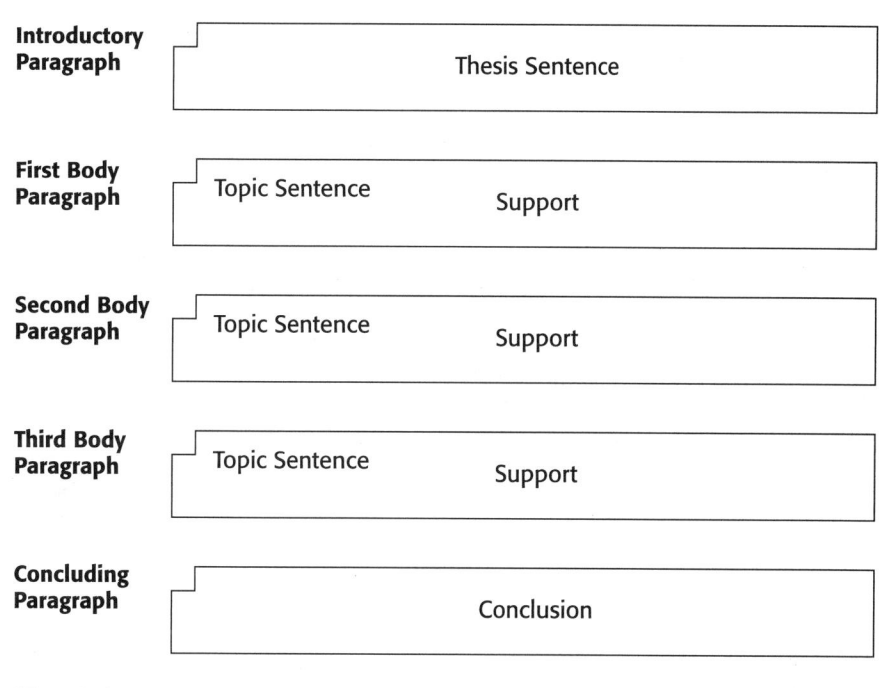

Introductory Paragraph	Thesis Sentence
First Body Paragraph	Topic Sentence — Support
Second Body Paragraph	Topic Sentence — Support
Third Body Paragraph	Topic Sentence — Support
Concluding Paragraph	Conclusion

Now let's apply the outline to the essay "A Double Standard."

Introduction Thesis sentence: "Just because he is male, [my brother] has many privileges and advantages that are denied me just because I am female." (The purpose of the next three paragraphs is to support or show the truth of the thesis sentence.)

First Support Topic sentence: "... [He] is much more free to stay out late and to come and go as he pleases." (This idea is *developed* by using specific examples and comparison. The next two paragraphs are developed in the same way.)

Second Support Topic sentence: "... [M]y brother doesn't have to do nearly as much work around the house as I do."

Third Support Topic sentence: (implied) He gets to use the car more than I do.

Conclusion (implied) It's a man's world.

Of course, not every essay is organized in just this way. An essay might have fewer or many more paragraphs to support the thesis. Essays written by professionals often do not contain a written-out thesis sentence; the thesis is only implied. But all essays have a thesis—a central point the writer wishes to make.

Why a thesis sentence? Using a thesis sentence forces a writer to decide ahead of time just what point is to be made. It helps the writer stay on track once the writing begins. On a smaller scale, the topic sentence offers the same kind of help in writing the paragraph. Of course, the thesis sentence also helps the reader by stating the main point of the essay.

Some writers (and instructors) like an essay to start with a thesis sentence that outlines the entire essay. Using that approach, the essay "A Double Standard" could have had the following thesis sentence:

Just because he is male and I am female, my brother has more freedom, has fewer household chores, and has first call on the family car.

That clearly sets up an essay with three developing paragraphs: one on freedom, one on chores, and one on use of the car.

Whichever method you use, it is important that you know before you begin your first draft just what it is you want to say. If you do not make a formal outline, at least jot down the main idea and the points you will use to support it, using the prewriting techniques discussed earlier.

WRITING ASSIGNMENT: AN ESSAY

Let's examine the three parts of the essay a little more closely.

The **introduction** (first paragraph) serves two purposes. One, as we have already seen, is to present the thesis or main idea of the essay. The other is to arouse interest so that the reader will want to continue. Perhaps the thesis sentence alone will do that. But often a more complex introduction is effective. The introduction to "A Double Standard," for example, puts one young woman's problems in the framework of recent progress made by women in general in North America.

Any introduction that sets the stage for the rest of the essay can be used. It might be a brief anecdote or description that leads into the thesis sentence. It might be an interesting quotation or a startling fact. A question can be an effective opener—but be sure it implies very clearly what point you intend to make in the essay and is not just a way of postponing that decision.

The **body** is the main part of the essay. It should be at least two or three paragraphs long. It is in these paragraphs that you support the thesis sentence. You prove your point with specific details, illustrations, examples, comparisons, and the other methods of paragraph development already studied. Each paragraph will consider one particular aspect of the general subject announced in the thesis sentence. Look again at "A Double Standard" for examples.

How long should a paragraph be? This is the logical answer: long enough to develop the idea it expresses in a way that satisfies or convinces the reader. In general, if a paragraph doesn't have at least four to six sentences, it needs more development.

The **concluding paragraph** should bring the essay to a satisfying close. Often it will summarize the main points made, as in "A Double Standard," although in a short essay this reminder of what has just been read may not be thought necessary. It might be appropriate to suggest actions based on what has been said or to predict future developments.

The **title** (for example, "A Double Standard") is usually a short, catchy phrase intended to capture the reader's interest and perhaps to give a hint about the subject of the essay. Centre the title about 1.5 inches (4 cm) from the top of the first page (on the top line of notebook paper). Capitalize the first word and other important words. Do not underline the title or put quotation marks around it (unless it is a quotation). The title is not really part of the main essay; any essential information it contains must be repeated in the essay itself.

WRITING ASSIGNMENT: AN ESSAY

Write an Essay with Introduction, Body, and Conclusion Paragraphs

Write an essay with two or three paragraphs of development on one of the following subjects:

1. Causes of family arguments
2. Why I would (not) want to be a police officer (or other occupation)
3. Three things (not people) I would hate to do without
4. Three desirable characteristics in an employee
5. Three types of pets—good and bad points
6. What makes a good parent

Use this outline planning form to help organize your essay:

Introduction

1. (The thesis statement for the essay) _____

Body I

2. (The topic sentence for the first body paragraph) _____

Body II

3. (The topic sentence for the second body paragraph) _____

Body III

4. (The topic sentence for the third body paragraph) _____

Conclusion

5. (Summary of the body paragraphs or a final statement) _____

Be sure that your essay:

- has a thesis sentence in the introductory paragraph.
- has a topic sentence at the beginning of each paragraph of the body.
- develops the thesis with interesting and convincing details.
- has a concluding paragrah.
- has a title centred at the top of page 1.

Writing Assignment Checklist

✓ To develop your thoughts on your chosen topic, ask how and why or use freewriting, clustering, or nonstop writing.

✓ Write a sentence outline of the essay.

1. Thesis sentence
   _____

2. First support—topic sentence
   _____

3. Second support—topic sentence
   _____

4. Third support—topic sentence
   _____

5. Conclusion
   _____

✓ Develop each support paragraph with at least three to five sentences, using interesting and convincing details.

✓ Centre a title on the top line of the first page.

✓ In revising the paper, look carefully for punctuation errors and those problems marked on recent papers.

✓ Proofread the final copy for errors in such things as spelling and punctuation.

SENTENCE MECHANICS: USING CAPITALS, FIGURES, AND ABBREVIATIONS

Can you identify the error in each of the following sentences?

Ruth is majoring in History.
Tom shouted, "we won the game!"
12 percent of the police force was sick.
She had two hundred and twenty-one old records.
That dog must weigh at least 50 lbs.
Dr. Cooper spoke after the dinner.

Knowing when and when not to use capital letters, figures, and abbreviations will make you feel more confident about your writing.

Capital Letters

Capitalize the first word of a sentence and the first word of a direct quotation that is a complete sentence.

> The store manager said, "We close at midnight."

Capitalize names and nicknames of persons and the word *I*.

> Do you remember that I called you "Elephant Breath" Smith in high school?

Capitalize names of *specific* places, structures, and school subjects.

> Asia   Yellowknife   Biology 256
> Gardiner Expressway   St. John's   Gaspé Bay
> John A. Macdonald High School   Modern Greek 101   Prince Edward Island

Don't capitalize names that are general rather than specific.

> He went to high school near here.
> They lived on an island last summer.
> Ruth is majoring in history.
> The Finleys live east of town.

Capitalize names of races, nationalities, languages, and religions.

> Caucasian   Russian   Swahili
> Presbyterian   Buddhism   Jewish

Capitalize names of organizations.

> Reform Party   Senate   Rotary Club
> Red Cross   General Motors   Mafia

Capitalize days of the week, months, holidays, and historical events.

> Tuesday   July   Canada Day
> New Year's Eve Thanksgiving   Korean War

Capitalize the first word, the last word, and every important word in a title.

> "She Don't Get the Blues"   *War and Peace*   "The Maple Leaf Forever"
> *The West Wing*   *Anne of Green Gables*

Capitalize a person's title only if it appears before a name.

> We saw Professor Mehta in the cafeteria.
>
> Alfred Mehta is a professor of economics.

Spotcheck 12-1

Supply capital letters as needed.

1. college of the jesuits is in quebec.
2. her father is catholic, and her mother is baptist.
3. my language professor can speak six languages, including tagalog.
4. the olsons vacationed on an island in lake superior.

5. the kids in elementary school called sam "sparky."

6. the band named loud and funky performed the beatles song "norwegian wood."

7. dave flunked math 1a, so i guess he won't major in accounting.

8. mr. and mrs. mcdonald saw the grand canyon when they went to arizona in june.

9. the salvation army building is on the corner of elm street and pine avenue.

10. vickie declared she would "never set foot in this town again."

Figures

In general, spell out numbers from one to ten, and use figures for the others. Ordinals are almost always spelled out.

| ten cookies | 11 cookies | fourth |
| three miles | 162 miles | thirteenth |

But always use figures to show times, dates, addresses, decimals, percentages, fractions, and statistics.

We have tickets for Flight 7, leaving at 3:15 a.m. on September 1.

Megan lives at 4 Spruce Street, Apartment 2.

Only 8 percent of the students know that in math *pi* equals 3.1416.

The Latin Club elected Liz president, 10–8.

Always spell out a number that begins a sentence. If the result is too long and awkward, rephrase the sentence.

(wrong) 123 bands marched in the parade.

(awkward) One hundred and twenty-three bands marched in the parade.

(rephrased) Members of 123 bands marched in the parade.

If two or more related numbers in a sentence call for different styles, use numbers for all.

The dictator's wife left behind 6 fur coats, 87 dresses, and 203 pairs of shoes.

Spotcheck 12-2

Cross out any incorrect uses of numbers and write the correct forms above them.

EXAMPLE: There were at least ~~8~~ *eight* chipmunks in the yard.

1. The mayor laid off three secretaries, 22 street cleaners, and 112 firefighters.

2. 12 percent of the police force was out sick.

3. Mimi wears shoe size six and a half.

4. Our candidate got only 9 percent of the vote.

5. The bus leaves at three p.m.

6. Ricky's birthday is on August third.

SENTENCE MECHANICS: USING CAPITALS, FIGURES, AND ABBREVIATIONS

Abbreviations

Only a few abbreviations are acceptable in formal writing. Here are some of them:

A.M. and P.M. (or a.m. and p.m.) B.C. A.D.
Mr. Mrs. Ms. Dr. (before a name)
Jr. Sr. M.D. (after a name)
B.A. M.A. Ph.D. (academic degrees)
GST

If any of these examples are unfamiliar, you can see the danger in using abbreviations: Your reader may not understand them.

It is generally safer to spell out a name once before switching to the abbreviation.

> We took poor Poochie to the Society for the Prevention of Cruelty to Animals. The workers at the SPCA said . . .

Some names are perhaps better known in abbreviated form: *CAA, CBC, RCMP, TV, VCR, IQ*. Use your judgment. Check a dictionary to see if periods are used with the abbreviation.

You may abbreviate titles such as *Gen., Gov., Prof.,* and *Dr.* when they appear before a full name. Spell them out when they appear with the last name alone.

> Sen. Amanda Cross will speak at the rally.

> Senator Cross was appointed by the prime minister last July.

Spell out (do not abbreviate) the names of provinces, countries, months, days, and units of measurement (grams, kilograms, centimetres, metres).

Spotcheck 12-3

Cross out any abbreviations that would be inappropriate in formal writing, and substitute full forms.

EXAMPLE: Phoebe was born in ~~Man~~. **Manitoba**

1. The police academy will hear a speaker from CSIS on Nov. 12.
2. At birth, the baby weighed seven lbs., three ounces (3.25 kg).
3. I've heard that Prof. Parsnip trains attack dogs.
4. The college will offer a new poli sci course next semester.
5. Two-thirds of the land in downtown T.O. is used for driving, parking, or servicing cars.
6. Singer Maureen Forrester was born in Montreal, Que., in 1930.

Doublecheck 12-1

Correct errors in capital letters, numbers, and abbreviations. Each sentence contains one error.

1. 12 years ago I moved to Regina.
2. Carrie is attending a University in the West.

3. Gilbert has studied spanish for four years.
4. Nick still owes me thirty-six fifty for a sports coat.
5. Did the second world war end in 1945 or 1946?
6. Joey lives at seventy-three Main Street.
7. Fatima earned a B.A. degree in Economics.
8. She attended High School in Moncton, New Brunswick.
9. That dog must weigh at least 20 kg.
10. The bartender told the boys to return "When you're 21."

Doublecheck 12-2

Correct errors in capital letters, numbers, and abbreviations.

1. The Earth's five billionth person was born in 1987, just 13 years after the 4 billionth person was born.
2. At that rate, there will be 6 billion people by the year 2000.
3. According to statistics Canada, the population of Canada was 26 833 million by the first day of 1991.
4. That was an increase of more than one million since new year's day, 1986.
5. Many canadian cities continued to grow, according to the Census Figures.
6. The Statistics show that, between 1981 and 1986, St. John's grew by 3%.
7. During the same time period, Sault ste. Marie declined by 0.4%.
8. According to Statistics Canada, as many women have their first baby after age 30 as those in their mid-20s.
9. In 1986, 63.1% of the Canadian population spoke english.
10. In the same year, 24.3% of Canadians listed French as their first language.

Doublecheck 12-3

Edit the following paragraph, correcting any errors in capital letters, numbers, and abbreviations.

[1]The Flea is a remarkable insect, says the magazine *national geographic*. [2]If there were olympic games for insects, fleas would win most of the gold medals. [3]Some fleas can jump one hundred and fifty times their own length. [4]That's equivalent to a human jumping nearly a thousand ft (300 metres). [5]One flea was observed jumping thirty thousand times without stopping. [6]Fleas are fast too. [7]A flea can accelerate 50 times faster than an Astronaut in a space shuttle after

liftoff. [8]Except for the creatures' athletic skills, Humans don't admire fleas. [9]3 plague epidemics, spread by rats and their fleas, have ravaged the World, killing more than 200 million people. [10]the last plague epidemic started in china in 1855 and was carried by steamships to all parts of the world. [11]In the U.S. in 1987 there were 12 cases of plague and 2 deaths.

SENTENCE STRUCTURE: BEING CONSISTENT

You will probably sense right away that there is something wrong with each of the following sentences. (The underlined words will give you some clues.)

1. The waiter <u>puts</u> our hamburgers on the counter and then <u>returned</u> to the kitchen.
2. When <u>one</u> drives into the Cabot Trail, <u>you</u> are overwhelmed by the magnificent scenery.
3. The prime minister walked slowly to the lectern, carefully adjusted his glasses, and delivered a <u>nifty</u> address on the state of the economy.

Each of the above sentences is inconsistent; each contains a confusing or annoying *shift*.

- Sentence 1 shifts from the present-time verb *puts* to the past-time verb *returned*. This is called a *shift of tense*.
- Sentence 2 shifts from the third-person pronoun *one* to the second-person pronoun *you*. (This use of *person* will be explained in a moment.)
- Sentence 3 shifts from a formal tone or style to the casual style *nifty*.

Be Consistent in Verb Tense

Be consistent in your use of the time (tense) of verbs unless there is a good reason to shift. Sentence 1 could have been written in either of these two ways:

> The waiter <u>puts</u> our hamburgers on the counter and then <u>returns</u> to the kitchen. (Both verbs are in present time.)

> The waiter <u>put</u> our hamburgers on the counter and then <u>returned</u> to the kitchen. (Both verbs are in past time.)

Sometimes a shift in time is necessary:

> Rosalia remembers [present time] that her parents owned [past time] a Plymouth station wagon when she was [past time] a little girl.

200 CHAPTER 12 WRITING THE ESSAY

Spotcheck 12-4

Make the subsequent verbs in each sentence consistent in time with the first verb.

                                                                                 opened

EXAMPLE: Jackie Robinson <u>was</u> an outstanding athlete who ~~opens~~ the door to professional sports for other black athletes.

1. Robinson joined the Brooklyn Dodgers in 1947 and becomes the first black player in modern major-league baseball.
2. Robinson went to high school in Pasadena, California, where he is a star in track, football, and baseball.
3. He attends the University of California at Los Angeles on a football scholarship and, in 1939, gained more yards than any other college player.
4. After service in the Second World War, Robinson joined the Kansas City Monarchs and plays for $400 a month in the Negro American League.
5. When Dodgers general manager Branch Rickey signs Robinson, he warned him to expect acts of prejudice from other players and the fans.
6. During the ten years he plays for the Dodgers, Robinson batted .311 and helped the team win six National League championships and a World Series in 1955.

Spotcheck 12-5

Rewrite the seven sentences in Spotcheck 12-4 (including the example) as a paragraph, leaving out the numbers. Make the verbs consistent—all in past time.

_____
_____
_____
_____
_____
_____
_____
_____
_____

Spotcheck 12-6

Cross out any verbs that are inconsistent, and write in the correct form above the crossed-out words.

[1]The first tinted glasses were not intended to protect eyes from the sun. [2]Darkened with smoke, the glasses are worn by judges in China in the fifteenth century. [3]The idea was to conceal a judge's eyes so that witnesses couldn't tell if

the judge thinks they are lying. [4]The earliest dark glasses were not vision-corrected, but by around 1430 judges are taking advantage of that feature too. [5]Outside the courts, others start wearing tinted glasses to reduce glare from the sun. [6]In America, the military played a major role in the development of sunglasses. [7]In the 1930s, the Army Air Force commissions Bausch & Lomb to develop glasses to protect pilots from high-altitude glare. [8]The resulting dark-green glasses became available to the public as Ray-Ban aviator glasses.

Be Consistent in Personal Pronouns

Pronouns are said to be in the first, second, or third *person*, depending on whether they refer to the person speaking, the person spoken to, or the person spoken about.

	Singular	*Plural*
First person	I, me, my, mine	we, us, our, ours
Second person	you, your, yours	you, your, yours
Third person	he, him, his she, her, hers it, its	they, them, their, theirs

(Third person also includes the names of persons, places, and things and indefinite pronouns such as *one, everyone,* and *anybody.*)

The point to remember is to avoid unnecessary pronoun shifts. Let's revise our earlier example.

(shift) When <u>one</u> drives into the Cabot Trail, <u>you</u> are overwhelmed by the magnificent scenery.

(consistent) When <u>one</u> drives into the Cabot Trail, <u>one</u> is overwhelmed by the magnificent scenery.

Watch out especially for the most common shift—from the first- or third-person pronoun to the second-person *you*.

Spotcheck 12-7

Eliminate shifts in person by making the second pronoun in each sentence agree with the first. Also, change verbs when necessary.

EXAMPLE: I used to think Lola was perfect, but as ~~one gets~~ **I get** to know her ~~one sees~~ **I see** she has a few faults.

1. People can usually solve a problem if you are willing to work at it.

2. In history class we had to bring the teacher an apple before one could get an A.

3. Oscar buys his clothes at flea markets because you can save money that way.

4. We tried to cheer Mike up, but there was only so much you could do.

5. When one watches television a lot, you get depressed at the poor quality of many of the programs.

Although newspaper and magazine writers often use the word *you* to address the reader directly, this informal approach is seldom appropriate in college writing. The only exception is the use of *you* in instructional writing, such as in textbooks.

(weak) You could easily understand the president's problem.

(better) A person could easily understand the president's problem.

(better) The president's problem was easily understood.

Spotcheck 12-8

Rewrite each of the following sentences to eliminate the inappropriate you. *Make the sentences as short as you can without leaving out information.*

1. You don't need a ticket to attend the Blue Rodeo concert.
   _____
   _____

2. After eating at Shopsy's restaurant, you feel you got your money's worth.
   _____
   _____

3. You can imagine how glad I was to see Ralph again.
   _____
   _____

4. Foreign travel helps you understand your own country.
   _____
   _____

5. If you drove to the sun at 100 kilometres per hour, it would take you 171 years to travel the 149.6 million kilometres.
   _____
   _____

Be Consistent in Language Tone

Your writing in college and later in your career will usually have a fairly serious or formal tone. Avoid slipping into overly casual and slangy language. Such shifts in tone are jarring to the reader, as in the case in our original example:

(shift) The prime minister walked slowly to the lectern, carefully adjusted his glasses, and delivered a <u>nifty</u> address on the state of the economy.

(consistent) The prime minister walked slowly to the lectern, carefully adjusted his glasses, and delivered a stirring address on the state of the economy.

Of course, if you are jotting a note to a good friend, you can be as informal as you want to be.

Change the italicized words to keep a fairly formal tone.

Spotcheck 12-9

EXAMPLE: Students who enrol in English 100 should expect to ~~keep their noses to the grindstone~~ *work hard* all semester.

1. Anyone who thinks Canadian schools will ever operate year-round is *full of beans*.
2. This year's top student is not only intelligent, she is a *foxy chick*.
3. The orchestra gave a *swell* performance of Beethoven's Third Symphony.
4. The members of the Seniors' Club *boogied* until midnight after installing their new officers.
5. Mr. Alberts was pleased to receive a raise of 50 *bucks* a week.

Doublecheck 12-4

*In the blanks, write **time**, **person**, or **tone** to identify the shift in each sentence. One of the sentences is correct as it stands.*

1. _____ If someone has visited Quebec City, they will have admired the interesting architecture.
2. _____ Quebec City is originally called Stadacona and was one of the oldest settlements in Canada.
3. _____ The beautiful city is a really cool place to vacation.
4. _____ It was always a tourist attraction because of its fascinating history.
5. _____ Anyone visiting Quebec will certainly see the famous Château Frontenac and they will also see the Legislative Assembly.
6. _____ Eating out in Quebec has been a gourmet experience because there is a variety of cuisine.
7. _____ Quebec is also famous for its yummy seafood dishes.
8. _____ Of course, visitors should speak French in Quebec if he wants to get around easily.
9. _____ Most Canadians learn French when they were at school.
10. _____ Even with only a little knowledge of French, visiting Quebec is an awesome experience.

Editing Check 12

Edit this paragraph to correct italicized errors in time, person, and tone. The first sentence has been done as an example.

¹~~If someone~~ Anyone who likes potato chips ~~you~~ should thank Thomas Jefferson and George Crum. ²Jefferson, the future American president, introduced french-fried potatoes after he *learns* to like them while serving as ambassador to France. ³The salted, thinly sliced chips so popular today *got a move on* because of a dispute between a chef and a customer. ⁴It happened in 1853 while chef George Crum *is* employed at a fancy resort in Saratoga, New York, and frying potatoes in the thick-cut French style. ⁵A diner sent his french fries back to the kitchen because they were too thick and *yucky*. ⁶If anyone has ever worked in a restaurant, *you* know how difficult some customers can be. ⁷Crum keeps cutting the potatoes thinner, and the diner *kept* sending them back. ⁸Finally the angry Crum slices the *spuds* so thin they are almost like strips of paper. ⁹The diner is delighted with the potatoes, other customers request them, and the restaurant *became* famous for its "Saratoga Chips." ¹⁰So when people sit down in front of the television set with a bag of chips in hand, *you* should say thanks to Thomas Jefferson and George Crum (and to Crum's fussy customer).

Checkpoint 12-1

Cross out the word causing a shift in time, person, or tone and write the correct or appropriate word in the blank to the left of the sentence.

EXAMPLE: __crashed__ The car sped around the corner and ~~crashes~~ into an ambulance.

_____ 1. As we neared the Rockies, you could see the snow on the mountain peaks.

_____ 2. If people have a real desire to win, you will often succeed.

_____ 3. Anthony came to the office wearing his new threads.

_____ 4. After he had studied most of the night, Curtis falls asleep during the exam.

_____ 5. Twice in the past week I took the bus to school and arrive late.

_____ 6. The judge sentenced the car thief to six months in the slammer.

WORDCHECK: PLACES AND THINGS   **205**

_____ 7. People should always eat a good breakfast because your mind doesn't function well when the stomach is empty.

_____ 8. When you jogged a lot, do your knees ever get sore?

_____ 9. Whenever Karen saw Kirk talking to another girl, she gets angry.

_____ 10. I never have trouble finishing my homework; the first thing you do is turn off the TV set.

Checkpoint 12-2

*In the blanks to the left of each sentence, write **time**, **person**, or **tone** to identify any shifts in the sentences. Write **C** if no shift takes place.*

_____ 1. The women's clothing in the store was too pricey for Anne.

_____ 2. If I shop at the Bargain Centre, you have to be careful.

_____ 3. Every time William sits down, the dog wanted to go out.

_____ 4. A person who writes a paragraph will find it easier to do if you organize your thoughts first.

_____ 5. Henry found the difficult history examination a real downer.

_____ 6. The mechanic opened the hood of the car and looks inside.

_____ 7. Whenever we plan a picnic, you can be sure it will rain.

_____ 8. The leaves turn brown and started to drop from the trees.

_____ 9. The sun was shining, but the wind was blowing.

_____ 10. The president discussed lots of stuff in his press conference.

No answers are given for Checkpoint quizzes.

WORDCHECK: PLACES AND THINGS

Among the many helps some dictionaries provide is information about sites throughout the world. Use a dictionary to answer the following questions.

1. How tall is the Eiffel Tower?
2. What is the capital of Nunavut?
3. What is the population of Zambia?
4. Where is the Blarney Stone? What is it?
5. What are the names of the Great Lakes?

13

THE CLASSIFICATION ESSAY

READING: USING CATEGORIES TO CONVEY INFORMATION

Precheck

Many people enjoy learning about their family's history—genealogy is becoming a very popular pastime. In some cases, knowing one's heritage and the history of one's ethnic group can be vital to the survival of future generations. In this essay, the Cree writer Pat Deiter-McArthur has classified the generations of First Nations people, starting from the time of the first contact with European settlers.

Journal Topic

Can you trace your family or ethnic group back several generations? Is there a significant event in your family's history? Are there many differences in how the generations lived?

Saskatchewan's Indian People—Five Generations —Pat Deiter-McArthur

It has been about five generations since Saskatchewan Indian people have had significant contact with European settlers. The first generation strongly influenced by Europeans were the treaty-signers. The key characteristic of this generation was their ability to have some input into their future. They retained their tribal cultures but realized that they had to negotiate with the Europeans for the betterment of future generations. They did not give up their language or religion or the political structures of nationhood. They were perceived by government as an "alien" nation to be dealt with by treaty.

alien foreign

The Second Generation (1867–1910) of Indian people were the objects of legal oppression by the government. This generation lived under the absolute rule of an Indian agent, a government employee. Through the Indian Act, this generation was denied their religion, political rights, and freedom to travel off their reserves. A pass and permit system was strictly adhered to on the prairies; every

adhered to followed

206

Indian person required a pass to leave the reserve and a permit to sell any agricultural produce. All children were required to attend residential schools run by the churches. The goals of their schools were, first, to make Christians out of their students and to rid them of their pagan lifestyles and, second, to provide a vocational education.

3 Tuberculosis was a major killer of Indian people during this time and contributed to decimating their population in Saskatchewan to a low of five thousand in 1910. This generation was treated as wards and aliens of Canada.

wards individuals under protection

4 The laws which served to oppress the Second Generation were in place until the early 1950s. The Third Generation (1910–1945) was greatly affected by these laws and schooling. This generation can be described as the lost generation. These people were psychologically oppressed. They rejected their Indianness but found that because of the laws for treaty Indians they could not enjoy the privileges accorded to whites. This third generation was our grandfather's generation. Many Indians at this time could speak their language but would not because of shame of their Indianness. They were still required by law to send their children to residential schools, to send their sick to Indian hospitals, and to abide by the Indian agent. They rarely had a sense of control over their own lives. This generation was considered wards of the government and denied citizenship.

oppressed kept under

5 Our father's time, the fourth generation since treaty-signing, can best be described as the generation of an Indian rebirth. This generation (1945–1980) is characterized by a movement of growing awareness—awareness that being Indian was okay and that Indian people from all tribes are united through their aboriginality, historical development, and special status.

6 This generation saw the rise of Indian and Native organizations across Canada, the return of traditional ceremonies, and an acknowledgement of the need to retain traditional languages and cultural ways.

7 Indian people of this generation were given the right to vote in 1960. The pass and permit system was abandoned in the late 1930s. In 1956, Indian children could attend either residential schools or the local public schools. However, the effects of this generation being raised within an institution and their parents being raised in the same way had a severe impact on these individuals. The residential school not only taught them to suppress their language but also to suppress their feelings and sense of individualism. The continued attack on Indian languages by residential schools left this generation with an ability to only understand their language, but many were not sufficiently fluent to call their Native language their first language.

8 During the sixties, there was a rise in Indian urbanization, a trend that continues today. This generation also contributed to an Indian baby boom that is estimated [to] be eight to ten years behind the non-Indian baby boomers. The federal and provincial vote allowed Indian people to legally consume alcohol. Alcoholism, suicides, and violent deaths were on the rise for this generation.

9 This was a period of experimentation by both the Indian communities and the government. Unfortunately, neither side was ready for each other. The intended government goal of assimilation was besieged with problems of racism, poverty, maladjustment, and cultural shock.

assimilation blending in with the rest of society

10 Today's Indian people are part of the Fifth Generation. The fifth generation is faced with choices: assimilation, integration, or separation. Indian people are now able to intermarry or assimilate with non-Indians without the loss of their

Indian status. Indian leaders across Canada are seeking a separate and constitutionally recognized Indian government. Indian government is to provide its own services within Indian reserves. Integration allows Indian people to retain a sense of their cultural background while working and living within the larger society.

The fifth generation people are the first children since treaty-signing to be raised by their parents. Many of this generation are not able to understand a Native language. Their first and only language is English. This generation is generally comfortable about their Indianness without strong prejudicial feelings to others. However, this generation is challenged to retain the meaning of Indian identity for their children.

Checking Meaning and Style

1. Which sentence contains the thesis statement?
2. How was the Second Generation denied freedom of travel?
3. Explain "the object of oppression."
4. What were the characteristics of the Fourth Generation?
5. What method does the writer use to describe these generations?

Checking Ideas

1. Why is the Third Generation described as "the lost generation"?
2. What began to happen during the Fourth Generation's time?
3. Explain the trend of "Indian urbanization."
4. What is the writer's attitude about the challenges facing the Fifth Generation?

Netcheck

Have you ever tried to trace your ancestry on the Internet? There are many Web sites that can help you find your roots. See what you can find by surfing genealogy sites.

WRITING MODELS: THE CLASSIFICATION ESSAY

In "Saskatchewan's Indian People—Five Generations," we noticed how the author organized her material—by breaking it into categories. You might use this approach in writing a paper on, say, four kinds of popular music (for example, rap, reggae, country, and jazz), or you might write a memo at work on three ways to increase company profits. The model essay that follows discusses three different perspectives on the college library.

Model Classification Essay

Library Privileges

Walk into the college library and you will see—and perhaps hear—at least three types of "customers": the scholars, the socializers, and the snoozers.

The scholars can be identified in a variety of ways. They wear serious expressions, as can be seen in those rare moments when they glance up from their work. As a rule, they have their noses in textbooks or are busy writing something, an essay for an English class, perhaps. Also in the scholar category are the students sitting at the library computers. Assuming that the solitaire games have been removed, they're probably looking for a book or magazine article that will offer help in writing a term paper in sociology on three types of football fans or the various categories of ethnic groups. If the library has a video collection, scholars will be the ones checking out the foreign films. They also look at their watches frequently to be sure they won't be late for their next class.

The socializers have other reasons for visiting the library. They find it a good place to go if the cafeteria is too noisy for a conversation with friends. Textbooks may be open on the study table, but they receive little attention. More important is chatting about the good-looking tennis instructor or last night's Academy Awards program on TV. The socializers can also be identified as the targets of annoyed looks from nearby scholars.

It isn't hard to guess what distinguishes the third category—the snoozers. They're the ones in the most comfortable chairs, or the ones with their heads resting on a study table. Sometimes they have a book in front of (or under) their faces; at other times, they don't even pretend to know the usual function of a library. The snoozers sometimes overlap with the socializers, as when there is a need to discuss last night's party that lasted until three o'clock. A conspicuous subcategory of the snoozers is made up of the snorers.

So, which are you—a scholar, a socializer, or a snoozer?

Notice that the first paragraph identifies the three classifications to be discussed and that each of the three body paragraphs begins with a topic sentence. Notice also the use of examples to explain each type.

WRITING ASSIGNMENT: A CLASSIFICATION ESSAY

In an essay, discuss a topic by breaking it into at least three classifications, as in the following suggested topics.

1. Types of popular music
2. Types of restaurants
3. Types of sports or attitudes toward sports
4. Types of children or parents
5. Types of television programs
6. Types of teachers

Writing Assignment Checklist

✓ Use prewriting techniques to come up with specific details, examples, and so on to develop the paragraphs. Clustering (Chapter 3) might work well here, with separate clusters for each type of item included in your topic.

✓ Be sure that the first paragraph has a thesis sentence and that each of the other paragraphs begins with a topic sentence that states how that paragraph will support the thesis.

1. Thesis sentence

   _____

2. First classification

   _____

3. Second classification

   _____

4. Third classification

   _____

5. Conclusion

   _____

✓ When revising the first draft, make sure that each classification supports the thesis and is developed with clear examples or illustrations.

✓ Watch out for inconsistent sentence structure (shifts) and the kinds of errors made in recent papers.

✓ Centre a suitable title at the beginning of the essay.

✓ Carefully proofread the final copy, bearing in mind all of the features we have covered to date.

SENTENCE STRUCTURE: ACHIEVING SENTENCE VARIETY

A speaker who always uses the same tone of voice becomes boring. A writer who uses the same sentence patterns over and over can also become boring. The ability to construct sentences in a variety of ways makes our writing more interesting and allows us to express our ideas more effectively.

Notice how the repetition of short sentences makes the following paragraph boring and even irritating:

More than a million earthquakes may take place in any one year. Most of them take place under the oceans. They usually don't cause any damage. Some earthquakes occur on land. Earthquakes near large cities may cause extensive property damage. They may even cause deaths.

With a variety of sentence patterns, the paragraph becomes smoother, more concise, and more interesting.

More than a million earthquakes may take place in any one year. Most of them take place under the oceans, so they usually don't cause any damage. When they occur near big cities, however, they may cause extensive property damage and even deaths.

We will study three of the basic sentence patterns: simple, compound, and complex sentences.

Using Simple Sentences

The simple sentence is made up of one independent clause, with no dependent clauses. Recall from Chapter 4 that a clause has a subject and a verb. The clause is independent if it expresses a complete thought.

The <u>detective</u> *left.*

Describing words (modifiers) may be added to form the complete subject. Words added to the verb make up the complete predicate.

<u>The uniformed detective</u> *left in a blue car.*

A simple sentence can have a compound subject (more than one) or a compound verb.

The <u>detective</u> and the <u>burglar</u> *left.* (compound subject)

The <u>detective</u> *left* but *returned.* (compound verb)

A simple sentence can combine all of these elements.

The uniformed <u>detective</u> and the <u>burglar</u> *left* in a blue car but *returned* within half an hour and *entered* the interrogation room.

That is a long sentence, but it is still, grammatically speaking, a simple sentence because it has only one independent clause and no dependent clause.

Spotcheck 13-1

Combine the short simple sentences into one longer simple sentence containing a single independent clause.

EXAMPLE: The apple was ripe. It fell. It fell to the ground.

The ripe apple fell to the ground.

1. The ripe apple fell. It fell with a crashing sound.

   _____

2. Lucinda washed dishes. Martin washed dishes.

   _____

3. Martin washed the dishes. He did it without complaining.

4. Martin washed the dishes. He dried them.

5. The baby was happy. The baby smiled. The baby gurgled. It was in the bathtub.

Using Compound Sentences

A compound sentence is made up of two or more independent clauses.

<u>The moon came up</u>, and <u>we set off through the woods</u>.

<u>Anthony got a raise</u>, so <u>he decided to celebrate</u>.

As in the examples above, the two clauses are usually joined by a comma and one of the connecting words and, but, or, for, nor, yet, or so. The two parts of a compound sentence are considered equal in importance.

Spotcheck 13-2

Change the simple sentences into compound sentences by joining them with one of the connectors and, but, or, for, nor, yet, *or* so. *Don't forget a comma after the first clause.*

1. Calgary has a population of more than 760 000. Edmonton has a population of about 615 000.

2. An early Greek named Stentor had a loud voice. Today we call a booming voice *stentorian*.

3. A penguin may look clumsy. It can swim faster than many fish.

4. Waldo couldn't do his homework. He had broken his glasses.

5. Roderick might go fishing. He might go sailing.

6. You should learn to swim. Almost three-fourths of the earth is covered by water.

_____

_____

Using Complex Sentences

A complex sentence has an independent clause and one or more dependent clauses.

       dependent clause   **independent clause**
<u>Because Mrs. Larson was sick</u>, her husband fixed breakfast.

    independent clause   **dependent clause**
Marian netted the fish <u>while Bill steadied the boat</u>.

A dependent clause begins with a dependent word such as *because*, *although*, or *since*. It needs an independent clause to complete its meaning. (See page 59 for a longer list of dependent words.)

In a compound sentence, the ideas in both clauses are given equal emphasis. In a complex sentence, the idea in the dependent clause is emphasized less than the one in the independent clause. In the second example just given, more importance is given to Marian netting the fish (in the independent clause) than to Bill steadying the boat. If we put Bill in the independent clause, his actions become more important:

      dependent clause   **independent clause**
While Marian netted the fish, <u>Bill steadied the boat</u>.

Remember to put a comma after a dependent clause that starts a sentence.

Spotcheck 13-3

Draw one line under the dependent clause and two lines under the dependent word.

    EXAMPLE: Ruth is tired <u>because</u> <u>she studied until three</u>.

1. While one American died onscreen in *Rambo*, 75 Russians and Vietnamese were killed.

2. Antonio will get a raise unless his sales decline.

3. Mr. Eden is the neighbour who owns two Dobermans.

4. Although many young baseball players are signed to professional contracts, 90 percent never appear in a major-league game.

5. The local team will win the pennant because its pitching staff is strong.

Spotcheck 13-4

Combine the two simple sentences to make a complex sentence. The result will contain one independent clause and one dependent clause. Start some sentences with the independent clause and some with the dependent clause. Put a comma after the dependent clause if it starts the sentence.

1. The dentist was upset. Sean missed his appointment.
   _____

2. Lisa was nervous. She was to meet her new in-laws.
   _____

3. Yousuf Karsh was a great photographer. He photographed Winston Churchill.
   _____

4. Gambling was legalized in Windsor. The crime rate went up 275 percent.
   _____

5. That is the bus driver. He returned my lost wallet.
   _____

- Don't assume that long sentences are always better than short ones. A mixture of long, short, and medium-length sentences is usually the most effective approach.

Spotcheck 13-5

Change these compound sentences into complex sentences.

EXAMPLE: Martin repaired his bicycle, and Claudette read a novel. (compound)
While Martin repaired his bicycle, Claudette read a novel. (complex)

1. The floor of the house shook, and Jack knew it was an earthquake.
   _____

2. The bank will give you a loan, and you can buy a car.
   _____

3. Yolanda got many Christmas gifts, but she didn't give any.
   _____

4. Claudette enjoys nature, so she spends her weekends camping.
   _____

5. Kimberly began giving money to friends, for she had won a lottery.

_____

_____

Quickcheck on Sentence Patterns

✓ A simple sentence has one independent clause and no dependent clause.

✓ A compound sentence has two or more independent clauses and no dependent clause.

✓ A complex sentence has one independent clause and one or more dependent clauses.

Doublecheck 13-1

Identify each sentence as simple (S), compound (C), or complex (X).

_____ 1. The giraffes and the bears are at the east end of the zoo.

_____ 2. The giraffes are fenced in, and the bears are surrounded by a moat.

_____ 3. Although the giraffes are interesting, I could watch the bears for hours.

_____ 4. My real favourites are the monkeys that live on Monkey Island.

_____ 5. Their antics amuse everyone but are a particular delight to the children.

Spotcheck 13-6

The following paragraph contains only simple sentences. Join sentences with a dependent word, as in the example, or with a connecting word (for, and, not, but, or, yet, so). Edit the paragraph to make all sentences either complex or compound. The sentences have been numbered as a guide to joining.

¹Thomas Edison (1847–1931) was a famous inventor~~,~~ **who** ~~He~~ played a major role in shaping today's society. ²For example, one of his most important contributions was electric light. He developed it in the nineteenth century. ³His electric light was of no use without something to plug it into. He developed power plants and wiring for lamps and switches. ⁴New York became the first city to have electric street lighting. Edison threw a switch in 1882 to turn on 800 bulbs

all over lower Manhattan. ⁵Among the many inventions in which he played a part are the phonograph and the motion picture projector. ⁶He attended school for only three months. He became famous throughout the world.

SENTENCE STRUCTURE: BUILDING EFFECTIVE SENTENCES

Many times, two or more short sentences can be combined to form a single sentence that provides variety, saves words, and gives more exact emphasis. **Prepositional phrases, participial phrases,** and **appositives** can be used in sentence combining.

Using Prepositional Phrases

Phrases, you'll recall from Chapter 4, are groups of related words that do not contain both a subject and a verb. A prepositional phrase begins with a preposition and ends with a noun or pronoun: *to the beach, with them, under the gnarled oak tree.*

Notice how prepositional phrases (underlined) are used in the following two examples:

The mechanic finally started the car. It took him about five minutes.

The mechanic finally started the car <u>after about five minutes</u>.

The lieutenant picked up the grenade. He didn't give it a second thought.

<u>Without a second thought</u>, the lieutenant picked up the grenade.

Remember to put a comma after a phrase that starts a sentence.

Spotcheck 13-7

Combine the following pairs of sentences by making one of each pair a prepositional phrase.

EXAMPLE: The trail guide built a campfire. She built it near a stream.

Near a stream, the trail guide built a campfire.

(or) The trail guide built a campfire near a stream.

1. The mechanic had grease all over his face. He looked like a creature from another galaxy.

   _____

   _____

2. The magazine had a picture of Marie. It was on page 34.

   _____

   _____

3. The rabbit hid. It hid between two boulders.

   _____

   _____

4. It had been a hectic day. Mrs. Farnaby was tired.

   _____

   _____

5. Crows were in the tree's highest branches. They were holding a meeting.

   _____

   _____

Using Participial Phrases

A **participle** is a word made from a verb. A *present participle* adds *-ing* to the verb. A *past participle* usually adds *-d* or *-ed*.

Verb	Present Participle	Past Participle
move	moving	moved
jump	jumping	jumped

Past participles of *irregular* verbs, you may recall, do not end in *-d* or *-ed*. Examples of irregular past participles are *begun, fought, eaten, sent, taught,* and *written*. (For a longer list, see pages 94–95.)

A participial phrase consists of a participle and its modifiers. Here are examples:

> moving into position
>
> encouraged by his parents
>
> having risen to the top
>
> written by a secretary

A phrase must be joined to an independent clause to make a sentence.

> Moving into position, the wrestlers await the referee's signal.
>
> Encouraged by his parents, Whitney did well in school.
>
> Having risen to the top, the new president turned his back on those who had helped him.

The first noun or pronoun after a participial phrase usually must name the person or thing referred to by the phrase. Otherwise, the error called a dangling modifier results.

> **(wrong)** Having risen to the top, those who had helped him were ignored by the new president.
>
> **(right)** Having risen to the top, the new president ignored all those who had helped him.

A phrase may appear before or after the word it describes.

(before) <u>Checking his watch frequently</u>, the nervous bridegroom waited for the bride.

(after) The nervous bridegroom, <u>checking his watch frequently</u>, waited for the bride.

Use commas to separate the participial phrase from the rest of the sentence.

An *-ing* word may also be used as a noun (the name of something). Then it is called a *gerund*.

<u>Walking</u> is good exercise.

Spotcheck 13-8

Underline the participial phrases in these sentences.

1. The mail carrier, terrified at the dog's snarling, retreated to the sidewalk.
2. Singing in the rain, Mark and Christine enjoyed their walk.
3. He remembered a poem taught to him by his mother.
4. Finished with his homework, Adrian went to bed.
5. Searching for a route to Asia, Cartier reached the St. Lawrence River.

Spotcheck 13-9

Underline the participial phrases in these sentences.

1. Played in India in the sixteenth century, the game we call Parcheesi was originally not a board game at all.
2. The game, enjoyed by the emperor Akbar the Great, took place in the royal garden.
3. Moving from bush to bush in the garden, the "pawns" were the most beautiful young women in India.
4. Their progress, determined by the throw of shells, finally brought them "home" to the emperor's throne in the centre of the garden.
5. The English, changing the Indian name *pacisi* to *Pachisi*, moved the game indoors and replaced the beautiful maidens with ivory pawns to mark progress around the board.

Spotcheck 13-10

Use participial phrases to combine the following pairs of sentences.

EXAMPLE: Norman backed the car out of the garage. He ran over Tim's bike. Backing the car out of the garage, Norman ran over Tim's bike.

1. Paul was exhausted from his hike. He wanted a hot bath.

   _____

2. The Selvadurais saved 10 percent of their salaries for ten years. They were finally able to make a down payment on a house.

   _____

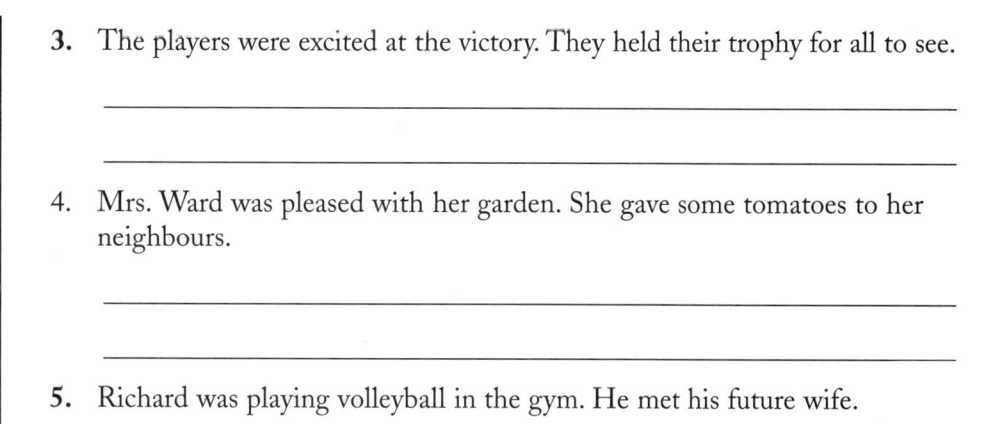

3. The players were excited at the victory. They held their trophy for all to see.
   _____
   _____

4. Mrs. Ward was pleased with her garden. She gave some tomatoes to her neighbours.
   _____
   _____

5. Richard was playing volleyball in the gym. He met his future wife.
   _____

Using Appositives

An appositive helps identify a noun or pronoun ahead of it.

>Dr. Eugenia Wilson, <u>a dentist</u>, needs a technician. (identifies Dr. Wilson)

>The Ashleys saw a statue of Sir John A. Macdonald, <u>the first prime minister of Canada</u>. (identifies John A. Macdonald)

Appositives are set off by commas if they are not essential to the meaning, as in the examples just given.

No commas are used if the appositives contain information essential to the sentence.

>**(no commas)** The store <u>Top Banana</u> sells expensive toys.

>**(no commas)** The movie <u>Austin Powers</u> stars Mike Myers.

Spotcheck 13-11

Underline the appositives in these sentences.

1. Vlad the Impaler, a fifteenth-century Romanian prince, was the inspiration for Dracula.
2. The seventeenth-century story "Bluebeard" was based partly on an actual Frenchman who killed several wives.
3. According to New England legend, the original Mother Goose of nursery rhyme fame was a Boston widow, Elizabeth Goose.
4. The first mechanically recorded human speech were the words of the nursery rhyme "Mary Had a Little Lamb."
5. The words were spoken in 1877 by Thomas Edison, inventor of the phonograph.

Spotcheck 13-12

Use appositives to combine these sentences.

EXAMPLE: Whitehorse is the largest city in the Yukon Territory. It has a population of about 19 200.

Whitehorse, the largest city in the Yukon Territory, has a population of about 19 200.

1. Elizabeth Kenny was an Australian nurse. She developed a method for treating polio.
   _____
   _____

2. The quartet played bebop. Bebop is a style of jazz developed in the late 1940s.
   _____
   _____

3. Elvis Presley was the "king" of rock 'n' roll. He died in 1977.
   _____
   _____

4. Alice Munro wrote *Open Secrets*. It is a collection of short stories.
   _____
   _____

5. Toronto's SkyDome has a retractable roof. The arena can hold 50 516 people.
   _____
   _____

Doublecheck 13-2

Identify the underlined words as a prepositional phrase (Prep), a participial phrase (Part), or an appositive (Ap).

_____ 1. Under her bed, Mary kept all of her childhood dolls.

_____ 2. Doctor Peterson, a sprinter in college, now runs marathons.

_____ 3. Renata, one of four sisters, had three brothers.

_____ 4. Having lived on a farm all of his life, Milton was eager to attend college in a city.

_____ 5. The Ricardos, annoyed by the poor sound quality, left the performance after the first act.

_____ 6. Clinging to a teddy bear, the child climbed onto her mother's lap.

_____ 7. Michael got a souvenir from his brother, a centre fielder for the Expos.

_____ 8. Encouraged by the appearance of the sun, the boys went to the beach.

SENTENCE STRUCTURE: BUILDING EFFECTIVE SENTENCES   221

Editing Check 13

Combine sentences in this paragraph by using prepositional and participial phrases and appositives. The sentences are numbered as a guide.

¹People have been trying to hide or get rid of body odour. They have tried for a long time. ²The ancient Egyptians were among the first to avoid "offending." They used scented oils under their arms. ³People favoured two spices. They were citrus and cinnamon. ⁴The body uses perspiration to cool off. The body can secrete several litres a day in hot weather. ⁵A product to fight underarm odour was introduced. It was introduced in 1888. ⁶It was called Mum. It was soon followed by other deodorants.

Checkpoint 13-1

In the first five sentences, identify the underlined words as a prepositional phrase (Prep), a participial phrase (Part), or an appositive (Ap).

_____ 1. One of the earliest eye drops, <u>used in China 5000 years ago</u>, was made from the mahuang plant.

_____ 2. The solution contained ephedrine hydrochloride, <u>an ingredient still used today to treat eye irritations</u>.

_____ 3. <u>In Germany in the late nineteenth century</u>, Hermann von Helmholtz made an important contribution to eye care.

_____ 4. He invented the ophthalmoscope, <u>a device for examining the eye's interior</u>.

_____ 5. In 1890, Otis Hall, <u>a banker in Spokane, Washington</u>, accidentally helped bring about one of the best-known eye solutions.

Identify the next five sentences as simple (S), compound (C), or complex (X).

_____ 6. As he looked at a horse's broken shoe, Otis Hall was struck in the eye by a flick of the horse's tail.

_____ 7. His cornea was cut by the blow, and it became infected.

_____ 8. His injury was treated by two eye specialists, brothers James and George McFatrich.

_____ 9. Impressed by his quick recovery, Hall joined the brothers in a firm to market their eyedrops, which contained muriate of berberine.

_____ 10. They combined the first and last syllables of the medicine for the market name Murine.

Checkpoint 13-2

Identify the underlined words as a prepositional phrase (Prep), a participial phrase (Part), or an appositive (Ap).

_____ 1. Between Susan and Fred was a low fence.

_____ 2. Angered by the remark, the cowboy rode away.

_____ 3. We vacationed in Jamaica, a wonderful country.

_____ 4. Old Faithful, a geyser in Yellowstone Park, spouts 125 million litres of water a day.

_____ 5. The judge, drinking lemon soda, gave a satisfied smile.

_____ 6. The family doctor, Edwin Goff, is away on vacation.

_____ 7. Lying in the sun, the cat was taking a nap.

_____ 8. The manager, disappointed by poor sales, locked the store.

_____ 9. Sylvia, my best friend, is changing jobs.

_____ 10. The book, covered by dust, had not been opened for years.

No answers are given for Checkpoint quizzes.

WORDCHECK: FOREIGN WORDS

Words and expressions from other languages make their way into English. Look up the meanings of the italicized words in these sentences. Note what language they come from.

1. Cedric had a sense of *déjà vu* as he entered the English class.
2. Rebecca shouted, "*Shalom!*" as her friends drove away.
3. Mark said he would repay Al's loan *mañana*.
4. His rude attitude made William a *persona non grata* at the party.
5. Marcia's wedding was a *fait accompli* by the time John arrived at the church to propose.

14

AN ESSAY USING PERSUASION

READING: PERSUADING OTHERS TO SHARE ONE'S VIEWS

Precheck

"You are what you eat" is an expression that has taken on a whole new meaning these days, as many of us don't know *what* we are eating! In the following article, Flora Lewis asks readers to think about the number of health risks they are confronted with. Writers often try to persuade readers to think or act in a certain way, and in this article, Lewis uses examples to argue that we need much more reliable information.

Journal Topic

What do you know about Dolly and the cloning of animals? What are your sources for scientific information? What is your point of view on topics such as genetic engineering and genetic modification?

Mad Cows, Funny Plants, Uranium Dust and Such –Flora Lewis

There is something that depleted uranium weapons, genetically manipulated plants and beef from countries exposed to mad cow disease have in common, and it is the reason for so much distress. They are all possible health dangers about which the public feels improperly informed, perhaps deliberately misled. 1

cumulative gradually increasing, becoming greater

This is a cumulative problem. It doesn't matter so much that these are specific questions with separate and unrelated causes, as that official explanations are no longer quite credible. 2

There have been too many cases of failure to be candid, whether from ignorance or in order to cover up embarrassment, as in the French incidents of HIV-contaminated blood being used for transfusions because locally produced tests were not ready and the authorities did not want to admit the need to import foreign ones. 3

223

The whole history of atomic weapons is dotted with cases of misinformation. Secrecy justified by security reasons has been used to hide risks to unwitting civilians, whether they were made to be guinea pigs or simply exposed to pollution.

There is no way that the ordinary person can verify any of the assertions about precautions that have been taken or the harmlessness of new scientific measures. In food production, industrial techniques are used more and more with questionable results—cows and chickens and pigs raised in tiny spaces and fed with dubious manufactured meal and drugs (antibiotics and hormones) to alter normal growth and fattening. It makes food cheaper but less reliable.

The reports on these various questions seem to trickle out, suddenly raising doubts about what had been assumed to be safe practices, and they are often contradictory. There is evidently a risk of conflict between significant economic interests and the basic interest of public health, and not adequate evidence that health is always put first.

In the case of depleted uranium, civilians have not been involved except in battle areas where the arms have been exploded, but large numbers of troops from many countries have been exposed.

There is convincing proof that the uranium metal in unexploded weapons presents no danger; the radiation level is low and the rays do not penetrate skin. But when it is pulverized into dust, it can be inhaled and accumulate to dangerous levels inside the body.

NATO has cited independent scientists assuring that there is no connection between these weapons and the cases of leukemia reported particularly among Italian soldiers, but what of other cancers? NATO itself is obviously an interested party, and the general record of officialdom in all these cases is such that the public is naturally skeptical.

There are so many complex new materials, inventions, techniques that the public uses in one way or another but cannot possibly know enough about to make rational judgments on the risk involved. José Bové, the French farm militant, rails against *"la malbouffe"* (mad cow), but the point is not whether we eat less well at less cost but whether we know what we are eating and its effects.

One way or another, individual governments have lost automatic public confidence in their pronouncements on a whole variety of issues that only recognized scientific experts can settle. Politicians don't know any more about the details than other citizens.

But there are no international organizations to which the questions can be referred. The World Health Organization does an impressive job fighting infectious and endemic diseases, a recognition of the principle that germs know no boundaries and neither should health. But it is not adapted to giving advice on new products, new drugs, new devices, advice which people need so as not to feel dependent on sources with interests involved.

This is another aspect of the globalization development, a new requirement because of the new patterns of trade, communications and even defense. The feeling that you can't trust what you are told, and can't find out for yourself, is an important element of the unease and discontent afflicting affluent societies and provoking protests that have no constructive proposals.

There has to be a good deal more effort to supply the kind of information that people can rely on as they go about their lives if they are not to believe only in fantasies. With so many bewildering claims and counterclaims demanding attention, credibility is more important than ever. It is a basis for peace and stability.

Checking Meaning and Style

1. What do depleted uranium weapons, modified plants, and mad cows have in common?
2. What was the embarrassment that the French tried to cover up?
3. What are animals fed with and what is the result?
4. What are Lewis's three main examples of possible public health risks?
5. What is an "important element of the unease"?

Checking Ideas

1. In many cases, how has secrecy been justified by authorities?
2. What is the conflict in interests that results in public ignorance?
3. Why is it not possible for the public to verify what they hear about harmlessness or safety precautions?
4. What is the problem with individual governments?
5. Why has the World Health Organization not been able to give advice?
6. Do you agree with Flora Lewis? Has she raised issues that you, too, would like to see addressed more openly?

Netcheck

Look up Dolly the sheep in a search engine and see how many sources of information you can find about the cloning event.

WRITING MODELS: USING PERSUASION

Writers often want to persuade others to share their views or to take a certain course of action—to buy a Spitfire SX, to vote for a certain political party, to oppose or support trade barriers. Flora Lewis wanted to raise awareness about the need for credibility in information sources.

In the following paragraph (condensed and paraphrased from an actual advertisement), Planned Parenthood Federation tries to persuade readers to pressure the television industry to change the way it handles commercials and programs that deal with sex.

Model Persuasion Paragraph

<u>Television is irresponsible in its treatment of sex, and viewers should complain to the networks</u>. Teenage viewers see thousands of sexual scenes each year that promote the idea of frequent and unprotected sex. The scenes rarely if ever suggest that the lovers are concerned about unintended pregnancies. These programs contribute to the more than 1 million teen pregnancies a year and to the resulting school dropouts, broken families, welfare costs, and abortions. Network executives should be told that they have other responsibilities in using the public airwaves besides pushing products and making money.

"Mad Cows, Funny Plants, Uranium Dust and Such" provides persuasive arguments that highlight the public's ignorance on important matters. You might want to use persuasive writing techniques—to convince income tax officials that you really don't owe more taxes, for example, or to convince a sweetheart in a distant city that she or he should marry you. Many of the paragraphs you have already written for this class were meant to persuade, even though you might not have thought of them in that way. If your topic sentence reads, "English classes are a waste of time," your paragraph should argue your point convincingly. In other classes you may need to "prove" in a term paper or exam that John Lennon was a greater composer than Mozart, or that NATO should not send troops to settle disputes in Europe.

Let's say that you want to write a paper showing that grades in college should be abolished. Here are some of the techniques of persuasion you might use:

1. Cite *facts or statistics* on student health problems or suicides blamed on grade worries.

2. Quote *expert authorities* who argue that grades inspire negative competition rather than positive cooperation.

3. Give *examples from history* showing that college students have not always been graded.

4. Offer *current examples* of colleges that don't assign grades.

5. Present a *narrative (anecdote)* about a rich and famous inventor who flunked out of college.

6. Give a *description* of a classroom full of students agonizing over an exam.

7. Describe a *personal experience*—the time you got a rash over a D in algebra.

Model Persuasion Essay

In this essay on work, notice that several techniques are used to persuade the reader.

Introduction with thesis statement underlined

Some observers say that North Americans work too hard. They point out that many workers put in longer hours on the job these days, sometimes for less money; moreover, increasing numbers of workers take second jobs to maintain their standard of living. To make matters worse, workers often find the drive to and from the job more and more time-consuming and frustrating. Is the solution a shorter work week with no reduction in pay, as some suggest? <u>Such a change could have both benefits and drawbacks, but is a good idea overall.</u>

Body with first support—topic sentence underlined

<u>A 30-hour work week could have many advantages for workers and their families.</u> For one thing, parents would have more time to spend with their children to strengthen the family ties that seem to be loosening these days. Not only would parents have the leisure to talk and play games with their children, they would also still have the energy to do so at the end of the workday. Increased leisure would permit workers to pursue hobbies and other interests that could enrich their own lives and refresh them for the return to work. There would also be more time for community activities. When the PTA at the children's school asks for help in the annual fundraiser, help is more likely to be offered.

Body with second support

A pessimist, however, might see a downside to a 30-hour work week and the increased leisure it would bring. Not everyone would use this time constructively. If more time off means more time in front of the TV drinking beer and eating chips, no great gain (except in weight) will be made. Increased leisure could lead to an increase in what often seems to be a favourite pastime: visiting the mall and buying items not needed with money better spent in other ways. Finally, increased time together could result in increased family tensions, arguments, and, in a worst-case scenario, family violence.

Body with third support

Rudy, my neighbour, is an example of both the good and the bad sides of increased leisure. He is now a "telecommuter," working at home four days a week and going to the office only on Fridays. Assuming that he actually does put in eight hours a day for his employer, he still saves four to six hours a week in driving time and another hour or so by not shaving as often. How does he use this new leisure? On the plus side, he plays tennis several times a week with his son. The other day Rudy attended a conference with his daughter's grade six teacher. And while Rudy and I were working in our yards last week (I'm glad to say he mows his lawn more often now), he told me how much fun the family was having in the evenings playing whist. However, his arguments with his wife seem to have increased. I heard her complain that since he was home so much, he should do more of the housework. She told my wife that Rudy spends far too much time and money surfing the Internet and buying the latest software. But I don't expect them to come to blows.

Conclusion

Increased leisure is a mixed blessing, but on the whole it's a benefit that more workers should receive.

WRITING ASSIGNMENT: A PERSUASION ESSAY

Persuade the reader to accept your viewpoint on one of these topics: work, education, marriage, television, popular music, or a topic you feel strongly about.

Writing Assignment Checklist

✓ Organize your essay with a thesis sentence and topic sentences similar to those that follow. Your thesis sentence should clearly state the point you intend to make.

> The growing scarcity of leisure, the lack of time for families to be together, and the hours spent commuting show the need for a 30-hour work week (a 4-day work week).
>
> My work and school schedules are too demanding.
>
> Many workers do (not) make good use of their leisure time.

Use this outline to organize your ideas:

Thesis _____

_____

First support _____
_____

Second support _____
_____

Third support _____
_____

Conclusion _____
_____

✓ Use prewriting techniques to make the preliminary outline and to develop the body of the essay. Asking how and why would have been helpful in developing the model essay.

✓ When revising the first draft, check to be sure that your thesis is clearly stated and developed with techniques to persuade readers.

✓ Do not only correct such things as grammar and punctuation, but also look for ways to improve the content and organization.

✓ Centre a title on the top line of the first page.

✓ Proofread the final copy carefully.

SENTENCE STRUCTURE: SOLVING SENTENCE PROBLEMS

We will now consider an assortment of problems that can weaken sentences: misplaced modifiers, dangling modifiers, nonparallel construction, other mixed constructions, faulty comparison, and passive constructions.

Notice what happens when we move the word *only* around in the following sentences:

Stan <u>only</u> borrowed five dollars. (He didn't steal the money.)

Stan borrowed <u>only</u> five dollars. (He would have liked more.)

<u>Only</u> Stan borrowed five dollars. (His friends had enough money already.)

We see that it is important to position words in a sentence carefully, especially words that change the meaning of other words. Such words are called **modifiers**.

A modifier should usually be near the word(s) it describes to avoid what is called a *misplaced modifier*. Sometimes the error is unintentionally amusing.

(misplaced) Antonia bought a used car from a local dealer with weak headlights. (The *dealer* had weak headlights?)

(revised) Antonia bought a used car with weak headlights from a local dealer.

(misplaced) Tony was given a horse by the rancher that was old and swaybacked. (The *rancher* was old and swaybacked?)

(revised) The rancher gave Tony a horse that was old and swaybacked.

The lesson is clear: Put modifiers near the words they modify.

Be especially careful with the modifiers *almost, only, just, even, hardly,* and *nearly*. They go in front of the words they modify.

Roderick ~~almost~~ ate almost the entire pizza by himself.

Kimberly ~~nearly~~ saved nearly six dollars by buying the dress on sale.

Spotcheck 14-1

Rewrite each of the following sentences to correct misplaced modifiers.

1. Leah bought a new handbag at a downtown store with a silk lining.
   _____

2. A cowboy's 10-gallon hat only holds 1.5 gallons of water.
   _____

3. Min saw an accident driving home from work.
   _____

4. Gloria even likes her new baby when he cries.
   _____

5. The average marriage in Canada only lasts 12.4 years.
   _____

Avoiding Dangling Modifiers

A modifier is said to "dangle" if it lacks a clear connection to the word it is supposed to modify.

(dangling) Arriving home from work, the dog greeted Elena at the front door.

Of course it was Elena, not the dog, who arrived home. The modifier "arriving home from work" dangles. A modifier that begins a sentence should usually be followed immediately by the word it modifies.

(revised) Arriving home from work, Elena was greeted at the front door by the dog.

(option) When Elena arrived home from work, the dog greeted her at the door.

(option) The dog greeted Elena at the door when she arrived home from work.

Spotcheck 14-2

Rewrite the following sentences to eliminate dangling modifiers.

1. Growing careless, the wrong name was entered by the clerk.
   _____

2. Although 21 years old, my father expected me to be in by midnight.
   _____

3. Able to bend steel bars with ease, I watched Mighty Mo in awe.
   _____

4. Vacation rushed to an end, playing tennis during the day and dancing at night.
   _____

5. Contentedly eating grass, Solomon took a photo of the cows.
   _____

Using Parallel Construction

Similar ideas are easier to read if they are in the same grammatical form—that is, if they have **parallel construction**. Compare the following pairs of sentences:

Not parallel	**Parallel**
Seeing is to believe.	Seeing is believing.
Kimberly likes to sail, to swim, and skiing.	Kimberly likes to sail, to swim, and to ski.
Naomi is not only smart, she has a lot of luck.	Naomi is not only smart, she is lucky.
Aspiring models should be attractive, tall, and not be overweight.	Aspiring models should be attractive, tall, and slender.

If the topic sentence of a paragraph or the thesis sentence of an essay lists several points, be sure to put them in parallel form.

(not parallel) Among the advantages of attending a community college are the low tuition, the small class size, and because it is close to my home.

(parallel) Among the advantages of attending a community college are the low tuition, the small class size, and the convenient location.

The first example has two nouns (*tuition* and *class size*) before switching to a dependent clause (*because it...*). The correction replaces the clause with a third noun, *location*.

Spotcheck 14-3

Revise the underlined segments to achieve parallel construction.

1. Whether right or when he is wrong, Larry likes to argue.
   _____
   _____

SENTENCE STRUCTURE: SOLVING SENTENCE PROBLEMS   **231**

2. After playing soccer all afternoon, Matty was tired, thirsty, and <u>he needed a bath</u>.

3. Henry believes that having a good family life is more important than <u>to have a lot of money</u>.

4. Working at Ajax Repair has taught me not only how to fix cars but also <u>getting along with people</u>.

5. Terrie was bright but <u>being lazy</u>.

6. Many industries are moving from the North to the South in the United States because wages are lower, the climate is often more pleasant, and <u>offers greater recreational opportunities</u>.

Avoiding Mixed Constructions

Do not start a sentence in one direction and then, without reason, go off in another.

(mixed) Because he was bored caused him to sleep in class.
(better) Because he was bored, he slept in class.

(mixed) When Tony gets home early pleases his wife.
(better) When Tony gets home early, his wife is pleased.

(mixed) The best part of a baseball game is where [is when] they hit home runs.
(better) Home runs are the best part of a baseball game.

Spotcheck 14-4

Revise the following sentences to eliminate mixed constructions.

1. Because she was hungry caused her to eat a late-night snack.

2. When Sally gets a raise pleases her family.

3. Although sunshine is forecast, but Rocky has his umbrella.

4. A good sale is when I am happy.

Avoiding Faulty Comparisons

Be sure that comparisons are completed.

(incomplete) Puffy cigarettes have less nicotine. (less than what?)
(better) Puffy cigarettes have less nicotine <u>than Gaspers do</u>.
(or) Puffy cigarettes have less nicotine <u>than tar</u>.

(incomplete) Plumbers charge more.
(better) Plumbers charge more <u>than they should</u>.

Be sure that comparisons are clear.

(unclear) The days in July are longer than December. (*Days* is compared to the month *December*.)
(better) The days in July are longer than <u>those</u> [or <u>the days</u>] in December.

Watch out for incomplete comparisons using the words *so*, *such*, and *too*. Careful writers will not stop short of the bracketed words in these sentences.

It was <u>so</u> hot yesterday [that I went swimming].

He is <u>such</u> an intelligent student [that he should do well in college].

The sunset was <u>too</u> beautiful [for me to describe].

(or) The sunset was beautiful.

Spotcheck 14-5

Revise the following sentences to eliminate faulty comparisons.

1. Polly is a lot smarter.

2. The trees in the spring are greener than the fall.

3. A Jeep Comanche looks better and goes faster.

4. The summers in Victoria are hotter than Vancouver.

5. A compact disc can hold more songs.

6. A sandwich from home costs far less than the cafeteria.

7. The dinner was so delicious.

_____

8. I asked Tim did he expect to make the team.

_____

Active vs. Passive Voice

Compare these two sentences:

Spike Owen hit two home runs Sunday.

Two home runs were hit by Spike Owen Sunday.

In the first sentence, the subject (Spike Owen) *acts;* in the second, the subject (home runs) *receives* the action of the verb *were hit*. The first sentence is in the *active voice*, the second in the *passive voice*.

You should generally use the more vigorous active voice. However, you may prefer the passive voice if the receiver of the action is more important than the doer. For example, the first of these two sentences might be preferred in some cases.

(passive) Thirty-two home runs were hit by American League batters in games Sunday. (emphasizes the home runs)

(active) American League batters hit 32 home runs in games Sunday. (emphasizes the American League batters)

Spotcheck 14-6

*In the blanks, write **A** if the sentence is in active voice, **P** if it is in passive voice.*

_____ 1. The country road was littered with bottles and paper.

_____ 2. Marietta read three novels during summer vacation.

_____ 3. The tire was removed by Robert.

_____ 4. The grass has been cut by Thomas only twice.

_____ 5. The fishermen repaired their nets.

Spotcheck 14-7

Change the following sentences from passive voice to active voice.

1. The holdup was seen by two customers.

_____

2. Carrie was praised by the teacher.

_____

3. All employees were notified of the layoffs by the company.

_____

_____

4. People over 65 were offered discounts at the store.

   _____

   _____

5. The essays were all written by students.

   _____

Doublecheck 14-1

Use the lettered items to identify the problem in each of these sentences.

A. Misplaced or dangling modifier D. Faulty comparison
B. Nonparallel construction E. Passive voice
C. Mixed construction

_____ 1. The wings of hummingbirds travel much faster.

_____ 2. Although the sun had gone down, the lake still shining in the distance.

_____ 3. The guide showed us the waterfalls, the lake, and where the trails went to the caves.

_____ 4. The window was closed by Raymond.

_____ 5. While studying in the library, the lights went out.

_____ 6. Ernie is good at ping-pong, chess, and playing backgammon.

_____ 7. The movie *Black Robe* was a lot longer.

_____ 8. The concert was attended by 10 000 fans.

Editing Check 14

Edit the following paragraph to correct any nonparallel or mixed constructions, dangling modifiers, passive voice sentences, and faulty comparisons.

¹The Academy Awards organization gave no prize for best sound effects at the first awards ceremony in 1928. ²That's because all the entries being silent films. ³Although thought of as "golden," mostly tin was what the statuette called Oscar was actually made of. ⁴The winning film that year, *Wings*, only had a small part for an actor named Gary Cooper, becoming better known when the "talkies" arrived. ⁵Originally broadcast on radio, the first television show wasn't aired until 1952. ⁶For creating Mickey Mouse, an award went to Walt Disney in 1932. ⁷One of the films that movie fans watch on TV more often, *Casablanca*,

SENTENCE STRUCTURE: SOLVING SENTENCE PROBLEMS   **235**

was named best picture in 1943. [8]A nonactor got much of the attention at the 1973 awards, when an advertising man got backstage, stripped off his clothes, and streaking past the footlights.

Checkpoint 14-1

Match the letter identifying the following sentence problems with the sentences below.

A. Misplaced or dangling modifier
B. Nonparallel or mixed construction
C. Faulty comparison
D. Passive voice

_____ 1. Stacy put the cookies back in the box she hadn't eaten.
_____ 2. The tennis player is quick and moves gracefully.
_____ 3. Ned would rather play basketball than to play football.
_____ 4. While driving to work, the radio announced a fire on Front Street.
_____ 5. Reginald Foster is a lot smarter.
_____ 6. To pay the rent is where my money goes.
_____ 7. Because he was tired was the reason Mr. Flores left the office early.
_____ 8. While away from the desk, the phone rang and rang.
_____ 9. The award was accepted by Jocelyn gratefully.
_____ 10. Nine out of ten housewives say Shiny is better.
_____ 11. Nguyen is a loyal friend, a diligent student, and good at tennis.
_____ 12. The exam was passed by most of the students.

Checkpoint 14-2

Match the letter identifying the following sentence problems with the sentences below.

A. Misplaced or dangling modifier
B. Parallel construction needed
C. Mixed construction
D. Faulty comparison
E. Passive voice

_____ 1. The paint on our house lasts longer.

_____ 2. Because he was hungry was why Andre hurried home.

_____ 3. The Flames only scored one goal against the Oilers.

_____ 4. The pencil was sharpened by the secretary.

_____ 5. He found the letter in a pile of trash from the governor.

_____ 6. Cynthia can't decide whether to go by train or should she fly.

_____ 7. The sunset was too beautiful!

_____ 8. Hiding behind the sofa, Angela found the kitten.

No answers are given for Checkpoint quizzes.

WORDCHECK: ABBREVIATIONS

The dictionary lists abbreviations just as it does words, in alphabetical order. For example, the airport abbreviation ETD ("estimated time of departure") appears right after the word *etching*.

Look up the meanings of these abbreviations:

1. etc.
2. e.g.
3. NATO
4. SPCA
5. mm

15 USING MIXED MODES

READING: AN INTERNET SUCCESS

Precheck For the past weeks, when you have done the Netcheck exercises, you probably used several different search engines. There are many to choose from, but in the following article Simon Crerar argues that only one is a winner: Google.com.

Why Google Should Be Your First Choice
–Simon Crerar

1 Consider these questions: Who left the last footprint on the moon? What was the name of Julius Caesar's wife? When was penicillin discovered? Where is the most isolated island on earth? Now think how you would find the answers. For those in the know, only one search engine will do, and 150 million times a day, this online sleuth delivers results at breathtaking speed.

indispensable something that one cannot do without

2 In the time it has taken for Google.com to become arguably the most indispensable website on the planet, the verb "to google" has appeared in the language. Little wonder that it has just been signed to power BBC's much-publicised search facility.

3 The great attraction? In the words of one convert: "Relevance, relevance, relevance." By a marvel of mathematics, Google is that rarest of search tools, one that responds intelligently and with cunning. If something succeeds, people use it. The research firm Nielsen/NetRatings calculates that Google is more than twice as popular as its nearest rival, Yahoo.

4 Arrive at Google's clutter-free home page and you can see why. Where blinking banner ads and World Cup betting offers irritate visitors to Lycos, and distracting auctions, ring tones and featured stories blight Yahoo, Google is efficiency itself.

raised the bar taken (quality) to a higher level

5 "There is no doubt that Google has raised the bar on the quality users should expect from a web search service," says Danny Sullivan, editor of the industry website SearchEngineWatch.com.

phenomenal astounding

6 Sullivan's readers agree: 66% voted Google the outstanding search service last year. In their words, Google is "easy to use and uncluttered," consistently gives good results despite the phenomenal growth in "coverage," and has "no pop-up

237

ads, or pop-unders." One enthusiast confirms what its legion of fans knows: "Usually, I find what I need in the first 10 results."

7 Does "googling" require any skill on the part of the user? It always pays to fine-tune terms according to the strengths of the chosen search engine, but that is much less necessary with Google. Follow our search tips over the page, enter your query and hit return. Nine times out of ten, this cheetah-like engine captures what you seek in the blink of an eye. This is no mean feat, because Google **rummages** through an index of more than two billion web pages, twice as many as its nearest rival, Sweden's Alltheweb.com. The answers to our sample questions? Easy: Gene Cernan, Calpurnia, 1928, and the isolated island of Bouvetoya, which is located 990 miles off Antarctica.

rummages skims

8 Set up in 1998 by Larry Page and Sergey Brin, two computer students then at Stanford University, near San Francisco, Google earned a reputation so rapidly that one rival after another has adopted it under licence.

9 What does Google have that its rivals do not? Its PageRank search technology, among other things. Put simply, this keeps tabs on the vast number of links between websites to indicate an individual site's true worth. In essence, when you link from www.mypage.com to www.yourpage.com, that is a vote. As well as the volume of votes, Google also considers the importance of the web pages that are voting. Married with sophisticated "text-matching" techniques that consider the content of each page, this egalitarian approach is well suited to the democratic nature of the web.

10 What scope is left for the competition?

11 "There is a lot of room for others," claims Paul Gardi of Ask Jeeves. "You may love Coca-Cola, but you wouldn't want to drink it at every meal." That is true, but like Coke, Google is leader of the pack. According to Sullivan: "The real fight is for who is number two."

12 Having redefined web searching, Google is determined not to rest on its laurels. Last year, Sullivan says, the engine "unveiled a dizzying array of new features and services."

13 Suppose little Johnny needs a photo of a killer whale for his school biology project. Click on Google Image Search and choose from more than 4,000 orcas (do ask for permission before copying one). Having problems attaching a zip to your daughter's graduation dress? Find help in the rec.crafts.textiles.sewing newsgroup in Google Groups (home to 700 million messages). Similar websites are gathered together in Google's Directory; it categorises 1.5 million web addresses and 20,000 volunteer editors summarise them. It is organised with an intelligence seemingly neglected by the directory pioneer, Yahoo, which struggles to fulfil its slogan: "The Only Place Anyone Needs to Go to Find Anything, Communicate With Anyone, or Buy Anything."

conspicuously clearly

14 Google is also **conspicuously** free, and you never feel pressured to buy a thing. If you do want to shop, however, you will find what you seek far more quickly with a Google search than through shopping directories such as uk.shopsmart.com. Simply enter your desired product and add UK, e.g., golf equipment UK. To the right of the results, based on popularity, will appear Sponsored Links, adverts that complement rather than distract from your search results.

15 According to the internet statisticians www.onestat.com, last month, 46% of web searchers began their hunt at Google, while only 20% started at Yahoo. That 20% were employing Google anyway, as it has powered all Yahoo inquiries since July 2000.

Can Google be improved? The superb map, stock price and telephone book search facilities are currently limited to sources in the United States, and with such a huge database, its SafeSearch filtering does not entirely eliminate sexual content. Google's Larry Page says that the perfect search engine "would understand exactly what you mean, and give you back exactly what you want." While Page and Brin's baby has made significant strides (no doubt helped by the 50 PhDs among Google's 150 technical staff), Brin concedes that "there is much more work to be done before it becomes the ultimate search engine." 16

Googlers are on board for the long haul. Rivals such as Ask Jeeves and Lycos blew millions of pounds advertising their services, but Google's growth has been fuelled by the infectious enthusiasm of converts. As one voter in the SearchEngineWatch.com awards said: "My girlfriend, who knows nothing about computers, tried Google once. Now not only does she exclusively use Google, but tells all her friends to as well. When was the last time a search engine provoked true word-of-mouth advertising?" 17

Google is currently testing a news search engine, which pools sources as diverse as the *Bangkok Post* and *The Jamaica Observer*. And last month, the company announced Google Answers, a paid-for service that enables you to ask trained researchers questions for a fee that you set. Master the engine effectively, though, and you will never need to part with your cash at all. 18

Checking Meaning and Style

1. Why does Crerar refer to Google as an "online sleuth"?
2. How does the opening paragraph attract the reader?
3. What statistics does Crerar use to support his argument?
4. In what paragraph do you find a process?
5. In paragraph 13, how is the topic sentence developed?

Checking Ideas

1. What is Google compared to, and where is "the real fight"?
2. In what ways has Google raised the bar on quality?
3. When you are doing a search, what is it always best to do, even on Google.com?
4. How does Google maintain its integrity with PageRank?
5. How does Google advertise?

HINTS FOR SUCCESSFUL GOOGLING

Idiot-Proof Searches

If you managed to master your ABCs at school, then learning to google will be a breeze. Simply type a few descriptive words in the search field at google.com and hit Enter. To research a holiday in Ibiza, for example, type "holiday Ibiza." To restrict the search further, simply include more terms, e.g., "holiday Ibiza San Antonio."

Brush Up Your Spelling

If you are a lousy typist, do not worry, because if you misspell your query (e.g., "corect my speling"), then, like a high-tech Dr. Johnson, Google automatically suggests an option (e.g., Did you mean: correct my spelling?) Click on the red link for a satisfactory answer. For each search word that Google recognizes, it also provides a link to a Dictionary.com definition; click on the underlined word in the blue Results bar.

Expect Options

Google ignores common words such as "where" and "it", because they slow down searches without improving results. If such a word is essential, include it by putting a + sign in front (e.g., +how does +it feel). If what you are searching for has more than one meaning, exclude a word by placing a - sign before it (e.g., bass -music, to find fish from the sea instead of Fish from Marillion). To search for words in a particular order, enclose them in quotes (e.g., "Atomic Kitten's official Web site").

Psychic Powers

Google is so confident it can find exactly what you are searching for that its "I'm Feeling Lucky" button goes directly to the top-ranking site for your query. This works best when looking for a company (e.g., Pret A Manger), institution (e.g., Houses of Parliament) or event (e.g., Royal Ascot).

It Never Sleeps

Not only is Google always on, but if your search reveals a suitable-sounding site that is temporarily unavailable, click on the Cached link to see how the site looked on the last occasion Google visited it; invaluable in bypassing the Internet's glitches.

Parlez-Vous Google?

You can google in 35 languages, from Arabic to Turkish. If you find an intriguing page in French, German, Italian, Portuguese, or Spanish, the search engine will do its best to translate it on the fly (click on Translate This Page). Those who cannot search in their own language, such as Afrikaan and Welsh speakers, can become a volunteer translator. To set your language, see www.google.com/preferences.

Local Sites for Local People

Although based in California, Google is the UK search engine *par excellence*, which is why it is the backbone of the BBC. For UK-focused results, simply add UK to your query or go to google.co.uk and click Pages from the UK. For services only in a specific city, type that city's name (e.g., Chinese restaurants Edinburgh).

Spice Up Your Life

More effective than Friends Reunited, googling is mushrooming among cyber-savvy daters, who run secret searches on potential dates to see if they are worth the effort. Simply enter the person's name and hit Search, remembering that common names will yield unmanageable results.

Netcheck

Go to the home sites of Lycos, Yahoo! and Google and compare their results on a search of your choice.

WRITING MODELS: THE MIXED MODE ESSAY

Using this text, you have practised a variety of methods for developing your ideas in paragraphs and essays—comparision, narration, description, process and other modes.

As you have seen in Simon Crerar's essay, most writers use a combination of methods. Crerar uses examples, statistics, and process to describe Google's success. His essay could be written in five paragraphs that follow this plan:

- Introduction—Google.com has had enormous success as a search engine, with good reason.
- Body 1—Google.com is "clutter-free."
- Body 2—Google.com is easy to use.
- Body 3—Google.com's PageRank explains its success.
- Conclusion—Google.com does not even have to advertise, but its innovations keep arriving.

Study the following essays.

Model Mixed Mode Essay #1

In an essay that she wrote in high school, Erica Van Gorder used an anecdote to introduce her thesis about the consequences of not informing teenagers realistically about alcohol abuse.

Let's Get Realistic about Teenage Drinking

Introduction with thesis statement

A few weeks ago, a younger friend of mine decided to have a little fun and get drunk before going to a high school dance. Her parents were away, so she consumed an entire 26-ounce [750 mL] bottle of vodka. When her friends got her to the hospital, she spent the night being closely monitored in case her heart stopped beating, a result of the tremendous amount of alcohol that had invaded her body. We as teenagers are all aware that alcohol isn't exactly "healthy," but when we think of death and alcohol, we think of drinking and driving and alcoholics. <u>What many teenagers need to be informed about is that alcohol has a lethal limit, and the consequences if they pass it.</u>

1st support with topic sentence and consequences

<u>Drinking is associated with the "good times," like partying and just letting loose.</u> Yet we are bombarded with messages from parents, teachers, and the media that unless we are 19 years old in this country we should "just say no." The result is we react by "just saying yes."

2nd support with topic sentence and reasons

<u>I ask you, is this a realistic request?</u> Teenagers have been drinking before our generation and they will after our generation, and all the public service messages in the world aren't going to change it. When are the media and government going to wake up to reality? Teenagers are going to drink, and that is why we should start to inform them about drinking responsibly.

3rd support with topic sentence and specific details

<u>What many teenagers are not aware of is that drinking has a lethal limit.</u> I'm not talking about the hangover in the morning or "puking the night of." I'm talk-

ing about the dangers of overdoing it. Many teenagers who have their first excessive drinking experience, which usually occurs at a house party, have no idea what their personal "limit" is. Many will drink themselves into oblivion until they either vomit or pass out. All of them are unaware of how close they are to possibly putting their lives at serious risk.

Conclusion with solution

I'm not here to condone teenage drinking; I'm here to say that teens are not made aware of the realities of excessive drinking and the dangers associated with it. <u>Let's get realistic about teenage drinking because if we are more aware of the possible outcomes, then maybe we'll make more informed choices.</u>

We can also see a variety of modes used in the following model mixed mode essay on the future. Study the organization of the essay.

Model Mixed Mode Essay #2

Looking Ahead

Introduction with thesis statement

Like everyone else, I have many goals in life. <u>Two of the most important are getting a solid education and leaving a healthy planet for those who come after me.</u>

1st support with topic sentence and specific details

<u>I want an education that will prepare me not only to get a well-paying and worthwhile career but that will also help me live a satisfying life outside my work.</u> To prepare myself to get a good job, I am majoring in X-ray technology. Careers in radiology (as the field is also called) pay quite well. I would be able to support myself and my family comfortably, and some day, perhaps, I would be able to buy a house in a safe neighbourhood with good schools. But I also want to get what is called a liberal education. For example, I want to take courses in literature and the arts to enrich my leisure time. I want to take courses in psychology and sociology to understand myself and my fellow citizens. I want to take courses in history to see where we humans have come from and where we are headed.

2nd support with topic sentence and specific details

<u>Protecting the environment is also important to me.</u> Like everyone else, I have a duty to leave our Earth in at least as good a condition as I found it. I believe we should all be like those Native Americans whose beliefs required them to consider how their actions would affect the seventh generation of those who followed. One small contribution I can make is to limit the size of my family so as not to contribute to the exploding population growth that threatens the environment and the quality of life for everyone. I can also vote for those political candidates who can look further into the future than the next election.

Conclusion

No one wants to live in poverty, but it is not necessary for us to be rich to be happy, especially if our education has prepared us to lead a full life. At the same time, we cannot be happy if we think we are leaving an unhealthy planet to our grandchildren.

Again, we see an essay organized with thesis and topic sentences. The first body paragraph (paragraph 2) gives specific reasons why the writer wants a good education. The next paragraph argues the need for a healthy planet.

WRITING ASSIGNMENT: AN ESSAY ON LIFE

Choose one of the following topics for your essay. The essay should have an introduction, two or three paragraphs of support, and a conclusion.

1. An essay discussing two or three goals you have that will make your life worthwhile.

2. An essay in which you discuss your life as a college student. You might discuss your weekdays, your weekends, and your summers.

2. An essay in which you discuss how your view of life differs from that of one or both of your parents. Support paragraphs might compare your parents' lives with your own life and goals.

Writing Assignment Checklist

✓ Use prewriting techniques such as asking how and why, freewriting, and journal writing.

✓ As was done in this chapter's reading, consider using different writing modes to develop your ideas. Use any of the methods discussed this term that will make your ideas interesting and convincing.

✓ Be sure to include in the first paragraph a thesis sentence that states what point you want to make in the essay.

✓ Start each support paragraph with a topic sentence.

✓ Revise the essay as many times as needed, watching especially for mistakes made on recent papers.

✓ Centre a title on the top line of the first page.

✓ Proofread the paper carefully before handing it in.

WRITING PROCESS: REVISING—ELIMINATING WORDINESS

Revision literally means to "re-envision," to "see again." If time permits, revise your writing only after you have laid your first draft aside for a while and given yourself a break from the writing process. By putting your work on the "back burner," you can return to it later with a fresh viewpoint, ready to see your work again and improve it.

There are several approaches to polishing a paper. One is to make sure that every word counts—that is, to eliminate wordiness.

Following are some tips for making your writing more concise.

1. Do not pad your writing with unnecessary words.

   (wordy) Due to the fact that her essay had been written with a pencil, Kayla was asked to write it once more, this time with a pen.

   (concise) Kayla was asked to rewrite her essay using a pen instead of a pencil.

2. Notice how one word can take the place of several.

   due to the fact that (because)
   during the time that (while)
   at the present time (now)
   in the near future (soon)
   hold a meeting (meet)

3. Get rid of unneeded words.

   After the class <u>ended</u>, we went to the cafeteria.
   The package was square <u>in shape</u>.
   Rich got home at 3 a.m. <u>in the morning</u>.

4. Do not waste space with such expressions as "it seems to me" and "in my opinion."

   In my humble opinion, (T)he mayor should be thrown out of office.

5. Sentences that begin with *It is*, *It was*, *There is*, or *There are* are often wordy.

   (wordy) There is a need for more widgets in Department B.
   (concise) Department B needs more widgets.
   (wordy) It is clear that Canada has great country music.
   (concise) Canada has great country music.

Spotcheck 15-1

Revise the following sentences to eliminate wordiness.

1. On account of being talented and a good musician, Sheila was chosen to play in the concert.

   _____
   _____

2. Agnes's dress was bright blue in colour.

   _____
   _____

3. Late in the month of June, heavy rain fell on the city and made everything wet.

   _____
   _____

4. Because of the fact that he is a pacifist, Eric opposes war.

   _____

   _____

5. As far as tomorrow night's game is concerned, it seems to me our team should win.

   _____

   _____

6. There are many occasions when we need good advice.

   _____

   _____

WRITING PROCESS: ADJECTIVES AND ADVERBS

Adjectives and adverbs are words that modify or describe other words. When you revise your first draft, use adjectives and adverbs to add colour and precision to your writing.

Adjectives

Adjectives describe nouns or pronouns, as in these examples:

> The campers watched the <u>beautiful</u> sunset. (*Beautiful* describes the noun *sunset*.)
>
> She was <u>optimistic</u>. (*Optimistic* describes the pronoun *she*.)

With most adjectives, add *-er* when comparing two things; add *-est* when comparing three or more things.

> Sheila is <u>taller</u> than Pat.
>
> Sheila is the <u>tallest</u> member of the team.

Longer adjectives become awkward when *-er* or *-est* is added.

> **(awkward)** The teacher is *intelligenter* than the banker.

With long adjectives, use *more* or *most* in front of the adjective instead of *-er* or *-est* at the end of it.

> The teacher is <u>more intelligent</u> than the banker.
>
> The plumber is the <u>most intelligent</u> person in town.

Never use *-er* and *more* together; never use *-est* and *most* together.

> **(wrong)** My dog is <u>more smarter</u> than your dog. (omit *more*)
>
> **(wrong)** That is the <u>most dumbest</u> thing I've ever seen. (omit *most*)

Some adjectives are irregular; that is, they are compared in a different way from the methods just discussed. Be sure to memorize the forms of these adjectives:

good	better	best
bad	worse	worst
many	more	most

Spelling Tip

Adjectives ending in *y* change the *y* to *i* before *-er* or *-est*.

happy   happier   happiest   easy   easier   easiest

Spotcheck 15-2

In the blanks, write the correct form of the adjectives shown in parentheses.

1. (faded) Robert's jeans are _____ than Pete's.
2. (bad) *Scream* was the _____ movie Natalie had ever seen.
3. (happy) Who is _____, Sara or Carrie?
4. (many) The Palladium holds _____ people than the Saddledome.
5. (intelligent) Of the three sisters, Chandra is the _____.

Spotcheck 15-3

Write sentences using the adjectives in parentheses.

1. (closest) _____
2. (less) _____
3. (more skilful) _____
4. (smallest) _____
5. (best) _____

Adverbs

Adverbs describe verbs. They usually end in *-ly*.

> The gas station attendant walked <u>slowly</u> to the pump. (*Slowly* is an adverb describing the verb *walked*.)

> The student <u>gladly</u> gave his bus seat to the old man. (*Gladly* describes the verb *gave*.)

Don't make the mistake of using an adjective instead of an adverb following a verb.

> Thomas spoke ~~angry~~ angrily to the dog's owner.

> The child ran ~~quick~~ quickly to her mother.

In writing, don't leave off the *-ly* in *really* and *easily*.

> The company president was ~~real~~ really angry when the vice-president contradicted him.

> Terry can make an apple pie ~~easy~~ easily.

Mistakes are often made with the words *well* and *good*. *Well* is an adverb; it describes verbs. *Good* is an adjective; it describes nouns and pronouns.

> Morgan is a <u>good</u> tennis player. (*Good* is an adjective modifying the noun *player*.)
>
> Morgan played <u>well</u> in the tournament. (*Well* is an adverb modifying the verb *played*.)

Spotcheck 15-4

Underline the correct word in parentheses.

1. Kevin (quick/quickly) picked up the phone.
2. Annie won the 100-metre dash (easy/easily).
3. The child gazed (envious/enviously) at the candy display.
4. It is (good/well) that Yuko had the spare tire inspected.
5. The basketball team played (good/well) in the conference finals.

The error called a **double negative** occurs when the adverb *not* is used with another negative word. (*Not* is often disguised in such contractions as *can't*, *won't*, *hasn't*, and *couldn't*.)

> **(wrong)** Jessica <u>didn't</u> have <u>no</u> time to go dancing.
>
> **(right)** Jessica <u>didn't</u> have <u>any</u> time to go dancing.
>
> **(right)** Jessica had <u>no</u> time to go dancing.

The words *hardly* and *scarcely* are negative and shouldn't be used with *not*.

> **(wrong)** The millionaire <u>didn't</u> pay <u>hardly</u> any taxes.
>
> **(right)** The millionaire paid <u>hardly</u> any taxes.

WRITING PROCESS: COHERENCE

When sentences and paragraphs follow each other in a clear and logical way, we say that they have **coherence**—they "stick together." When revising your writing, be sure to present your ideas in the most effective order.

Spotcheck 15-5

Number the following lists of items in the most coherent order.

1. An essay on your experience as a student

    _____ High school

    _____ Elementary school

    _____ College

    (This is an example of time order.)

2. A descriptive essay about Orchestra Hall

   _____ Auditorium

   _____ Lobby

   _____ Stage

   (This is an example of space order.)

3. A narrative essay about Little League

   _____ Striking out

   _____ Getting up to bat

   _____ Pitcher throwing ball

   (This is an example of climax order.)

4. An essay with the following thesis statement: "It isn't fair that my brother is allowed to stay out later, do nothing around the house, and take over the car."

   _____ Chores

   _____ Car

   _____ Curfew

   (This is an example of logical order.)

Another way to tie your ideas together is to use **transition words** such as these:

Time-Order Words:
   first   before   then   next   during   meanwhile   afterwards   finally

Space-Order Words:
   next to   nearby   across from   to the left   to the right   above   below

Climax-Order Words:
   consequently   thus   therefore   as a result   in the end

Logical-Order Words:
   first of all   moreover   in addition   furthermore   finally

Spotcheck 15-6

Write appropriate order words in each of the blanks.

1. An essay on your experience as a student (time order)

   _____ I attended grade school.

   _____ I attended high school.

   _____ I attend college.

2. An essay on the view from your front door (space order)

   _____ I see the Quicks' house.

   _____ I see the Baptist church.

   _____ I see Leech Lake.

3. An essay on your uncle's career (time and climax order)

   _____ He was a grocery bagger for 18 months.

   _____ He worked hard.

   _____ He became assistant manager.

WRITING PROCESS: FAULTY LOGIC

Your writing should be logical. If your reader's response is "That doesn't make sense," you have lost your reader. Here are eight common logical fallacies or errors in reasoning:

1. **Hasty Generalization**—A sweeping statement about a group that doesn't take into account likely exceptions; a conclusion based on little evidence ("jumping to a conclusion").

   (illogical) Women workers are underpaid.

   (illogical) French bread is the best in the world.

   Yes, *some*, *many*, *a few* women are underpaid. But the sentence implies that *all* are underpaid, and the reader knows that isn't true. As for the second example, it seems unlikely that the writer has sampled all the breads in the world. Watch out for sentences that use or imply the words *all, every, none, always, never*. Instead use qualifiers such as *many, some, most, the average, sometimes*.

2. **Non Sequitur**—These Latin words mean "it doesn't follow." Here's an argument in which the conclusion "doesn't follow" the evidence offered:

   (illogical) Maria had a frown on her face yesterday, so she must have flunked her history exam. (Her frown has many possible explanations.)

3. **Bandwagon**—The fact that most people favour something is not necessarily a reason for everyone to "get on the bandwagon."

   (illogical) The Reform candidate is leading in the polls, so I guess I should vote for him.

4. **Either–Or Fallacy**—Saying there are only two choices or possibilities when there are actually more.

   (illogical) Either I get some new clothes, or I'll never get a girlfriend.

5. **Circular Reasoning**—"Proving" a point by restating it (going around in a circle).

   (illogical) Professor Jones is a poor teacher because his classes are no good.

6. **Ad Hominem**—"To the man." Attacking a person's ideas by attacking the person. Also, appealing to the emotions rather than to reason.

   (illogical) How can you agree with Joe Smith's politics? He's been divorced three times.

   (illogical) Vote for Margaret Smathers; she lost both her children in a car accident.

7. **Post Hoc, Ergo Propter Hoc** (*Post Hoc*, for short)—"After this, therefore because of this." Wrongly assuming that because one event follows another it is caused by the first event.

   (illogical) It's no use washing my car. The last two times I did, it rained.

8. **Glittering Generalities**—Gaining favour with nice-sounding words that have little meaning by themselves.

   (illogical) If elected, I will restore liberty, honour, and patriotism to this great nation.

Spotcheck 15-7

Identify the logical fallacies in these examples.

1. Everyone else cuts class, so why shouldn't I do it?

   Fallacy:_____

2. Either everybody stops using paper products, or we soon won't have any more trees.

   Fallacy:_____

3. The reason I like that band's music is that it sounds so good.

   Fallacy:_____

4. You just know that anyone on welfare is lazy.

   Fallacy:_____

5. Angela has a nice smile, so she will be good in sales.

   Fallacy:_____

6. Football players advertise beer, so drinking must improve athletic ability.

   Fallacy:_____

7. If we don't go to a movie tonight, the evening will be wasted.

   Fallacy:_____

8. Since everyone is getting a personal computer, I should too.

   Fallacy: _____

9. I went to a movie last night, and today I got an A in algebra. I'm going to go to a movie before all of my tests.

   Fallacy: _____

10. You look like a smart person. You'll probably want to buy some life insurance.

    Fallacy: _____

Doublecheck 15-1

Match the letters identifying the following sentence errors with the appropriate sentences that follow.

A. Wordiness

B. Adjective or adverb misused

C. Logic error

_____ 1. No other woman can match Gloria's sense of humour.

_____ 2. John can't hardly read without his glasses.

_____ 3. Many people believe that exercise helps them think clear.

_____ 4. Randolph tipped the scales at 190 pounds in weight.

_____ 5. Abdul had been married for five years at that point in time.

_____ 6. Both Mr. and Mrs. Jones play tennis, but she has the best serve.

_____ 7. My fight with Franklin is past history.

_____ 8. Joe Pugilist can't never remember his last boxing match.

_____ 9. Pete studied for a week for the English exam, and now he has an ulcer.

_____ 10. If you don't marry me, my life will be a disaster.

Doublecheck 15-2

Rewrite or edit the sentences to correct problems with wordiness, misuse of adjectives and adverbs, and faulty logic.

1. The firefighters put out the blaze quick.

   _____

2. Swedes are blondes.

   _____

3. It seems to me that Jennifer should head the committee.

4. Alaska is more bigger than Texas.

5. Greg had the worse batting average on the team.

6. Due to the fact that Christmas will be here in the near future, I'm saving my money.

7. Ricky would make a good surgeon because he doesn't mind the sight of blood.

8. The company's sales figures are real good this year.

9. Although they are twins, Sonia is tallest by three inches.

10. Everett doesn't phone his parents hardly ever since he moved to South Carolina.

Editing Check 15

Edit the following paragraph to take care of problems with wordiness, logic, and adjectives and adverbs. Not all of the sentences contain errors.

[1]In 1885, George Eastman gave up his bank clerk's comfortable salary of $15 a week to gain time to develop a small and simple camera that would be easy to use. [2]Up until that time in the past, cameras were large and complicated. [3]Three years later he produced a camera that in size was only 9 centimetres wide and 16 centimetres long. [4]The small size was possible in part because the camera used rolled, paper-backed film, instead of the bulky glass plates generally used at that time. [5]Eastman called it the "Detective Camera" because it was more smaller than other cameras, and its small size might enable someone like the popular fictional detective Sherlock Holmes to use it without being noticed.

⁶The camera had a button on the side and a key to advance the film forward. ⁷The camera came loaded with enough film to satisfy anybody, enough to take 100 pictures. ⁸When all the pictures had been taken, the photographer returned the entire camera back to Eastman's Rochester, New York, factory. ⁹Some time later, 100 circular pictures, 6 centimetres in diameter, were returned. ¹⁰Returned, too, was the camera, loaded with film for another hundred photos. ¹¹"You press the button—we do the rest" was the company's slogan. ¹²No one can think of a more better one. ¹³In 1888, Eastman changed the camera's name to Kodak, a name that could be pronounced easy anywhere in the world. ¹⁴The business itself soon before long became the Eastman Kodak Company. ¹⁵It was the more successful camera company for many years.

Checkpoint 15-1

Match the letter identifying the following sentence errors with the appropriate sentences that follow.

A. Wordiness

B. Adjectives or adverbs misused

C. Faulty logic

_____ 1. Stinger is the most fastest racehorse I've ever seen.

_____ 2. Either I play professional basketball or I'll end up on skid row.

_____ 3. The final payment on Jill's coat is due in the month of June.

_____ 4. Professor Daley is smiling, so she'll probably let us out early today.

_____ 5. That test on grammar was real easy.

_____ 6. In order to succeed in birdwatching, one will find that one needs patience.

_____ 7. It's always windy in Chicago.

_____ 8. In the opinion of this writer, smog control standards should be the same in all states.

_____ 9. Jennifer is more kinder than Constance.

_____ 10. The car moved slow through the parking lot.

Checkpoint 15-2

Edit the following paragraph and try to identify all of the errors.

My brother Bill. My brother Bill is older than me, so he is more smarter. He went to college, but I went straight from high school to my first job. The hairdressing salon was quite a nice place. Bill became an accountant, he worked for a downtown firm. At the end of last year in December; he married the boss doughter. Called June. I will never be so success like Bill.

No answers are given for Checkpoint quizzes.

WORDCHECK: MISCELLANEOUS FACTS

How well do you know the language of the Web? See if you understand these items.

1. What is URL?
2. What do you do when you "download"?
3. Define HTML.
4. What is MP3?
5. What is the difference between ISDN and ADSL?

ADDITIONAL READINGS

EDUCATION AND WORK

Studying Science, Playing Politics

Deborah Skilliter

Women have found it difficult to study in nontraditional areas such as engineering and other science and technology courses. When a woman does enrol in these areas, she often must overcome enormous barriers. Here is one woman's story; perhaps you know of others.

1 I'd been thinking of a career in science for about four years when I broached the subject of studying geology in university to my high-school guidance counselor.

2 "You wouldn't be any good at it," he opined. "Besides, women don't belong in science."

3 Dutifully, I enrolled in an arts program, but still felt a little wistful about geology. That summer I worked as a field assistant on a geological mapping project in Cape Breton. The project geologist—a woman—and I talked about the experiences of women studying science while we hammered at rocks amid clouds of black flies. She presented me with the novel idea that women could have careers in science. She also exploded my fear that science was beyond my mental capacities. Geology has traditionally been a man's field, but she encouraged me to find my place.

4 I made the switch.

5 I quickly learned that women were far from welcome in the lab. Two of the men in my geology class decided to make me the target of a series of more and more threatening practical "jokes" combined with a constant barrage of insulting remarks about women in general. I quickly learned to wear jeans on campus after an incident in which my skirt was yanked over my ears while I stood talking with some classmates. One day I returned to my microscope to find the specimen replaced by a condom. I decided that I'd had enough.

6 It didn't occur to me that the university might have some means of dealing with the problem. The only thing I could think of was to threaten to involve the police. This didn't so much reduce the level of harassment as change its style. From now on I was regarded as a "feminist with fangs."

7 Despite all this, the geology department had started to feel like home to me, mostly because of the encouragement I got from the professors and because of the

small classes. But I still felt nervous about chemistry and math because of my shaky background and the huge classes.

I was slightly reassured when the chemistry professor, Dr. Jekyll (not his real name), suggested in the first class that the $95 textbook was really worth the money because it was written by a female and that women in science needed more role models.

A few weeks into the first semester, several incidents began to make me uneasy. A young woman passed in an assignment unstapled. Dr. Jekyll threw the unstapled assignment into the air and beckoned the woman to come forward and retrieve the pages that were now strewn about the front of the classroom. Reluctantly, the woman began collecting her papers. While she was walking back to her desk, Dr. Jekyll exclaimed, "My, you're cute when you blush."

Shortly into second semester, we began a unit on the properties of light. Dr. Jekyll asked for a "volunteer" to demonstrate the reflectivity of light. These "volunteers" were actually conscripts and were generally female. By now the class had become somewhat wary of the call for volunteers and there was intense scrutiny of shoelaces and notebooks. He singled out a woman and began to explain.

"We are able to see Eve because light reflects off her. Light reflects off her head. Light reflects off her ears. Light reflects off her eyes, and my, what beautiful eyes she has! Light reflects off her seductive lips, and light reflects off her A-HEMS."

This was accompanied by loud mock throat clearing. I heard a suppressed noise of protest from a woman sitting behind me. We exchanged sympathetic glances. My first thought was to get out of the classroom as quickly as possible and hope not to have to return. My second thought was that this style of teaching shouldn't be allowed to continue.

Eventually I tracked down the phone number of the university's adviser on sexual-harassment complaints and then spent several days agonizing over whether or not I should phone. I discussed it at home and was advised to forget about it. What right did I have to question the lecturing style of a professor? I should simply go to class, take notes, and leave. Ignore comments that were unrelated to chemistry.

I tried this approach without success. I was unable to concentrate on the course material. I kept waiting for Dr. Jekyll to drop the next bomb, and was in a constant state of anxiety that I could be the next "volunteer." I dialled the number.

The adviser assured me that my complaint was valid. I knew this, but I had a purpose in visiting her office: I wanted out. I was able, with the adviser's assistance, to transfer into another section of the same subject. Within days, I was happily settled into my new class.

But not without cost. All the bureaucratic wrangling involved in changing classes had eaten into time I should have been spending studying. I had several hours of work to catch up on and I had developed an intense hatred and fear of chemistry.

The academic year has come to a close and I am left with lots of questions. I've realized that behaviour like Dr. Jekyll's is fairly common. It has also occurred to me that Dr. Jekyll is unconscious of the impact his classroom power games have on his students. Or it may be that he doesn't care.

During exams I literally bumped into Dr. Jekyll in the hallway. He asked to speak to me. Fighting down a mixture of panic and anger, I tried to make my escape. He would have none of it. "This won't take a minute," he said, then proceeded to offer what he called an "apology." He liked, he said, to use everyday examples when he taught, to help students better understand the subject. This sounded to me more like self justification than an apology. But all I could think of was that I just wanted to get away. Fast.

Afterwards it bothered me that he could have identified me so easily from a class of close to 100 students when my complaint was supposed to have been confidential. It also bothered me that even what passed for an apology was something imposed on me against my will.

Was my guidance counselor right? Do I belong in the world of science? I think I do. But I think that those who teach the subject have to consider the power they have. For this to happen means that science has to change, and I plan to be part of that change.

Checking Meaning and Style

1. Why did Skilliter first enrol in an arts program? What changed her mind?
2. What sorts of harassment did she encounter in the geology department?
3. How did she handle the initial attacks?
4. What were the effects of the professor's behaviour on the classes?

Checking Ideas

1. What is the significance of the title of Skilliter's essay?
2. Why did she name the professor "Dr. Jekyll"?
3. What were the most frightening aspects of this experience?
4. What would you have done had you been in that class?

Shedding Light on Confucius: A Window to East Asians in Canada

Douglas Todd

Everyone has values based on influences from families, teachers, peers, and other sources. In this essay, Douglas Todd presents a view of the Chinese value system that is based on the philosopher Confucius.

Restaurant manager Joseph Siu does a double-take when he sees a copy of *Confucius Speaks.*

"Ah, Confucius," Siu says. "I learned all about him as a child. I have tried to tell my children about him too. Confucius is so tender. He believes in peace. He doesn't believe in fighting."

Siu calls over a Chinese Canadian waitress, who asks where she can get a copy of the new philosophical comic book illustrating Confucian thought.

Such a flurry of interest by East Asian folks reveals how Confucius is still revered.

It's impossible to understand the world view of Canada's East Asian immigrants without understanding Confucianism, a complex ethical tradition that's grown out of the aphorisms of the 6th-century BC philosopher. Many consider Confucius one of the most influential thinkers in history, mainly because so many people—a couple of billion Asians—have been shaped by his teachings on family, society, authority, respect for elders, education, order, and virtue.

Confucius Speaks (subtitled *Words to Live By*, Anchor, $14.95) is written and drawn by Tsai Chih Chung. A former maker of animated movies, Tsai is already a publishing star in Asia, particularly China. Tsai spends most of his time in Taiwan and the rest in West Vancouver, with family.

Confucius Speaks is the latest English title in a series of Tsai's spiritual comic books, which aim to bring alive the abstract teachings of great Asian philosophers. Some of Tsai's other books in English include *Zen Speaks: Shouts of Nothingness*, *Sunzi Speaks: The Art of War* and *The Tao Speaks: Lao-Tzu's Whispers of Wisdom*.

Tsai doesn't speak English and doesn't give interviews. However, Tsai's English translator, philosopher Brian Bruya of Seattle, says the new book on Confucius will help North Americans understand why people from Chinese cultures are so different.

It's a crucial undertaking.

Harvard's Tu Weiming was invited to speak at a major University of B.C. conference on the economics, politics, and business of Asia recently because organizers believed it was essential to kick off the event with a Confucian expert.

Confucian ideals lie at the root of Asian society, Tu explained.

"Industrial East Asia, under the influence of Confucian culture, has already developed a less adversarial, less individualistic, and less self-interested modern civilization," he said.

Confucianism's emphasis on respecting others and fulfilling one's duty to the family, society, and the cosmos is bred in the Chinese person's bones in much the same way Christian values about free will, social justice, and charity penetrate the Western psyche, whether one practises Christianity or not.

Confucius Speaks, which avoids stuffy scholasticism, offers one route to understanding East Asian codes of conduct on everything from benevolence to modest facial expressions.

You are not really an individual in a Confucian-based society, it explains, but someone who fulfils a role. Confucianism teaches that people should be defined, first and foremost, by the place they occupy in the interrelated network of society.

In Confucian culture, it's most important for people to fulfil their roles as fathers, mothers, aunts, children, teachers, students, employees, and leaders. They must perform their roles with virtue—respecting order and hierarchy. They must avoid bringing shame on themselves, their family, their society, and their ancestors.

This anti-individualistic approach is the opposite of what happens in Western society, where individual rights and freedom are cherished and duties are rarely discussed.

Confucianism, with its emphasis on duty, also helps explain some of the remarkable business success in East Asian countries.

Its stress on discipline and patience, Bruya says, helps East Asian business people prevail over Western entrepreneurs, with their hunt for quick fixes. As well, Chinese business people gain from the Confucian belief in education and hard work.

Confucian thought has some pitfalls, however.

Essentially backward looking, Confucius thought everyone should be striving to recreate a mythological utopian society, says Bruya.

Bruya and Tu also believe Confucianism may have made many East Asians too deferential to authority and tradition. East Asian scholars, steeped in the Confucian mentality, often lack a sufficiently critical spirit to challenge the dictatorial tendency of strong rulers, Tu says.

Confucianism, in an adulterated form, is also being manipulated by authorities to support oppression all over East Asia, including Hong Kong and Taiwan, Bruya says. Partly as a result of Confucian culture, human rights and democracy are not highly valued in East Asia, even in those countries that officially allow freedom of thought. 23

Paradoxically, as East continues to meet West, the influence of some Confucian beliefs may be waning. The rapidly expanding economic clout of Asia flows in part from East Asians rejecting Confucius' conservative dream of returning to a perfect past, Bruya says. East Asian industry has mushroomed partly because East Asians are adopting the Western ideal of progress. 24

Nevertheless, the hope of many, including Bruya and Tu, is that the blending of Eastern Confucian wisdom with Western values will result in more fertile, balanced, and compassionate cultures. 25

Eastern and Western spiritual traditions not only promote ethical values that they can share—including the Golden Rule, which Confucius cites as: "Do not do unto others what you would not want others to do unto you"—they also have things to teach each other. 26

Many Asians need to learn more from the West about spontaneity, freedom, and equality. And Westerners can learn from Confucius about fulfilling responsibilities, respecting others, and being a good member of the family, society, and the globe. 27

Checking Meaning and Style

1. What is the writer's definition of Confucianism?
2. What is the name of Tsai's latest comic book? How is it written?
3. What occurred at the beginning of the University of British Columbia conference?
4. What parallels can be drawn between Confucianism and Christianity?
5. On what is Confucian society based and what is its approach?

Checking Ideas

1. Why is the teaching in Confucianism considered opposite to Western thinking?
2. How does this Chinese philosophy enhance business practices?
3. What are the possible disadvantages of Confucianism?
4. What might be the advantages of a fusion between Western practices and Confucianism?

How to Find Your First Job

Lyric Wallwork Winik

Most people would agree that in the last decade the idea of job satisfaction disappeared; finding a job and holding on to it became the crucial issues. For people in their early twenties, this has been an especially difficult time. Here is some advice on finding a job.

Even in a good economy, finding that first job can be tough. "No one has a sure thing anymore," said Owen Tseng, 21, of Houston, who graduated from UCLA last 1 month with a degree in economics and spent his senior year looking for a job in marketing. But he added, "The worst thing you can do is to give up."

In Cincinnati, Megan France, 21, has a similar story. "I know there are a lot of people worse off than me," she said, "but I can't believe that I have nothing after nine months of searching. It's discouraging and depressing."

Megan, who graduated in March from Ohio State University with a degree in Spanish and criminology, is primarily interested in undercover narcotics work, but she broadened her job search to include business and translating jobs. In addition to private companies, she applied to ten government agencies. So far, one has responded. Megan's only other job offer was as an airline ticket agent—a job that did not require a college degree. "Companies don't want to hire you if you don't have experience, but you can't get experience if they don't hire you," she said. "I worked during school, I graduated cum laude, and that hasn't meant anything to any of the employers. What incentive is the work world giving us?"

Indeed, whether you are graduating from a two- or four-year college, a trade school or high school, the work world may seem mystifying. This year, 1.16 million Americans will graduate from college, and most will enter the job market. If past years are any guide, only 42 percent will have a job upon graduation, according to the National Association of Colleges and Employers. In the association's 1993 survey of recent graduates, however, the percentage with jobs rose to 83.7 percent after about six months. And U.S. Department of Education statistics show that 84 percent of students were employed one year after graduation.

It helps to be focused. "There are two kinds of graduates," said Marilyn Moats Kennedy, a career counselor based in Chicago. "Those who know what they want to do and those who don't."

If you know the field you want to work in, Kennedy said, doing extra research is key. Having more information will make you a better job candidate and help you find openings.

If experience is a problem, Kennedy recommends joining a temporary employment agency. "Temp agencies send you on short-term assignments, but you can get a feel for what really happens inside a business," she explained. "You should also use this as an opportunity to gather additional information. Stop by the company's human-resource office and look for job postings."

Temp agencies also area good strategy for those who are unsure about what they want to do, Kennedy added, because they often offer assignments in a variety of industries. "Your first job helps you gain perspective," she said.

That is what happened to David Taylor of Lima, Ohio, who graduated from Ohio State in 1991. Unable to get a job as an electrical engineer, he taught at a vocational high school and discovered that he liked working with computers. Taylor, now 27, went back to school, got a second degree in computer science and landed a job as a computer programmer. "If I hadn't gone into teaching, I wouldn't have known I like computers," he said.

Computers and data processing are among the fast-growing segments of the economy. According to the Bureau of Labor Statistics, other areas (needing varying levels of education) expected to have high job growth over the next decade are health and education services and retailing. There will be a demand for registered nurses, nurses' aides and home health aides. America also will need more salespersons and restaurant workers, as well as teachers, teachers' aides, truck drivers, veterinarians and pharmacists. Overall, such service-related jobs will account for 24 million of the 25.1 million new jobs expected to be created by 2005.

Employers say their questions for job applicants are: Can you do the job? Will you do the job? Will you fit in? Betty DeVinney of Eastman Chemical, which hires new college graduates each year, likes applicants who are enthusiastic, pay attention to detail, can work with others and know about the industry and the company. "Nothing turns off an interviewer more than an unprepared or disinterested candidate," she said.

"I have big aspirations," said Dawn Netherton, 22, a UCLA graduate who hopes to work in broadcasting. "I know I'll end up having at least five different careers." But while Dawn is not sure where she will end up, she has carefully catalogued what her strengths are and where her interests lie. From temporary work, she learned that she didn't like large corporations, while working as a cocktail-server to pay her college bills taught her that she likes dealing with people. She landed a summer internship in broadcasting but said she may have to settle for a less-than-perfect first job.

"What you really need," said Marilyn Moats Kennedy, "is to find an employer who will take a chance on you."

Checking Meaning and Style

1. What is the thesis of this essay? Is it stated or implied?
2. How many examples does Winik use to develop the thesis? Which example provides the most useful information on the process of preparing a strategy for finding a job?
3. What are the areas of highest job growth predicted for the next ten years?
4. What are the two kinds of graduates (Paragraph 5)? What strategies are most effective for each kind of graduate?

Checking Ideas

1. What strategies would you advise someone to follow to be successful in finding a job?
2. Why do you think Dawn Netherton says she knows she'll end up having at least five different careers? Do you expect you'll have several different careers?
3. How can you find out what kinds of jobs would be most interesting to you?

RELATIONSHIPS AND PARTNERSHIPS

Babies Having Babies

Jocelyn Elders

In Canada, teenage pregnancy is a growing social issue. Teenage mothers face huge problems, and in this article U.S. Surgeon General Jocelyn Elders argues that until everyone is concerned enough to do something about it, the problem will not go away.

Working as a physician in rural or inner-city America can be a heart-breaking experience, particularly if your patients are children. In Arkansas hardly a day passed that I didn't see a child who bore the age-old scars of poverty, hopelessness and despair. I saw babies whose broken bones and bruised bodies were grim testimonies to child abuse and neglect. I saw children with dull eyes and sullen faces, who were not only physically, but also emotionally and spiritually, deprived. I saw children with sexually transmitted diseases and girls as young as 12 having babies. Life had dealt these kids double and triple whammies. Theirs was a warped pattern of growth and development. Neglected as infants, they grew into children with behavioral problems and went on to become school dropouts, violent offenders and child parents.

These tragedies are particularly prevalent in communities where there is a high incidence of teenage pregnancy. In fact, studies show a direct relationship between teen pregnancy and many of our most serious social, economic and health-related problems. Teenage pregnancy is a major contributor to the nation's high infant-mortality and abortion rates. It starts young mothers and their families on the fast track to joblessness and welfare dependency. Children born into families begun by teenage mothers are more likely than other children to use drugs, alcohol and tobacco, to do poorly in school and to exhibit the kind of antisocial behavior that results in incarceration. Simply put, teenage pregnancy is the wellspring for much of what ails us in this country. When a young girl from the South Side of Chicago or from rural Appalachia becomes pregnant, it's not only her future and that of her child that's imperiled. It's also yours and mine. It's the health of our pocketbooks, the safety of our streets and the security of our homes.

Teenage births increased by more than 65 percent during the 1980s. What else can we expect, given our archaic policies'? We wait until young people become sexually active or already have a baby on the way. Then we become concerned. Then we exhaust our resources on remedial services, welfare and Medicaid. Wouldn't we be smarter—and more compassionate—to invest our precious dollars in programs that *prevented* teenage pregnancy and reduced the need for costly medical and social bandages?

The key is to reach children early, while they are in the process of developing their habits and attitudes. We need to arm our youngsters with age-appropriate information about human sexuality and development. We need to help them develop the confidence and the skills to overcome peer pressure to have sex. We need to provide them with the services that will help them avoid unnecessary risks. Youngsters need to know there are consequences to premature sexual activity beyond the birth of a baby—consequences that are not only far-reaching and hazardous to their futures, but, in the case of AIDS, hazardous to their very lives.

Every day, as we debate the issue, nearly 8,000 new children become sexually active, 3,000 become pregnant, 1,500 terminate their pregnancies, 700 contract syphilis or gonorrhea, and a small but tragic and growing number acquire the HIV virus.

Personally, I have never seen anything moral or virtuous about writing off young people who don't follow our counsel on abstinence. I believe we need school-based clinics that provide comprehensive primary-care services, including the local option for family-planning services for sexually active teens. And I believe young people should be taught the ABC's of healthy behavior with the same intensity they are taught their academic ABC's.

Only when teenage pregnancy becomes everybody's concern will we make real headway. Only when we care enough can we lift our youth above this tragedy and give them hope for the future.

Checking Meaning and Style

1. What is the thesis or main point of this article?
2. What social, economic, and health-related problems does Elders relate to teenage pregnancy?
3. What statistics does Elders give to support her argument?
4. What is the topic sentence of Paragraph 4? What are the supporting details?

Checking Ideas

1. What do you think are some reasons for the high incidence of teenage pregnancy?
2. Do you agree with Elders that we need school-based clinics and that schools should teach healthy behaviour? Give reasons for your opinion.
3. What kinds of information about human sexuality should children be taught?

Raising a Feminist

Sarah Vaughn Snyder

In this newspaper article, Snyder discusses how to give a young child positive images of what women are capable of doing.

It was the ponytail under the batting helmet that caught my 3-year-old son's attention. It belonged to the only girl among the two dozen or so 7- to 10-year-olds playing Little League that day.

"Is that lady a man?" Ben asked.

Never missing an opportunity to lecture on gender equality, I pointed out that the player in question was indeed a girl, and that girls can play quite a good game of baseball, too.

I wanted to hug the ponytailed player, whose name was Carly, for helping me nudge one boy's world-view a little closer to where I'd like it. Children, I've learned, are excruciatingly literal: They believe what they see, not necessarily what they're told. This can make convincing a toddler that there are no substantive differences between boys and girls a challenging proposition.

When Ben announced one morning that "mommies don't mow lawns," I knew only one image could change that keenly observed conclusion. So, on a hot Saturday in May, I supplied the missing image, and suffered a smirking husband to do it.

The burden of providing the "right" images to satisfy a toddler's stern judgment of what men and women do isn't limited to chores. When Ben asked me to set up his favourite computer game one day, I was trapped.

"You'll have to wait until Daddy comes home," I admitted, clearing my throat. "I'm not sure how to do it."

"Why does only Daddy know?" he asked, exasperated.

The next day, I signed up for a computer class.

Fortunately, making the case for gender equality is easier thanks to the Carlys of the world. Ben sees or hears about so many women in the course of a day who hold positions that once belonged only to men that I have to believe his views on gender will be far more grounded than my male peers'.

All of Ben's pediatricians, by coincidence, have been women. His dentist is a woman. His mother's boss is a woman. His mother is an editor, his aunt is a lawyer, his friend's mother is an amateur carpenter. Each provides an image more enduring to a child than any amount of preaching.

Some of my parents' generation might think it silly for a mother to master computers to impress her son or make a lecture out of a girl playing baseball. But while I remember much talk as a child about what women could do, I recall precious few images of what women actually did besides run households.

Until my teens, I never met a professional woman who was not a teacher or a nurse. Women did not hold positions of authority. They were not principals or managers. Meeting such women after college had the bracing effect, and novelty, of visiting a foreign country for the first time.

One friend recalls her mother, while teaching her how to iron, telling her conspiratorially, "Successful men like well-organized households." Another, now an editor, still remembers a speech class in junior high school in which the assignment was to "demonstrate a task." She demonstrated the artful wrapping of a gift—only to be given a C for her poor choice of topic. Since only girls would ever wrap packages, the teacher reminded her, the demonstration was useful to only half the class.

In only one generation, the images children are fed of what women do have changed dramatically.

Will my son be more comfortable working for a woman one day if he has mowed lawns with her as a kid or watched her play baseball? I think so. The images remembered by the child are surely part of the prejudices of the man.

Walking away from that baseball field, I wanted to thank not just Carly but my sister, my son's pediatricians, even the woman he was once fascinated to see waving flags and wearing a hard hat at a construction site. Most women I know feel frustrated by the glass ceilings they still face. But perhaps they can find comfort in knowing that by simple virtue of how they lead their lives, they are changing the world-views of the next generation of men—the one still in diapers.

Checking Meaning and Style

1. What is the thesis of the essay? Is it stated or implied?
2. What does the writer say is the best way to convince a child of something?
3. What examples does Snyder use to point out the differences between what women did in her mother's generation and what they do now?
4. How does Snyder say women are changing the world views of the next generation of men?

Checking Ideas

1. Do you think there are differences between the jobs that men and women are capable of doing? Use details or examples to support your opinion.
2. What does Snyder mean by the statement, "The images remembered by the child are surely part of the prejudices of the man"?
3. Do you think the next generation will have a different view of gender equality? Why or why not?

The "I Don't Care" Game

Susan Jacoby

In this article, Susan Jacoby discusses the many different meanings of the response "I don't care" and the communication problems it can create in relationships.

A friend and I are making plans for dinner. When she insists, "Oh, I don't care," I suggest Chinese or Italian. "It doesn't matter to me," she says. "You choose."

My mouth waters when I think about hot-and-sour soup and steamed meat dumplings, so I say, "I've found a great new Chinese place. Let's go there." My friend agrees. Then, in an ever-so-casual voice, she adds, "You know, I'm on a diet. They always have good salads at Italian restaurants."

Grrrrr. Why didn't she just say she wanted Italian? Or would she have picked Chinese if *I'd* chosen Italian? Is there a right answer to, "I don't care—you choose"?

Of course, "I don't care" sometimes means exactly that. In most instances, though, the expression covers an emotional agenda that ranges from a misguided notion of agreeability to outright manipulation.

Women are most likely to confuse "I don't care" with agreeability—probably because so many of us were brought up to believe that it's not nice to ask for what we want.

At age 12, when I was first allowed to sleep over at friends' houses, my mother warned me against stating a preference for breakfast. "Just say anything will be fine with you," she cautioned, "because if you ask for something they don't have, it will be embarrassing." After years of being served eggs—which I loathed—I changed my response to "anything that doesn't have to be cooked."

On teenage dates, the rule against expressing a too definite preference was even stronger. Boys were supposed to do the choosing because they did the paying. I never made my own choice. I always asked what he was having, then ordered a smaller portion. "I don't care" wasn't just a courtesy, but a statement conveying the powerful message, "You're in charge—you decide."

The implicit "you decide" message, which surfaces most frequently in intimate relationships, may be one reason why "I don't care" irritates me so much. The phrase reminds me of a less confident, less honest, more manipulative younger self—and I dislike being on the receiving end as much as I once disliked being on the giving end.

Many people—men as well as women—use "I don't care" as a way to shift responsibility for uncomfortable choices. Celia, who has been married to an I-don't-care man for more than 20 years, says, "My husband's standard response is, 'It's all the same to me.' I waste a lot of energy trying to figure out what he wants—and I also worry that I'll be blamed if my choice turns out to be a disaster."

Celia finally broke the pattern when she and her husband decided to take a trip to celebrate their anniversary. "The choice was between Ireland—a place we'd always dreamed of visiting—and a less expensive trip. When he started in with his usual 'I don't care,' I said, 'Oh, no you don't, not this time.' I told him to collect the travel brochures and we'd make the decision together."

Celia's husband, who hates to spend money, agonized over the decision but finally admitted he wanted to go to Ireland. Celia believes his I-don't-care habit was really a way to avoid responsibility for any decision that might prove to be a mistake. "He hasn't stopped it entirely," she says, "but now when he says 'I don't care,' we both realize that what he means is, 'This is hard for me.'"

For some people, the I-don't-care stance is really a childlike test of love. The unspoken agenda is: "If you really love me, if you're really my friend, you'll *know* what I want."

Even when the overt issue is trivial—as in the case of Italian versus Chinese food—the underlying issue may be important. When my friend finally admitted she wanted Italian food, I asked why she hadn't said so in the first place.

"You don't have a weight problem," she replied in a hurt tone. "You never consider how hard it is for me to control what I eat with all those servings in Chinese restaurants."

In other words, I'd been selfish and thoughtless. A true friend would have read her mind.

"I don't care" mind-reading games usually ensure that no one gets what he or she really wants. Janet's widowed mother lives 1000 miles away in a tiny apartment. When Janet made her first visit after her son's birth, she wanted to stay in a motel.

Fearful of offending her mother, Janet began by saying, "It doesn't matter to me, but wouldn't it be more convenient for you if I stayed in a motel?" Her mother countered with, "I don't care; do what makes sense for you." Janet interpreted that comment to mean, "I really want you to stay with me, but I don't want to insist." So Janet and her baby slept on a rollaway bed in the living room—and the visit turned into a nightmare of inconvenience. Both women would have been happier if one had had the courage to tell the other what she wanted.

Life is so much easier without these guessing games. If you want to be an agreeable guest, remember that it's *not* easy for a hostess to watch a guest struggle to eat something she doesn't enjoy. And even if you don't have a strong preference, you can help by saying, "Anything but eggs." Because if you don't care, why should anyone bother trying to please you?

Checking Meaning and Style

1. What is Jacoby's purpose for writing this essay?
2. Where does Jacoby state the thesis?
3. According to Jacoby, for what reasons do people play the "I don't care" game? What examples does she give to support those reasons?
4. What are the effects of not telling others what you want? In which paragraphs does Jacoby discuss these effects?

Checking Ideas

1. Do you agree with Jacoby that "Life is so much easier without these guessing games"? Give reasons for your answer.
2. Discuss a time when you or someone you know played the "I don't care" game.
3. How would you advise a friend to say clearly what he or she wants to do without being overbearing or disagreeable?

COMMUNITY AND SOCIETY

Lessons Learned During Ramadan

Ameena El Jandali

Most of us celebrate religious festivals of particular significance. In this reading, Ameena El Jandali explains what the holy month of Ramadan means to Muslims, and why it is of importance to her personally.

1   The holy month of Ramadan ended a couple of days ago. As Muslims throughout the world have abstained from food and drink between sunrise and sunset for the past 30 days, many of the things that were taken for granted have taken on special value and meaning.

2   Among the obvious, of course, are the dual blessings of food and drink. We are so accustomed to having these in abundance that we rarely think twice about the fact that they are bounties that millions are deprived of. We forget that in countless countries, meat, milk, or sugar are not staples, but luxuries, afforded only to the rich. We forget that throughout the world, including [the United States], there are millions of people who cannot sleep at night from pangs of hunger or gnawing cold. We forget, not only to share what we have with those less fortunate, but to feel remorse for their plight, and thankfulness for our own good fortune.

3   Fasting in Ramadan was also a month-long lesson in discipline and self-control. In today's world in which the rule is "if it feels good, do it," Ramadan is an opportunity to practice that long lost art of abstinence, sacrifice, and endurance. Brainwashed into believing that we cannot function without our morning coffee, midday candy bar, or constant train of snacks, many of us find incomprehensible the idea of going without food or drink for over 12 hours. That Muslims fast, not to lose weight or for medical reasons, but for a higher spiritual cause is what makes fasting in Ramadan possible for people who in normal circumstances cannot miss a meal.

4   Ramadan is not only a time to exert control over our physical side, but over the mental and spiritual as well. While negative thoughts and ill behavior toward others should be avoided year round, in Ramadan special effort is made to eschew such destructive vices as back-biting, cursing, arguing, or lying. Combined with the emphasis on generosity and sharing in Ramadan, the outlook of the fasting person should be on doing good toward others, while improving one's own shortcomings.

Ramadan is a time for Muslims to remember the less fortunate, not merely in thoughts or prayers, but with financial support.... Even here, in the bastion of democracy and freedom, poverty, homelessness, and hunger are affecting growing numbers of the population.... But in Ramadan, even rich Muslims experience the pangs of hunger and the taste of thirst. At least in the month of Ramadan, they walk in the shoes of their less fortunate brethren.

In today's competitive and self-centered world, Ramadan is a time to remember qualities and people we tend to forget. Let us learn from the lessons of Ramadan, the lessons of thankfulness, sharing, and caring....

Checking Meaning and Style

1. What is the main point of the essay? In what paragraph is it expressed?
2. How do the first sentences of Paragraphs 2 to 5 help the reader?
3. What "blessing" is mentioned in Paragraph 2?
4. What lesson does Ramadan teach, according to Paragraph 3?
5. What kinds of controls does the holy month emphasize? (Paragraph 4)
6. What kind of charity is emphasized in Paragraph 5?
7. How are Americans "brain-washed"? (Paragraph 3)

Checking Ideas

1. Would an observance similar to Lent and Ramadan be good for all Canadians?
2. Do you ever feel that North Americans take too much for granted?
3. What practices have you ever observed that have taught you lessons (yoga, martial arts, meditation, etc.)?

Finding a Nationality That Fits

Isabel Vincent

It can be argued that the greatest bond that Canadians share, since the settlements of the Inuit and First Nations, is that they are all immigrants. Settling in a new country, adapting to a new culture, and using another language are particularly difficult for the first two generations. In this essay, Isabel Vincent describes the cultural conflicts between her home and the outside world.

We started to become Canadian the day my mother got her first pair of pants.

They were grey-green gabardine with a high waist, and came wrapped in tissue paper in an Eaton's box. My mother reluctantly modelled them for my brother and me, all the while declaring that she couldn't imagine ever feeling comfortable with the stretchy cloth hugging her hips. Portuguese women didn't wear pants, only the *canadianas* dared wear anything so revealing. But in the same breath she'd rationalize that she spent too much money not to wear them, and besides they'd probably be warm in the winter.

3   That was in 1975, a few years after my family had made the big break and moved from the poor immigrant enclave of Kensington Market to the more upscale neighbourhoods of North York, where pockets of European immigration were just beginning to emerge. We were pioneers in a way. My father had been among the first wave of Portuguese immigrants to Canada in the early fifties, working a bleak stretch of railroad near Port Arthur—now Thunder Bay, Ontario—to earn enough money for my mother's passage across the Atlantic. My mother arrived sea-sick in Halifax in 1955, and took a slow train to Toronto, where she joined my father in a roach-infested flat on Nassau Avenue in the market.

4   My mother still speaks of those early *sacrificios*: living in a cold climate with cockroaches and mutely shopping for groceries, pointing out items to a local shopkeeper because she couldn't speak English. Her language skills were so tenuous that she once interpreted a greeting from an Orthodox Jew who lived in the neighbourhood as an offer to buy my brother.

5   In those days, Toronto police used to disperse small crowds of Portuguese men who lingered too long outside cafés. Despite a burgeoning group of immigrants, there were few Portuguese speakers, even in the market.

6   But by 1975, the market became a Saturday-morning diversion for us, a place to shop for salted cod and fresh vegetables. To the hearty Portuguese immigrants who still worked the factories and construction yards, and rented windowless basements in the market, we were on our way up. After all, there were very few Portuguese families north of Eglinton Avenue. Although we lived in a mostly Jewish and Italian neighbourhood, we were finally becoming Canadian. Or so I thought.

7   I learned English in my first year of school. Multiculturalism was just beginning and hyphenated Canadians were beginning to flourish. I played with Italian-Canadians, Lithuanian-Canadians and Chinese-Canadians, but at that time nobody—especially suburban seven-year-olds—seemed able to pronounce "Portuguese-Canadian," so I told people I was Greek; it was easier to say. My brother went even further, changing his name to something faintly Anglo-Saxon, so his teachers and classmates wouldn't get tongue-tied around those sloshy Portuguese vowels and embarrass him. It seemed a very practical idea at the time, and I reluctantly followed suit.

8   But we still had problems, and didn't seem to belong. We never quite fit into the emerging Portuguese community, growing up around the parish of St. Mary's Church and the Toronto branch of the popular Benfica soccer club on Queen Street West. We were strangely aloof with our compatriots, most of whom had emigrated from the Azores, and whose guttural form of Portuguese we had difficulty understanding. My brother and I balked at heritage-language classes and remained passive spectators at the annual religious processions.

9   But if we had trouble dealing with our peers in downtown Toronto, in North York we were not much better off. My mother and aunts spoke disparagingly of the *canadianas*, Canadian women who (they were sure) knew nothing about how to keep a clean house or cook a decent meal. My mother taught me to cook and sew, and she and my aunts teased my brother, saying someday he'd marry a *canadiana* and would end up doing all his own housework.

10 For all her predictions, my mother was delighted to find out that she had been wrong. My brother, a physician, did marry a Canadian, but he doesn't do much of the housework. These days, my mother's biggest problem is pronouncing the name of her new grandson, Matthew Loughlin MacLean Vincent.

As I grew older I developed a nostalgia for my Lusitanian past, and tried desperately to reintegrate into the community. But I soon grew to hate the hypocrisy of some of my compatriots, most of whom were immigrants who chose to spend several years working in Canada, only to retire to the Portuguese country-side and build their palatial retreats with the fat pensions they collected from the Canadian government. Like my father, who learned English quickly and severed ties with his homeland, I became a staunch Canadian. I could sing "The Maple Leaf Forever" before I was ten, and spent my childhood years in French immersion. I became so good at masking my heritage that a few years ago when I applied for a job at a Toronto newspaper I was turned down because I was perceived as being too Anglo-Saxon. 11

"If you were ethnic, I'm sure they would have hired you on the spot," the wife of the paper's managing editor told me a year later. 12

But for most of my life being Portuguese seemed to me a liability. And then my mother bought that important first pair of pants. For a while it seemed that my life had changed. I was proud of my mother: she was becoming like all of the other mothers in the neighbourhood. 13

But my excitement was short-lived. A few days later, she decided they just wouldn't do. She carefully wrapped them back up in the tissue paper, placed them in the cardboard Eaton's box, and returned them to the store. 14

Checking Meaning and Style

1. How does Vincent describe her parents' early years in Canada?
2. What does she mean by "hyphenated Canadians"?
3. What made Vincent's family different from the other Portuguese?
4. What did the children do to their names?

Checking Ideas

1. Was Vincent's parents' immigration experience typical?
2. What were the pants supposed to be symbolic of?
3. Why was Vincent's failure to get the newspaper job ironic?
4. What does Canada's multiculturalism mean to you and your city?

Hang the Rich; Improve the Herd

H. S. Bhabra

You are about to read a novel idea about whom to punish for crimes. What kinds of white-collar crime are common? What punishment do you think criminals such as Alan Eagleson or the Bre-X scam perpetrators should be given?

The late right-wing British columnist George Gale—whose work, by an excellent irony, ran under the general rubric The Voice Of Reason—once published a pro-hanging piece under the headline "Let The Bastards Swing!" 1

I couldn't agree more. All we disagree about is who the bastards are. 2

I don't mean common hoodlums—the vermin who mug and rape old ladies, the scum who knock over corner stores. What would be the point? They're too stupid to 3 know any better, too lame-brained to be deterred by the threat of future woe. If hanging deterred murderers, murder would have stopped by now. It didn't even stop petty theft in 18th-century England. Nothing did—not even transportation to Australia.

If people are desperate, demented, or angry enough—if they feel they have nothing to lose—no threat of retribution, however condign, will stop them. And some of them are just too dimwitted to know that what they're doing is wrong.

No, I think we should keep hanging for people who *do* know. For people whose behaviour would be improved by the deterrent of the rope.

It's time to hang the rich. Not all of them. Just the ones who take their smug, self-regarding sense of privilege and use it to pillage the rest of us.

Think about it: How many victims of violent crime do you know? Now think: How many people do you know who are affected by something like the collapse of a major company. Millions of Canadians suffer when incompetence, misapplication, or malfeasance strikes a financial institution or professional body. Only a few hundred are victims of violent crime on any given day.

It isn't the morons on the street who are a danger to most of us, it's the men in suits. But what happens? Idiot villains get threatened with chain gangs while white-collar criminals do 20 minutes at a country club, or get their licence to practice suspended for a weekend or get put into a penal day-release program. I've had meals more punitive than that.

Yet it's these people—the powerful, the established, the ones beyond sanction, the ones society is for—who damage us all when they go bad, weakening the very structure of civil order.

It's time to teach a lesson to the felons in French cuffs—the stock promoter who massages his accounts, the lawyer who siphons off her clients' trust funds, the doctors who seduce patients, the raiders who skim a pension fund. It's time to show them the rope.

And yes, I know, this is the point at which the bleeding-heart conservatives step forward and say it isn't their fault—it's their upbringing, the damage done by Upper Canada College, McGill, and University of Toronto Law School; it's the psychological distress created by power, rank and privilege; you can't hold people responsible for their actions when they have the Empire Club and Simon Fraser and Georgian Bay cottages and a ski lodge in Banff in their background.

I say: In a pig's ear, friend.

Two hundred and fifty years ago, Voltaire mocked the English for killing one admiral from time to time to put courage in the others, but the practice must have had something to recommend it, because a generation later it produced, in Horatio Nelson, the greatest fighting captain the world has ever seen and a navy that ruled the waves for over 100 years.

We all know that capital punishment works not when it fits the crime but when it grotesquely exceeds it. If the punishment for drunk driving were the electric chair, who would risk frying for one last beer?

Insider trading would stop cold if we hanged a half-dozen culprits at the corner of King and Bay. (Well, maybe two dozen in Vancouver.) No estate agent would ever misrepresent a property again if the price were a bullet in the brain-pan.

Company directors asleep at the wheel while their company is run into the ground? Let them dance the Tyburn jig. Psychiatrists jump their patients' bones? Let them trip the Newgate polka. Stock promoters, crooked lawyers, bent accountants, unethical ministers and MPs, manipulators of the widow's mite and orphan's pence—let them waltz with Doctor Death. It doesn't take much culling to improve the herd.

Why stop there?

Lawyers who get their snouts in every loophole defending those charged with capital crimes... if their clients are found guilty, hang the lawyers.

I'll even compromise to get the whole thing off the ground. Let's take advantage of no baseball. Let's set up the stocks in Olympic Stadium and the SkyDome. Let's fetter white-collar malefactors there and sell tickets for the privilege of heaving ordure, muck, and sewage at the fallen rich. Let's televise it. If it sells, not only will it make up the shortfall in downtown revenues and television advertising, it will also give us the opportunity to poll the people for their opinion of hanging the rich.

It's time to teach the pointy-headed, lily-livered right that we liberals represent the people's wishes.

In the meantime, remember this: Jack Ketch can cure the ills the College of Physicians cannot remedy; and wrongs beyond redress by the Stock Exchange Council and the Law Society can be solved by Captain Swing.

Checking Meaning and Style

1. Where is the thesis of this article?
2. What kinds of people does the writer suggest should be hanged?
3. What is the writer's tone? What is the effect of his irony?
4. Why does he use one-sentence paragraphs?
5. What do the references to the "Tyburn jig" and "Newgate polka" mean? What would be the equivalent expression in your area?

Checking Ideas

1. Why does the writer think "men in suits" are a danger?
2. What excuses are made for these villains?
3. Why does he think muggers should not be hanged?
4. What is your reaction to this idea?

Kick 'Em Again

Judy Rebick

Judy Rebick is a well-known television and radio commentator. In this essay, she uses examples and statistics to argue that our democratic society is flawed when it allows huge differences in wealth to occur.

Poor bashing is becoming a national sport in this country, with politicians outdoing each other in blaming welfare recipients for their own poverty. Ontario premier Mike Harris went further than most this spring when he cut the prenatal benefit to pregnant women on welfare, saying that he didn't want them to spend it on beer. Prime Minister Jean Chrétien has also equated those who don't have paid work with drunks. "In my judgment," he told a black-tie audience in 1994, "it is better to have them at 50 percent productivity than to be sitting at home, drinking beer, at zero percent productivity." Even NDPers have joined in. Former B.C. premier Mike Harcourt announced his welfare reforms in September 1993 by explaining: "We want to clean the cheats and deadbeats off the welfare rolls.... Where there is work and where there are training programs, people who are able to work who won't take those training programs, who are taking advantage of the goodwill of British Columbians, who refuse to get into the workforce—those people will be cut off of welfare."

What's the reality of people on welfare? The highest welfare fraud figure I have ever seen is 6.8 percent. There is more fraud going on in Toronto's SkyDome on any given Saturday when businessmen take their families to tax-deductible boxes that are supposed to be for business associates than in all the welfare offices across the country.

This spring, the National Council of Welfare produced an important document entitled *Profiles of Welfare: Myths and Realities*. Contrary to the notion that most welfare recipients are lazy good-for-nothing young people looking for a free ride, people under 20 living on their own account for only 4 percent of welfare recipients and only another 12 percent are between 20 and 25. Another powerful myth is that teenage women get pregnant to qualify for welfare. In fact, only 3 percent of single parents on welfare are under age 20 and nearly half of all single-parent families on welfare have only one child; another 31 percent have only two children.

Jean Swanson, former president of the National Anti-Poverty Organization, now with End Legislated Poverty in Vancouver, says that poor bashing goes beyond the crass comments of politicians and media pundits. "Even the questions we ask about the poor show our prejudice," she says. "We ask: How can we help the poor? How can we get people off welfare and on to work? What we should be asking is: How can we reduce poverty? How can we get the rich to share? How can we get jobs with adequate income?"

Swanson points out that all the welfare-to-work experiments are simply moving people from one form of poverty to another, because the decreasing value of minimum wage and difficulty in finding full-time work mean staying well below the poverty line even with a job. "Poor people have as much control over these experiments as lab rats," she says.

Meanwhile, social assistance is disappearing as a public issue. A CBC/Environics poll in February listed a series of public policy issues and asked people to prioritize their concerns. The "welfare poor" is not even on the list, even though every person I know who lives in a big city is more and more disturbed by the extent of homelessness and despair.

A new book called *Confronting the Cuts: A Sourcebook for Women in Ontario*, edited by Luciana Ricciutelli, June Larkin, and Eimear O'Neill, describes some of the impact of Mike Harris's Ontario on women and children. After the 21.6 percent cut to welfare when Harris came into office, a mother of two now receives $1239 a month. When you consider that the cost of a two-bedroom basement apartment in Toronto is about $800 a month, that means struggling to survive on $4.88 a day for each person in the family. In a recent Health Canada study, 80 percent of mothers reported cutting down on their own meals and 20 percent said they went hungry for an entire day. Over half had to give up the telephone or other basic services in order to have money for food. According to the Daily Bread Food Bank in Toronto, 29 percent of mothers report that their children go without food at least once a week. A Thunder Bay study revealed that a couple with two young children now have to make do with $43 a week for food after other expenses are paid. Before the cuts, they had $104 a week. How can anyone live on $43 a week for food for four people? And this is in the province where the economy is supposed to be booming.

In 1997 Robert Gratton, the CEO of Power Financial Corporation, earned 8
more than $27 million. Six other CEOs made more than $10 million each.

How can a society call itself democratic when some people can't afford to put food 9
on the table and others make so much money they couldn't spend it in ten lifetimes?

Checking Meaning and Style

1. What is the significance of this article's title? How does it reflect the article's thesis?
2. What examples does Rebick give to support her thesis?
3. What are the sources of the statistics?
4. Why does Rebick conclude with a rhetorical question?

Checking Ideas

1. What does Rebick compare welfare fraud to?
2. Why are welfare-to-work projects often unsuccessful?
3. Why does Rebick believe that "social assistance is disappearing as a public issue"?
4. Would you agree with Rebick's conclusions about our society and the issue of welfare?

Our Own Native Hong Kong

Meaghan Walker-Williams

Hong Kong is a prosperous island with a thriving business in banking and trade as well as being an Asian cultural centre. "Borrowed" by the British until 1997, it is now part of mainland China again. In this article, Meaghan Walker-Williams argues that our First Nations people should repeat the model of Hong Kong in Canada.

Members of First Nations, who own large amounts of land and vast natural 1
resources, should be some of the richest people in the world. They aren't. On average they are massively unemployed, desperately poor and extremely disenfranchised. Hong Kong, a barren rock in legal limbo, sort of belonging to Britain and sort of belonging to China, should have become a garbage dump. It didn't. In 50 years it went from Third World poverty to a higher income per capita than England.

Those First Nations who never signed a treaty, never ceded their rights, and 2
never gave up their title, are—like Hong Kong was—in a sort of legal limbo. Not exactly Canadian, and not exactly sovereign entities either. After 200-plus years of legal shenanigans by Canadian politicians and leaders with all the integrity of circus sideshow barkers, First Nations have become almost as barren as Hong Kong was.

Since there are some interesting parallels—legally and economically—between 3
First Nations and the Hong Kong situation, why not have a little Hong Kong here?

Oh Canada, can you imagine it? Indian reserve shanty towns of Third World 4
conditions, with 85% unemployment, squalor, poverty and massive dependency, would be transformed into meccas of economic growth, boom and prosperity. Pockets of free trade zones all across our home "on native land," where Canadians

and Indians and international interests alike can come to do business, trade, shop, tour and create wealth for all those involved. Just as occurred in Hong Kong.

In that context, the question is not, "What do Indians have to trade?" The question is, "How could First Nations in Canada, with very little to trade themselves, take advantage of their constitutionally protected rights to become the place where other people trade?" Now that is a situation ripe for wealth creation.

How would it work? There are a number of political, legal and economic hurdles to overcome. The Coast Salish Free Trade Model, which I developed with the help of various other Salish, and law and economics professor David Friedman of the University of Santa Clara, follows.

A First Nation in Canada that never signed a treaty could assert its right to engage in free trade with other nations from around the world under sections 25 and 35 of the Canadian Constitution. On reserves, First Nations and those visiting would not be subject to any form of taxation. Businesses and individuals seeking such an environment would be welcome.

The niches likely to find this free trade zone attractive are financial services, including foreign banking, tourism and hospitality, imports of raw materials, light manufacturing, exports, software and various technology outfits and entertainment.

We would require every business that comes to a free trade zone to do three things only. First, they would need to provide modest equity in their operations to individual band members, giving band members an interest in the success of the foreign business and creating a higher expectation of success than currently exists in most First Nations joint ventures with outside enterprises. Next, they would have to provide employment and training that is culturally sensitive to the needs of First Nations in that territory, and hire a percentage of First Nations to work in that business. We see this as a voluntary exchange: Businesses would provide skills development in exchange for protection from intrusive, tax-hungry non-native governments.

Third, as businesses taking advantage of the opportunities afforded by a free-market economy in North America become profitable, we would require that a portion of the dividends be distributed to all band members via the establishment of a perpetual trust. This trust, similar to the Alaska Permanent Fund, would replace government spending, giving the federal and provincial governments an incentive to cooperate in our move to laissez-faire.

Ultimately, the Coast Salish Free Trade Model would provide good economic results, and not just for First Nations. Land values around reserves would naturally go up—as well as lease values on reserves. Reserves would become magnets for international investment, which would ultimately benefit Canada's economy. Look at how Hong Kong's economy provided prosperity and uplift to its neighbours. Permitting First Nations this level of autonomy would allow non-native Canada to keep its mixed market economy—whatever you non-natives decide—while enjoying the benefits of a free market in its backyard.

The solution gives no special group more rights and privileges than any other group. If non-First Nations of the Canadian population wish to engage in free trade, they are more than welcome to come and do business in our territory. We not only won't stop them, we will embrace them with open arms. Not only does the "Hong Kong Here" idea suggest that First Nations should enjoy these rights, it suggests that ALL people, of every nation should enjoy these rights, and we are the first nation that wants to make that happen.

Checking Meaning and Style

1. How does the author compare the First Nations' situation and Hong Kong's?
2. Explain "circus sideshow barkers" and "legal shenanigans."
3. How are the First Nations towns described now?
4. What is the *process* Meaghan Walker-Williams outlines?
5. What would be the voluntary exchange?

Checking Ideas

1. Why are the First Nations in a "legal limbo"?
2. What is the proposal outlined here?
3. How would these zones be legal?
4. What would be the result of this venture?
5. What do you think of this as a business idea?

ENVIRONMENT AND SCIENCE

Exposing a Mysterious Development

Geoffrey Rowan

In the same way it was predicted that CDs would supersede tapes, and DVDs replace videos, the demise of the Polaroid is often announced—especially now that digital cameras are here. However, as Geoffrey Rowan explains, the Polaroid should be appreciated for its ingenious technology.

1   Dire prediction from the world of photography: Polaroid's latest model, the Captiva, may be its last. After 50 years on the market, the instant camera is in danger of falling prey to its younger, slicker, and increasingly easy-to-use cousin, the video camera.

2   However, we shouldn't forget that this potential victim of the video revolution is a remarkably complicated bit of technology. It is no mean feat to have a mechanism capture an image and then replicate it within seconds right before your eyes.

3   Instant photography relies heavily on advanced chemistry: each snapshot involves more than 200 reactions taking place on film consisting of as many as 20 different layers, depending on the type used.

4   Here's how it goes. As with any photograph, the process starts with the push of a button which opens the camera's shutter and allows light to pour in through the lens and bathe the film for about one one-thousandth of a second.

5   In that split second the light travels through the film's top layer—a clear plastic sheet—and into the layers below that will create a negative image. The negative alone is made up of 16 layers, each about a millionth of an inch, or one micron, thick. (The combined thickness of these layers is about half that of a groove in a vinyl record.)

6   The bottom layer of the film is opaque and serves as one wall of the miniature darkroom in which the negative will be developed. Other layers contain silver halide crystals, which darken when exposed to light. Stuck to their surface are dyes— yellow, magenta, or cyan—which allow the crystals to absorb blue, green, or red light, respectively.

7   But so far, all that split-second exposure has done is make a ghost image. More chemicals are required to amplify what the light has begun and thus produce a fully detailed negative.

These chemicals are contained in a tiny pouch on one edge of the film. Immediately after the shutter snaps, the camera forces the film through a pair of metal rollers, which apply enough pressure to rupture the pouch and spread out its contents.

Floating in this chemical soup are tiny pieces of white pigment, which stay on top as the other ingredients soak into the layers of film. In this way they form the other wall of the darkroom in which the negative can develop without being exposed to more light. (They also account for any whites that appear in your finished picture.)

As the chemicals from the pouch spread, they join those already in the various layers, vastly amplifying the ghostly image into the final negative. At this point, the film sets to work on the positive image you'll eventually stick to your refrigerator door.

From the negative layers, three other "image" dyes—this time, yellow, magenta, and cyan—move up through the cloud of white pigment. When they reach the underside of the top sheet of clear plastic, they will form the final image.

The yellow is activated by the negative's blue crystals, the magenta by the green, and cyan by the red. They move because they carry a negative charge that draws them to the positive charge given to a thin layer of polymer on the underside of the plastic.

All this—from the click of the shutter to the finished picture—takes about three minutes. But unless the chemical processes are turned off, it will be a picture that lasts just a few hours.

That's the task of an acidic polymer that sits sandwiched between the film's opaque bottom and a latex barrier that separates it from all the silver halides. About five minutes after hitting it, the chemicals from the pouch, which are highly alkaline, begin to soak through the latex barrier.

This brings them into contact with the acidic polymer, which neutralizes them—and freezes the chemical action.

This leaves you with something that no video camera can match. Granted, the camcorder and company are changing modern society forever by adding home movies to people's television diet (along with such dubious entries as *America's Funniest Home Videos* and, thanks to the Rodney King footage, America's unfunniest police forces). But nothing they can produce will ever knock the Polaroid from its vantage point on the refrigerator door.

Checking Meaning and Style

1. What dire prediction does the author begin with?
2. How does the author develop his argument about the inimitable quality of the Polaroid?
3. With a partner, can you make a flow chart of the Polaroid's mechanism?
4. How do the chemical processes turn off?
5. What words does the author use to describe the processes of the Polaroid? What can you tell about his attitude to the camera?

Checking Ideas

1. What makes the Polaroid absolutely unique?
2. In what way has the video recorder changed our modern society?
3. Explain the reference to the refrigerator door.
4. What kind of a camera, if any, do you prefer to use?
5. What do you consider a unique invention?

Individual Actions Can Have Huge Consequences

Ian Burton

Do you listen to the weather forecast? Have you noticed any changes in our weather patterns? In this essay, environmentalist Ian Burton writes that our behaviour is having drastic effects on the weather. Think of an action you took and assess its consequences.

It is easy to accept the idea that the large-scale affects the small. What is not always so obvious is that the small-scale affects the large. Take the weather. "Everybody talks about the weather, but nobody does anything about it." This has long been a common complaint. The weather affects us in many ways. Too little rain and farmers are clamouring for drought relief. Too much rain and they are complaining again. The success of the office picnic, the garage sale, the baseball game, the weekend at the cottage, is affected by the weather. Our very moods reflect the weather—the ennui of a dull, rainy afternoon; the spring in our step on a warm, sunny morning. The large-scale affects the small. We are creatures of the weather.

It's not true, however, that nobody does anything about it. Environment Canada goes to great lengths to try to predict it. The weather forecast is the news with the highest number of listeners.

Evidence shows that we act on this information. Farmers choose the time to plant and the time to harvest depending upon the weather. Tour operators, managers of ski resorts, golf courses, marinas, in fact the whole leisure, vacation, and tourist industry responds in critical ways to weather forecasts. The whole economy is strongly influenced by weather. So we have been "doing something about it," even if it has been largely linked to attempts to predict.

But now we are discovering something new in the weather equation. People are actually changing the weather, and in a really big way.

This has been a long-standing human ambition. Traditional societies developed elaborate rituals, such as rain-dances, to influence the weather. Greek sailors in classical times made sacrifices for a favourable wind. In modern times, cloud seeding has been tried to produce rain or deflect the track of hurricanes. Smoke canisters are used in Florida to prevent frost, and burners were once used at London's Heathrow airport to try to disperse fog.

All these attempts have had minimal results. But in the next 50 years or less we are set to transform our weather beyond recognition. By the middle of the next century the weather in southern Ontario will probably be like that of Kentucky today. The Maritimes could be more like southern New England or New Jersey; southern British Columbia like Oregon or northern California, and the Prairies like Nebraska or Kansas. And all this the result of human behaviour. The small-scale is affecting the large.

The mechanism for all this is the well-known emission of carbon dioxide from the use of fossil fuels like oil, coal, and natural gas, as well as other greenhouse gases. The aggregate effect of our innumerable small-scale decisions is changing our world.

Is this bad or good? Many Canadians might relish shorter and less severe winters. Heating bills would be down but air-conditioning bills would be up. Drought might become more frequent in the Prairies, the level of the Great Lakes might fall, and the level of the sea rise on all three coasts—Atlantic, Pacific, and Arctic.

Economic impact studies carried out by the Canadian Climate Centre suggest that, on balance, the costs would be greater than the benefits, the risks greater than the opportunities. But all the evidence is not yet in.

What should we do in the meantime? Many nations, Canada included, are moving toward an approach that will try to change people's behaviour as a precaution against changing the weather. But it's a far cry from international agreements to the behaviour of the person on Main Street.

This means that the small has to begin to think seriously about how it affects the large. Our everyday behaviour has suddenly become powerful enough to change the weather.

Who says nobody is doing anything about it? It's rather like casting a vote in a democratic election. One single vote appears to matter very little. But good citizens take the responsibility to vote very seriously, and that changes governments and the direction of the country.

Changing the weather is something we each do every day. As prophets and philosophers have told us for millennia, the behaviour of each individual is significant. Now science is showing us a new version of this eternal message.

Checking Meaning and Style

1. What does Burton mean by "the large-scale affects the small"?
2. What have we mainly attempted to do about the weather?
3. What have we suddenly discovered?
4. In what way has changing the weather "been a long-standing human ambition"?
5. Why is the weather going to change "beyond recognition"?
6. What are the effects of the changed climate going to be?

Checking Ideas

1. What is Burton's attitude toward the way we are influencing the weather?
2. Have you noticed any differences in the environment over the past few years?
3. In what ways are you personally affecting your environment?

The Good, the Bad and the Ugly of Skepticism

David Suzuki

In this essay, the popular scientist David Suzuki describes the skeptics' view of environmental changes, and the effects that this might have on important policies. This article comes from Dr. Suzuki's Web site, www.davidsuzuki.org, where he publishes his magazine, Science Matters.

Skeptics are a strange bunch. Certainly, a healthy dose of skepticism is essential to science and crucial to helping us all weed out truth from the everyday noise of media and advertising. But there are those who, in spite of overwhelming evidence, still cling to theories and beliefs that have little basis in fact. Some of these "skeptics" deny evolution, others deny that the world is round and, increasingly, some deny that human impact on the environment poses a serious threat to society, and to life in general.

Intuitively, that just doesn't fly. Every day, it seems, there's another troubling news report about pollution, global warming or species extinction. It's depressing. Actually, some analysts say that the "eco-guilt" brought on by all these news stories is what's fuelling the popularity of skeptics, as people search for more comforting worldviews.

Skeptics often label people (like me) who disagree with them as "doomsayers." Skeptics are tired of doomsayers, who they say espouse nothing but bad news. And they offer an enticing alternative: everything you hear about the sorry state of our environment is wrong. The doomsayers are wrong; the scientists are wrong; the news stories are wrong. The environment is actually improving.

Perhaps that uplifting conclusion explains why a new book by Bjorn Lomborg received so much publicity when it arrived in North America. His book, *The Skeptical Environmentalist* claims to measure the "real state of the world" which, according to Mr. Lomborg, is just fine.

Of course, another possible reason the book received so much publicity is because of the deep pockets and influence of some big businesses that have vested interests in maintaining the status quo. Indeed, Mr. Lomborg's take on the state of the planet is very similar to the positions of some large industry-funded institutes and groups, such as the Global Climate Coalition. These groups wage big budget campaigns to confuse the public about issues like air pollution and global warming.

So it was strange to see Mr. Lomborg's book and his views go largely unchallenged in the media, who often completely ignored the fact that his beliefs ran contrary to the vast majority of scientific opinion. In fact, before the release of his book in North America, Mr. Lomborg's views had already been widely discredited by many of his colleagues at Aarhus University in Denmark. Some had even written articles with titles like, *Lomborg's claims are untrue and dangerous* and *Lomborg's facts are absurd and irrelevant*.

Yet, in spite of this criticism from his peers, one of Canada's national newspapers recently ran an unchallenged series of full-page essays from Mr. Lomborg as well as numerous editorials and a book review so over-the-top in terms of praise that it was almost comical. The reviewer even had the audacity to conclude, "After Lomborg, the environmental movement will begin to wither."

Such outrageous claims should immediately raise suspicion. Recently, a much different review of the book appeared in *Nature,* one of the world's most respected science journals. It describes *The Skeptical Environmentalist* as, "a mass of poorly digested material, deeply flawed in its selection of examples and analysis." The review goes on to say that Mr. Lomborg's "bias towards non peer-reviewed material over internationally reputable journals is sometimes incredible...At other times it seems fictional."

A critical eye is a valuable tool and the media are supposed to help us in this regard by presenting information in a balanced way so the reader, viewer or listener can make an informed decision. Unfortunately, balance is often lost in the desire to be controversial, shocking, or meet a desired editorial slant. That's a shame, because issues that pertain to the health of the planet are far too important to be treated as mere journalistic fodder to appease the skeptics.

Checking Meaning and Style

1. Define "skeptic" according to David Suzuki. What important issue do these skeptics deny above all?
2. What seems to be happening every day?
3. What were some of the reactions to Lomborg's writings in Europe? How did this differ from the national newpaper's reaction?

Checking Ideas

1. Why do some people wish to ignore environmental warnings?
2. Why did Lomborg receive increased publicity?
3. Why are Lomborg's ideas considered dangerous by scientists like Suzuki?
4. What is the important step that, as a science writer, Lomborg should have taken?
5. In what way does this article support the need for readers to check the sources of what they read?

Will *Survivor* Replace *Lord of the Flies*?

Christine McGovern

Does television viewing have an impact on our reading habits? Is it changing our world view? In this article, Chrisitne McGovern expresses concerns about the impact of the television program Survivor on her teaching of the novel Lord of the Flies by William Golding.

1   One of the great joys of teaching ninth-grade literature is in serious jeopardy now that *Survivor* has crept into our national consciousness. No longer will my students become acquainted with the "darkness of man's heart" through William Golding's *Lord of the Flies*. Thanks to this summer's television phenomenon, man's inhumanity-to-man will seem old hat—or will it?

2   For eleven years, I have taught the novel to freshmen at Georgetown Visitation, a Catholic girls' school in Washington, D.C. The journey is rough, so I begin with a pre-reading activity. I tell them: Your plane has crashed on a desert island, which has a mountainous area, a forest, a sandy beach, and a lagoon. All adults have perished. The plane has drifted out to sea. You have only the items on your person and the clothes on your back. Your job is to organize to survive.

3   I then retreat to the corner of the room and record what happens next. After witnessing this exercise more than thirty times, I never fail to be amazed by the students' resourcefulness. Their concerns mirror the boys' on the island as they plan for basic survival and rescue. Usually they, like the boys in the novel, elect a leader who organizes them into work groups to feed, shelter, and sometimes entertain each other. They build a fire for warmth, protection, and roasting interesting flora and fauna. Only once did they attempt to cook one of their own.

4   Mostly they work cooperatively—a characteristic some label as a "feminine" value. Sometimes they follow their leader while other times the leader is usurped by a power-hungry rival. Occasionally a small band will break off from the group, bored or overwhelmed by the chaos of the classroom/island.

They tend to injuries, personal hygiene, and once in a while they even say a prayer to stave off any "beasts" who might attack them at night. Danger and fear emerge early on, foreshadowing the evil that lurks in the hearts of the characters and themselves. All sorts of monsters invade their idyllic paradise, but usually they fend off the aggressor.

Only once has a class succeeded in getting off the island. Pooling their talents, they made a "boat" from desks with a sail made by linking their plaid uniform kilts and moved their vessel full mast toward the door and safety.

The results of the exercise almost always reinforce the virtues of selflessness, courage, team work, and kindness. So they are in for a surprise when the characters rebel from rules and even plot to kill each other.

Now having met the evil Richard, vengeful Sue, and traitorous Kelly, I'm not sure they will believe that savagery, if left unchecked, is a bad thing. Worse, I fear that they will identify the television show with the novel. Richard becomes the choirboy-turned-murderer, Jack. The revulsion against rat cuisine replaces reluctance to eat raw pig meat, and the $1 million pot of gold seems a far more desirable reward than the triumph of virtue.

I have been assured by my sophomores, who read *Lord of the Flies* untainted by *Survivor*, that the novel's impact will not suffer by comparison. Yes, they say, students may foresee a breakdown in society sooner as alliances forge enmities. Yes, they might recognize earlier the danger of peer pressure to betray their friends. But, no, human beings can still tell the difference between a hoked-up TV show and a fictional life-and-death situation with no escape hatch.

I'm not so sure. Golding's title, *Lord of the Flies*, refers to the ancient Hebrew name for the devil. And the devil is a snake. And the snake ate the rat.

Checking Meaning and Style

1. What exactly does the title of this article mean?
2. Explain the phrase "man's inhumanity to man." What teaching strategy does McGovern use to engage her students?
3. Summarize the kinds of reactions the class has to the task McGovern set.
4. What hideous act did the boys in *Lord of the Flies* commit?

Checking Ideas

1. What role do you think you would play in a simulation of survival after a plane accident?
2. What does fear foreshadow?
3. What similarities are there between the cast on *Survivor* and the boys in the novel?
4. Why do you think a class might not be so surprised by the boys' actions any more?

HEALTH AND SPORTS

So What's the Problem with *Wussy* Sports?

Mary Louise Adams

What's a "wussy sport"? Is it one in which any male participants are considered weak or effeminate? Recently, figure-skating males from Kurt Browning to Elvis Stojko have taken the lead in pushing the sport into a macho, hockey-like sport, forsaking skating's other focus: artistic development. In her essay, Mary Louise Adams argues that this is not a positive direction for skating to take.

I first noticed it about ten years ago—not on the ice but in an issue of *Saturday Night* magazine. After a childhood and adolescence spent immersed in figure skating, I had been away from the sport, as participant and spectator, for a number of years. I certainly wasn't prepared for an image of Kurt Browning, a figure skater, done up as the epitome of urban cool—cocky black beret, tight jeans, leather bomber jacket. The adjective used to describe him was "macho." I had never seen the words "macho" and "figure skating" in such close proximity.

Five years later, the "macho turn" in skating was well underway. In 1994, the *Globe and Mail* included Browning on its year-end list of the 25 most powerful personalities in Canadian sport. Not only had he won four world titles and landed the first quadruple jump in competition, apparently he'd also "wiped away the stereotype of effeminate male skaters."

Although the pronouncement was a bit premature, it is true that since Browning became world champion in 1989, male skaters have been taken more seriously. Browning, for instance, was the first male skater to land endorsement contracts with major corporations such as Toshiba and Coca-Cola. Elvis Stojko, who succeeded him, has long-term contracts with McCain's, McDonald's, Canon, and Roots. Much of this commercial success comes from winning world championships. But Brian Orser was also a world champion and no comparable endorsement contracts ever came his way, suggesting that there is more to gaining corporate support than medals.

Skating is being straightened up. The straighter it gets, the more marketable its skaters become. And, I suspect, the more marketable it becomes, the straighter are the skaters. To read the sports section of your daily newspaper it would seem that this is a great thing—finally male skaters are getting the respect they deserve. They are being taken seriously as athletes. No one snickers about Elvis Stojko.

How is it that yesterday's sissies are coming to be today's jocks? After Kurt Browning won his first world championship, University of Alberta sports sociologist Garry Smith claimed, rightly I think, that Browning, despite his success, would still not be considered a sports hero. It was mainly, said Smith, "because of the sport he's in. A lot of people think of it as more of an art form than a real sport. Skating is seen as kind of feminine, so to what extent can he really be a hero to guys?" This is the former life of men's figure skating in Canada, where the term "kind of feminine" used in relationship to men means kind of gay and where fear that they might be perceived as gay is still enough to keep many boys out of the sport.

Unlike their predecessors—Toller Cranston, Brian Pockar, Brian Orser—Browning and Stojko come across as real guys, fellows a sports writer can spend some time with. Certainly both men have been portrayed by the press as fitting easily into mainstream notions of heterosexual masculinity. Son of an Alberta rancher and trail guide, Browning's cowboy background was rarely left unmentioned by journalists and television commentators. He was presented as the boy-next-door, a gosh-gee kind of ladies' man, an athlete who, had he been bigger, might have had a shot at the NHL. Here clearly was a guy who challenged the notion that skating is for sissies.

While sports journalists appreciated Browning, Stojko makes them weak in the knees. He's the three-time world champion and, as of Nagano, a two-time Olympic silver medalist. Not an article is written about him that doesn't mention his black belt in karate: few overlook his fondness for dirt bikes. Stojko does the biggest tricks. He plays hurt. He does not point his toes (as Browning eventually learned to do). During the recent Olympic games he was widely and favourably quoted when he said, "I'm a powerful skater. I'm a masculine skater, not a feminine skater... I don't skate feminine and I'm not going to be that way. I don't have a feminine side." Tough Guys: 2, Sissies: 0.

Stojko is, unquestionably, one of the best jumpers the sport has ever produced. But in the skating world he has been criticized over the years for the artistic quality of his programs: his often simple choreography, his tendency to take obvious rests, to telegraph his big jumps. In response to such criticisms, Stojko, his coach, and supportive journalists suggest that skating judges just don't appreciate his overtly masculine style. The assumption behind the claim is that an effete "skating establishment" rewards effeminacy rather than athleticism, that Stojko is a misunderstood underdog who is simply being true to his nature as a man.

Some underdog with those three world championships and two Olympic medals. A recent issue of *Saturday Night* magazine—obviously a great champion of the new macho skating—included an article called "Skating Is No Wussy Sport." Writer David Staples goes to fabulous lengths to construct Stojko as uniquely tough and masculine among skaters. Staples is probably the first writer ever to describe Stojko's American rival, the stiff and formal Todd Eldredge, as a "graceful" skater. The description helps Staples to maintain the tough guy vs. sissies comparison upon which he bases his argument.

Staples uses verbs like "sniff" and "natter" when citing skating officials. He finds it shocking that ties in skating are broken by artistic and not technical marks. He claims that skaters who have received artistic marks higher than Stojko's have simply been "boosted" by the judges—as if the artistic component to skating is merely incidental and has no value of its own. There's an assumption that looking "balletic"—being stretched, pointing your toes—is physically easy. And that comes, I think, from an assumption that the men who skate like that do it "naturally." That's just the way they are. They look like sissies because they are sissies.

11   Staples, like others, writes of Stojko's rejection of dance training: "Determined not to look effeminate on the ice, [Stojko] refused to be a ballet dancer, polishing the air with sweeping arm movements." We learn that Stojko's dad thinks ballet is only for "ladies and Russians who [can't] skate."

12   In interviews, Stojko visits the same theme, as if that is what sets him apart from his competitors. In one pre-competition profile on CTV, Stojko says, "I was never into taking ballet. That's not me. That's not where I'm at. How can I say—Of course you can be powerful in ballet, but I try more to be the macho kind of guy. That's the way I am." That many male skaters do not take ballet is less important here than the way Stojko implicitly counterposes macho-ness with ballet and the way he suggests that the difference between them is somehow present within skaters themselves.

13   Constructing an opposition between athleticism and dance is a standard device of figure skating commentary. It is used as a means of distinguishing male skaters from female skaters and also as a means of distinguishing the various skaters within these events. In men's competitions, commentators talk about "showdowns" or, unbelievably, about "shootouts" between the "jumpers and the artists," as if one could not be both at the same time—a position belied by Ilia Kulik who landed a clean quad and took the gold medal in Nagano.

14   This athleticism/dance—or sport/art—opposition isn't only used to differentiate between skaters, it also structures the meaning of skating in relation to sports more generally. Could something that actually demands interpretive—that is, artistic—skill really be a sport?

15   This is the question I hear under the defences of Stojko's artistry written by journalists such as Staples. If skating could just rid itself of expectations of expressiveness, if it could be less like dance, if it could evolve into a "jumping contest," then its position as a sport would be secure. There would cease to be a need to promote the virility of its male competitors.

16   In the past, skaters such as Toller Cranston, John Curry, and Robin Cousins considered it the highest praise to be called artists. By contrast, many people currently involved in skating go to great lengths to play down its connection to art or dance in order to underline the definition of skating as sport. Australian sociologist R. W. Connell has argued that sport is the leading marker of masculinity in mass culture. It is assumed that masculinity can be forged through athleticism and that real jocks and real men are synonymous categories with no room in them for anything homosexual. Art, by contrast, is often assumed to pose a threat to masculinity. Hence, the overwhelming need to portray male figure skaters as athletes, as tough competitors, as anything but artists (which can lead to interesting contradictions in a sport that demands some level of artistry from its participants).

17   This emphasis on the athletic as a means of downplaying the de-masculinized image of the artist is something that also affects male dancers. But while dancers try to blur the boundaries between athletes and themselves, skaters and the people who represent skaters reinforce them, clinging to and augmenting, where possible, the definition of their performances as athletic.

18   There are a number of ways to do this: One can, for instance, talk about how hard skating is. A few years back, in a short documentary on CBC's *Prime Time*, Elvis Stojko complains that, "People don't realize that you come to the rink and you train everyday—you stumble, you fall. We don't have pads like hockey players do. We hurt ourselves pretty bad sometimes and it's a hard sport. That's all a part of it and I want to show a bit of that on the ice." As he speaks, viewers watch him falling and crashing into the boards.

19 Another way to shore up the athleticism of skating is to borrow vocabulary from other sports. Many a tired cliché has found a new, if ill-fitting, life in a skating context: "We [Stojko and coach] want to keep squeezing him [Browning] to get into an overtime situation and score." Verbs like crush, attack, overpower, gun, as in "gunning for a medal," are now common—despite their inappropriateness to the format of figure skating competitions—in coverage of men's (but not, of course, women's) skating.

20 Not surprisingly, the sport most commonly referenced by this jock talk is hockey. In Canada, hockey remains (recent Olympic losses aside) the definitive macho sport, the mark of a tough northern masculinity. Pat Burns, coach of the Boston Bruins, has been quoted as saying, "An avowed homosexual, that would never be accepted in hockey—never.... A wall would go up because it's a macho sport."

21 While hockey and figure skating both take place on the ice, it is hard to imagine two sports that are more different. Nevertheless, hockey impacts on the language of skating in a number of ways. As far back as 1970, the Department of Health and Welfare was using hockey as a reference to encourage boys into skating: "Figure skating is definitely for the 'He-man' too. The amount of energy used in a full free-skating competitive program can easily equal that needed for a hard-played game of hockey. You need only watch the spectacular speed and agility of a top male skater to be convinced."

22 Hockey-talk about individual male skaters positions them closer to the centre of the sports world, closer to the centre of Canadian maleness—as if to say there is more to these boys than costumes and camel spins. A *Maclean's* article about Browning starts out by noting that "Until he was 15, Browning was a slick, high-scoring centre in minor hockey...." After the Lillehammer Olympics, *Morningside's* Peter Gzowski made sure to ask Browning, "Do you ever wonder what would have happened if you had stayed playing hockey?... You're a clever hockey player." In *Chatelaine*, Sandra Martin writes that Stojko "looks more like rookie of the year for the Toronto Maple Leafs than the king of figure skaters." On television Lloyd Eisler is profiled playing hockey—and getting injured while he scores a goal. It's hard to imagine similar talk or similar images of Brian Orser or Toller Cranston, of Josée Chouinard or Shae-Lynn Bourne.

23 In the skating world, the macho-ization of male skating is a hit. The Canadian Figure Skating Association says that enrollment of little boys in its skating programs has increased substantially over the last few years. Sponsorship of both the sport and individual athletes has increased and now comes from a broader range of companies. Coverage of skating in newspaper sports sections has improved in terms of both quantity and quality.

24 Some of this is, of course, related to the international success of Canadian men in figure skating. But it is also the case that sports journalists are more comfortable talking about skating when the guys they have to interview speak their language, when they revel in being jocks. One can only wonder how sports writers will cover the skating of rising star Emmanuel Sandhu whose image is more reminiscent of John Curry or Toller Cranston than of Elvis Stojko. Covering Sandhu, a former student of the National Ballet School of Canada, there will be no room for dissing the art side of the sport/art divide; there will be no way to establish his "guy quotient" by contrasting him to his arty competitors.

25 I worry about attempts to paint skating as a sport for guys, as an athletic rather than an artistic activity. In the past, skating was a place that permitted, indeed rewarded, certain kinds of "feyness." Skating (despite official CFSA assertions to the

contrary) was a good place for sissy boys to express their own kind of masculinity. There are too few social sites where this remains a possibility.

In blurring the line between sport and art, skating also helped to blur the polarities related to a sport/art opposition, that is the lines between male and female and straight and gay. Male skaters, for a time, were able to reject the rigid gender dichotomies of the sporting world. Stojko and those who fawn over him will have none of this.

What I find especially unnerving and homophobic about moves to construct skating narrowly as sport is the way these moves are presented as progressive, as "the right thing," as if in discounting much of what makes skating unique, the macho-skating camp is finally getting male skaters the respect they deserve.

Elvis Stojko is portrayed as an underdog, a radical, for what are, in essence, attempts to jump into line with a hegemonic masculinity—the same hegemonic masculinity that has made it difficult for male skaters to get respect in the first place. To me this marks a closing down of possibilities for how men can use their bodies. It marks a small victory for the lowest-common denominator of guyness in a world that could benefit from a lot more effeminacy.

Checking Meaning and Style

1. What did the writer notice about Kurt Browning's image in *Saturday Night*?
2. What does "kind of feminine" refer to?
3. What has characterized Elvis Stojko's skating?
4. What is David Staples' attitude to skaters who get high artistic marks?
5. What kind of language is now used to describe male skaters?
6. What position did skater Ilia Kulik "belie" at Nagano?
7. Explain the expression "shore up the athleticism of skating."

Checking Ideas

1. Why does Brian Orser not get the endorsements other sports people do?
2. In what ways does Stojko reinforce the idea that skating is a sport?
3. What are two consequences of the "macho-ization" of skating?
4. What is the writer's attitude to these trends in male skating? What are her reasons for this view?

Alternative Medicine Gains Ground in Canada

Wallace Immen

Many practitioners of Western medicine are beginning to support the use of alternative types of medicine. The proliferation of "wellness" courses, massage therapy clinics, chiropractors, and other alternative practitioners all indicate the growing desire to use alternative medicine, often in combination with Western medical practices. Here, statistics on the use of alternative medicine across Canada are outlined.

Joan Watterson of Vancouver has gone from being in a wheelchair to being a regular jogger, and she says it is all because she "basically fired my doctor."

After being diagnosed with multiple sclerosis, Ms. Watterson spent years going to neurologists. "What I disliked is they were treating me as symptoms rather than a whole person," she said, and through a referral from a friend she found an M.D. who also is trained as a homeopath.

Homeopathic medicine added to conventional medical treatment and massage therapy brought enough relief that six years later she can say, "I'm not perfect, but I'm fine."

Ms. Watterson is not alone. At least 15 percent of Canadians aged 15 and older, or about 3.3 million people, seek out alternatives to conventional medicine, but most have not given up on doctors, according to figures being released today by Statistics Canada.

Only about 2 percent of people rely exclusively on alternative medicine, the study found, while 65 percent of Canadians used doctors only and about 12 percent had alternative care in addition to visits to a doctor. More than 20 percent said they consulted no one about their health problems.

While there is evidence that there is substantially more interest in alternative approaches to healing than there was a decade ago, this is the first time Health Canada has compiled numbers on their use, said Wayne Millar, senior analyst in the agency's health statistics division in Ottawa.

The National Population Health Survey asked 17 626 people in all provinces and territories whether they had consulted an alternative practitioner at some time within a year of the time the survey was taken. The options included: massage therapist, acupuncturist, homeopath, naturopath, Feldenkrais or Alexander Method teacher, relaxation therapist, biofeedback specialist, rolfer, herbalist, reflexologist, spiritual healer, or participation in a self-help group such as Alcoholics Anonymous.

Women were much more likely than men to seek out alternatives. Use of alternative therapies tends to be more common the farther west people live in Canada and is more frequent among those with higher levels of education and income. While the rate is only 5 percent of people in the Atlantic provinces, it is 14 percent in Quebec, 12 percent in Ontario and 21 percent in the Prairies and British Columbia. B.C. women were the most frequent users in the country, with 24 percent reporting at least one visit to some type of practitioner.

The Statistics Canada report, being published today in the *Canadian Journal of Public Health*, points out that chronic diseases that do not respond to medical treatment are often a factor in seeking other types of therapy. Only 9 percent of people with no long-term complaints consulted alternative-care providers, compared with 16 percent who had one chronic condition, 20 percent who had two lingering problems and 26 percent who had three or more.

Chiropractors were the largest category of alternative practitioner, often accounting for about two-thirds of consultations. Next most favoured were massage therapists and homeopaths, each used by about 2 percent of people surveyed.

In general, alternative treatments are not covered by provincial health-insurance plans, and the analysis concludes that inclusion of an alternative practitioner's services under existing health plans could result in higher health costs. "The key question is whether the extension would bring a reduction in the use of the conventional health system," Mr. Millar said.

"For many years now, there has been growing criticism of, and some would say rebellion against, technology and the perceived impersonalization of medical care," notes an accompanying analysis in the public health journal of the difference between users and non-users of alternative medicine. The analysis, by a group from the University of Montreal, found that in Quebec users of alternative care tend to be in better health than non-users.

However, that may not necessarily reflect the effectiveness of the treatments they receive. "If you're dying or have just been run over by a car, it doesn't make sense to look to complementary medicine first," commented Dr. David Gering, a Vancouver M.D. who incorporates homeopathy into his practice.

Dr. Gering said he believes that Statistics Canada's estimate is extremely low. He pointed to a 1993 U.S. survey that found 33 percent of people had used alternatives, although many in that poll said they had not even told their doctors about it. "I think this shows that people are using the resources that are available," Dr. Gering said.

Once they are diagnosed, people may then seek out unorthodox practitioners who can take more time with them than doctors in busy practices.

"Many people [who] come to me say they don't feel listened to" and have become disappointed by a system that treats them as an unhealthy body part rather than a whole person, Dr. Gering said.

The Canadian numbers are based on surveys taken in 1994 and 1995, and a follow-up study is being done to determine how use of alternative medicine is increasing, Statscan's Mr. Millar said.

Checking Meaning and Style

1. How does the writer begin the article?
2. What kinds of practices are labelled "alternative"?
3. What is the profile of people who visit alternative-care providers for help?
4. Why might Statistics Canada figures on usage be low?
5. What were the overall findings of the survey about usage (a) regionally? (b) by gender? Can you put these findings on a chart?

Checking Ideas

1. Why might people not tell their doctor they are using alternative medicine?
2. Why are people becoming disillusioned with Western medical practices?
3. Many Canadians have been concerned about their provinces' level of health care. What are some of these concerns?

Home Ice

Paul Quarrington

Have you ever skated on a homemade garden rink? In this process essay, Paul Quarrington shows us how to make such a skating rink.

Think of it as wintry gardening. Focus on the magical aspects, for on a more worldly level, we are about to discuss standing outside on the most bitter of nights with a spurting garden hose in your hand, likely frozen there forever. We are about to discuss how to make a backyard skating rink.

2   It seems to me that the backyard rink ranks right up there with frozen duck ponds and ice-locked rivers. Which is to say, they have a home not only on earth but also in our frostbitten imaginations. Dreams of Stanley Cups and figure-skating championships are born there. Local arenas are nice enough places, I suppose, but the important thing is the sense of community. When I think of local arenas, I think of the benches, the snack bars, the people huddled together eating cold hot dogs and blowing on cups of hot chocolate. The ice itself is nothing special—it is quiet and subdued, not like the unruly ice you find in a backyard rink. The ice of a backyard rink is welted and scarred and unable to smooth the wrinkled face of the planet. It is elemental, having as much claim to the land as rocks or wind.

3   That is why the process is not really so much "making" or "constructing" a backyard rink; it is more along the lines of allowing one to come into being, a sort of shivering midwifery. Some people conceive of the process as imposing the rink on the ground, which results in the most mundane and dreary objection to the backyard skating rink: it will ruin the grass. That is not true. I even checked with a landscape gardener who assured me that although the grass may grow in opposite directions for a time the rink won't ruin the grass.

4   I propose to pass on the recipe for the definitive, the quintessential, the perfect backyard skating rink. I did not arrive at such a recipe without a lot of help. I turned to my friend Peter Hayman, a Toronto filmmaker and father of three young boys. I have skated on Hayman's rink and know it to be first-class (I have a simple test: any ice that does not immediately flip me onto my dustcover is first-class). Also, I went to Ronn Hartviksen, the creator of perhaps the most ambitious and beautiful rink in the world, and I also consulted the guru of the backyard rink, Walter Gretzky.

5   The first step in making the rink is to find the right site. If you are going to make a rink, decide early in the season, well before winter is actually in sight. This is the easy part, walking outside and choosing the likeliest spot. It may be that you have a smallish backyard and are simply going to flood the whole thing. The guiding principle should arise from the fact that you are going to have to shovel, resurface, and otherwise groom your backyard rink, so you should keep it to a manageable size. Twenty by forty feet seems reasonable: large enough for skaters to manoeuvre, even to play a spirited, congested, game of shinny, but small enough to care for.

6   A prime consideration is flatness. It is not necessary that the ground be perfectly smooth (you will be surprised at how hilly and full of cavities your lawn really is), but there is no getting around the fact that it must be level. Some depressions can, of course, be built up with snow, and small rises will just become part of the rink.

7   The last consideration is proximity to a water source. Tapping into an inside source is best. If you can run a hose into the basement, for example, and hook up with the washing-machine taps, you will reap a number of benefits. Remember that no nozzle/hose connection is perfect, and imagine some of the nasty things that could happen at an outside connection—such as finding the thing encased in block of ice. Even if you avoid nightly chipping and hacking, any outside terminal is going to require a bucket or two of hot water just to get the tap cranked. So, if you can get to the water inside, so much the better, especially because in the maintenance stages, you can employ the hot water for resurfacing, a technique I call "the poor man's Zamboni" (a machine used to resurface the ice in arenas).

8   But let's not worry about maintenance right now; let's get the thing started. Just a couple of quick points here: make sure you have plenty of good-quality, thick, heavy rubber hose. Having selected the site, and got the hose, make sure the ground is properly tended, which means mowing and raking. If you don't you may face what

proved to be the bane of my childhood backyard rinks: errant blades of grass popping through the ice surface. I know this does not seem likely or even possible, but, believe me, little green Ninjas will sprout up and flip you onto your backside. So give your lawn a marring cut late in the fall.

Here is an optional step. In Thunder Bay, Hartviksen hoses down the naked earth in late fall but in more southerly climes, watering your lawn in fall serves no purpose except to demonstrate to the neighbours that you are fairly strange, so they will not think twice the first time you are out there at midnight and 40 below. **9**

Now you wait. You wait for cold temperatures. You are more than likely going to have to wait for the cold temperatures in January. So you wait for the requisite cold temperatures, and you wait for snow. Wait until there is a whole lot of snow, maybe two or three good dumpings. Then clear some of it away from your rectangle, leaving behind anywhere from four to six inches. This clearing supplies you with a little border, something to aid in water retention while flooding. It also gives a comfortable sense of containment and might even keep a puck on the ice, although you and I both know that the puck will hit your little ridge of snow, pick up torque, and be gone into the neighbour's yard. **10**

Now you are ready to make your base. It is best to flatten the snow. Hartviksen sends out troops of kids to play "boot hockey." He also possesses a heavy piece of wood that he can drag behind him, smoothing the surface. The foundation of the base you are making is snow. Snow plus water and the chilly, chilly air. I am going to advocate the "slush" approach to base building. I am the proponent of the most active sort of base building, getting out there with a hose and creating slush, which is then smoothed flat. You want the slush to be more solid than a slurpee, just watery enough that snowball construction is out of the question. Do small sections at a time: water the ground, work it into slush with a snow shovel, use the back of the shovel to smooth it out, move along, do it again. Work lanes, walking backward across the rink-to-be. Once you get that done, have someone carry you inside to thaw you out in a dry, warm corner. In the morning, it will be slightly hilly—well, let's face it, your rink at this point would baffle most topographical mapmakers. But that's all right. You have done most of the heavy human work now; it is time to turn things over to Mother Nature and let her smooth everything out. **11**

The next night, go out there armed with your hose. Just the hose, no fancy nozzle or sprayer: you have to have the open-ended hose because you want to get as much water on the ground in as short a time as possible. You should be able to hit most places without stepping on the ice surface, but if you can't, go ahead and step on it. Depending on how cold it is you might be able to do two or even three floodings that first night. When you have finished, do yourself an enormous favour: take the coil of hose inside the house with you. **12**

The next morning, you will find a vaguely flat sheet of ice, although it might be alarmingly pitted, cracked, and ravined. Now, in Peter Hayman's words, you "make like a referee." No, don't get small-minded and petty and order people around for no good reason (just joking); he means that you get out there on hands and knees—as referees often do during games—grab handfuls of snow and start stuffing the cracks and holes. Stuffing and tamping, tamping and stuffing. It's amazing how much snow even the smallest crack can hold, so don't imagine this is the work of a few moments. However, the more patching you do the better your rink will be. **13**

Now you have to do your flood that evening, taking care to find the air pockets that undermine the structure and correct them at this stage. In the morning, you have something that looks like a skating rink. There is still some patching to do, but **14** it seems less fundamental—more like polishing than anything else—and after another couple of floodings that evening you will have, if not a proper skating rink, what Hayman refers to with caution as "a skateable situation."

Put the lightest family member out there. Hold your breath. As the person skates around the outer edges there will be some creaking and cracking. Make like a referee and flood again that evening. And the next. And the next. You need an ice thickness of perhaps six inches to survive sudden thaw. In time you will not have to flood every evening, or even every other night, but many nights will find you out there, hose in hand, practising some wintry gardening. 15

Checking Meaning and Style

1. Where is the thesis statement in Paul Quarrington's essay?
2. How does Quarrington introduce many of the steps in the homemade-rink process?
3. What factors should you consider in choosing the site?
4. Why must you make sure the ground is "properly tended"?
5. What steps are involved in making the base?
6. What do you do when you "make like a referee"?
7. What is the tone of this essay? Where would you be likely to find an article of this kind?

Checking Ideas

1. In making a backyard rink, why is it advisable to focus on the magical aspects?
2. How does Quarrington view the backyard rink?
3. Why is skating so popular in Canada?
4. Do you participate in winter sports?

Dentistry Self-Drilled

Dave Barry

Columnist Dave Barry comments here on something many of us dread: a visit to the dentist!

I bet you rarely stop to think how important your teeth are. This is good. America is in enough trouble as it is, what with inflation and all; we just can't afford to have people stopping to think how important their teeth are, especially on major highways. 1

Nevertheless, you owe a lot to your teeth. They are your best friends. Think about it: while you're out here, playing tennis and reading novels, they're sitting patiently in your mouth, a foul-smelling, disgusting place almost devoid of recreational facilities, dealing with Slim Jims and Cheez-Its and the other crap you give them to chew. 2

You ought to apologize to your teeth for the way you treat them. You ought to go up to a mirror, right now, and bare your teeth and look them straight in their eyes 3 and say: "I'm sorry." You may want to practice a bit so you can say this clearly with your teeth bared. Don't let the children see you.

Now I know what you're thinking. You're thinking: "I don't have to apologize to my teeth. I take good care of my teeth."

That's what *you* think. That's what I thought, too, until I started going to the dentist again recently after a brief absence of about twelve years. I stopped going because I didn't trust him. For one thing, he wore an outfit that buttoned on the side, the kind the spaceship crews wear in low-budget science fiction movies. For another thing, he and his cohorts *always left the room* when they X-rayed me. They'd make up flimsy excuses, like "I have to go put my socks in the dryer," or "I think the cat is throwing up." Then they'd flip the X-ray switch and race out of the room, probably to a lead-lined concrete bunker.

When he came back, the dentist would jab me in the gums sixty or seventy times until my mouth was full of blood and I had to spit in what appeared to be a miniature toilet. Then he'd show me what he claimed was an X-ray of my mouth, knowing full well I would not be able to distinguish an X-ray of my mouth from a color slide of the Parthenon, and he'd tell me I had a cavity and he was going to fill it. I would tell him I hadn't noticed any so-called cavity, and that it was, after all, *my* mouth. And he would give me this long routine about how if he didn't fill it, all my teeth would fall out and I'd lose my job and end up drooling on myself in a gutter, which is what they taught him to say in dental school. Then he would spend several hours drilling a hole in my tooth.

Answer me this: A cavity is a hole in your teeth, right? So if the dentist is so *upset* about this hole in your teeth, why does he spend so much time making it *bigger?* Huh? Does he need more money so he can buy more space-uniform shirts?

Finally I decided I could save some money if I stopped going to the dentist, got a sharp implement and, in the privacy of my own home, jabbed *myself* in the gums a couple of times a year. I figured I could ward off cavities by brushing after every meal with an effective decay-preventive dentifrice. I mean, that's what they told us for years, right? "Brush your teeth after every meal," they said. Parents said it. Teachers said it. Bucky Beaver said it.

Never trust a talking beaver. I found this out the hard way when after twelve years of brushing like a madman, I returned to the dentist. The Dental Hygienist looked at my mouth the way you would look at a full spittoon. "You haven't been flossing," she said.

It seems that while I was home jabbing myself in the gums, the Dental Community was losing its enthusiasm for brushing and getting into flossing. These days the Dental Community regards anybody who merely brushes as a real bozo. This is blatantly unfair. In all those years of going to school and watching Bucky Beaver and Mister Tooth Decay, I never heard *one word* about flossing.

Flossing does not come naturally to human beings. If the Good Lord had wanted us to floss our teeth, He would have given us less self-respect. But the Dental Community says we have to do it, because otherwise we'll get gum disease.

Pretty slick, isn't it? If we can't even see cavities, how the hell are we going to dispute them when they tell us we have gum disease?

I was about to point all this out to my dentist when he gave me this gas, nitrous oxide I believe, and all of a sudden I felt *great.* I began to really *appreciate* the Dental Community for coming up with flossing and all the other fine things it has done for me over the years. I even began to soften toward Bucky Beaver.

I think this was part of the plan.

Checking Meaning and Style

1. What is the purpose of the introduction (Paragraphs 1 through 4)?
2. What is the tone of the selection? Which parts do you find particularly humorous?
3. What reasons does Barry give for having stopped going to the dentist?
4. Why, at the end, did Barry start to appreciate the Dental Community?

Checking Ideas

1. How is Barry's description of his dentist appointment similar to or different from your own experiences at the dentist's office?
2. Have you changed the way you think about your teeth and the dentist after reading this selection? Why or why not?
3. What new discoveries can you think of that have prompted the medical or dental community to change its recommendations for staying healthy?

WRITING RESOURCE A
WRITING A SUMMARY

What Is a Summary?

After you have seen a good movie, you tell your neighbour what it was about—that is a summary. Giving a brief account of something is making a summary. To summarize is to concentrate on the main points rather than on the details of a piece. It could be a summary of a news item, a novel, a film, or a scientific feature in a newspaper, for instance. A summary does not change the meaning of the original or reinterpret the author's view in any way. It is generally one-third the length of the original and includes only the essential points—the main ideas—and *not* the specific examples or details of the article. Unless quotation marks are used to indicate where the author's actual words are quoted, in a summary, writers use their own words.

Why Summarize?

The ability to summarize is a very useful study skill. It helps in recalling the main details of a textbook. For students, a quick summary on index cards can reinforce a text's or lecturer's main points and provide an easy review before finals. Summaries convey essential information about material to others who have not read or seen what the writer has. In research papers, a summary of a writer's work or opinion is essential if the report is an argument, a discussion, or an opinion about particular material. In addition, summaries are useful in writing comparisons of the plot, characters, or style in novels or films. Lastly, summaries help students focus concisely on the main ideas.

READING: FINDING THE MAIN POINTS OF AN ESSAY

In her article "Lack of English, Not Good Will, Is the Culprit," Anna Nike Mineyko explains why many immigrants have problems. Read the article and then examine the model summary, which has been taken from the main points of the article.

Lack of English, Not Good Will, Is the Culprit

–Anna Nike Mineyko

1   Did you ever have to look for a job in a new, unfamiliar environment, especially during a recession, while hardly being able to understand English, your second language?

2   A lot of immigrants in Canada could answer yes. They are afraid to make phone calls and are frightened by interviews because they lack communication skills. They are unsure if their résumé was written correctly or whether a covering letter might

contain errors. Many of these new Canadians are educated, some with university degrees. They are proud of their knowledge but are shy about what they perceive to be their poor English.

They seek employment because they are motivated and responsible. They have not arrived in Canada to collect welfare.

In Poland, I was a journalist and an editor. When I came to Canada three years ago, I didn't know English at all. During my first year, I learned by myself and then I took courses. One day I realized, "Okay, I am not a journalist right now. I can't write because I don't know sufficient English, but I can stay in my chosen field and experience the special, exhilarating tension involved in the print and publishing environment."

Today, my first Canadian job in a printing store came to an end. I found this job placement after completing a desktop publishing course. Because I also worked in Poland as a graphic designer, it wasn't difficult to change tools—from drawing by pencil to drawing by computer software. Much more difficult to learn, however, was how to understand the customers who visited the store.

Clients would order letterheads, business cards, envelopes, logos, invitations, résumés, newsletters, and flyers. They wanted to be advised by a designer and needed professional artwork.

It took time until I understood why the customer was the most important thing in the world. I remember one customer who stood over me while I created two complicated forms for him and a logo using CorelDraw.

The whole time he advised me that this job was supposed to take only 15 minutes. To behave properly in this context I should have smiled and been polite. I didn't smile. Instead, I asked him to go for coffee and come back after 20 minutes. Should I feel guilty? Yes; because the customer was paying for my work.

Customers expect not only nice, appropriate behaviour but also excellent communication skills. The Polish language expresses itself differently from English. We shear words; I make small breaks after each word I speak. My parents and teachers taught me how to speak properly in Poland because educated people have to speak Polish very clearly.

But English is a river. Words flow together. If somebody is nervous, or excited, he or she may speak in the same clipped manner, but I do that because English is my second language, not because I am nervous. The result is that Polish people often are thought to be aggressive because they speak English the same way they speak Polish.

A nice woman visited our store quite frequently. After a few visits, I felt she barely tolerated contact with me. One day I understood why: I sounded rude.

It happened when I couldn't open her electronic file in the software memory. I told her about my difficulties simply: "I can't open your file." I said this sentence clearly. As usual, I sheared words. My accent caused what I said to sound harsh. Even though I smiled, she may have thought I meant, "I won't open your file."

I wanted to say, "Although I can't open your file, don't worry. I will redo this job quickly. I'll give you a call, when I am finished."

Unfortunately, she did not give me enough time to communicate further. The woman was furious. "You know what?" she said, "I'll come back at 6 o'clock to pick up this job!" The work ended up being done well and on time, but I felt the woman now thought I was her enemy. This was a terrible misunderstanding.

It's very important to understand and to be aware of why new immigrants might appear as if they're from outer space. No one is at fault. Each culture is beautiful. And here in this wonderful country we can meet and enjoy people from other cultures.

If a woman from Jamaica doesn't speak before a man during a meeting at work, it doesn't necessarily mean that she is passive. If a Polish man doesn't smile too often, it doesn't mean he doesn't like people. It's important to be aware of these differences. 16

"Take it easy, Anna," my friend, a designer at the print shop, said after a discussion about my artwork. "I will," I said, but I was upset the whole weekend before I came to realize that there is nothing wrong with me. 17

Many other immigrants have the same problem—we suffer from culture shock. 18

WRITING MODELS: THE SUMMARY

Following is an example of a summary, taken from the reading about the importance of understanding a language and cultural problems many immigrants experience. The main points of the article have been selected, paragraph by paragraph, and the article is shortened to about one-third of its length.

Model Summary

Summary of "Lack of English, Not Good Will, Is the Culprit" by Anna Nike Mineyko

Anna Nike Mineyko, in her article "Lack of English, Not Good Will, Is the Culprit," from the *Toronto Star*, February 1994, writes about the difficulties of immigrants who speak little English. It is hard to find a job in a "new, unfamiliar environment, especially during a recession."

She maintains that, because of their lack of English, immigrants are hesitant about their job application skills, even though they may be very highly qualified. They want to find work rather than be on welfare, states Mineyko, who was a journalist in Poland. When she arrived here she had to teach herself English before taking courses. She found a job in a printing store, realizing that she could not be a journalist without adequate English.

Her printing job was stressful, mainly because of her difficulty in understanding the customers. She had no idea of the importance of smiling and being polite to the customer. Mineyko explains that Polish makes sharper sounds than English, which is more flowing, like a river. To the customers, to whom she thought she was being polite, she actually sounded aggressive and rude. With one particular customer, for example, as a result of Mineyko's lack of English, a serious misunderstanding arose: the customer thought Mineyko was "her enemy."

Mineyko pleads for understanding of new immigrants' situation. She says that every culture is beautiful and can be enjoyed in our country if we are aware of cultural differences and of the culture shock from which many immigrants suffer.

WRITING ASSIGNMENT: A SUMMARY

Select a reading from Checkpoints, and follow these seven steps.

1. Carefully read the passage to be summarized, considering the main topic, the thesis of the article, and the main point of each paragraph. The main point should be conveyed in the topic sentence in each paragraph. If you cannot find the main point in one sentence, imagine that you are telling a friend about what you have just read, without going into great detail: what you say will be the main point.

2. Read the passage again and highlight the topic sentence, or main point, of each paragraph.

3. Take the highlighted parts and write them in sequence into one paragraph on a separate paper.

4. Consider whether you need to add any details to make proper sense. Fill in any "gaps," keeping your sentences as lengthy and as complex as possible. Two ideas can often be conveyed in one sentence. This approach will help keep the summary brief.

5. Count the words to ensure that you have the desired length, usually one-third of the original.

6. Make sure that your first sentence includes the author's name, the article's title (correctly punctuated), with a present-tense verb, clearly stated before the introduction of the topic of the item.

    EXAMPLE: E. M. Forster, in *Aspects of the Novel,* defines two types of literary characters.

    OR: In "Legalize Marijuana," Frank Jones suggests that the drug should no longer be illegal.

7. Check that you have a sufficient conclusion in the last sentence, with no additional, personal opinions.

    EXAMPLE: Ian Burton concludes that we must all be aware of our behaviour and how it affects the global situation.

WRITING RESOURCE B
REVISING AND EDITING

USING A COMPUTER

If you have your own computer, you probably already know it can be a big help in your writing. If you don't have one, you perhaps can gain access to one in a computer lab on campus. A lab technician may be available to help you get started, and the "Help" option found on the top bar of many word processors can take you to on-screen instructions.

Deleting and Moving Copy

It is a simple matter to *remove* a sentence, a paragraph, or a larger unit. First "select" the material by running the cursor over it while the left mouse key is pressed. Or take the Edit and Select route at the top of the screen. The material you have now highlighted will be removed when you click Delete on the keyboard. To *move* material to a different spot, first select it, then use Edit/Cut. The selected material will disappear. Place the cursor at the desired insertion point and dick Edit/Paste to restore and move the material. Since making changes is so easy; you have the advantage of trying several versions of a sentence—especially a thesis or topic sentence—without a lot of erasing or crossing out.

Spelling

Many word-processing programs will check your spelling for you. Either select the material you wish to check or place the cursor at the point where you wish to begin checking. Click the spelling icon at a screen-top bar, or dick Tools/Spelling. The program will identify any questionable spellings and present a list of alternatives. Remember, the computer doesn't know that your seemingly correct "their" should have been spelled "there."

Vocabulary

If you think that a word you have written isn't quite the right one—or if you think you would like to use a more impressive word (let's hope not!)—some word processors will show you a list of words that have a similar meaning. For example, if you're dissatisfied with "car," you might have access to a pull-down menu that will list these synonyms, among others: auto, limousine, convertible, sedan, jalopy, lemon. A dictionary may be needed to help you figure out which of the words best fits your needs. (If you are connected to the Internet, you can turn to online dictionaries, such as Merriam-Webster's at www.m-w.com.)

Grammar

Your computer may even be able to check your grammar—after a fashion. First, select the content you wish to check, or place the cursor at a starting point. Click the grammar icon. Then see if you agree with the computer on any of the "errors" found.

Prewriting

If a keyboard is faster for you than a pen, the computer can be an advantage in brainstorming, nonstop writing, list making, and other quick methods of coming up with topics, as well as details, for paragraphs and essays. Word processors can simplify outlining. The "columns" and "divide page" features are useful when, for example, you want to set up side-by-side lists for comparison prewriting.

Editing and Revising

Some writers prefer to print out a paper copy of the material for this stage of the process. Be sure to leave space in the margins and between the lines for your corrections and improvements.

REVISING AND EDITING A PARAGRAPH

Revising and editing are two different steps in the process of writing. Revise a paragraph by making sure that your words communicate what you actually think and that readers will understand your points. Edit a paragraph to check for sentence sense. When you are finished with revising and editing, print a new copy of your paragraph and read it one last time to make sure everything is the way you want it to be.

Revising

Here are questions to ask as you revise a paragraph:

- Does it communicate your ideas clearly?
- Does it have a topic sentence that says what the paragraph is about?
- Is it unified? Do all of the other sentences stick to the topic?
- Is it adequately developed with specific details to make it interesting and convincing?

Lynn Quesnel was using a college writing assignment to explore the following question about her personal life: Should she work longer hours to be able to afford nicer things, or should she work fewer hours to have more time with her children?

Lynn used clustering and then journal writing to develop a first, rough draft of a paragraph. Here it is.

Rough Draft

What is more important, having money or having time? If I work longer hours at my job, I can earn a lot of money. That money *should* buy me a lot of great things—like a nice house, new cars, and vacations! But how many hours of work a week would it take to get them—fifty? Sixty? I already work 35 hours a week, and I'm nowhere near a new car or a vacation, although I do have a nice fat mortgage. And then if I worked longer hours, what about the kids—spending time with them, teaching them, just being with them? If I work less hours, so I can stay home with the kids. Then will I have any money to take them places, feed them, give them stuff they need, or will I just be sitting around worrying; about having enough money to pay the bills?

Lynn's Observations about the Rough Draft

Lynn read her draft after she wrote it. She decided to write down what she learned about her own ideas when she read the paragraph. Here is what she wrote.

REVISING AND EDITING   303

—The paragraph seems to say that I think of time and money as opposites—are they really? Is there a real choice here, or am I painting the situation as too black and white?

—What are the possible solutions? The draft seems to be a long rant!

—There isn't really a topic sentence. Instead, I ask a question. The paragraph has some details.

Instead of taking her rough draft and trying to "fix" it bit by bit, Lynn started a whole new paragraph. This time, she wrote more slowly and thought about her observations. She decided to start with what time and money have in common.

Second Draft

I love both time and money. I love time because it gives me chances to relax, to just "be" with my children, time to cook. Time to play, time to dance and run. But I also love money, and more importantly than money, I love my job. My job gives me space to myself away from my family, a chance to be creative, it gives me a lot of satisfaction because I do my job pretty well. I also like to have money to spend, to get my kids the toys they want (and that they learn from). If I had money but didn't have any time to spend it, or if I had time but didn't have any money to spend, I wouldn't be happy. When I really think about it, compared to a lot of folks, I have a lot of both time and money right now.

Lynn's Thoughts about the Second Draft

The second draft seemed better to Lynn. It seemed less like nonstop writing and more thoughtful. The act of writing this second draft also changed how Lynn was thinking about the topic. Lynn decided to start her next draft by writing a topic sentence. She also decided to make the paragraph sound less personal. Realizing that a lot of working mothers probably share her dilemma, she started out with a new topic sentence.

Third Draft with Topic Sentence

For a working mother with children, time and money seem to be two opposing choices, but they are actually both important for different reasons. She needs time so she can be with her children, to teach them the values that she finds important, and simply playing with them. By not working too many hours, she can still have time to cook and do other household tasks. She can have time for herself—to dance, run, relax, whatever. But money is also important so Mom can have a share in the Canadian dream. Live in a nice place, drive a decent car, and buy the things that her family wants, such as music CDs and books.

Even more important, mothers need their work. I for one love my job. It gives me a chance to be creative. And a lot of satisfaction because I do my job pretty well.

Even though it sometimes seems that a working mother needs to choose either time or money—staying home or going to work—the real question is how to find a balance between them, because neither one offers all the benefits that she needs.

Lynn was pleased with this draft. She thought it communicated her ideas well and that the details she had added explained her ideas better. The details also seemed to fit with the topic sentence for the most part. Lynn did make changes to the last few sentences, shown above in handwriting, because they seemed to go too far off the topic. She decided the draft was ready for editing.

EDITING

Editing a paragraph means examining it for "sentence sense."

- Look at each sentence to make sure that it is logical, grammatical, and error-free. For example, ask these questions about your sentences:
  - Are all of the sentences complete, or are there some fragments that need to be revised?
  - Do the subjects and verbs agree?
  - Is there some variety in the sentences?
- Check each word to be sure it is the best word for what you want to say.
- Check the punctuation, capitalization, and other small matters to make sure everything is correct.

Lynn read her paragraph and wrote notes to herself in the margin. (The notes are circled in the paragraph below.) Then she went back and edited each sentence in response to the notes.

Paragraph with Editing

> For a working mother with children, time and money seem to be two opposing choices, but they are actually both important for different reasons. She needs time so she can be with her children, to teach them the values that she finds important, and simply playing with them. By not working too many hours, she can still have time to cook and do other household tasks. She can have time for herself—to dance, run, relax, whatever But money is also important so Mom can have a share in the Canadian dream. Live in a nice place, drive a decent car, and buy the things that her family wants, such as music CDs and books. Even though it sometimes seems that a working mother needs to choose either time or money—staying home or going to work—the real question is how to find a balance between them, because neither one offers all the benefits that she needs.

Lynn improved her paragraph with careful editing. Notice, however, that she did not begin editing until she thought she had a strong draft. By keeping revising and editing separate, Lynn maintained her focus, first on the big issues and later on the smaller ones.

WRITING RESOURCE C USING OUTSIDE SOURCES IN WRITING

Writing in college is like joining a conversation that people are already having about your topic, only the conversation is written on paper instead of being spoken. To show how your ideas fit into the discussion, you will need to refer to specific details of other people's written work. These ideas and words have to be handled with the utmost integrity if one is not to be accused of **plagiarism.** Plagiarism is the use of someone else's ideas, words, or work as one's own. It is regarded as cheating because it is dishonest to take another person's work without acknowledging the source. Any idea you wish to use in your own writing must be documented regarding its source. This means that works must be cited, or listed, in an index—usually a Works Consulted—at the end of the paper and documented within the paper.

Here are some easy guidelines to follow:

- Keep your own ideas and words separate from your outside sources

- Tell your readers exactly where you came across the ideas you are quoting.

- Use an approved citation style. This is often the MLA (Modern Language Association), which is generally used in fine arts and humanities, while the APA (American Psychological Association) is used in social sciences. In natural and applied sciences, the Council of Science Editors offers a choice.

Here, the examples are all in MLA style. This includes an in-text citation, also called a parenthetical citation, and a corresponding Works Cited (Consulted) entry at the end of the paper.

KEEP YOUR IDEAS SEPARATE FROM YOUR SOURCES' IDEAS

Only refer to other people's ideas by quoting their exact words, paraphrasing their ideas (in your own words, that is) or summarizing the most important points.

When you include a source's exact words, there are three ways of indicating this:

- Introduce the material with a phrase including the name, qualifications, and publication of the quote

- Enclose the exact words from the source inside quotations

- Give the page number of the source in which you read the words you are quoting

> **EXAMPLE:** William Damon, director of the centre on adolescence at Stanford University, defines the youth charter as "a coherent set of standards and expectations for youth behaviour, shared by all the important people in a young person's life" (43).

In this case, obviously the source is a reliable one as he is an expert on youth behaviour with an important position as a director. It is easy to see where Mr. Damon's words are used because of the clear use of quotation marks. In addition, at the end of the quote, the page number where the words are located is cited. The book that the quote came from is listed in "Works Cited" at the end of the essay.

> **Grammar Check:** Be careful to ensure that the quote does not sound confusing because of your introductory sentence.
>
> **EXAMPLE:** Ellen Goodman, a writer for the *Boston Globe*, disagrees with this view and "for openers, 38 percent of all poor children already live in two-parent homes" (A13).

This is a confusing statement because the quote is not well introduced. Using the word "noting" helps smooth the transition:

> Ellen Goodman, a writer for the *Boston Globe*, disagrees with this view, noting that "38 percent of all poor children already live in two–parent homes" (A13).

Note that in the revised version, the writer left out words at the beginning of the quote. If you leave out words in the middle of a quote, you need to indicate this with three dots, like this ". . .". Some instructors may wish you to surround these dots with brackets [. . .].

> **EXAMPLE:** Gene Logsdon states that one type of "biological degradation" on today's farm is human: "the quiet despair of farmers today is plainly due to the . . . strain of economic pressures" (41).

If you are not quoting directly, to avoid plagiarism, you must give the author's name and the page number of the source, but you do not need quotation marks if you are paraphrasing, or summarizing the work.

> **EXAMPLE:** Linguist Deborah Tannen has found that men and women have different habits of speech, and this difference can lead to misunderstanding. For example, women may appear to be at fault when they are not because they have a habit of apologizing (284). Men may appear to be harsh if they have a habit of giving direct criticism (285).

In this example, Tannen is identified as a linguist; no quotation marks are used since her direct words were not quoted, but her ideas were summarized and page numbers for her work are included. As a result, the reader knows when Tannen's ideas are being stated.

Alternatively, Tannen could have been cited in the parenthesis with the page number:

> **EXAMPLE:** Men and women have different habits of speech (Tannen 284–285).
>
> **Note:** A range of page numbers is given because Tannen discusses this issue over a few pages.

In order to form their own opinions, readers need to know where your outside material came from, including:

- Who wrote it?
- Where did it appear?

The answers to these questions help the reader know how much **credibility** to give the material—there is a difference in quality between *The Enquirer* and *The Globe and Mail!*

- What is the page reference?

Once they have this, they can read the entire source for themselves.

Direct Quotes

If a quote is less than four lines, use quotation marks, check the grammar so that the statement flows from your introduction, and add the parenthetical note before the final period of the sentence.

If the quotation is longer than four lines, use a block format.

> **EXAMPLE:** Judy Rebick attempts to describe the people on welfare: What's the reality of people on welfare? The highest welfare fraud figure I have ever seen is 6.8 percent. There is more fraud going on in Toronto's SkyDome every given Saturday when Toronto businessmen take their families to tax deductible boxes that are supposed to be for business associates than in all the welfare offices across the country (Rebick 5).

Works Cited

At the end of your essay, a separate page lists all of the other works you have consulted and quoted from. Consult the style sheet in your college for exact directions.

In most Works Cited, the following patterns are observed.

Book

The author's name, then title of the book, followed by the publisher's name, place of publication, and date.

> **EXAMPLE:** Kogawa, Joy. *Obasan.* Penguin: Toronto, 1991.
>
> > NOTE: Authors' names are always listed by the surname, and in alphabetical order. If there are more than three authors, usually only the first one is named, followed by *et al.* (meaning *and others*).

If there is no author, alphabetize the book by its first word, not including articles such as *an* or *the.*

Article

Many of your quotes will be from articles you have read on a particular topic.

> **EXAMPLE:** Landsberg, Michelle. "Beauty Myth Preserves Male Dominance," *Toronto Star* (May 7, 1998): C-1.
>
> > NOTE: All months are abbreviated except May, June, and July. The date order is day, month, year.

Web Site

There are many variations for Web site entries, depending of course on the actual site. If no author is given, name the Web site itself. If two dates are given, include both—one is the date of the site, and the second is the date you accessed the site. You will find the name of the institution sponsoring the site between the dates, and the complete URL will be given at the end. So as not to be accused of plagiarism, be very careful to acknowledge your sources from the Web as you would from any other source.

> **EXAMPLE:** "Camping with the Sioux: The Fieldwork Diary of Alice Cunningham Fletcher." 2001. *National Anthropological Archives, Smithsonian Institution.* 9 July 2002 <http://www.nmnh.si.edu/naa/fletcher/fletcher.htm>.

For an example of Works Cited, please see the list of texts in the Acknowledgements section of this book.

Plagiarism

In order for you to be certain that you understand the difference between plagiarism and quoting your sources, here is an example to help you.

> **Original Source:** The issue of undocumented or illegal immigrants in the United States is of recent vintage. It hardly entered public thinking during the first hundred years in the history of immigration in the United States, because no federal laws restricted immigration. (Source: Bischoff, *Immigration Issues*, p. 265.)

> **Plagiarized:** The dispute of <u>undocumented or illegal immigrants</u> in the United States of America is of <u>recent</u> age. The <u>public hardly</u> thought about it <u>during the first</u> century of the <u>history of immigration</u> to America—<u>no federal laws</u> limited immigration (Bishoff 265).

Using synonyms, or the same words exactly, is unacceptable.
Here are two acceptable versions, one without using a direct quote:

> Bischoff comments that public debate over illegal immigrants is fairly new. There was no reason to discuss it previously because there were no federal laws governing immigration (265).

Bischoff comments that public debate over illegal immigrants is fairly new: "The public hardly thought about it during the first century of the history of immigration to America because no federal laws governed immigration" (Bischoff 265).

Example of Works Cited

The Basic Guide to Resume Writing and Job Interviews. Videotape. Advantage Video, 1998.

Burton, Ian. "Individual Actions Can Have Huge Consequences," *Globe and Mail* (13 July 1990): A13.

Carver, Raymond. "Cathedral." *An Introduction to Fiction.* Fifth Edition. Ed. X.J. Kennedy. Toronto: Little Brown, 1991.

WRITING RESOURCE D FOR STUDENTS OF ESL

Non-native users of English sometimes have a problem choosing from the articles *a* and *an* and the adjective *some*.

Using *A, An,* and *Some*

The article *a* is used before words that do not begin with a vowel (*a, e, i, o, u*): a book, a scary movie.

An is used before words that do begin with a vowel: an alligator, an open door. (It often is helpful to say the two words together. It is easier to say "an apple" than "a apple." It is easier to say "a banana" than "an banana.")

A and *an* have no plural forms:

> Singular: There is an apple in the refrigerator. Plural: There are apples in the refrigerator. (no article)

The word *some* can be used before plural nouns: "There are some apples in the refrigerator."

A and *an* are not used before nouns that cannot be counted, such as gasoline, weather, and music: "Be sure to buy flour at the store." Or, "It looks as if we'll have good weather for the parade."

The word *some* can be used before both "countable" and "uncountable" words:

> Countable: I need some new socks.

> Uncountable: Some geometry should be required in high school.

Spotcheck D-1

Write a, an, *or* some *in the blanks.*

1. She's buying _____ dress.
2. He's studying _____ English textbook.
3. I'm looking for _____ blueberries.
4. She is eating _____ ice cream cone.
5. He is writing _____ letter.
6. Farmer Brown is selling _____ wheat.

Using *The* Instead of *A* or *An*

Use the article *the* before things already mentioned.

> There is a clock on the cabinet. The clock is ten minutes slow.

Use *the* before specific things.

> **(nonspecific)** We saw a movie at a downtown theatre.

> **(specific)** We saw the movie *Jaws* at the Paramount Theatre.

Spotcheck D-2

Write a, an, the, *or* some *in the blanks.*

1. Rafael has _____ cap on backwards. _____ cap has "Astros' sewn on it.
2. There are _____ fishing reels in the box. _____ reels are new.
3. There is _____ bread dough in the bowl. _____ dough is ready for the oven.
4. Wilhelmina knows _____ author of children's books. _____ author will speak in the student lounge tomorrow.
5. _____ car is parked at the side of the road. _____ car has a flat tire.

Spotcheck D-3

Write a, an, the, *or* some *in the blanks.*

Although he is 5 feet, 8 inches tall, Tony Figueroa weighs 180 pounds. ¹_____ doctor told him his weight was too high and that he should try to get ²_____ exercise.

Now Tony goes to ³_____ Downtown YMCA gym three times a week where he does ⁴_____ variety of exercises. ⁵_____ gym has ⁶_____ indoor running track and Tony begins his exercise each day with 20 laps around ⁷_____ track. Then he works out on ⁸_____ stair-climbing machine. ⁹_____ machine develops ¹⁰_____ leg muscles and is good for his heart. Rather than "pump iron" like ¹¹_____ more serious exercisers, Tony uses ¹²_____ machines that develop upper body muscles, such as ¹³_____ pectorals, ¹⁴_____ abdominals, and ¹⁵_____ biceps. On ¹⁶_____ days, when he is feeling especially good, he finishes with ¹⁷_____ 20-minute swim in ¹⁸_____ gym's pool.

Verb-Preposition Combinations (Phrasal Verbs)

Non-native speakers of English may run into combinations of verbs and prepositions that seem odd. In the preceding sentence, *run into,* meaning "encounter," is an example of this. Here are similar expressions that are often used:

be or get back by—return: I'll <u>be back by</u> midnight.

be out of—not have any: The cafeteria <u>is out</u> of boiled spinach.

blow up—inflate: Maria's mother <u>blew</u> up 20 balloons for the party.

break down—stop working (machines): The motorcycle <u>broke down</u> near Saskatoon.

break up—end a relationship: Is it true that Glenn and Gloria <u>have broken up</u>?

call back—return a phone call: I'm busy now. I'll <u>call</u> you <u>back</u> at noon.

carry on—continue an activity: When Juana comes back, just <u>carry on</u> as if nothing had happened.

carry on—act emotionally: Bill <u>carried on</u> like a six-year-old when he didn't get the promotion.

clean up—put things in order: Who will be <u>cleaning up</u> after the banquet?

clear up—improve (weather): I hope it <u>clears up</u> before the game Saturday.

come on or hurry up—move faster: <u>Come on!</u> We don't want to be late for class again.

come across or bump into—meet unexpectedly: Guess who I <u>came across</u> in Florio's Cafe this morning?

cut down on—do or eat less: Boris lost ten pounds after he <u>cut down on</u> eating sticky buns.

cut in—interrupt: Antoine was talking to Becky when Felicity rudely <u>cut in.</u>

do with—related to: Ecology has something to <u>do with</u> protecting the environment.

do without—give up something: The pioneers had to <u>do without</u> sugar.

get back—return or have returned: I have to <u>get</u> that book <u>back</u> to the library by Monday.

give up—surrender or lose hope: I'm afraid that Ng will just <u>give up</u> if he doesn't get an "A" in the class.

give up—quit a behaviour: Luana sings much better since she <u>gave up</u> smoking.

go ahead—do it (but you shouldn't): <u>Go ahead</u>! Spend your rent money on beer!

go against—oppose: Our debating team <u>goes against</u> Springhaven in the tournament.

go away—leave: Are you staying in the dorm over spring break or <u>going away</u>?

go back—return: Rosa is <u>going back</u> to college in the fall.

go in for—enjoy: Jorge <u>goes in for</u> classical music.

go out—leave (to have a good time): No more TV viewing! I'm <u>going out</u> this weekend.

go up—increase: The price of gasoline has <u>gone up</u> again.

keep up with—match, equal: The Smiths can't <u>keep up with</u> the Joneses in buying expensive clothes.

leave behind—abandon: Tim had to <u>leave</u> his dog <u>behind</u> when he joined the navy.

let in or out—allow to enter or leave: Be sure to <u>let</u> the cat <u>out</u> before you leave for work.

look after—take care off: The neighbour <u>looks after</u> our children each Tuesday.

look out—be careful: <u>Look out</u>! That dog looks mean.

look up—do research: I'll have to <u>look up</u> *anthropomorphism* in the dictionary.

put in—deposit: Remember to <u>put</u> a quarter <u>in</u> the parking meter.

put on or turn on—<u>Put on</u> the light. It's too dark to read.

put up with—permit, tolerate: Cristina can't <u>put up</u> with her neighbour's loud music.

run out of—exhaust the supply: We'll stop at the next filling station. We're about to <u>run out of</u> gasoline.

send for—order (by mail, phone, etc.): My wife <u>sent for</u> a back scratcher that was demonstrated on the shopping channel.

set off—cause to sound: The burglar <u>set off</u> the car alarm.

stop at—go to a place: <u>Stop at</u> the supermarket on your way home and pick up a loaf of bread.

take after—resemble a relative: Little Jimmy <u>takes after</u> his dad; they both have freckles.

take off—leave the ground (aircraft): The plane <u>took off</u> two hours late.

take off—remove clothing: Spike's mother told him to <u>take</u> his cap <u>off</u> at the dinner table.

take out—display: The drug dealer <u>took</u> a hundred-dollar bill <u>out</u> of his wallet.

take out—remove: Don't forget to <u>take out</u> the garbage before going to work.

turn down or up—lower or increase the volume: <u>Turn down</u> the TV, please, so I can study.

turn on or off—cause or cease to function: <u>Turn on</u> the radio, and find out if the Oilers won today.

be up to—be capable of: Are you <u>up to</u> the challenges of army training?

Spotcheck D-4

Write the correct prepositions in the blanks.

1. Who will clean _____ the mess after the party?
2. Frasier was worried when he realized that he was _____ money.
3. I hope this old car doesn't break _____ before we get home.
4. Melanie was surprised when she bumped _____ Alex in the nightclub.
5. Doesn't quantum theory have something to do _____ mathematics?
6. I hope Zu Shah doesn't go _____ before Sam comes home from college.
7. Lisa hopes the weather clears _____ for her wedding day.
8. When Anatol comes in, shout "Surprise!" and then turn _____ the light.
9. Claudette said the theatre is already _____ tickets, so we can't attend.
10. How much money did you put _____ your savings account?
11. Lourdes got _____ the money Margarita had borrowed to buy books.
12. I could really go _____ a nice cool drink right now.

WRITING RESOURCE E GRAMMATICAL TERMS— THE PARTS OF SPEECH AND TRANSITION WORDS

Words are classified into eight *parts of speech* based on their use in a sentence.

Noun A word such as Patricia, New York, sofa, or patriotism that names a person, place, thing, or idea.

Proper nouns name particular people, places, etc., and are capitalized: *Professor Kinski, Lake Louise, Pepsi, Buddhism.*

Common nouns name people and things in general and are not capitalized: *doctor, river, soft drink, religion.*

Group (collective) nouns refer to groups of people or things as if they were a single unit: *team, audience, flock.*

Verb **Action verbs** say what the subject does: "The boy *ran* home." **Linking verbs** connect the subject to a word that identifies or describes it: "The boy *was* tired."

Transitive verbs have an object that receives the action of the verb: "The car *hit* the hydrant." **Intransitive verbs** do not take an object: "Birds *fly*."

A **verb phrase** is a verb made up of more than one word: *has run, could have run, will be running.*

A verb in **active voice** shows the subject acting: "The singer also *played* a guitar." A verb in **passive voice** shows the subject being acted upon: "A guitar *was played* by the singer."

Adjective A word that describes a noun ("*talented* actress") or pronoun ("she is *talented*"). An adjective tells which one, what kind, or how many.

Adverb A word that describes a verb ("ran *slowly*"), an adjective ("*very* beautiful"), or another adverb ("moved *rather* quickly"). An adverb tells how, when, where, or to what extent.

Pronoun A word that takes the place of a noun: "The students entered slowly. *They* dreaded Professor Higgins' exams."

Personal pronouns refer to people or things: *I, we, you, she, he, it, they.* Besides those subject forms, pronouns also have object forms (*me, us, you, her, him, them*) and possessive forms (*my, mine, our, ours, your, yours, his, her, hers, their, theirs, its*). Example: "*We* gave *them* *our* tickets."

Indefinite pronouns (*each, neither, anyone, everybody,* etc.) do not refer to a specific person or thing: "*Nobody* knows the answer."

Interrogative pronouns (*who, whom, whose, what, which*) begin questions: "*Whose* book is that?"

Relative pronouns (the interrogative pronouns, plus *whoever, whomever, whichever, whatever*) begin dependent clauses: "The books were free to *whoever* needed them."

Intensive pronouns (words ending with *-self* or *-selves*) give emphasis to a noun or other pronoun: "The doctor *himself* said it." "We *ourselves* will pay the bill."

Reflexive pronouns (words ending with *-self* or *-selves*) show the subject acting upon itself: "The carpenter hit *himself* on the thumb."

Demonstrative pronouns (*this, that, these, those*) point to a particular person or thing: "*These* are my favourite flowers."

Preposition

A word such as *to, for, of, in, with,* or *between* that connects a noun or pronoun (its object) to the rest of the sentence and forms a prepositional phrase: "They went swimming *in the river.*"

Conjunction

A word that joins other words.

Coordinating conjunctions ("connectors") are *and, but, or, for, nor, yet,* and *so*. They join grammatically equal units, such as two independent clauses: "Sylvia attended the concert, *but* Glenn was out of town."

Subordinating conjunctions ("dependent words") include words such as *although, because, since,* and *unless*. They join dependent (subordinate) clauses to independent clauses: "We went by train *because* Ernie doesn't like to fly."

Conjunctive adverbs ("transitional words") join independent clauses: "Bernice got a pay raise; *however,* she remained unhappy." Other conjunctive adverbs include *moreover, nevertheless, finally,* and *meanwhile.*

Interjection

A word showing strong feeling, such as *wow, oh,* or *well:* "*Oh,* I could hardly believe my eyes!"

Transition Words

These words are extremely important for sentence variety when writing in any particular rhetorical mode.

For reference, here is a list of transitions in their usage categories.

Additional Information
additionally
also
besides
furthermore in other words (use for restatement of same idea)
moreover

then
finally

Comparison
equally important
likewise
similarly

Time Reference
afterwards
eventually
later
meanwhile
next
now
soon
subsequently

Effect
as a result
accordingly
because of this
consequently
otherwise (negative effect)
therefore
thus

Contrast
conversely
despite this
however
instead
in contrast
nevertheless
on the contrary
on the other hand
still

Example
as a matter of fact
for example
indeed
in fact
truly

The following is a list of the most common subordinate conjunctions:

after	in order that	though
although	like	unless
as	no matter how	until
because	once	when
before	provided (that)	whenever
even though	since	where
if	so (that)	whereas
in case	than	while

ANSWER KEY

Spotcheck 1-1

1. its
2. its
3. It's
4. it's, its
5. It's

Spotcheck 1-2

1. their
2. They're
3. Their, there
4. There, their
5. they're, their, there

Spotcheck 1-3

Answers will vary.

1. The gas company fired its president.
2. It's been a long time since I last saw Harry.
3. There are at least two ways of looking at most things.
4. The Smiths lost their Doberman.
5. The Guccis say they're going to move.

Doublecheck 1-1

1. their
2. There
3. It's
4. its
5. their
6. They're
7. its
8. their
9. there
10. their

Spotcheck 1-4

1. Are, our, or
2. have
3. hear
4. here
5. than
6. too
7. Where
8. were
9. You're
10. here
11. Then

Doublecheck 1-2

Answers will vary.

1. June is taller than April.
2. We're in trouble now.
3. Sam is in trouble, too.
4. There's a song in my heart.
5. Your lunch is ready.
6. I hear a lark singing.
7. I eat an apple every day.
8. Where is our car?
9. Bill is too tired to play tennis.
10. You're in biology class at 11 o'clock.

Doublecheck 1-3

1. too
2. It's
3. our
4. too
5. there's
6. have
7. your, its
8. then
9. than
10. There's
11. than, theirs
12. its
13. Your
14. its
15. You're, or

Editing Check 1

1. are two
2. when they're putting salt and pepper on their food they're using
3. were paid in salt
4. was very precious too
5. are still very expensive today as pepper heightens our desire to eat
6. would never have begun; might never have happened

ANSWER KEY 317

Spotcheck 2-1

1. (Example) The Olympic Games have become highly controversial. First, many judging decisions have been suspected of being fixed; many athletes' drug abuses are detected and governments go into debt on the taxpayers' dollars.
2. Answers will vary.
3. Answers will vary.

Spotcheck 2-2

Answers will vary.

Spotcheck 2-3

Sentences 3 and 9

Spotcheck 2-4

Answers will vary.

Spotcheck 2-5

1. good
2. good
3. weak
4. good
5. weak

Spotcheck 2-6

Answers will vary.

Spotcheck 2-7

1. weak
2. weak
3. weak
4. good
5. weak
6. weak

Spotcheck 2-8

Answers will vary.

1. My favourite sport is tennis.
2. My neighbourhood has several attractive front yards.
3. Christmas shopping is Valerie's favourite pastime.
4. My English class was boring on Monday.
5. My cousin is a fancy dresser.

Spotcheck 2-9

1. electricity
2. swimming
3. Ms. Jackson
4. calendar
5. plumber
6. person
7. Air conditioning
8. George Ferris
9. Jupiter
10. snow

Spotcheck 2-10

1. fought – action
2. were – linking
3. looked – linking
4. hit – action
5. cheered – action

Spotcheck 2-11

1. eat – action
2. are – linking
3. look – linking
4. have – action
5. live – action

Doublecheck 2-1

1. soldiers fought
2. soldiers threatened
3. river was
4. cause seemed
5. army needed
6. reinforcements arrived

Spotcheck 2-12

Answers will vary.

Spotcheck 2-13

1. ~~Of the three singers,~~ Charles is best.
2. ~~Between the tall buildings,~~ a tree turned ~~to the sunlight~~.
3. One ~~of the ducks on the pond~~ is tame.
4. ~~For some reason,~~ the instructor gave an "A" ~~to everyone in the class~~.
5. ~~Between you and me,~~ the award should go ~~to Sylvia~~.

Doublecheck 2-2

1. neighbours have
2. queen removed
3. Chevy is
4. stew tastes
5. Lawrence was

Spotcheck 2-14

1. athletes
2. player
3. chance
4. career
5. [You]
6. athletes

Spotcheck 2-15

1. appeared, achieved
2. was invented
3. had resembled
4. developed
5. would have
6. were offered
7. was taking
8. were named

Doublecheck 2-3

1. (s) Education, (v) is
2. percent drop out
3. rate is
4. quality is credited
5. education has been
6. schools stress
7. values are reinforced
8. status depends
9. half attend
10. They worry
11. hours is
12. colleges receive
13. Americans have been
14. emphasis may hamper

Checkpost 2-1

1. The
2. The
3. A / a
4. A / the / the
5. *no article* / a
6. a
7. The / *no article*
8. the
9. The
10. *no article*
11. *no article* / an
12. *no article*
13. A
14. an
15. an

Checkpost 2-2

1. *no article* / the / the / *no article* / The
2. *no article* / *no article* / a / a / a
3. *no article* / *no article* / the / *no article* / *no article* / *no article*
4. *no article* / a / *no article* / a / *no article*

Spotcheck 3-1
Answers will vary.

1. oatmeal
2. indoor sports, table tennis
3. languages
4. *Checkpoints*
5. oranges, lemons, or grapefruit

Spotcheck 3-2
Answers will vary.

1. Larry got red in the face, slammed the table with his fist, and stormed out the door.
2. Yolanda has a new Nissan 200 SX "XE" coupe, with power steering, power windows, and power locks.
3. Naomi brought a turkey sandwich on whole wheat bread with mayonnaise, mustard, tomato, onion, and sprouts.
4. Carlos is six feet tall, weighs 170 pounds, and has dreamy dark eyes.
5. Jonathan had three cheeseburgers, a jumbo order of fries, and a vanilla milkshake; he finished the meal off with an apple turnover and a medium Coke.

Spotcheck 3-3

1. (B) lacks both
2. (B) lacks both (D) lacks both
3. (B) lacks verb
   (D) lacks verb (or both)
4. (F) lacks both
5. (C) lacks subject

Spotcheck 3-4

1. (B) lacks both
2. (C) lacks subject
3. (D) lacks both
4. (D) lacks verb
5. (B) lacks both
   (E) lacks verb

ANSWER KEY 319

Spotcheck 3-5

Answers will vary.

1. A small airplane flew overhead.
2. I spilled my soup while eating lunch.
3. After the movie, Jennifer and Jim went dancing.
4. The dog was barking at passing cars.
5. A clerk in the shoe department smiled at Annie.

Spotcheck 3-6

Answers will vary.

1. The officer stopped a red convertible.
2. Tim saw a shooting star while driving home.
3. Angelo studied all night before the exam.
4. The plumber is fixing the sink.
5. Willie married a cashier at the theatre.

Spotcheck 3-7

1. ... Cheops, the largest....
2. ... of desert, it is....
3. ... stone blocks, some weighing....
4. ... for 20 years to build....
5. ... made of reeds and their own....
6. ... being built, the pyramid....

Editing Check 3

1. Fragments: 2, 4, 5, 8, 9, 11, 13

Helen Keller provides an inspiring example of a person who overcame great physical handicaps. She was made deaf and blind by illness before the age of two. With the help of a teacher, Anne Sullivan, Helen learned to communicate by spelling out words on a person's hand. She learned to speak by the time she was 16 as a result of her own hard work and Miss Sullivan's patience. Graduating from Radcliffe College in 1904 with honours, she began working to improve conditions for the blind by writing books, lecturing, and appearing before legislative bodies. Two movies tell of her life: *The Helen Keller Story* and *The Miracle Worker*.

Checkpost 3-1

1. much
2. any
3. some
4. any
5. any
6. many/any
7. Many/Some
8. many
9. some
10. any/many

Checkpost 3-2

Answers will vary.

Spotcheck 4-1

1. When
2. Although/Even though
3. because
4. where
5. Whenever

Spotcheck 4-2

2, who
4, where
6, while
8, which
11, when
12, although

Spotcheck 4-3

1. F – Because
2. C
3. C
4. F – Even though
5. F – Before
6. C
7. F – Since
8. C
9. C
10. F – Although

Spotcheck 4-4

Answers will vary.

1. <u>Although</u> the wind was blowing, we went to the beach.
2. Sally planned a party <u>because</u> it was Ahmed's birthday.
3. <u>Whenever</u> Kimberly entered the classroom, Sam smiled.
4. Mary screamed <u>as</u> Curtis picked up the phone.
5. <u>Since</u> it was raining, we cancelled the picnic.

Spotcheck 4-5

1. which is the day taxes are due
2. who knows more and more about less and less
3. that we sing
4. which was scheduled to appear in many cities
5. that has many mountains

Spotcheck 4-6

1. who
2. that (*also* who)

3. that
4. which
5. that

Doublecheck 4-1

Answers will vary.

Doublecheck 4-2

1. who
2. that, which
3. while
4. which
5. which
6. where
7. while / which / that

Doublecheck 4-3

1. <u>which</u> is the largest country in the Western Hemisphere
2. <u>which</u> is a distance of 5514 kilometres.
3. X
4. <u>which</u> is also known as the Precambrian Shield
5. <u>which</u> is composed of ancient rock
6. <u>Although</u> the Shield's rock is ancient
7. X
8. X
9. X
10. <u>Where</u> erosion has not yet worn away the sharp peaks

Editing Check 4

Sections showing editing are underlined.

[1]The term *martial arts* covers a variety of fighting methods based on ancient Asian combat skills. [2]The martial arts are practised today for a number of <u>reasons, including</u> self-defence, physical fitness, and sports competition. [3]Styles, techniques, and teaching methods <u>vary, even</u> within a given branch of martial arts, such as <u>karate, although</u> adherence to ancient traditions is usually emphasized.

[6]Although the exact origins are <u>uncertain, the</u> Asian styles of the martial arts seem to have come to China from India and <u>Tibet, where</u> they were used by monks for exercise and protection against bandits. [9]The arts flourished in <u>Japan, although</u> Japan was among the last of the Asian nations to learn them. [11]For a time, practice of martial arts was restricted to the Japanese warrior class, but the peasants practised in secret.

[12]Martial arts can be divided into two <u>categories, those</u> that use weapons and those that don't. [14]In the weaponless methods, such as karate and kung fu, the contestant depends on kicks and hand and arm <u>blows, as well</u> as various holds, chokes, and twists, to subdue an opponent. [16]In one of the branches using weapons, kendo, based on ancient Japanese sword <u>fighting, contestants</u> today use bamboo swords cased in leather.

[18]T'ai chi is the most gentle of the martial arts. [19]<u>It uses</u> slow, graceful movements that bear little resemblance to the original blows and blocks on which the movements are based. [20]<u>T'ai chi is used</u> today for conditioning and flexibility. [21]Some use it as a form of meditation.

Checkpost 4-1

1. a lot of/few/no/lots of/a few
2. no
3. a little
4. lots
5. a little

Checkpost 4-2

1. are
2. Are
3. is
4. Are
5. are

Spotcheck 5-1

1. ... the Second World War. Its empire....
2. ... the English. They hold....
3. ... in 1952. She has been....

Spotcheck 5-2

1. ... the Second World War, so its empire....
2. .. the English, and they hold....
3. ... in 1952, and she has been....
4. ... England, for many....
5. ... in London, or they may....

Spotcheck 5-3

1. believe, but today's
2. exhaust, and they
3. rugs, or they
4. setup, so the
5. mixer, for its
6. women, but it

Spotcheck 5-4

Answers will vary.

1. One brother is a banker, and the other is a forest ranger.
2. Andrea takes vitamins, but she doesn't need them.
3. Sara will move to Victoria, or she will stay in Vancouver.
4. My car is ten years old, so I am looking for another one.

ANSWER KEY   **321**

Spotcheck 5-5

1. If mother gets home early, we will....
2. The bulldozer knocked down the trees, as the neighbours....
3. Since she was already ten minutes late, Yolanda decided....
4. We always have a good time when we go camping.
5. Because the electricity went out, Terry lit some candles.

Spotcheck 5-6

Answers will vary.

1. The class bell rang before Mark finished the test.
2. We're going skiing this weekend unless it rains.
3. Bill enjoyed the stew although he hates parsnips.

Spotcheck 5-7

1. ... in education; they believe....
2. ... "get ahead"; it produces....
3. ... children; those children....

Spotcheck 5-8

1. ... in education; in fact, they....
2. ... "get ahead"; moreover, it....
3. ... small children; as a result, those....
4. ... in schools; however, we....
5. ... "educational"; for example, television....

Spotcheck 5-9

Answers will vary.

1. Ricky doesn't eat sweets; furthermore, he avoids fatty foods.
2. You should go to bed; otherwise, you will be tired tomorrow.
3. The loan is due this month; however, I hope to get an extension.
4. Ned usually does well on tests; for example, he got a 96 on yesterday's history quiz.

Doublecheck 5-1

1. C—automobile was introduced it brought
2. C—Farmers could drive dwellers could go
3. RTS—Highways, motorways made motels were built
4. C—families owned they could move
5. C—Cars made movies, restaurants, banks became

Doublecheck 5-2

1. C—you are you eat
2. RTS—Indians brought Pilgrims liked
3. C—Popcorn is litre contains
4. C—you add popcorn compares
5. RTS—popcorn has it has

Doublecheck 5-3

Bathing suits did not make an appearance until the middle of the 1800s <u>because</u> recreational bathing was not popular before then; <u>however</u>, at that time doctors began to prescribe the "waters" for a variety of ailments. Europeans flocked to the streams, the lakes, and the ocean <u>where</u> they sought relief from "nerves" or other disorders. Standards of modesty were different in those days, <u>so</u> bathing suits covered more of the body than they do today. Women wore knee-length skirts in the water; <u>in addition</u>, they wore bloomers and black stockings under the skirts. <u>Since</u> a wet bathing suit could weigh as much as the bather, the accent was on *bathing*, not swimming.

<u>If</u> she wanted greater privacy, a woman could use a "bathing machine" at the ocean. Attendants would wheel her and the portable dressing room into shallow waters. <u>After</u> she had changed into a loose head-to-toe gown, she would step down a ramp into the surf <u>while</u> attendants shooed away any interested males.

A Danish immigrant to the United States named Carl Jantzen revolutionized swimwear in 1915 <u>when</u> he invented a knitting machine that yielded a stretchy fabric. The fabric resulted in a body-clinging fit; <u>however</u>, swimsuits still had sleeves and reached to the knees. Swimsuits became more revealing in the 1930s <u>when</u> narrow straps and backless models paved the way for the two-piece suit.

It wasn't until 1946 that the bikini made its appearance. The Second World War had recently ended, <u>and</u> the United States was testing an atom bomb in the Pacific. A French designer was about to introduce a skimpy swimsuit model, <u>but</u> he didn't have a catchy name. <u>Thus</u>, the atomic blast at Bikini Atoll on July 1, 1946, gave him the name for the "explosive" suit he displayed to the world four days later.

Doublecheck 5-4

1a. .... five years, so she....
1b. Since Mrs. Frisbee has been with the company five years, she....
1c. ... years; therefore, she will....
2a. ... worker, but she....
2b. Although Ruth is a hard worker, she will....
2c. ... hard worker; however, she....

Editing Check 5

Answers will vary.

1. remarkable, for it
2. top, and it

3. enemies; it once
4. material; that is
5. labourers; for example, when
6. Although hundreds of thousands of workers

Checkpost 5-1

Answers will vary.

1. Canada is larger than the USA.
2. Niagara Falls has more tourists than Lethbridge.
3. The Mississippi River is more polluted than the St. Lawrence Seaway.
4. Margaret Atwood is more interesting than Farley Mowat.
5. Sean Connery is more famous than Keanu Reeves.

Spotcheck 6-1

1. fly, flew, flown
2. eats, ate, eaten
3. forget, forgot, forgotten
4. goes, went, gone
5. hurt, hurt, hurt

Spotcheck 6-2

1. bought
2. given
3. threw
4. told
5. brought
6. began

Spotcheck 6-3

1. taught
2. sung
3. flew
4. eaten
5. drunk
6. spoken
7. saw
8. written
9. spent
10. paid

Spotcheck 6-4

Answers will vary.

1. Priya had never seen a porpoise before.
2. The toddler became restless during the baseball game.
3. The phone rang three times.
4. Shania had known Fran in Timmons.
5. The owner had driven the car 240 000 kilometres.

Spotcheck 6-5

1. excited
2. frightened
3. grown
4. annoyed
5. prejudiced

Spotcheck 6-6

1. is
2. has
3. has
4. does
5. did
6. have
7. were
8. has
9. was
10. did

Spotcheck 6-7

1. knows
2. supposed
3. asked
4. says
5. run

Doublecheck 6-1

1. Wilbur Wright introduces...he makes
2. the bicycle maker discovers
3. he flies
4. He travels
5. he completes
6. the brother watches
7. he builds
8. he receives
9. he is

Doublecheck 6-2

1. was
2. lived
3. went
4. returned
5. took
6. goes
7. begins
8. produces
9. meets
10. receives

Editing Check 6

Sam walks over to the library because he needs some information to write a psychology class paper on hypnotism. He asks a librarian for help. He is told that the *Readers' Guide to Periodical Literature* lists articles from about 200 magazines. He looks under "hypnotism" and sees the titles of many articles on the subject. He decides to request the April 1982 issue of *Essence* because he is attracted to an article called "Hypnosis: Put Your Mind Power to Work."

Checkpost 6-1

Answers will vary.

1. Lying on a massage chair is one of the most pleasant sensations I've ever had.
2. The murder of innocent women and children is the worst war crime.
3. In 1999, Toronto had the most snow days in a hundred years.
4. Voting is the most important civic duty.
5. SuLyn is the quietest girl I know.
6. Of all the board games, Trivial Pursuit is the most fun.
7. Einstein was not the smartest student in his class.
8. The elephant is the most intelligent of the animal species.
9. The whole world had the most terrific millennium party.
10. Donovan Bailey was the world's fastest man at one time.

Spotcheck 7-1

1. are
2. play
3. run

Spotcheck 7-2

1. plans
2. expects
3. enjoy

Spotcheck 7-3

1. (s) one; (v) is
2. cause; is
3. banana; adds
4. workers; are
5. woman; thinks

Spotcheck 7-4

1. (s) house; (v) is
2. remains; are
3. tombstones; are
4. quality; is
5. feelings; are

Spotcheck 7-5

1. (s) One; (v) owns
2. Both; have
3. Everyone; was
4. Each; tastes
5. Nobody; is

Spotcheck 7-6

1. has
2. don't
3. drive
4. love
5. costs

Spotcheck 7-7

1. gives
2. plans
3. is

Spotcheck 7-8

1. seems
2. has
3. is

Doublecheck 7-1

1. knows
2. was
3. are
4. were
5. watches
6. are
7. was
8. need
9. are
10. has

Editing Check 7

1. people are
2. one has
3. answer lies
4. first means
5. (sports) that stimulate
6. Activities are
7. They increase
8. Lifting is
9. walking, swimming produces
10. experts say

Checkpost 7-1

Answers will vary.

1. from mine
2. haircut
3. most thorough
4. this book is derivative
5. were worse
6. taller
7. talkative
8. faster
9. as Sylvia
10. active

Spotcheck 8-1

1. him
2. they
3. it
4. she
5. me
6. we
7. you
8. he

Spotcheck 8-2

1. IO
2. S
3. IO
4. OP
5. DO
6. S
7. IO
8. DO

Spotcheck 8-3

1. They–subject
2. it–direct object
3. him–indirect object
4. him–object of preposition
5. them–direct object

Spotcheck 8-4

1. Sam and I
2. Justin and him
3. We NDPers
4. us tourists
5. my wife and me
6. the other hikers and us
7. The Laflairs and she
8. the senator and him

Spotcheck 8-5

1. I
2. I
3. we
4. he

Spotcheck 8-6

1. Whom
2. who
3. who
4. whom

Spotcheck 8-7

1. himself
2. me
3. themselves
4. you

Doublecheck 8-1

1. We
2. me
3. I
4. who
5. himself
6. whom
7. themselves
8. I
9. her
10. who
11. they
12. us
13. we
14. who
15. The auditor and I
16. We
17. us
18. who

Doublecheck 8-2

Answers will vary.

1. Lucy will paint the picture herself.
2. Whom did you recommend for the prize?
3. The bee stung me on the finger.
4. The children gave themselves a party.
5. It was Fred who won the race.
6. Patrick and she shared first place.
7. The honours were shared by Kimberly and me.
8. Do it yourself.

Editing Check 8

1. You and me
2. Correct
3. Francine and me
4. Francine and I
5. Correct
6. him and the other guys
7. he himself
8. he being
9. themselves
10. than I

Checkpost 8-1

Answers will vary.

1. …I would help more people in need. (H)
2. …I will be very happy. (P)
3. …I'd be on the Honours List. (H)
4. …it plays an annoying tune. (P)
5. …I'd make March break a two-week period. (H)
6. …everyone has to shovel. (P)
7. …I'd invite all the gang in. (H)
8. …had my mother not cooked dinner for me. (P)
9. …I always flip channels with the remote. (P)
10. …I'd be a star by now. (H)
11. …had I studied. (H)
12. …buy me a souvenir. (P)
13. …she'd appoint more women in key positions. (H)
14. …I'll look you up. (P)
15. …they'd be more popular. (H)

Spotcheck 9-1

1. its
2. their
3. his
4. her
5. his
6. her

Spotcheck 9-2

Answers will vary.

1. All the office workers brought their own lunches.
2. Each of the drivers had to show a licence.
3. A person who showers uses only half as much water as a person who bathes.
4. Fans who bring their ticket stubs from the rained-out game will get in free.

Spotcheck 9-3

1. its
2. its
3. its
4. it
5. its

Doublecheck 9-1

1. a
2. b
3. b
4. b
5. b
6. b
7. a
8. b
9. a
10. b

Spotcheck 9-4

Answers will vary.

1. As the umpire and the coach argued, the coach's voice got louder and louder.
2. Frank told the instructor, "You have a poor understanding of the subject."
3. Ms. Stemley gave a big smile when she saw Ms. Wright.
4. The truck wasn't damaged when it hit the police car.
5. The wind that followed the hail caused extensive damage.

Spotcheck 9-5

Answers will vary.

1. Johanna did weight training for a year before the change in her body became noticeable.
2. Jeffrey wants to be a rodeo rider, but he has never attended a rodeo.
3. When driving on a highway, the driver must stay alert.
4. People always listen to the one who complains the loudest.
5. Not responding to her invitation was impolite of me.
6. Mr. Chan goes to the gym every day because exercising is good for him.

Doublecheck 9-2

Answers will vary.

1. Visitors to Paris should see the Louvre museum.
2. Don't buy a car that needs premium gasoline.
3. This magazine says the polar ice cap is melting.
4. Anyone suffering dizzy spells should see a doctor.
5. The radio announcer said rainy weather is expected.
6. The Jayanathans did not meet their neighbours until the neighbours invited them to a PTA meeting.
7. The committee finally made its recommendation at 1 a.m.

8. Neither of the golfers lost a ball in the rough on the final round.
9. Emile told Winston, "I am certain to win the race."
10. Not all drivers know their way around the Trans-Canada Highway.

Editing Check 9

1. Moviegoers would have...if they had actually lived
2. For one thing, historians say cowboys were greatly outnumbered...by their neighbours
3. at least a quarter of the cowboys
4. residents...would scratch their heads
5. town had...bodies in its
6. because such incidents were so uncommon.
7. Studies of the period say
8. Correct
9. Correct
10. They included
11. they're often found

Checkpost 9-1

Answers will vary.

1. ...removing your hat so I can see the board?
2. ...buying a condo.
3. ...playing squash.
4. ...meeting until later.
5. ...financing a ball game.
6. ...reading as soon as you can.
7. ...smoking.
8. ...trying acupuncture.
9. ...killing the traitor.
10. ...to admit he stole the apple.

Spotcheck 10-1

Answers will vary.

1. thin, skinny
2. hyper, rowdy
3. compulsive
4. mature
5. youthful
6. talented
7. loud, gaudy
8. stubborn, pigheaded

Spotcheck 10-2

1. mother
2. cottage
3. ambulance chaser
4. studious
5. intoxicated

Spotcheck 10-3

1. ready, so you
2. late, and he
3. raise, for you
4. apologize, or I
5. pets, but they

Spotcheck 10-4

Answers will vary.

1. Mary has a cold, and Bill has a headache.
2. It's raining, but sunshine is forecast.
3. Jan's shoes were too small, so she gave them to Sonia.

Spotcheck 10-5

1. Grown in California and Oregon,
2. juice of a coconut,
3. as "the poor man's fruit,"
4. No, breadfruit

Spotcheck 10-6

1. fresh, preserve them, or make them
2. Florida, Texas, Hawaii, Mexico, or Puerto Rico.
3. Figs contain calcium, phosphorus, and iron.

Spotcheck 10-7

Answers will vary.

1. At the time of Confederation, Ontario, Nova Scotia, Quebec, and New Brunswick were united.
2. Casa Loma, the CN Tower, SkyDome, and the Air Canada Centre are familiar landmarks in Toronto.
3. When you visit a new city, you plan to explore your surroundings.
4. After you go for a jog, make sure to stretch.

Spotcheck 10-8

1. Bill's Diner, which looks like it survived a tornado, is a favourite student hangout.
2. My history teacher, Mr. Jefferson, has written a book on the Charlottetown Referendum.
3. The mating call of the Mediterranean fruit fly, according to experts, has the same frequency as the musical note F-sharp.
4. Correct
5. Pound cake, which is one of my favourite desserts, got its name from the pound of butter used in making it.
6. That fact, of course, won't keep me from enjoying pound cake—and putting on pounds.
7. Money is a bad master, it has been said, but a good servant.
8. Billy Bishop, who failed RMC, became Canada's ace pilot in 1917.

Spotcheck 10-9

1. ... 45°C, recorded July 5, 1937, at Midale and Yellowgrass, Saskatchewan.
2. ... –63°C, at Snag, Yukon Territory, on February 3, 1947.
3. ... Robert Wong, 213 West Pender Street, Vancouver, British Columbia.
4. ... Lethbridge, Alberta, on January 4, 1962.

Doublecheck 10-1

1. ... McLuhan, usually known as Marshall McLuhan, was....
2. ... on July 21, 1911, and... on December 31, 1980.
3. ... media, he became....
4. ... in 1943, and he was....
5. ... man, he formulated....
6. ... significant, but....
7. ... media where television, for example, conveys....
8. ... in 1964, he became....
9. In 1967, *The Medium Is the Message* was published, and....
10. ... at University of Toronto, and... in 1983 in his memory.
11. Correct
12. ... information, but also....

Spotcheck 10-10

1. anyone,
2. admitted,
3. is,
4. list,
5. Correct
6. found,
7. canoe,
8. and,

Editing Check 10

1. According to archeologists,...
2. ... men, and graves....
3. ... bronze, razors....
4. Correct
5. Correct
6. In the New World, Indian....

Checkpost 10-1

1. interesting
2. disappointed
3. puzzling
4. embarrassing
5. annoying

Checkpost 10-2

Answers will vary.

1. It's hard to put up with snow for seven months.
2. Susan put off her wedding because she hadn't saved enough money.
3. Justin set up his roommate with a friend of his.
4. George comes across very sociable.
5. The government form was difficult to fill out.
6. Maria has to take up Spanish as a second language.
7. The plane touched down in Montreal on its way to Newfoundland.
8. The artist touched up the old painting in order to make it more attractive.
9. Students who hand in work on time obtain the best results.
10. The organization hands out condoms to promote safe sex.

Spotcheck 11-1

1. fact
2. fact
3. opinion
4. opinion
5. opinion
6. fact
7. opinion
8. fact

Spotcheck 11-2

1. beautiful
2. talk
3. enthusiastic
4. poorly acted
5. ask
6. looked healthy
7. car
8. house
9. Regardless
10. envious of

Spotcheck 11-3

1. ... gas tank?
2. Look out! That gun is loaded. (or)
3. ... spare dime.
4. "What time is it?" William asked.
5. ... it was.

Spotcheck 11-4

1. ... Frye, "Literature... mythology."

2. "Marriage... institution," said Mae West. "But... institution."
3. "I did... Canada," said...
4. "No, Mr. Speaker," said Elijah Harper.
5. ... said, "We are... folly."

Spotcheck 11-5

1. "What... tonight?" Mary asked.
2. "Oh, I don't know," Cathy answered. "I'll... Star Trek on TV."
3. Correct
4. "So what... Miss Intellectual?"
5. Mary said, "I'll probably do some reading. There's an article called 'Lipstick and You' in the new Teen World that looks good."

Spotcheck 11-6

1. I've
2. can't
3. hasn't
4. they're
5. you're
6. There's
7. couldn't
8. You've
9. won't
10. we'll

Spotcheck 11-7

1. men's
2. horses'
3. week's
4. countries'
5. radio's
6. flowers'
7. cars'
8. lifetime's

Spotcheck 11-8

1. book's
2. Duncan's
3. Correct
4. boys'
5. women's

Spotcheck 11-9

Answers will vary.

1. The men's faces were brightened by smiles.
2. The two farmers' trucks collided.
3. Jennifer's dance class meets on Tuesdays.
4. Both players won athletic scholarships.

Doublecheck 11-1

1. "Why... morning?"
2. ... Shakespeare's The Taming of the Shrew.
3. I'm; Joe's
4. McCrae's poem "In Flanders Fields"...
5. "Surely," Joyce said, "you don't expect me to drink day-old coffee."
6. Correct
7. Charles'
8. cowboys'
9. "Look... leap" is...
10. school's

Spotcheck 11-10

1. The sun came up; the dew quickly dried.
2. ... baseball; however, he...
3. ... Kids on the Block, $115 million; TV comic Bill Cosby, $113 million; talk-show host Oprah Winfrey, $80 million; and singer Madonna, $63 million.

Spotcheck 11-11

1. ... picnic: paper plates...
2. ... admire: enthusiasm.
3. Correct

Spotcheck 11-12

1. ... Marsha—a knockout!
2. ... Seaway (completed in 1959) was....
3. ... Mildred—I mean Agnes—went....
4. ... Brad (who owes me money, by the way) was...
5. Tina's brother—in fact, her whole family—is a little odd.

Doublecheck 11-2

1. ... are Bombay, India; Cairo, Egypt; Jakarta, Indonesia; London, England; and Tokyo, Japan.
2. Uncle Alfred (he's my mother's late brother) once....
3. The curtain rose; the performance began.
4. ... trip: a knife....
5. ... Beethoven (1770–1827) was....
6. Allison lost—would you believe it?—ten pounds....
7. ... two months; however, she....
8. ... owned—furniture, clothing, family keepsakes—was....
9. ... the World Series in 1992; moreover, they won....
10. Katharine Hepburn (do you remember her?) won....

Editing Check 11

1. I'll...didn't...beef; however,
2. form of—you guessed it—hamburger
3. hamburger's
4. success?
5. it's McDonald's
6. Correct
7. we're...McDonalds—[or colon] the drive-through....labour (one task per person).
8. "Over 1 Million Sold."
9. aren't...we're
10. McDonald's
11. you're...who's...McDonald's...company—[or semicolon] about 10

Checkpost 11-1

1. might
2. should
3. should
4. would
5. may
6. may
7. could / would
8. need / must
9. can / must
10. need
11. must

Spotcheck 12-1

1. College, Jesuits, Quebec
2. Her, Catholic, Baptist
3. My, Tagalog
4. The, Olsons, Lake Superior
5. The, Sam, "Sparky"
6. The, Loud and Funky, Beatles, "Norwegian Wood"
7. Dave, Math 1A, I
8. Mr. and Mrs. McDonald, Grand Canyon, Arizona, June
9. The, Salvation Army Building, Elm Street, Pine Avenue
10. Vickie

Spotcheck 12-2

1. 3 secretaries
2. Twelve percent
3. size 6½
4. Correct
5. 3 p.m.
6. August 3

Spotcheck 12-3

1. November
2. pounds
3. Professor
4. political science
5. Toronto
6. Quebec

Doublecheck 12-1

1. Twelve
2. university
3. Spanish
4. $36.50
5. Second World War
6. 73
7. economics
8. high school
9. kilograms
10. when

Doublecheck 12-2

1. four
2. six
3. Statistics Canada
4. New Year's Day
5. Canadian, census figures
6. statistics, percent
7. Ste., percent
8. Correct
9. percent, English
10. percent

Doublecheck 12-3

1. flea, *National Geographic*
2. Olympic Games
3. 150
4. feet
5. 30 000
6. Correct
7. astronaut
8. humans
9. Three, world
10. The, China
11. United States, two

Spotcheck 12-4

1. (joined) became
2. (went) was
3. (attends) gains
4. (joined) played
5. (signs) warns
6. (plays) bats, helps

Spotcheck 12-5

(**past time**) Jackie Robinson was an outstanding athlete who opened the door to professional sports for other black athletes. Robinson joined the Brooklyn Dodgers in 1947 and became the first black player in modern major-league baseball. Robinson went to high school in Pasadena, California, where he was a star in track, football, and baseball. He attended the University of California at Los Angeles on a football scholarship and, in 1939, gained more yards than any other college player. After service in the Second World War, Robinson joined the Kansas City

Monarchs and played for $400 a month in the Negro American League. When Dodgers general manager Branch Rickey signed Robinson, he warned him to expect acts of prejudice from other players and the fans. During the ten years he played for the Dodgers, Robinson batted .311 and helped the team win six National League championships and a World Series in 1955.

Spotcheck 12-6

1. Correct
2. were worn
3. thought they were
4. were taking
5. started
6. Correct
7. commissioned
8. Correct

Spotcheck 12-7

1. ~~you~~ they
2. ~~one~~ we
3. ~~you~~ he
4. ~~you~~ we
5. ~~you~~ one gets

Spotcheck 12-8

1. No ticket is needed to attend the Blue Rodeo concert.
2. Diners at Shopsy's Restaurant feel they get their money's worth.
3. I was glad to see Ralph again.
4. Foreign travel helps one understand one's own country.
5. A person driving 100 kilometres per hour would take 171 years to travel the 149.6 million kilometres to the sun.

Spotcheck 12-9

1. mistaken
2. attractive
3. an exciting
4. danced
5. dollars

Doublecheck 12-4

1. person
2. time
3. tone
4. Correct
5. person
6. time
7. tone
8. person
9. time
10. tone

Editing Check 12

1. Anyone who
2. learned
3. originated
4. was
5. unappealing
6. he or she
7. keeps
8. potatoes
9. becomes
10. they

Spotcheck 13-1

1. The ripe apple fell with a crashing sound.
2. Lucinda and Martin washed dishes.
3. Martin washed the dishes without complaining.
4. Martin washed and dried the dishes.
5. The happy baby smiled and gurgled in the bathtub.

Spotcheck 13-2

1. ... 760 000, and Edmonton....
2. ... voice, so today....
3. ... clumsy, but it....
4. ... homework, for he....
5. ... fishing, or he....
6. ... swim, for almost....

Spotcheck 13-3

1. While <u>one American died onscreen in Rambo</u>
2. unless <u>his sales decline</u>
3. who <u>owns two Dobermans</u>
4. Although <u>many young baseball players are signed to professional contracts</u>
5. because <u>its pitching staff is strong</u>

Spotcheck 13-4

Answers will vary.

1. The dentist was upset when Sean....
2. Lisa was nervous because....
3. Yousuf Karsh is a great photographer who photographed Winston Churchill.
4. After gambling was legalized in Windsor, the crime rate....
5. That is the bus driver who returned....

Spotcheck 13-5

Answers will vary.

1. When the floor of the house shook, Jack knew....
2. If the bank will give you a loan, you....

3. Although Yolanda got many Christmas gifts, she....
4. Because Claudette enjoys nature, she....
5. Kimberly began giving money to friends after she....

Doublecheck 13-1

1. S
2. C
3. X
4. X
5. S

Spotcheck 13-6

1. ... inventor who played...
2. ...electric light, which he developed...
3. ...plug it into, so he...
4. ...street lighting when Edison...
5. Correct
6. Although he attended school for only three months, he became famous...

Spotcheck 13-7

1. With grease all over his face, the mechanic looked....
2. ... picture of Marie on page 34.
3. ... hid between two boulders.
4. After a hectic day, Mrs. Farnaby....
5. In the tree's highest branches, crows were....

Spotcheck 13-8

1. terrified at the dog's snarling
2. Singing in the rain
3. taught to him by his mother
4. Finished with his homework
5. Searching for a route to Asia

Spotcheck 13-9

1. Played in India in the sixteenth century
2. enjoyed by the emperor Akbar the Great
3. Moving from bush to bush in the garden
4. determined by the throw of shells
5. changing the Indian name *pacisi* to *Pachisi*

Spotcheck 13-10

1. Exhausted from his hike, Paul wanted....
2. Having saved 10 percent of their salaries for ten years, the Selvadurais were finally....
3. Excited at the victory, the players held....
4. Pleased with her garden, Mrs. Ward gave....
5. Playing volleyball in the gym, Richard met....

Spotcheck 13-11

1. a fifteenth-century Romanian prince
2. "Bluebeard"
3. Elizabeth Goose
4. "Mary Had a Little Lamb"
5. inventor of the phonograph

Spotcheck 13-12

1. Elizabeth Kenny, an Australian nurse, developed....
2. The quartet played bebop, a style....
3. Elvis Presley, the "king" of rock 'n' roll, died....
4. Alice Munro wrote *Open Secrets*, a collection of short stories.
5. The Toronto SkyDome, an arena with a retractable roof, can hold....

Doublecheck 13-2

1. Prep
2. Ap
3. Ap
4. Part
5. Part
6. Part
7. Ap
8. Part

Editing Check 13

1. ... body odour for a long time. (prepositional phrase)
2. ... avoid "offending," using scented... (present participle)
3. ... two spices, citrus and cinnamon. (appositive)
4. The body, using perspiration to cool off, can... (present participle)
5. ... was introduced in 1888. (prepositional phrase)
6. Called Mum, it was soon... (past participle)

Spotcheck 14-1

1. Leah bought a new handbag with a silk lining at a downtown store.
2. A cowboy's 10-gallon hat holds only 1.5 gallons of water.
3. Driving home from work, Min saw an accident.
4. Gloria likes her new baby even when he cries.
5. The average marriage in Canada lasts only 12.4 years.

Spotcheck 14-2

1. Growing careless, the clerk entered the wrong name.
2. Although I was 21 years old, my father....
3. Able to bend steel bars with ease, Mighty Mo filled me with awe.

4. Vacation rushed to an end as we played tennis....
5. Solomon took a photo of the cows contentedly eating grass.

Spotcheck 14-3

1. wrong
2. dirty
3. having a lot of money
4. how to get along with people
5. lazy
6. recreational opportunities are greater

Spotcheck 14-4

1. Because she was hungry, she ate a late-night snack.
2. Her family is pleased when Sally gets a raise.
3. Although sunshine is forecast, Rocky has his umbrella.
4. A good sale makes me happy.

Spotcheck 14-5

Answers will vary.

1. Polly is a lot smarter than Victoria.
2. The trees are greener in the spring than in the fall.
3. A Jeep Comanche looks better and goes faster than a GMC truck.
4. The summers in Victoria are hotter than those in Vancouver.
5. A compact disc can hold more songs than an LP.
6. A sandwich from home costs far less than one from the cafeteria.
7. The dinner was so delicious I could hardly stop eating.
8. I asked Tim if he expected to make the team.

Spotcheck 14-6

1. P
2. A
3. P
4. P
5. A

Spotcheck 14-7

1. Two customers saw the holdup.
2. The teacher praised Carrie.
3. The company notified all employees of the layoffs.
4. The store offered discounts to people over 65.
5. Students wrote all the essays.

Doublecheck 14-1

1. D
2. C
3. B
4. E
5. A
6. B
7. D
8. E

Editing Check 14

1. Correct
2. ...all the entries were silent....
3. ... "golden," the statuette called Oscar was actually made mostly of tin.
4. ...had only a small part...Gary Cooper, who became....
5. First broadcast on radio, the program wasn't aired on television until 1952.
6. For creating Mickey Mouse, Walt Disney received....
7. ...watch on TV most often....
8. ...and streaked....

Spotcheck 15-1

Answers will vary.

1. A talented musician, Sheila was chosen to play in the concert.
2. Agnes's dress was bright blue.
3. Late in June, rain drenched the city.
4. Eric is a pacifist.
5. Our team should win tomorrow night's game.
6. We often need good advice.

Spotcheck 15-2

1. more faded
2. worst
3. happier
4. more
5. most intelligent

Spotcheck 15-3

Answers will vary.

1. Of my three best friends, Antoine is the closest.
2. You should put less sugar on your cereal.
3. In archery, Muhammad is more skilful than William.
4. That is the smallest apple I've ever seen.
5. What is the best team in the NFL?

Spotcheck 15-4

1. quickly
2. easily
3. enviously
4. good
5. well